TV Times Kathie Webber Cookbook

TVTimes Kathie

Webber Cookbook

COLLINS LONDON & GLASGOW
TVTIMES LONDON

WILLIAM COLLINS SONS & CO. LTD.
LONDON . GLASGOW . SYDNEY . AUCKLAND
TORONTO . JOHANNESBURG

TVTIMES LONDON

ISBN 0 00 435109 6

PRINTED IN GT. BRITAIN BY SIR JOSEPH CAUSTON & SONS LTD.
PUBLISHED BY WILLIAM COLLINS SONS & CO. LTD.
LONDON AND GLASGOW

Contents

Introduction

When I was first learning to cook, I was lucky to learn directly from my mother—watching everything she did and helping out on every possible occasion. Later, I went to a technical college where I worked from worthy text books. I would have loved a book which consisted of basic information just as my mother taught, yet included lots of super recipes showing how to use all those basics in more advanced ways.

Most people, like me, want this kind of book; one which chooses the middle course between a cooking ABC and those advanced tomes which assume you know it all. So I've packed into this book as much information as I could and as many recipes as possible, plus lots of colour photographs to whet your appetite and show what the finished dishes should look like.

The book opens with kitchen know-how which explains all about lining cake tins, making paper piping bags and covering pudding basins. I've also included recipes for making your own meat and fish stocks and instructions for skinning and boning fish, for making croûtons and a bouquet garni.

The next part consists of recipes for all the pastries and sauces you'll want to use in your cooking. In this chapter are step-by-step instructions so you'll make perfect puff pastry and smooth mayonnaise the first time.

To follow the basics are chapters on soups and starters, vegetables and salads, fish, meat, poultry and puddings to take you right the way through all the courses of the meal. Here you'll find simple recipes, plain traditional recipes, exciting recipes from abroad, not so easy recipes for the more adventurous and every one of them tried and tested so you know they'll work if you follow the instructions to the letter.

Next come the cakes—large and small, plain and fancy, traditional and up to date. Here are recipes for all occasions from a wedding in the family to cut and

come again fruit loaves which are ideal for packed lunches and picnics.

In the bread section you'll find more cakes and buns, all of which are raised by yeast. Here too are bread recipes including how to make a Cottage Loaf, an Almond Plait and Christmas breads from other lands. Quick breads using baking powder rather than yeast can be made too.

For the very practical cooks there are chapters on making your own sweets and preserving, using all the traditional methods such as jam-making, bottling, pickling and making chutneys. I've included the newer art of freezing because more and more freezers are being sold each year and more and more frequently I'm asked for instructions on how to freeze this or that. This preserving chapter gives explanations of how and why each method works, so if you've had problems in the past, you'll be able to work out just where you've gone wrong and avoid the same mistakes. Tried and tested preserving recipes will give you no problems and you can fill your store cupboard cheaply with pots of preserves for the year to come.

I have included a chapter of drinks recipes so that real favourites such as Irish Coffee can be made. These pages also include drinks for the children, mulled wines for winter, chilled punches for parties and some non-alcoholic mixtures for those who don't like alcohol.

Now that you know a little bit more about this cookery book, I hope you'll find it's just the one you've been looking for. I've tried to include something for everyone and I hope I've succeeded. But mainly I hope beginners to the fascinating art of cookery will pick up this book and learn a lot, and still find lots to absorb their interests when soufflés and spun sugar have long been mastered.

Kathie Webber

Kitchen know how

These tips and hints will help you achieve marvellous results from your cooking all the time. Knowing the correct methods, cooks' short cuts and why things are done just so will save you money, and hours of preparation time in the kitchen too

Yorkshire pudding batter
This can be made in exactly the same way as pancake batter, but I prefer to add ¼ pint milk and ¼ pint water instead of all milk. Also I leave the batter to stand for 30min., before using it.
Bake the batter above the Sunday joint, turning the oven to 425 deg. F. or Mark 7. Pour about 2 tablespoons fat from the meat dish into an 8in. square tin. When it is just beginning to give off a haze, stir the batter and pour it into the tin.
Cook at the top of the oven over the meat for 45–50min., or until well risen, brown and very crisp.

Perfect boiled rice
It's not difficult to make and serve perfect plain boiled rice, but it seems all too easy to get a soggy mass. Buy Patna or long grain rice and the best quality you can find. Long grain rice fluffs up and separates, unlike Carolina or short grain rice, used for puddings, which sticks together.
Allow 1½-2oz. rice per person. Half fill a large saucepan with water and add a good pinch of salt. Ideally use 1 pint of water to 1oz. rice, but this needs such an enormous pan. I use an 8in. diameter pan, when I'm cooking a large quantity. Bring the water to a fast rolling boil. Rinse the rice under running cold water to remove any excess starch, and drain thoroughly. Add to the pan, and boil, uncovered, for 12-15min.
When cooked, the rice should have a bite to it. Test a grain by pressing it between your fingers. It should still feel slightly firm.
Drain the rice well, then rinse with plenty of running hot water. You can serve it once it's drained, or you can dry it further, by spreading it on baking trays and leaving it in a very cool oven, set at 225 deg. F. or Mark ¼, until required for serving.

Good gravy
This is best made using the fat and juices from the pan the meat or poultry was roasted in.
Transfer the roast on to a hot serving dish. Pour off most of the fat, leaving behind 2 tablespoons fat and all the juices, and bits of meat or poultry.
Add 1-2oz. plain flour depending on how thick you like your gravy and stir it round with a wooden spoon.
Cook it gently on top of the stove for 2min. Gradually pour in stock or water from cooked vegetables, stirring and cooking all the time. Bring the gravy to the boil, season well and let it simmer for 5min.
You can use a spot of gravy browning but the gravy should be a good colour because of the browned deposits in the meat tin.

Making a bouquet garni
A bouquet garni is a small bunch of herbs tied together so that they're easy to find when you want to remove them. I've used a bouquet garni in many of the recipes consisting of 1 bay leaf, 3 parsley stalks, 1 sprig of thyme and 4 peppercorns and I usually tie these herbs and spices in a small muslin bag with a long string which can hang outside the pan. If you like you may also include 1 blade of mace in your bouquet garni.

Using gelatine
It's not the problem you might think. The easiest gelatine to use is the powdered variety and I prefer Davis. Dissolve it by measuring the amount into a small basin, adding 3 tablespoons cold water and standing the basin over a pan of gently boiling water.
Don't let the basin touch the water and don't let the gelatine boil or you'll have to start again. Pour the gelatine into the mixture at a height, so that it cools down and becomes almost the same temperature as the mixture. If it's too hot the cold mixture will cool it too quickly and it will go into strings. Pour it slowly and in a thin stream so you don't get set blobs in the mixture.

Using a piping bag
This is something you get used to so don't be dismayed if the results aren't too good the first time. It's important to remember four things.
1. Don't have any lumps or you will block the pipe.
2. Use an even pressure all the time and use only one hand.
3. Don't overfill the bag or you'll not be able to manage. For the beginner, it's easiest to pipe a little, re-fill the bag and pipe a little more.
4. Check the consistency before you fill the bag. This is most important with icing. If it won't hold a shape in the bowl, it won't on the cake. Potato is easy to pipe if it's a little softer than you would have it for serving.

Seasoning foods
I expect that you season foods with salt and pepper automatically as you cook. But do you taste your dishes before you serve them? It's easy enough to add too little, when a dash more of either salt or pepper could really lift the flavour. It's important, too, to taste again after food has cooked with its seasoning in and just before you serve. Seasoning tends to vanish during long cooking, but don't put in double the amount to start. Check the taste and season again before serving.

Keeping a sauce warm
Preferably sauces should be made and served immediately, but you can keep them warm without a skin forming. When the sauce is cooked and seasoned, wet a circle of greaseproof paper, remove the spoon from the sauce and press the wet paper on to the surface of the sauce. This prevents air getting to the mixture which in turn prevents a skin forming. When you reheat, remove the paper, scrape any sauce off the paper and stir all the time.

Skinning and boning fish

The fishmonger will ask you if you want fish prepared, but it's usual for them to leave the skin on fish fillets and the bones in herrings.

To skin plaice fillets, lay the fillet skin side down on a board. Cut the flesh from the skin at the tail end. Dip your fingers in salt to get a good grip on the skin, then saw the flesh off the skin keeping the blade of the knife flat to the skin. Use a very sharp knife for this.

To skin sole, put the fish skin side up on a board. Cut the skin away at the tail end, grip the skin with salty fingers and rip it off. Sole is much easier to skin than plaice.

Boning herrings isn't difficult either. Lay the open herrings skin side up on a board and press down on either side of the backbone to loosen it with your fingers. Turn the fish and ease away the bone from the tail end. It will come away cleanly taking with it the small bones.

Cutting citrus fruit for fruit salad

Cut off a slice at the top and bottom cutting through to the flesh.

Stand the fruit on a wooden board on one cut side and using a sharp stainless steel knife, cut downwards to the board, taking peel and pith together. You'll cut off a little flesh, but it can't be helped, and it is preferable to having the look of the fruit spoiled by bits of white.

Hold the orange in your left hand and cut to the centre by the side of each segment skin, turning the flesh and juice into a bowl. Squeeze the segment skins left in your hand so none of the juice is wasted. If you like, you can cut the pith off some of the pieces of orange and lemon peel and boil the peel only with a little water and some sugar to make a syrup for the fruit salad.

Allow it to cool before you strain it and pour it over the cut fruit.

FISH STOCK
(Makes one and a half pints)

bones, head and skin of filleted white fish
1 small onion
1 stick of celery
1 small carrot
½ level teaspoon salt
4 peppercorns
1 clove
3 parsley stalks
1 bay leaf

☐ Wash the bones, head and skin and put them in a large saucepan with 1½ pints cold water. Skin the onion and leave whole. Wash the celery and cut in half. Peel the carrot and leave whole. Add the vegetables to the pan with the salt, peppercorns, clove, parsley stalks and bay leaf.

☐ Bring slowly to simmering point and simmer gently for 20min. Don't cook for longer or the stock becomes gluey. Strain the stock and use the same day; storing just makes it bitter.

CROUTONS

four ½in. thick slices of white bread
oil for deep frying

☐ These are small cubes of bread which are fried until they're golden brown and crisp.

☐ Remove the crusts from the bread and cut the bread into exact ½in. cubes using a very sharp knife.

☐ Heat the oil to the correct temperature —see page 15—and fry the bread cubes for about 1min., or until light golden brown in colour and very crisp.

☐ Drain on plenty of crumpled kitchen paper. Serve with soups to sprinkle on top, with Veal Marengo—see page 103— or with meat stews and casseroles.

PANCAKES
(Makes about eight pancakes)

4oz. plain flour
good pinch of salt
1 large egg
½ pint milk
1oz. lard

☐ Sift the flour and salt into a bowl. Make a well in the centre. Add the egg and a little of the milk and beat to make a thick smooth batter, drawing in the flour from the sides as you beat.

☐ Lightly beat in the rest of the milk and the batter is ready for use.

☐ Melt a small piece of the lard in a frying pan and pour in some batter to make a thin coating on the pan. Turn the pan so that the batter runs round rather then cooking in a lump in the centre. Cook for 1min., then turn or toss and cook the other side until golden brown.

☐ Keep hot while you use the rest of the batter to make more pancakes in the same way.

MEAT OR CHICKEN STOCK
(Makes about two pints)

2-3lb. raw or cooked bones, skin and gristle of meat, bacon and poultry, or poultry giblets
1 small onion
1 small carrot
1 stick of celery
¼ level teaspoon salt

☐ Use only fresh ingredients and if the bones are raw ask the butcher to cut them into convenient sizes.

☐ Remove all fat from the meat and cut scraps of meat into pieces. Put all meat, bones, skin and gristle in a saucepan. Cover with 2 pints cold water, add the salt and bring to simmering point. Simmer for 1 hour.

☐ Skin the onion and leave whole. Peel the carrot; leave whole. Wash the celery. Add to pan and cook for 1 hour more.

☐ If the bones are raw, simmer the stock for another 2 hours. Don't mix the various bones and meats unless you want general stock for homely soups.

☐ Strain the stock and remove the vegetables. Cool it as quickly as possible and store in a fridge or larder for not more than 2 days. It's always best to use it on the day you make it. Remove the solidified fat before you use stock.

Lining a round cake tin. 1. Cut a piece of greaseproof paper as long as the tin is round. Fold 1in. on one long side. Cut to fold at ½in. intervals.

Lining a rectangular cake tin. 1. Stand the tin in the middle of a large piece of greaseproof paper.

Lining a square cake tin. 1. Stand the tin on a large piece of greaseproof paper. Grease the tin.

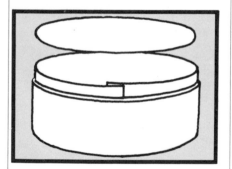

2. Grease the cake tin. Place the strip of paper inside the tin, with the cut edge on the base. Trim the greaseproof paper to stand 1in. above tin.

2. Make cuts from each corner of the paper to each bottom corner of the tin. Grease the cake tin.

2. Cut the paper from one edge to the bottom corner of the tin exactly in line with the side of the tin. Make three more cuts in the same way.

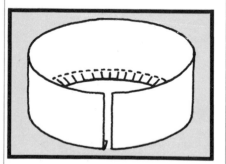

3. Cut a round of greaseproof paper the same size as the cake tin. Place it in the bottom over the cut edges. Grease the paper well.

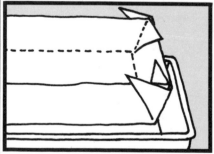

3. Arrange the paper in the tin, folding corners made by the cutting, one behind the other so that they lie flat. Grease the paper well.

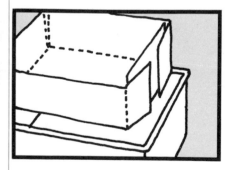

3. Fold the short sides upwards and the long sides of the paper behind the short sides. Place in the tin and grease the paper well.

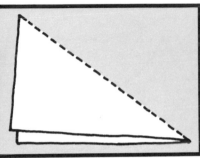

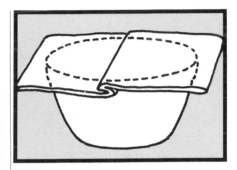

Lining a Swiss roll tin. 1. Cut a large piece of greaseproof paper and stand the tin in the middle.

Making a paper piping bag. 1. Cut a 10in. square of greaseproof paper and fold it in half diagonally.

Covering a pudding basin. 1. Cut a large piece of greaseproof paper and make a pleat in the middle. Place the paper on top of the basin.

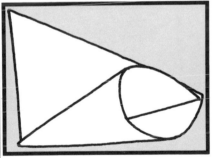

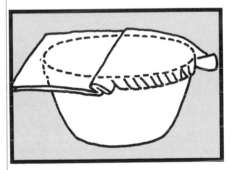

2. Cut the paper from each corner to the corresponding bottom corner of the tin. Grease the tin.

2. Place one finger in the centre of the long side and hold the point nearest you. Roll it over away from you to meet the next point.

2. Starting at the point farthest from you, roll paper towards the basin under itself and continue all the way round. Tuck under to secure.

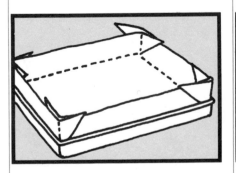

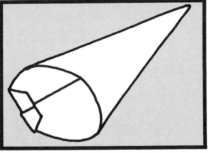

3. Place the paper in the tin and fold the corners made by the cutting, one behind the other to make a neat corner. Grease the paper.

3. Hold the two points and roll the third point towards you and behind the other points. Fold twice to secure and cut off a little of the cone's tip.

3. Fold a large piece of greaseproof paper three or four times to make a long thick strip. Put under basin and use to lift out of the saucepan.

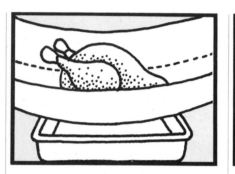

Wrapping a chicken for cooking. 1. Cut a large piece of foil and lay it in the roasting tin. Place the chicken or joint of meat in the middle.

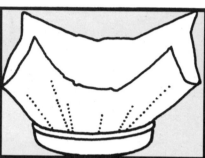

Cooking a casserole in foil. 1. Cut a large square of foil and mould it in a shallow dish. Leave the edges standing up.

Wrapping fish for cooking. 1. Cut a large piece of foil. Lay the fish or other flat foods in the centre.

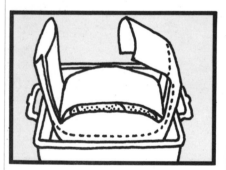

2. Fold over the long sides to enclose the chicken or meat loosely.

2. Fill the foil with all the dry ingredients for the casserole. Transfer the foil to a baking tin and pour in any liquid.

2. Bring two longest sides to meet over the middle. Fold them over twice and press to seal, laying the folds flat.

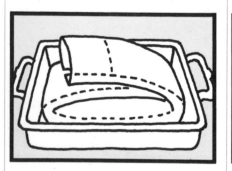

3. Bring short sides together over the chicken or meat and press them firmly together to prevent them opening.

3. Loosely gather the top of the foil to make a swag bag shape. Don't tighten too much, but allow room for steam.

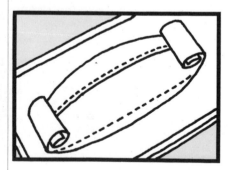

3. Fold the ends twice and press the folds firmly to seal in the fish. Lay the parcel on a baking tray for cooking.

Wrapping a roly-poly pudding. 1. cut a large piece of foil and make a pleat in the centre. Lay the roly-poly on the pleat in the foil.

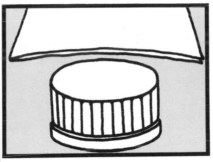

Making a soufflé dish. 1. Choose a soufflé dish of the right size and cut a large piece of foil.

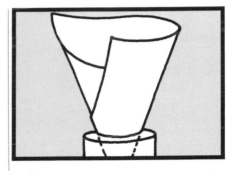

To make a funnel. Cut a double thickness of foil and twist it as you would make a paper piping bag. Cut off the point to fit a bottle or jar.

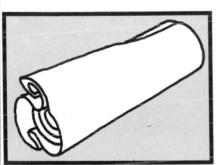

2. Bring the long edges to meet in the middle and fold them twice, pressing the folds to seal. Lay the folds flat.

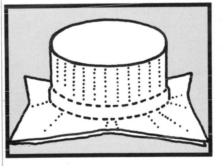

2. Mould the foil over the dish, pressing all the folds flat and squaring off the corners at the base.

To make sweet cases. Mould a double thickness of foil over a jam jar or other suitable object and cut the top into fancy shapes for parties.

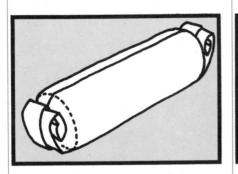

3. Fold the ends of the foil twice and press to seal. Steam or boil, putting the pudding on the fold rather than on the pleat which allows for rising.

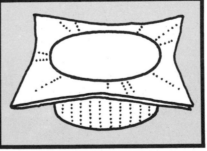

3. Remove the dish and place the case on a baking tray. You can use this method to make a mould for a cake, if you want to bake two the same size.

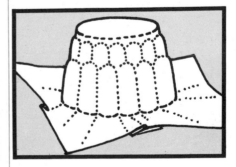

Making small dishes. Mould a double thickness of foil over an old jelly mould, fancy dish or anything with a pattern. Use for children's parties.

13

Handy Measures

Breadcrumbs—fresh 2 heaped tablespoons	1oz.
Breadcrumbs—toasted 2 heaped tablespoons	1oz.
Cornflour 2 heaped tablespoons	1oz.
Currants 1 heaped tablespoon	1oz.
Caster sugar 2 level tablespoons	1oz.
Cocoa 3 level tablespoons	1oz.
Grated cheese 3 level tablespoons	1oz.
Coconut—desiccated 1 heaped tablespoon	1oz.
Demerara sugar 2 level tablespoons	1oz.
Flour 1 heaped tablespoon	1oz.
Granulated sugar 2 level tablespoons	1oz.
Oatmeal 2 level tablespoons	1oz.
Raisins 2 level tablespoons	1oz.
Rice 1 heaped tablespoon	1oz.
Sultanas 1 heaped tablespoon	1oz.
Golden syrup 1 rounded tablespoon	1oz.
Treacle 1 rounded tablespoon	1oz.
Dried yeast 2 level teaspoons	$\frac{1}{2}$oz.
Fresh yeast 1 level tablespoon	$\frac{1}{2}$oz.
Eggs Large Medium Small	2oz. $1\frac{3}{4}$oz. $1\frac{1}{2}$oz.
Liquids 32 tablespoons	1 pint

Food storage times in the refrigerator

FOOD	TIME	HOW TO STORE
MEAT		
Joints	4–5 days	Refrigerate straight away. Wipe off any blood with a clean, damp cloth. Cover lightly with foil.
Steaks	3–4 days	
Chops	3–4 days	
Stewing veal	2–3 days	
Offal and mince	1–2 days	
Sliced bacon	7–10 days	
COOKED MEATS		
Joints	2–5 days	Wrap in foil or leave in the covered dish they were cooked in or any other container.
Casseroles and made-up dishes	2–3 days	
POULTRY		
Whole fresh poultry	2–3 days	Draw, rinse, dry and cover with foil. Remove wrappings from oven-ready birds.
Cooked poultry	2–3 days	Cool and refrigerate straight away. Remove stuffing, wrap or cover with foil.
Cooked and made-up poultry dishes	1 day	Cool and refrigerate in covered dish or container.
FISH		
Raw	1–2 days	Covered loosely in foil.
Cooked	3–4 days	Covered loosely in foil, or placed in covered container.
FRUITS AND VEGETABLES		
Soft fruits	2 days	Clean and refrigerate in a covered container.
Hard and stone fruits	3–7 days	Lightly wrap or in the crisper.
Bananas		Never refrigerate.
Salad vegetables	3–5 days	Clean and drain. Store in crisper or lightly wrapped in polythene or in plastic container.
Greens	3–7 days	Prepare ready for use. Wrap lightly or place in the crisper.
MILK		
Fresh milk	3–4 days	In bottle or covered container.
Milk sweets, custards, etc.	2 days	In covered dishes.
Cultured milk	7–10 days	In original container.
Yogurt	2–5 days	In original container.
CHEESE		
Hard cheese	1–2 weeks	Original pack, polythene, greaseproof or foil.
Cream cheese	1 week	In covered container, polythene or foil.

Frying foods in deep oil

It is most important to test the temperature of the oil before adding food for deep frying. If you are frying cooked foods such as fishcakes, all that is required is that the oil should give a crisp coating and heat the inside thoroughly, so you would use a higher temperature than you would for frying uncooked foods. Ideally use a thermometer, one which registers up to 400 deg. F. and stand it in the pan from the moment you start to heat the oil.

Choux pastry mixtures such as Whiting Quenelles
330 deg. F. rising to 375 deg. F. during cooking

Chips—first frying
330 deg. F.–340 deg. F.

Batter-coated fish fillets, fritters, rissoles
360 deg. F.–390 deg. F.

Chips—second frying, small fritters, croûtons
390 deg. F.–400 deg. F.

If you do not have a thermometer you can test the temperature of the oil another way. Cut a cube of bread about ⅓in. square and drop it into the oil. It should rise and frizzle and brown in 1 minute if the oil is really hot—about 390 deg. F. Obviously this method is not very accurate but it is much more reliable than the blue haze test. Oil doesn't give off a haze until it's burning, and if it does burn, the oil is unusable.

Oven temperature table

Food	Gas setting	Elec. setting	Heat of Oven
Meringues, warming jars for jam, warming plates	¼	225	Very cool
Warming food, slow stewing, fruit bottling	½	250	Very cool
Rich fruit cakes, milk puddings	1	275	Very cool
Casseroles	2	300	Cool
Pâtés, slow roasting, shortbread	3	325	Warm
Large plain cakes, Victoria sponge	4	350	Moderate
Whisked sponges, small sponge cakes	5	375	Fairly hot
Choux buns and éclairs, shortcrust pastry and pies, quick roasting	6	400	Fairly hot
Bread, flaky pastry, scones	7	425	Hot
Meringue-topped pies, puff pastry, Baked Alaska	8	450	Very hot
Small puff pastry items	9	475	Very hot

Refrigerator star markings

	Maximum Temperature of Frozen Food Compartment	Maximum Storage Time for (a) Frozen Foods	(b) Ice Cream
***	0 deg. F.	2–3 months	2–3 months
**	+ 10 deg. F.	4 weeks	1–2 weeks
*	+ 21 deg. F.	1 week	1 day

Weights and measures metric conversions

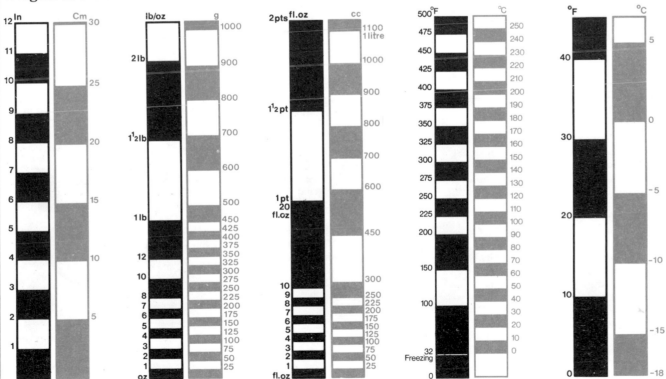

15

Basics Step by Step

Pastries and sauces are used so much in cookery—they're included in all kinds of dishes, they occur in all courses of a meal and at all times of the day. Here are simple step by step picture instructions for the ones you'll be using the most

Everybody thinks that the person who makes crisp, light pastry is a wonderful cook. This isn't always true and nor is the opposite—that the good cook who hasn't had much success with pastry, never will succeed. Pastry-making is something you learn just as you learn about sauces and soups and everyone can learn. Naturally some people will always make better pastry than others, but this is true of everything we do. I want to take some of the mystery out of this subject and show you how to make pastry to beat everyone you know.

The whole idea of pastry-making is to introduce air into the mixture and the more air the better. So sieve the flour and salt first of all. The fats should be rubbed into the flour using your fingertips. Gather up flour and fats each time and lift them about four inches from the surface so that they fall back as you rub in and trap air.

Mixing must be done quickly and lightly so that the air isn't knocked out. Don't add too much liquid because you'll get a soft, sticky dough that can only be corrected by adding more flour and that makes pastry tough. A good guide is one teaspoon of water for every ounce of flour. Too little liquid makes a dry hard pastry. Sprinkle the liquid over the rubbed-in mixture evenly. Knead the pastry on a lightly floured board just until it becomes smooth. Kneading should take you about ¼min., no more. Your finished pastry should be a smooth, pliable but stiff dough that rolls out evenly without cracking.

The fats that are recommended for pastry are lard because it shortens or makes pastry crisp, and butter, which has the best flavour, although margarine is a good substitute. Ideally, mix lard and butter and then you get the best of both worlds.

Cool hands are an asset when making pastry. Although not noticeably so when making shortcrust, the difference can be seen when making puff pastry. If you have warm hands, you can cool them by running cold water over the inside of your wrists—particularly over the pulse. If you have a marble pastry board so much the better.

When you roll out pastry, roll only in one direction at a time, then turn the pastry and roll in another direction. All pastry except for hot water crust which must be kept hot and therefore is best used straight away, and choux pastry, benefit from a rest in a cool place after they're made. Pastry does become stretched during the rolling and it's much better to let it shrink back in the fridge while it's resting than on top of your pie during the cooking. If this has happened to your pastry, allow time for it to sit in the fridge for at least 30min. Lift the pastry on to a pie or into a flan using your rolling pin and don't let the excess hang over. Cut it off because the hanging excess is heavy and stretches the remainder. When you have laid the pastry in a flan ring, lift the excess pastry with one hand until it's vertical and push in with the other hand. Then you won't find your flan case walls half the depth after baking.

When you see a recipe which refers to 8oz. shortcrust or 8oz. puff pastry, this figure 8oz. always refers to the amount of flour used. So 8oz. shortcrust pastry consists of 8oz. plain flour, 4oz. mixed fats plus a pinch of salt and the water for mixing. It never means weigh 8oz. of the finished pastry and use this. Bought pastries are referred to by their finished weights because this is the way they are bought.

Here and on the next two pages are step by step recipes for all the pastries you'll want to make, including some variations of shortcrust pastry. Try potato pastry for a fish or meat pie—it makes a delicious topping.

SHORTCRUST PASTRY

This pastry is the foundation of many pastries. It's the most useful one because it's made very quickly and it can be used for both sweet and savoury dishes, for covering pies and for making large and small tarts. Variations of shortcrust pastry include cheese pastry, flan pastry and oatmeal pastry. All the recipes are here.

1. You will need 8oz. plain flour; a pinch of salt; 2oz. lard; 2oz. butter or margarine; fresh cold water. Sift the flour and salt into a mixing bowl.

2. Rub in the lard and butter using your fingertips as shown. The mixture should look like fine breadcrumbs. Measure in 8 teaspoons cold water.

3. Mix quickly and lightly to a stiff dough. You may need a little more water because some flours absorb more than other kinds. Knead lightly.

SUET CRUST PASTRY

Use this pastry for sweet and savoury puddings. Generally suet crust pastry is steamed or boiled which gives the best results, but it can be baked and although I think it's a bit too crisp, you may like to try this.

4. Roll out the pastry on a lightly floured board to a round ⅛in. thick and a little larger than the pudding basin.

4. Cheese pastry is made by adding a pinch of pepper and 4oz. finely grated Cheddar cheese. Sift pepper with flour; stir in cheese after rubbing in fats.

1. You will need 8oz. self-raising flour; a pinch of salt; 4oz. shredded suet; fresh cold water. Sift the flour and salt into a mixing bowl.

5. Cut out a quarter as shown and line the basin with the large piece. Moisten the cut edges and press them well to seal. Roll the quarter into a round for the top.

5. Flan pastry can be made by stirring 1½oz. caster sugar into the rubbed-in mixture and mixing with 1 large egg yolk and about 5 teaspoons cold water.

2. Stir the shredded suet into the flour. I use packet suet because it's quick and easy, but fresh grated butchers' suet makes a very good pastry.

6. You can line a basin another way. Reserve a quarter of the pastry for the top. Roll remainder and fold it into quarters. Gently roll the point.

6. Oatmeal pastry is made by stirring the oatmeal into the sifted flour and salt. Rub the fats into this mixture. Mix to a stiff dough with cold water.

3. Add about 8 tablespoons cold water and sprinkle it over the mixture. Mix quickly and lightly to a soft dough.

7. Flour your fist and put it into the pastry supporting the folds with the other hand. Line the basin and gently smooth the folds. It should fit perfectly.

PUFF PASTRY

A light, flaky, very rich pastry that's really delicious if homemade. Like flaky pastry it needs cool hands or the butter oozes out, and lots of rest in the refrigerator between each rolling. Try to keep to a good oblong shape and the corners square each time you roll so that the finished pastry layers will rise evenly. Don't roll over the edge or you'll push out the butter. Use to make vol-au-vents and mille feuille.

4. Turn the dough on to a lightly floured board and roll it out to an oblong twice as long as it is wide. Keep the corners square.

HOT WATER CRUST PASTRY

This is the only pastry which must be kept hot rather than cool during the making and using. The pastry sets when cool which is why it's used to make pastry cases for meat pies.

1. You will need 8oz. unsalted butter; 8oz. plain flour; ½ level teaspoon salt; ½ teaspoon lemon juice; fresh cold water.

5. Place the remaining butter in a block on one half of the pastry and fold the other half over to enclose. Don't seal the pastry edges.

1. You will need 8oz. plain flour; 1 level teaspoon salt; 2oz. lard; ¼ pint milk and water mixed.

2. Sift the flour and salt into a mixing bowl. Cut a piece off the butter the size of a walnut and rub it into the flour.

6. Press the middle twice with your rolling pin. Roll out the dough to an oblong three times as long as it is wide. Don't roll over the edges.

2. Sift the flour and salt into a mixing bowl. Put the lard and milk and water mixed into a saucepan.

3. Mix to a stiff dough with the lemon juice and enough cold water. Knead lightly until smooth and no longer sticky to touch.

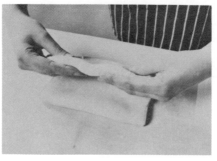

7. Fold the dough in three as you would for flaky pastry and put it in the fridge to rest for 15min. Roll and fold the pastry seven times in all.

3. Bring the lard and milk and water to the boil. Don't let it go off the boil but pour it immediately into the flour.

4. Mix quickly using a wooden spoon until the dough begins to stick together.

5. As soon as it's cool enough to handle, turn the dough on to a lightly floured board and knead until it's smooth.

6. If it isn't as smooth as the dough shown here, add a few drops of boiling water until it becomes smooth. It's difficult to raise if it's dry.

7. Place the dough on a lightly floured plate over a basin of boiling water. Cover the dough to keep it hot while you raise the remainder.

POTATO PASTRY

Use this pastry to cover meat and fish pies. This is a good pastry for adding extra nourishment to a dish.

1. You will need 6oz. peeled potatoes; salt; 3oz. margarine; 5oz. plain flour; 1 level teaspoon baking powder.

2. Cut the potatoes into quarters and cook for 20min. in boiling salted water until tender. Push the potato through a ricer or sieve until smooth.

3. Put the margarine into a large mixing bowl. Cream it until smooth and lighter in colour using a wooden spoon.

4. Add the sieved potatoes and stir them lightly into the margarine.

5. Sift in the flour and baking powder.

6. Mix well using a wooden spoon until the dough begins to stick together. Knead lightly with your hands until it is smooth.

7. Turn the dough on to a lightly floured board and roll out to a ½in. thickness.

FLAKY PASTRY

This pastry is very similar to puff pastry although it's not quite as rich and it's easier to make. If you can allow the time, wrap the finished pastry in greaseproof paper and leave it in the fridge for 30min. or longer to rest. Use it for covering sweet and savoury pies and for making small tarts.

4. Roll out the dough to an oblong three times as long as it is wide. Dot a quarter of the mixed fats over two thirds of the rolled out pastry.

CHOUX PASTRY

Use this pastry for making éclairs and large choux buns. Very small choux buns —the size of a walnut—can be filled with cream, piled into a pyramid and coated with chocolate sauce for a very special party sweet.

1. You will need 8oz. plain flour; a pinch of salt; 3oz. butter; 3oz. lard; 1 teaspoon lemon juice. Mix the butter and lard together to soften them.

5. Fold the plain third over the middle, fat-dotted third, keeping the edges square.

1. You will need 4oz. plain flour; a pinch of salt; 2oz. butter; 2 large eggs; ½ pint cold water. Sift the flour on to a piece of greaseproof paper.

2. Sift the flour and salt into a mixing bowl. Divide the mixed fats into quarters and rub one quarter into the flour, using your fingertips.

6. Fold the remaining third over the other two to make three layers, again keeping the edges as square as you can. Turn the pastry so the edges face you.

2. Put the salt, butter and water in a pan and bring to boiling point. Remove immediately from the heat.

3. The rubbed-in flour and fat mixture should look like fine breadcrumbs. Mix to a stiff dough with the lemon juice and fresh cold water.

7. Press the sides gently with your rolling pin to seal in the air. Repeat steps 4, 5 and 6 twice more, turning the pastry each time.

3. Add the flour to the butter mixture all at once and beat, using a wooden spoon.

4. Beat until the mixture is smooth and comes away from the sides of the pan and forms a ball. Allow to cool until you can stand the pan on your hand.

5. Beat the eggs and beat them very gradually into the mixture, making sure one lot is incorporated before you add any more.

6. Spoon the mixture into a nylon piping bag fitted with a large plain pipe. For ease, stand the piping bag in a jug with the top folded over.

7. Pipe the choux pastry on to greased and lightly floured baking trays either in blobs for buns or 3in. lengths, cutting the mixture off with a knife.

ROUGH PUFF PASTRY

Another light, rich, layered pastry similar to puff pastry. It can be used to cover sweet and savoury pies.

1. You will need 8oz. plain flour; a pinch of salt; 3oz. butter; 3oz. lard; 1 teaspoon lemon juice. Sift the flour and salt into a mixing bowl.

2. Cut the margarine and lard into pieces the size of a walnut. Don't cut them smaller or your pastry will be short rather than flaky.

3. Add the fats to the flour with the lemon juice and fresh cold water and mix lightly to a stiff dough. Press the pastry lightly together; don't knead it.

4. Roll out the pastry to an oblong, three times as long as it is wide.

5. Fold the pastry into three layers by folding one third over the middle and the remaining third over the top. Turn the pastry so the edges face you.

6. Press the edges of the pastry hard with your rolling pin to seal in the air. Press the centre two or three times to distribute the air.

7. Repeat steps 4, 5 and 6 three times more then wrap the pastry in greaseproof paper and put it in the fridge to rest for 30min., or more.

COVERING A PIE DISH

When covering a pie dish with pastry make sure the filling is right up to the rim of the dish. If it isn't, it's better to use a smaller dish, or the pastry will sink in the middle. Use a pie crust raiser or an egg cup if in doubt.

4. Hold the large piece of pastry over your rolling pin and place it over the pie.

LINING A FLAN RING

Lift the pastry into the flan ring. If you stretch it you'll find the walls of your flan half the size you want them. Press the pastry into the flutes and roll off the excess. Press again into the flutes making sure the pastry goes right into the corners to give your finished case a neat look. Trim edge again.

1. Roll out the pastry to the correct thickness and 1 in. larger than the dish. Cut off a ½ in. strip all round.

5. Press the edges to seal and trim them using a sharp knife.

1. Lift the pastry on your rolling pin into a greased flan ring standing on a baking tray. Press lightly into flutes and roll off.

2. Grease the edge of the pie dish and press on the strip of pastry.

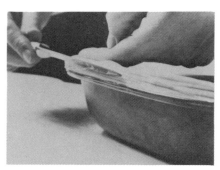

6. Using the back of the knife, knock up the edges. This is making cuts in the pastry edge so that it resembles cooked puff pastry.

2. Press again into the flutes making sure you press the pastry well into the bottom corner. Trim off the top, if necessary, using a sharp knife.

3. Moisten the edge of the pastry on the edge of the dish using a pastry brush and cold water.

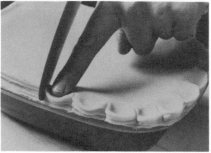

7. Decorate the edge using a knife and your forefinger. Brush the pie with egg or milk and bake.

3. Lay a piece of greaseproof paper on the pastry and fill it with baking beans which keep the pastry flat. Bake—see the flan recipes.

LINING TART PLATES AND TINS

Cut out your round first and then lay it on the plate. Decorate the edge as I have done with a teaspoon bowl, or you can cut lots of tiny circles and use to decorate the edge. Pastry leaves arranged round the edge will also make your large plate tarts look interesting.

1. Lay the plate upside down on the pastry and cut out a round ½in. bigger all round than the plate.

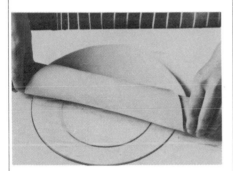

2. Grease the plate. Lift the pastry on your rolling pin on to the plate. Trim edges again if necessary.

3. Cut out rounds of pastry using a cutter and press them into greased tartlet tins. You can use a plain or fluted cutter.

MAKING PASTRY TWISTS

Large jam tarts are traditionally decorated with pastry twists. Here's how they're made. Again be careful that you don't stretch them or they may break, or worse, shrink back during cooking.

1. Roll any trimmings a little thinner than usual and cut ½in. wide strips, one for each twist.

2. Hold one end firmly on the board and lift the other end. Twist gently.

3. Moisten the edge of the pastry on the tart plate and press a twist on to the pastry.

MAKING LEAVES AND TASSELS

Pastry decorations are added to both sweet and savoury pies although tassels are generally used for savoury pies.

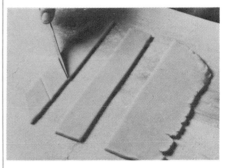

1. Roll out any pastry trimmings and cut into 1in. wide strips. Make diagonal cuts along these strips to make leaf shapes.

2. Mark the veins on each leaf using a sharp knife. You can make these leaves as big or small as you like. Just cut narrower or wider strips.

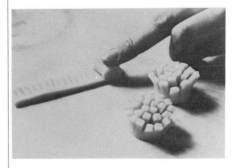

3. Cut a ½in. wide strip of pastry from the trimmings and make cuts just over ¼in. long down one side. Roll the pastry and seal the end.

WHITE SAUCE

This plain white sauce is the most useful of all the sauces. Serve it well-seasoned with fish and chicken or sweetened with puddings. If you alter the amount of milk you add you can have a thick sauce for coating food, a thinner one for pouring or a very thick mixture called a panada which is the basis for soufflés.

VARIATIONS

Once you have made a basic white sauce, it's easy to make lots of different sauces. Most of the ingredients are simply stirred into the made white sauce—see parsley and mushroom sauces. Béchamel sauce is a more flavoursome white sauce and is made by boiling flavouring ingredients with the milk.

CORNFLOUR SAUCE

Making a cornflour sauce is a little easier than using plain flour, and cornflour, being finer than ordinary flour won't go into lumps. You can substitute cornflour for plain flour when making a white sauce or you can make a sauce simply with cornflour and milk as is shown here.

1. You will need 1oz. butter; 1oz. plain flour; ½ pint milk; salt and pepper. Melt the butter in a pan, but don't let it burn.

Parsley sauce is made simply by stirring 1 level tablespoon finely chopped parsley into the finished white sauce before adding the seasoning.

1. You will need 1 level tablespoon cornflour; ½ pint milk; salt and pepper. Blend the cornflour in a 1 pint basin with 1 tablespoon of the milk.

2. Stir in the flour and cook the mixture (or roux) for 1min., or until it becomes sandy coloured and textured. Remove the pan from the heat.

Béchamel sauce—boil 1 small onion stuck with cloves, 1 carrot and 1 bouquet garni with the milk. Allow to stand for 30min., before using.

2. Boil the rest of the milk and pour it on to the cornflour, stirring all the time. Pour it back into the pan, bring to boil and boil for 3min., stirring.

3. Gradually stir in the milk, making sure the sauce is smooth. Bring to the boil, stirring, then simmer for 2min., stirring occasionally. Season well.

Mushroom sauce can be made by adding 2oz. button mushrooms. Rinse and slice them and fry in 1oz. butter until tender. Drain well; add to sauce.

Cheese sauce can be made by adding 2 heaped tablespoons grated cheese to the sauce with the salt and pepper. Take the pan off the heat and stir well.

VELOUTE SAUCE

This is a sauce which is made with white stock rather than milk. Velouté sauce can be made with fish, veal or chicken stock to be served with the appropriate food. It's a lighter textured sauce than a milk sauce and it should have a lot more flavour, although this does depend on how flavoursome the stock is. It is finished with lemon juice and cream. Don't add more than 8 tablespoons double cream to this amount of sauce, although you can add less or substitute single cream.

BROWN SAUCE

This is the basic brown sauce recipe from which all kinds of variations are made. The brown sauce takes its colour from the fat and flour which are cooked together very, very gently for about 20min., or until they have turned a rich brown. It's very easy to catch the mixture at this stage and this will give the sauce a bitter taste, so cook it on the lowest possible heat and stir it occasionally.

VARIATIONS

When you have made a basic brown sauce you can make the following sauces quite easily. Espagnole sauce is a brown sauce with more flavour and either brown sauce or Espagnole can be used to make other sauces such as Piquant and Robert shown here.

1. You will need 1oz. butter; 3 button mushrooms; 3 peppercorns; pinch of mixed herbs; 1oz. plain flour; ½ pint stock; lemon juice; salt and pepper.

1. You will need 1 onion; 1 carrot; 1oz. dripping; 1oz. plain flour; ½ pint brown stock; salt and pepper. Skin the onion, peel the carrot; dice both. Melt dripping.

Espagnole sauce—fry 1oz. chopped bacon with the vegetables. Add stock, 2 tablespoons tomato purée and 1 bouquet garni. Simmer for 1 hour and strain.

2. Melt the butter and fry the mushrooms without browning them. Add the peppercorns and herbs and stir in the flour. Gradually stir in the stock.

2. Add the vegetables to the pan and fry them for 10min. Stir in the flour and cook the mixture very gently for 20min., or until a rich brown colour.

Piquant sauce can be made simply by adding 3 roughly chopped gherkins and a few roughly chopped capers to the finished brown sauce. Stir well.

3. Bring the sauce to the boil, cover and simmer for 1 hour. Sieve the sauce and stir in the juice of ½ lemon, salt and pepper and 8 tablespoons double cream.

3. Gradually stir in the stock, bring to the boil. Cover the pan and simmer gently for 30min. Season with salt and pepper and strain the sauce to serve.

Robert sauce—fry 1 onion in butter, add ¼ pint dry white wine and 1 tablespoon vinegar; boil to reduce. Stir in sauce, pinch of mustard and sugar.

25

BREAD SAUCE

Traditionally served with roast chicken, bread sauce is very simple to make. It's flavour comes from the additions to the milk. You could also add 1 small piece of carrot, 1 pinch of mixed dried herbs and 1 blade of mace.

1. Skin 1 small onion and stick it with 2 cloves. Put it in a pan with ½ pint milk, 1 bay leaf and 6 peppercorns. Bring to the boil.

2. Allow the milk to stand for 1 hour to infuse. Drop 3oz. bread gradually into a liquidiser until it is crumbled. Strain the milk through a nylon sieve.

3. Stir the breadcrumbs and 1oz. butter into the milk. Bring to the boil, then simmer for 20min. Season with salt and pepper and nutmeg.

VINAIGRETTE

Also known as French dressing. I always make up a pint at a time and keep it in a bottle in the fridge. If liked you can skin and crush a clove of garlic and add it, or if you prefer a less strong taste, just skin the clove and add to the bottle. Leave it there all the time.

1. Put 3 tablespoons vinegar into a bowl. Add a pinch of mustard powder, a pinch of caster sugar and salt and pepper.

2. Whisk the mixture until blended, then gradually add 6 tablespoons oil, whisking all the time.

3. Serve the vinaigrette in a small jug. It will be necessary to whisk it each time before serving.

MAYONNAISE

This sauce causes more problems than any other I know. The emulsion of the egg yolk and oil breaks down if the oil is added too quickly. Add it drop by drop until you've added at least half. Beat well all the time and if it looks like separating, stop adding oil and beat like mad until it's smooth again.

1. Drop 1 large egg yolk into a basin. Add ¼ level teaspoon mustard powder, ¼ level teaspoon salt, a pinch of pepper and a pinch of sugar.

2. Whisk well until blended then drop by drop add ¼ pint olive or salad oil, whisking all the time until the mayonnaise is thick.

3. Whisk in 1 tablespoon vinegar and 1 teaspoon lemon juice until the mayonnaise is thinned slightly and season to taste with salt and pepper.

HORSERADISH SAUCE

The real thing nearly blows your head off so it should be used sparingly. The more cream you add to this sauce, the milder it will be.

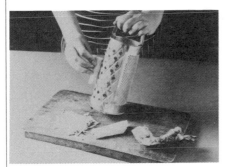

1. Wash a horseradish root; dry and peel. Grate the root coarsely. Put 3 tablespoons horseradish in a bowl with 2 teaspoons lemon juice; mix well.

2. Add 1 teaspoon vinegar, a pinch of mustard powder, 3 tablespoons single cream, 3 tablespoons double cream and salt and pepper to taste.

3. Mix well until blended and serve with roast beef or with steaks.

ORANGE SAUCE

This is an arrowroot sauce and it shows you how to use arrowroot. Use 2 level teaspoons arrowroot to ¼ pint liquid. Use tinned fruit juices, fresh juices, sugar syrup with flavourings or milk with flavourings.

1. Thinly peel off the rind from 1 orange and cut the rind into thin strips. Squeeze out and strain the juice from 2 oranges.

2. Bring the orange juice to the boil. Blend 2 level teaspoons arrowroot with 2 teaspoons cold water. Pour on a little hot juice and stir well.

3. Return to the pan and stir until boiling. Add the rinds and simmer the sauce for 2min., or until thick and clear.

CHOCOLATE SAUCE

This chocolate sauce is dark and rich and can be served hot over suet and steamed puddings or cold over ice cream.

1. Break 3oz. plain chocolate into a saucepan. Add 2oz. caster sugar, 1 rounded teaspoon cocoa and ¼ pint cold water.

2. Heat the mixture gently until the chocolate has dissolved, then simmer for 3min. Add another ¼ pint cold water.

3. Bring to the boil, reduce the heat and simmer the chocolate for 20min., or until thick and syrupy. Serve the sauce hot or cold.

Soups & Starters

Starters often cause problems simply because they're the first thing a hostess sets before her guests. Everyone wants this first course to be different, exciting and absolutely delicious so here, for you to choose, are dozens of interesting recipes

KIDNEY SOUP
(Enough for four-six)

8oz. ox kidney
1oz. lard
1 medium-sized onion
1 medium-sized carrot
1 stick of celery
1oz. plain flour
2 beef stock cubes
2 pints boiling water
1 small bay leaf
1 blade of mace
¼ level teaspoon dried thyme
6 peppercorns
salt
2 tablespoons sherry—optional
2 thick slices white bread

☐ Skin and wash kidney. Cut into small pieces, removing white core. Melt lard. Fry kidney gently for 5min. Skin and chop onion. Wash and peel carrot. Slice thinly. Wash celery and slice fairly thinly. Remove kidney from the pan leaving behind the fat. Add vegetables; fry for 5min. Stir in flour. Lower heat and cook gently until the flour is golden.
☐ Dissolve stock cubes in the boiling water. Pour into the pan. Bring to the boil slowly, stirring until liquid thickens.
☐ Tie herbs and peppercorns in a piece of muslin. Add to pan with kidney and a good pinch of salt. Cover and simmer for 2 hours.
☐ Remove herbs. Liquidise or push soup through a nylon sieve. Pour back into pan. Check seasoning. Add sherry and heat for 5min. Toast the bread. Cut into small dice. Serve soup in hot bowls and top with cubes of toast.

MINESTRONE
(Enough for four-six)

1½oz. haricot beans
1 large onion
1 clove of garlic
1 large carrot
1 small turnip
1 stick of celery
1oz. butter
2 medium-sized potatoes
2 chicken stock cubes
1 level tablespoon tomato purée
boiling water
1 bay leaf
1 sprig of thyme
6 peppercorns
good pinch of salt
4oz. white cabbage
2 tomatoes
2 courgettes
½ small packet frozen beans
1oz. macaroni

☐ Cover the haricot beans with cold water. Leave them to soak for 24 hours.
☐ Skin and chop the onion. Skin and crush the clove of garlic. Peel carrot and slice into pieces about the size of matchsticks. Thickly peel the turnip. Cut into matchstick-sized pieces. Wash celery and slice thinly.
☐ Melt the butter in a large pan. Add the onion and garlic. Fry gently for about 5min. until tender but not brown. Peel potatoes. Cut into ½in. dice.
☐ Dissolve the stock cubes and tomato purée in 2 pints boiling water. Pour into the pan. Drain water from the haricot beans. Add the beans, carrot, turnip, potato and celery pieces. Tie the herbs and peppercorns in a small piece of muslin and add to the pan with salt. Cover and simmer for 1 hour.
☐ Shred the cabbage finely. Drop the tomatoes into boiling water; leave for 1min., then drain. Skin and chop the tomatoes. Dice the courgettes. Add rest of ingredients to pan. Cover and simmer for a further 20-30min. Remove the bag of herbs.

CREAM OF CELERY SOUP
(Enough for four)

1 large head of celery
1 medium-sized onion
1oz. butter
1 chicken stock cube
1¼ pints boiling water
4 peppercorns
1 small blade of mace
1 small bay leaf
1 small sprig of thyme
¾oz. cornflour
¾ pint milk
salt
2 tablespoons single cream or top of the milk
1 level tablespoon finely chopped parsley

☐ Cut off the leafy parts from the celery. Break the head into sticks and wash well. Slice into 1in. pieces. Skin and chop the onion. Melt butter in a large pan. Add the vegetables and fry for 8min. or until tender, but do not allow to brown.
☐ Dissolve the stock cube in the boiling water. Pour into the saucepan. Tie peppercorns, mace and herbs in muslin. Add to vegetables. Cover and simmer for 30-40min.
☐ Remove bag of herbs. Pour vegetables and liquid into a liquidiser and blend them for 1min., until smooth, or push through a nylon sieve. Blend the cornflour and milk. Bring to boil in a large pan, stirring all the time. Add celery purée. Check seasoning. Cover and simmer gently for 5min.
☐ Serve the soup in hot bowls. Swirl a little cream or top of the milk on top and sprinkle with the parsley.

Top to bottom: Kidney Soup, Minestrone, Celery Soup

GAZPACHO
(Enough for four)

1lb. tomatoes
boiling water
1 medium-sized onion
1 small green pepper
1 clove of garlic
2 tablespoons vinegar
4 tablespoons olive oil
salt and pepper
14oz. tin tomato juice
2 tablespoons strained lemon juice
croûtons

☐ Drop tomatoes into boiling water, leave for 1min., then drain and skin. Cut one in half. Remove seeds and save flesh for garnish. Put seeds with rest of tomatoes and chop roughly. Skin and roughly chop the onion. Save half for garnish. Wash pepper, cut in half and remove core and seeds. Chop flesh into small dice and save a quarter for garnish. Skin and chop clove of garlic. Blend the vegetables, vinegar, oil, salt, pepper, tomato juice and lemon juice in a liquidiser for 1min. Chill for 30min., then serve.
☐ Dice reserved tomato flesh. Serve the tomato, reserved onion, green pepper and the croûtons in separate bowls.

SCOTCH BROTH
(Enough for four)

1 hough or shin bone or ¾lb. mutton
1½oz. pearl barley
2 large carrots
1 small turnip
1 medium-sized onion
1 large leek
salt and pepper
4 tablespoons peas or shredded cabbage
1 level tablespoon finely chopped parsley

☐ Put the meat bone or meat in a pan and add 2 pints cold water. Bring to the boil, skim when necessary. Pour a little boiling water on to the barley, stir and then drain. Add barley to pan. Cover and simmer for 1 hour.
☐ Peel and dice the carrots and turnip. Skin and roughly chop the onion. Cut off root and discoloured leaves from leek. Cut leek into ½in. slices. Wash well. Add the root vegetables to the pan; season with salt and pepper and simmer for 30min. Then add the peas or cabbage and simmer for a further 30min.
☐ Remove the bone, if used, or mince the meat. Skim away as much of the fat from the surface of the soup as possible. Return meat to pan; check the seasoning and stir in the chopped parsley.

WELSH MUTTON COWL
(Enough for four)

1½lb. scrag end of mutton
2 large carrots
½ small turnip
4 medium-sized potatoes
2oz. pearl barley
salt and pepper
3 medium-sized leeks
1 level tablespoon finely chopped parsley
4 thick slices white bread

☐ If you can't buy mutton, and it's scarce nowadays, use lamb. Wipe and cut into serving pieces. Put in a pan with 1½ pints cold water. Peel carrots and thickly peel turnip. Cut into dice. Peel potatoes and leave whole. Bring meat quickly to the boil and skim the top. Add carrots, turnip and potatoes, pearl barley and salt and pepper to season. Cover and simmer for 1½ hours.
☐ Remove roots from leeks and damaged leaves. Cut into ½in. slices and separate into rings. Wash well in salted water. Add to pan with parsley and cook for 5min. more.
☐ Cut the bread into small dice. Add to the soup and serve while the leeks are still crisp.

ICED AVOCADO PEAR SOUP
(Enough for four)

½oz. butter
1 level teaspoon chopped onion
1 level teaspoon plain flour
1 chicken stock cube
½ pint boiling water
1 large avocado pear
1 tablespoon lemon juice
½ pint milk
4 tablespoons plain yogurt
salt and pepper
mint sprigs

☐ Melt the butter in a pan, add the onion and fry gently for 5min. Do not allow the onion to brown. Stir in the flour and cook for 2min. Dissolve the stock cube in the boiling water. Add gradually to the saucepan, stirring. Bring to the boil, stirring all the time. Remove from the heat.
☐ Cut the pear in half using a stainless steel knife and remove the stone. Scoop all the flesh from the skin. Mash with the lemon juice until smooth. Stir in half the milk. Add the hot sauce to the avocado, stirring well until smooth.
☐ Stir in the rest of the milk and the yogurt. Season to taste with a little salt and pepper. Cover and chill for 2 hours. This soup discolours if left overnight. Pour into bowls and garnish with mint.

TOMATO SOUP
(Enough for four)

1 small carrot
1 small onion
1 rasher streaky bacon
2oz. butter
1 chicken stock cube
1 pint boiling water
2lb. 4oz. tin peeled tomatoes
salt and pepper
pinch of caster sugar
croûtons

☐ Peel and chop the carrot. Skin and chop the onion. Cut off the bacon rind. Chop the bacon into small pieces and heat it gently in a pan until the fat runs.
☐ Add 1oz. butter and the vegetables and cook gently for 5min.
☐ Dissolve the stock cube in the boiling water. Add to the pan with the tomatoes and their juice. Bring to the boil and simmer gently for 30min.
☐ Push through a nylon sieve into a clean pan. Add salt, pepper and sugar and reheat. Garnish with croûtons.

MUSHROOM CREAM SOUP
(Enough for five-six)

2oz. butter
1 shallot or 1 small onion
10oz. mushrooms
2oz. plain flour
1 chicken stock cube
1 pint boiling water
2 teaspoons lemon juice
½ pint milk
1 level tablespoon chopped parsley
salt and pepper
5 tablespoons single cream

☐ Melt the butter in a saucepan. Skin and finely chop the shallot or onion and add to the pan. Fry gently for 5min. Wash the mushrooms and slice finely. Add these to the saucepan and continue to fry gently for a further 5min., stirring. Sprinkle in the flour and cook for 2min., stirring occasionally. Remove the saucepan from the heat. Dissolve the stock cube in the boiling water. Stir in the stock, adding it slowly at first, and stirring all the time. Stir in lemon juice.
☐ Return to the heat and bring to boiling point, stirring until the soup has thickened. Blend in the milk, cover and simmer for 20min. Add most of the parsley and season well. Add the cream just before serving. Sprinkle each bowl of soup with rest of parsley.

CHILLED WATERCRESS SOUP
(Enough for six)

2 bunches of watercress
1 small onion
¾lb. potatoes
2oz. butter
1 chicken stock cube
1 pint boiling water
½ pint milk
salt and pepper
1 blade of mace—optional
5oz. carton single cream

☐ Wash and shake dry the watercress. Discard coarse roots and stalks. Trim off a small bunch of top leaves for garnish. Skin and thinly slice the onion. Peel and roughly slice the potatoes. Melt the butter in a heavy saucepan and gently fry the vegetables for 3-4min.
☐ Dissolve the stock cube in the boiling water. Add to the pan with the milk. Season with salt and pepper and the mace if used. Simmer very gently for 15min., or until the vegetables are nearly cooked. Add the watercress and simmer for a further 10min. Remove the mace.
☐ Push through a nylon sieve or liquidise. Finely chop the reserved watercress. Allow soup to cool then chill in the fridge for 1 hour. Just before serving stir in the cream and watercress.

ICED CUCUMBER SOUP
(Enough for four)

2 medium-sized cucumbers
¼ small onion
1oz. butter
1oz. plain flour
2 chicken stock cubes
1½ pints boiling water
salt and pepper
2 large egg yolks
4 tablespoons single cream
chopped parsley

☐ Wash and thinly peel the cucumbers. Cut 12 slices for decoration. Cut rest into 1in. pieces. Skin and chop the onion. Melt the butter in a large saucepan. Fry the cucumber and onion for 10min. Stir in the flour and cook for 3min.
☐ Dissolve the stock cubes in the boiling water. Add gradually to the vegetables. Season with salt and pepper. Cover and simmer for 20min.
☐ Liquidise the soup for 1min., or push through a nylon sieve. Rinse out the pan and pour in the soup. Beat the egg yolks and cream and stir into the soup. Heat gently until the soup is nearly at simmering point; pour into a large bowl. Leave to cool, then cover and chill in the refrigerator. Pour into bowls. Lay 3 slices cucumber on top of each bowl of soup.

MULLIGATAWNY
(Enough for four)

1lb. scrag end neck of lamb
1oz. lard
1 large onion
1 medium-sized cooking apple
1 level tablespoon curry powder
1oz. plain flour
salt and pepper
pinch of mixed dried herbs

☐ Wipe meat and cut it into small pieces. Melt lard in a saucepan, add the meat and fry until browned. Remove meat from pan; drain meat well and keep aside. Skin and finely chop the onion. Peel, core and chop the apple. Add onion and apple to the pan. Fry gently for 5min.
☐ Stir in curry powder and flour and cook gently for 2min. Remove pan from heat and gradually stir in 1½ pints cold water. Add meat. Bring to the boil, stirring. Add salt and pepper and the herbs.
☐ Simmer the soup for 1 hour, then strain soup into a clean pan, discarding apple and onion. Cut meat from bones and chop finely. Return to soup. Reheat soup and serve.

CHICKEN AND BAMBOO SHOOT SOUP
(Enough for four–six)

3oz. raw chicken meat
2oz. bamboo shoot
2oz. raw ham or green bacon
2 chicken stock cubes
2 pints boiling water
3oz. egg noodles
salt and pepper
1 tablespoon sherry

☐ Slice the chicken meat, bamboo shoot and ham into matchstick strips, 1½in. long. Dissolve the stock cubes in the boiling water in a saucepan and simmer the bamboo shoot and chicken for 10min.
☐ Add the noodles and 1 level teaspoon salt and simmer for a further 5min. Add the sherry and pepper to taste. Sprinkle on the strips of ham and boil soup gently for 3min. more. Serve in small hot bowls.

CARROT SOUP
(Enough for four)

12oz. carrots
1 large potato
½ small onion
1oz. butter
salt and pepper
pinch of caster sugar
1 level teaspoon finely chopped parsley
pinch of dried chervil—optional
1 chicken stock cube
1 pint boiling water

☐ Peel the carrots and potato; skin the onion, and grate vegetables coarsely. Melt the butter in a large saucepan. Add the prepared vegetables and stir. Add a little salt and pepper to taste, the sugar, parsley and chervil, if used. Cover the saucepan and cook very slowly for 15min., or until the carrots are very soft. Shake the pan occasionally to prevent the vegetables sticking to the base.
☐ Dissolve the stock cube in the boiling water and stir into saucepan. Bring to the boil; cover and simmer for a further 15min. Sieve or liquidise the soup into a clean saucepan. Check the seasoning and reheat soup. Garnish with croûtons.

LENTIL SOUP
(Enough for four–six)

6oz. lentils
2 pints boiling water
1 small onion
2 sticks of celery
1 medium-sized potato
1oz. lard
1 level teaspoon mixed dried herbs
1 blade of mace—optional
½ pint milk
salt and pepper

☐ Wash the lentils and place in a large bowl. Pour the boiling water over the lentils. Leave to soak overnight. Skin and finely chop the onion. Wash the celery and cut into 1in. lengths. Peel the potato and cut into pieces. Cover with cold water.
☐ Melt the lard in a saucepan and add the onion and celery and cook gently for 10min. Add the herbs, mace, if used, and lentils, together with their water. Bring rapidly to the boil, then reduce the heat to simmering. Cook for 2 hours, or until the soup thickens. Drain the potato.
☐ Add the potato and milk; bring to the boil again and cook for 10min., or until the potato is soft. Sieve the soup, through a nylon sieve, or liquidise. Season well with salt and pepper and reheat. Serve very hot.

CHICKEN SOUP
(Enough for six)

1 small onion
1oz. butter
6oz. cooked chicken
1½oz. plain flour
2 chicken stock cubes
1½ pints boiling water
¾ pint milk
salt and pepper
1 bay leaf
whole blanched almonds

☐ Skin and finely chop onion. Melt butter in a large saucepan. Add onion. Cover and fry for 5min. Cut chicken into small pieces. Stir flour into onion in saucepan and cook for 2min. Dissolve stock cubes in the boiling water. Remove pan from heat and gradually stir in the stock and milk. Bring to boil, stirring all the time. Add chicken meat, seasoning and bay leaf. Cover and simmer for 30min.
☐ Toast almonds until golden. Before serving soup, remove bay leaf and float almonds on top.

SPINACH SOUP
(Enough for four)

1 small onion
1oz. butter
1oz. plain flour
½ chicken stock cube
½ pint boiling water
¾ pint milk
12oz. packet frozen creamed spinach
salt and pepper
2 tablespoons single cream

☐ Skin and finely chop the onion. Melt butter in a medium-sized saucepan, add onion, cover and fry gently for 5min., or until tender. Stir in the flour and cook for 2min. Remove from heat.
☐ Dissolve the stock cube in the boiling water and gradually add to pan with the milk. Return to heat, bring to the boil and add the spinach and seasoning. Cover and simmer for 30min. stirring from time to time.
☐ Check seasoning and add cream before serving the soup. Serve garnished with fancy shapes made from Cheese Pastry—see page 17.

CHICKEN AND LEMON SOUP
(Enough for six-eight)

2 large chicken joints
1 small onion
1 celery top
salt and pepper
2oz. Patna rice
3 large eggs
juice of 2 large lemons
1 level teaspoon chopped mint

☐ Wipe the chicken joints and put into a large pan. Skin the onion. Wash the celery. Add to pan with 3 pints cold water and a good pinch each of salt and pepper. Bring to the boil, cover and simmer gently for 2 hours. When cooked, lift out chicken and strain the stock. Cut the chicken from the bones into small pieces.
☐ Return stock to pan and when it is boiling, add the rice and cook for 12min.
☐ Beat the eggs with 2 tablespoons cold water and lemon juice until frothy. Take a ladleful of hot stock and stirring all the time, pour it on to the eggs. Add another ladleful and pour it back into the soup, stirring all the time and taking care not to let the soup boil or it will curdle. Add the chicken pieces and mint and heat through. Serve at once.

BEETROOT SOUP
(Enough for six)

1 large onion
1 large carrot
1oz. butter
1oz. plain flour
2 chicken stock cubes
2 pints boiling water
1 bay leaf
16oz. tin beetroot
5oz. carton soured cream

☐ Skin and roughly chop the onion. Peel carrot and cut into slices. Melt butter in a medium-sized saucepan and fry vegetables for 5min., or until tender. Stir in the flour and cook for 2min. Dissolve the stock cubes in the boiling water. Remove pan from heat and gradually stir in stock. Add the bay leaf, cover and simmer for 20min.
☐ Drain off liquid from beetroot; add beetroot whole to the soup. Cover and simmer for a further 20min.
☐ Strain and reserve stock. Push the vegetables through a nylon sieve into the stock, or, remove bay leaf and blend the stock and vegetables in a liquidiser until smooth. Return to pan. Bring to the boil and check seasoning. Pour into bowls and stir soured cream into each bowl. Serve hot.

OXTAIL SOUP
(Enough for six)

1 oxtail
1 medium-sized onion
1 medium-sized carrot
2 sticks of celery
1oz. butter
1 rasher streaky bacon
salt and pepper
1 bay leaf
1 blade of mace
2 level tablespoons plain flour
3 tablespoons sherry
juice of 1 small lemon
1 packet potato crisps

☐ Ask the butcher to cut the oxtail into joints. Wash and dry the joints and trim off any excess fat. Skin and chop the onion. Peel and grate the carrot; wash the celery and cut into 1in. lengths.
☐ Melt the butter in a medium-sized saucepan. Add oxtail and fry until golden on all sides. Add vegetables and lightly fry for 5min., or until golden brown. Cover with 3 pints cold water and bring to the boil. Cut off the bacon rind and cut rasher into small pieces. Add to the meat and vegetables. Add salt and pepper, the bay leaf and mace. Reduce the heat. Cover and simmer gently for 4 hours, or until the meat is tender. Remove from the heat and allow the liquid to cool so that fat forms on the surface.
☐ When the fat has solidified, carefully remove it with a draining spoon. Remove the meat and strain the liquid. Pour the liquid into a clean pan. Cut the meat into small pieces and remove the bones. Blend the flour with the sherry and add a little of the stock. Pour the flour mixture into the saucepan and add the pieces of oxtail. Add the lemon juice. Bring to the boil slowly, stirring all the time. Simmer for 5min.
☐ Ladle the soup into hot bowls and just before serving garnish with some potato crisps.

CREAMY VEGETABLE SOUP
(Enough for four)

1 medium-sized onion
1 large leek
1 large carrot
1½oz. butter
1oz. plain flour
1 chicken stock cube
¾ pint boiling water
¾ pint milk
1 bay leaf
1 blade of mace
1 large potato
salt and pepper
2 heaped teaspoons finely chopped parsley

☐ Skin and finely chop the onion. Cut off leek root and discoloured leaves. Wash well and slice thinly. Wash and peel carrot, cut into slices. Melt butter in a large saucepan, add onion, leek and carrot. Cover, reduce heat and cook for about 10min. Stir the flour into the vegetables and butter and cook gently for 2min.
☐ Remove from heat. Dissolve the stock cube in the boiling water and gradually add to pan with milk. Return to the heat and bring to the boil, stirring all the time, until the sauce thickens. Add the bay leaf and mace, tied in a piece of muslin. Cover and simmer for 10min.
☐ Meanwhile, wash and peel the potato and cut into ½in. dice. Add to the soup. Season to taste and cook for a further 20min. or until tender. Remove the muslin bag and sprinkle soup with finely chopped parsley just before serving.

CORN CHOWDER
(Enough for four)

6oz. salt pork or green bacon
1 large onion
4 large potatoes
6 large cream crackers
½ pint milk
12oz. tin sweetcorn
1 level teaspoon salt
dash of paprika

☐ Cut the salt pork into small cubes or remove the bacon rinds and snip the rashers into pieces. Fry the pork or bacon in a saucepan until crisp and lightly browned. Skin and slice the onion. Peel and slice the potatoes. Stir onion into the bacon and cook until golden, then add potatoes and 1 pint water. Continue cooking for 20min., or until potatoes are tender.
☐ Crumble the cream crackers into a bowl, pour in milk, and leave to soak. Add to the cooked potatoes, then add corn, salt and paprika. Simmer over a low heat for 8-10min., then serve hot.

COLD CHERRY SOUP
(Enough for four)

1lb. 14oz. tin or 1½lb. fresh cherries
1 small lemon
2in. piece of cinnamon stick
5oz. caster sugar
¼ pint hot water
1 tablespoon port

☐ Drain liquid from tinned cherries. Add enough water to juice to make 1 pint. Remove peel from lemon leaving all pith behind. Put half the tinned cherries in a pan with the juice, cinnamon and lemon peel. Bring to boil and cook for 20-30min.
☐ Put the sugar in another saucepan with the hot water. Heat gently to dissolve the sugar, then bring to the boil. Add rest of cherries. Cook for 5min.
☐ Remove cinnamon and peel from first cherries, then stir all cherries and syrup together, adding the port. Allow to cool, then chill in the fridge.
☐ If the fruit is fresh, wash and stone cherries and cook as above using 1 pint cold water.
☐ If using sweetened tinned cherries, proceed as described, but add the strained juice of the lemon.
☐ This soup is Polish and is served there with croûtons as a starter to a meal, or just on its own for breakfast.

FISH CHOWDER
(Enough for four)

1 small onion
2 rashers streaky bacon
3 small potatoes
1lb. fresh haddock
15oz. tin peeled tomatoes
1 pint fish stock, or water
salt and pepper
1 bay leaf
2 cloves

☐ Skin and finely chop the onion.
Remove the rinds from the bacon and
fry until the fat runs. Chop bacon
roughly. Add onion and bacon to pan
and fry gently for 5min., or until soft but
not coloured.
☐ Meanwhile, peel and slice the
potatoes. Remove the skin from the
haddock and cut the flesh into cubes.
Beat the tomatoes until they are mashed.
Add potatoes, fish, tomatoes, fish stock
and all the seasonings to the pan. Cover
and simmer gently for 30min., or until
the fish is cooked. Remove the bacon
rinds, bay leaf and cloves to serve.

CAWL
(Enough for six-eight)

2lb. piece salty bacon
3 pints boiling water
3 medium-sized potatoes
2 large carrots
1 small swede
2 large leeks
½ small cabbage
4oz. peas or beans
2oz. oatmeal

☐ Put the bacon in a large pan; pour on
the water. Peel the potatoes and carrots.
Thickly peel the swede. Cut vegetables
into fairly large pieces. Add to pan,
cover and simmer for 1½ hours.
☐ Remove roots and damaged leaves
from leeks. Cut in half downwards and
wash well. Remove damaged leaves from
the cabbage. Wash the cabbage and
shred cabbage and leeks.
☐ After 1½ hours, remove the bacon—
keep hot. Add the cabbage, leeks and
peas or beans to the pan and cook for a
further 15-20min. Blend oatmeal with a
little of the soup. Pour into rest of soup,
stir well and cook for 10min. The
oatmeal thickens the liquid and absorbs
any fat from the bacon.
☐ Serve soup as a first course, then
follow with the bacon.

BORSCH
(Enough for ten)

8oz. white cabbage
2 medium-sized carrots
¾lb. raw beetroot
1 small leek
1 medium-sized onion
1 stick of celery
¼ medium-sized turnip
3 chicken stock cubes
3 pints boiling water
salt
1 level teaspoon finely chopped parsley
1 small bay leaf
3 peppercorns
2 level tablespoons tomato purée
1 level teaspoon caster sugar
2 tablespoons lemon juice
5oz. carton soured cream

☐ Remove any damaged leaves from the
cabbage. Wash and shred the cabbage.
Peel the carrots and cut them into fine
strips. Peel the beetroot; reserve 1 small
one and cut the rest into fine strips.
Remove root and damaged leaves from
the leek. Wash well. Cut leek in 2in.
pieces, then into fine strips. Skin and
finely chop the onion. Wash the celery
and cut into fine slices. Peel the turnip
thickly, cut into strips.
☐ Dissolve the stock cubes in the boiling
water and put into a large saucepan. Add
strips of beetroot, a good pinch of salt,
parsley and the rest of the vegetables.
Bring to the boil, cover and simmer for 2
hours, stirring occasionally.
☐ Tie the bay leaf and peppercorns in a
piece of muslin and add to the pan with
the tomato purée, sugar and lemon juice.
Simmer for 30min. more, or until the
vegetables are soft. Grate the rest of the
beetroot and add it to the soup 10min.
before serving.
☐ Push soup twice through a fine nylon
sieve or liquidise. Strain back into the
saucepan and heat through to boiling
point. Serve with 1 dessertspoon of
soured cream to each plate.

LEEK SOUP
(Enough for four)

1½lb. lamb bones
2 large leeks
½ pint milk
salt and pepper
1lb. potatoes
2 tablespoons single cream

☐ Make this soup after boning breast of
lamb, or ask your butcher for the bones.
Put bones in a pan with ½ pint cold
water and bring to the boil. Skim when
necessary. Trim off roots and damaged
leaves from the leeks. Cut in half
downwards and wash well. Cut into
½in. slices. Put leeks in a pan with the
milk, 1 pint cold water and salt and
pepper to season. Add bones and their
water. Bring to the boil, cover and
simmer for 2 hours.
☐ Peel and cut the potatoes into small
dice. Add to pan after 1 hour's cooking.
Stir in the cream just before serving and
add more seasoning if necessary.

FRENCH ONION SOUP
(Enough for six-eight)

1½lb. onions
1½oz. butter
1 tablespoon olive oil
salt and pepper
1 level teaspoon caster sugar
1½oz. plain flour
2 beef stock cubes
3 pints boiling water
¼ pint dry white wine
½in. thick rounds French bread
4oz. grated Parmesan cheese

☐ Skin and thinly slice the onions. Melt
the butter with the oil in a large heavy
saucepan. Add the onions and cook for
15min. over a low heat with saucepan
covered. Stir occasionally. Take off the
lid, raise the heat and stir in 1 level
teaspoon salt and the sugar. Cook for
30-40min., stirring frequently, until the
onions have turned a deep golden brown.
☐ Sprinkle in the flour and stir for
2min. Dissolve stock cubes in the boiling
water. Gradually stir in the stock. Add
the wine and salt and pepper to taste.
Simmer for 30min.
☐ Just before serving, toast the French
bread, allowing 1 round per person.
Place in the bottom of a tureen. Pour on
the soup. Sprinkle the cheese over the
bread when it comes to the top.

GIBLET SOUP
(Enough for four)

3 lots of chicken giblets or 1 lot turkey or goose giblets
1 small onion
1 small carrot
1 stick of celery
1 level teaspoon mixed dried herbs
1 clove
1 small blade of mace
6 peppercorns
1 level teaspoon salt
1oz. butter
1oz. plain flour

☐ Clean the giblets; put them into a pan with 2 pints cold water. Bring slowly to simmering point. Skin the onion, peel the carrot; wash the celery. Add them whole to the pan with the herbs, clove, mace, peppercorns and salt. Cover pan and simmer for 2 hours.
☐ Strain the stock and make it up to 1½ pints with water. Melt the butter in a saucepan, stir in flour and cook very gently for 20min. or until brown. Don't let it burn. Stir in the stock, bring to the boil, stirring and cook for 5min.
☐ Cut tiny pieces from the best giblets and reheat these in the soup. Season well and serve hot.

POTATO SOUP
(Enough for six)

1 large onion
4 medium-sized potatoes
2½oz. butter
1½ pints milk
salt and pepper
pinch of mixed dried herbs
2 tablespoons single cream
finely chopped chives

☐ Skin and very thinly slice the onion. Peel and thinly slice the potatoes. Melt butter in a pan but do not allow it to brown. Add potatoes and onion and stir until coated in butter. Put on lid and cook very gently for 12min. without burning. Stir in milk, salt, pepper and herbs. Cover and simmer for 35min. then check seasoning.
☐ Liquidise or push soup through a nylon sieve. Stir in cream and garnish with chopped chives.

GARLIC SOUP
(Enough for six-eight)

6oz. stale white bread
4 cloves of garlic
1 tablespoon olive oil
1 level teaspoon paprika
2 level teaspoons salt
2 pints boiling water
1 large egg

☐ Slice the bread very thinly and put it in a bowl. Skin the cloves of garlic. Heat oil in a frying pan and fry garlic until golden. Add paprika. Stir and remove from the heat or the paprika will go black and taste bitter.
☐ Add the salt to the boiling water and pour over the bread. Add garlic mixture, cover bowl and leave to stand for 5min.
☐ Beat the egg with a little water and stir into the soup. Reheat but do not boil. Remove garlic. Check seasoning, adding more salt if required. Serve hot with croûtons.

VICHYSSOISE
(Enough for four)

4 large leeks
2 medium-sized potatoes
1 medium-sized onion
2oz. butter
salt and pepper
2 chicken stock cubes
1¾ pints boiling water
5oz. carton single cream
finely chopped chives

☐ Wash leeks and remove roots, and discoloured leaves. Use only the white parts. Cut into 1in. pieces. Wash and peel the potatoes and slice thinly. Skin the onion and cut into slices.
☐ Melt the butter in a saucepan. Add the leeks and onion and fry gently for 10min., or until soft but not coloured. Add salt and pepper and the potatoes. Dissolve the stock cubes in the boiling water. Add to the vegetables. Cover pan and bring to boiling point. Reduce heat and simmer for 40min., or until vegetables are tender.
☐ Liquidise soup or push it through a nylon sieve using a wooden spoon. Stir in the cream. Leave to chill in a fridge for 2 hours then sprinkle with chopped chives to serve.

THICK ONION SOUP
(Enough for four)

1lb. onions
1oz. butter
1 chicken stock cube
1 pint boiling water
½oz. plain flour
salt and pepper
2 tablespoons top of the milk

☐ Skin and finely chop all but one onion. Melt ½oz. butter. Fry chopped onions gently until soft but not coloured. Dissolve the stock cube in the boiling water. Add to the pan, cover and simmer gently for 40min.
☐ Mix the flour to a smooth paste with a little cold water. Stir into the soup.
☐ Bring to the boil and simmer for 10min. more. Season well with salt and pepper.
☐ Skin and slice the remaining onion. Divide into rings. Melt the rest of the butter. Fry the rings for 5min., or until soft but not coloured. Drain on crumpled kitchen paper.
☐ Stir top of milk into soup and serve garnished with onion rings.

NORWEGIAN FISH SOUP
(Enough for four-six)

1¼lb. cod fillet
salt and pepper
1½oz. butter
1½oz. plain flour
¼ pint milk
5oz. carton single cream
1 tablespoon Marsala or sherry
2 level teaspoons finely chopped parsley

☐ Wash cod fillet and cut off as much of the skin as possible. Put in a pan with 1½ pints cold water and a good pinch of salt. Cover and simmer for 1 hour. Drain and reserve stock.
☐ Melt butter in a pan; stir in flour and cook gently for 2min. Remove from heat and gradually stir in milk and fish stock. Bring to boil, then simmer for 3min. Put fish and some of the liquid into a liquidiser and blend for 1min. Pour into remainder of the soup. Stir in cream and season to taste. Stir in Marsala or sherry. Simmer for 3min. Serve hot, sprinkled with chopped parsley.

RISOTTO
(Enough for four)

1 large onion
1lb. mushrooms
2oz. butter
4oz. Patna rice
1 chicken stock cube
1 pint boiling water
salt and pepper
pinch of saffron powder
4 tablespoons white wine
4 tablespoons olive oil
parsley
2oz. grated Parmesan cheese

☐ Skin and finely chop the onion. Wash and quarter the mushrooms. Heat the butter in a large frying pan and add the rice. Cook, stirring all the time until the rice has browned. Add the onion and fry for 3min.

☐ Dissolve the stock cube in the boiling water. Add stock to pan a little at a time, then bring to the boil, stirring. Season and add the saffron. Reduce heat, and cook gently until the rice has absorbed all the liquid. Add the wine and stir very gently. Turn rice into a bowl and steam over a pan of hot water until dry.

☐ Heat the oil in a saucepan and fry the mushrooms gently for 5min. Drain and season to taste.

☐ Pile rice in the centre of a hot dish and spoon the mushrooms round to make a border. Garnish with parsley and sprinkle Parmesan cheese on the rice, or serve separately.

ANTIPASTO

☐ Antipasto is the name the Italians give to appetisers at the beginning of a meal. There's no set recipe, but a plate of antipasto should be colourful and contain a variety of ingredients. Here are some typical antipasto ideas.

1. Finger-sized pieces of brown toast rubbed with a cut clove of garlic. On top of each, three fillets of anchovy each rolled round a caper.

2. Slices of salami rolled and secured with cocktail sticks.

3. Black olives, drained and rinsed and mixed with vinaigrette—see page 26.

4. Parma ham slices.

5. Slices of salami with a green or black olive in the centre, secured with sticks.

6. Tinned brown beans, prepared as for black olives.

7. Green olives prepared as for black olives.

8. White beans (tinned or boiled) prepared as for black olives, then mixed with drained tuna fish and topped with finely chopped parsley.

CHICKEN LIVER PATE
(Enough for ten)

½lb. streaky bacon
1 clove of garlic
1lb. chickens' liver
1lb. lambs' liver
1 large egg
1 tablespoon brandy
3 tablespoons double cream
pinch of mixed dried herbs
salt and pepper
3 olives
6 gherkins

☐ Cut off rinds from bacon. Stretch rashers by scraping them with a knife. Line a 9in. loaf tin with the bacon rashers. Skin and finely chop the clove of garlic. Coarsely mince the livers and garlic once. Lightly beat egg add to livers with brandy, cream and herbs. Season with salt and pepper.
☐ Pour into prepared tin. Cover with foil and stand in a baking tin, half-filled with cold water. Cook for 2 hours in centre of oven, pre-heated to 325 deg. F. or Mark 3. Cool for 30min. Cover with greaseproof paper and put a weight on top; leave overnight.
☐ Turn out. Slice olives; cut gherkins into fan shapes. Arrange the olive slices and gherkin fans on the pâté.

GREEK FISH SALAD
(Enough for four)

1lb. fresh haddock
½ small onion
1 large lemon
1 bay leaf
6 peppercorns
4 tablespoons olive oil
salt and pepper
1 level tablespoon chopped parsley

☐ Wash haddock. Skin and chop onion roughly. Cut off a little lemon peel leaving any white pith behind. Cut 4 thin slices for garnish.
☐ Put fish into a large saucepan. Cover with 1 pint cold water. Add onion, bay leaf, peppercorns and the piece of lemon peel. Cover and bring to the boil. Reduce heat, simmer for 15min. or until cooked. Do not overcook or fish breaks up too much. Remove from liquid and allow to cool on a plate.
☐ Remove skin from fish. Squeeze and strain lemon juice. Whisk olive oil and lemon juice together, until mixture thickens slightly; add salt and pepper to taste. When fish is cold, flake it roughly, leaving fair-sized pieces. Put into serving dishes.
☐ Just before serving pour oil and lemon dressing over. Sprinkle with chopped parsley. Garnish with lemon slices.

TOMATO ICE
(Enough for four)

2lb. ripe tomatoes
½ small onion
1 level dessertspoon tomato purée
Worcester sauce
lemon juice
1 level teaspoon caster sugar
lemon slices
cucumber slices

☐ Turn freezer to lowest setting. Wash and cut up tomatoes. Skin and roughly chop onion. Put into a large saucepan, cover and cook for 20min., or until tomatoes are soft. Push through a sieve into a bowl. Add tomato purée, Worcester sauce, lemon juice to taste and sugar. Leave to cool.
☐ Pour into ice trays or plastic boxes. Place in freezer compartment for 3–4 hours. When frozen dip base of tray in hot water, turn out. Crush with a rolling pin. Pile into glasses.
☐ Garnish with slices of lemon and cucumber.

PRAWN COCKTAIL
(Enough for four)

8oz. packet frozen prawns
1 small lettuce
2 level tablespoons mayonnaise—see page 26
2 level tablespoons tomato ketchup
2 tablespoons single cream
salt and pepper
½ teaspoon lemon juice
lemon wedges

☐ Leave the prawns to thaw in a bowl of cold water. Wash the lettuce carefully and dry in a tea towel. Using a large knife, shred finely. Put the mayonnaise, tomato ketchup, cream, salt and pepper into a mixing bowl and beat well. Add the lemon juice.
☐ Put some of the lettuce into the bottom of 4 small serving glasses. To the remaining lettuce add the piquant sauce and most of the prawns, saving a few for garnishing. Mix the lettuce and sauce well and put it into the small glasses.
☐ Garnish with lemon wedges and the remaining prawns.

POTTED SHRIMPS
(Enough for four)

4oz. butter
pinch of ground mace
pinch of pepper
pinch of ground nutmeg
6oz. peeled shrimps
lemon slices

☐ Melt 3oz. butter in a small pan. Stir in the spices and shrimps. Heat gently for 1min. Turn mixture into 4 small pots, smooth the tops and cool.
☐ Melt remaining butter and pour over the shrimps. Allow to set. Garnish with lemon slices.

KIPPER CREAMS
(Enough for six)

½lb. frozen kipper fillets
¼ very small onion
4oz. butter
1 large lemon
5oz. carton double cream
salt and pepper

☐ Cook the kipper fillets according to the instructions on the packet, poaching rather than grilling them. Skin and finely chop the onion. Melt 1oz. butter and fry the onion until cooked and transparent but not browned. Finely grate the lemon rind and squeeze out and strain the juice.
☐ Put the kipper fillets in small batches through your liquidiser including a little of the kipper liquid from the pan, lemon juice and cream. Continue until all the kippers are liquidised. Stir in the lemon rind and any cream and lemon juice that may be left, then the onion, melted butter and plenty of pepper.
☐ Taste before you add any salt. Spoon into 6 individual pots and smooth the tops. Melt the remainder of the butter and pour it over the kipper creams.
☐ Leave in the fridge to set for 10min. Garnish with lemon slices if liked.

POTTED HERRINGS
(Enough for four-six)

4 large herrings
1 blade of mace
1 bay leaf
2in. strip of lemon rind
salt and pepper
6oz. butter

☐ Cut off the heads and slit and clean herrings. Place on a board, open side down and press thumbs along backbone to loosen from the flesh. Turn fish over and lift backbone and small bones away. Rinse the herrings.
☐ Lay the fish in a large ovenproof dish. Add ¼ pint cold water, the mace, bay leaf, lemon rind, salt and pepper. Cover with the lid or a piece of foil. Cook for 20min. in centre of oven, pre-heated to 350 deg. F. or Mark 4. Leave to cool in the liquid.
☐ Drain off the liquid. Put the fish into a bowl and mash thoroughly with a fork, removing all small bones. Season again to taste. Melt 3oz. butter in a saucepan and add the fish. Mix thoroughly. Press into a 7in. dish. Leave until cold.
☐ Melt remaining butter over a low heat. Pour over cold herring mixture and leave until set.

SHRIMP-FILLED VOL-AU-VENTS
(Enough for six)

½lb. puff pastry—see page 18
6oz. peeled shrimps
½pint white sauce—see page 24
salt and pepper
1 level dessertspoon chopped parsley

☐ Roll out pastry on a floured board to about 1in. thickness. Use a 2in. fluted cutter and cut out the cases. Using a smaller cutter, press it into each case, but press only halfway through. This will form the lid. Place the cases on a baking tray. Cook for 30min., in centre of oven, pre-heated to 450 deg. F. or Mark 8.
☐ Add the shrimps to the white sauce and season well. When the vol-au-vent cases have cooked allow them to cool slightly.
☐ Use a teaspoon and carefully remove the lids and any uncooked pastry inside the cases.
☐ Spoon a small amount of sauce into each case and replace the lids. Garnish with the chopped parsley.

POTTED CHICKEN
(Enough for four)

4oz. cold cooked chicken
3oz. cooked ham
salt and pepper
ground nutmeg
3oz. butter

☐ This is a good recipe for using up the trimmings of cold roast poultry as an alternative to making a soup.
☐ Mince the chicken and ham very finely. Season with salt and pepper and some ground nutmeg. Gradually work in 2oz. butter and mix to a smooth paste. Press the paste into small glass pots and smooth the tops. Melt remaining butter and pour over the chicken. Leave to set.
☐ Serve with toast.

CHEESE AIGRETTES
(Enough for six)

2oz. grated Cheddar cheese
choux pastry—see page 20
oil for deep frying

☐ Add 1½oz. cheese to the choux pastry after you've beaten in the eggs.
☐ Heat the oil to the correct temperature—see page 15. Form the choux pastry into small balls and carefully lower them into the pan. Fry for about 5min., until the aigrettes are well puffed and golden brown. Drain well and serve with the remainder of the grated cheese.

CHEESE CROQUETTES
(Enough for six)

1oz. butter
1oz. plain flour
¼ pint milk
6oz. grated Gouda cheese
salt and pepper
dash of Worcester sauce
1 level tablespoon finely chopped chives
2 large eggs
fresh white breadcrumbs
oil for deep frying

☐ Melt the butter in a pan, stir in the flour and cook gently for 2min. Remove from the heat and gradually stir in the milk. Bring slowly to the boil, stirring, and cook gently for 2min. until thick. Stir in the cheese, salt and pepper to taste, Worcester sauce and chives. Beat 1 egg and beat into mixture.
☐ Spread mixture on a large plate, cover and leave to cool overnight.
☐ Using 2 tablespoons form the mixture into 12 small croquettes. Beat the remaining egg. Dip the croquettes first in egg, then in breadcrumbs. Shake off excess and repeat the process. Heat the oil to the correct temperature—see page 15. Fry 6 at a time in hot deep oil until golden brown on all sides. Drain on kitchen paper and keep hot. Fry remaining croquettes. Serve hot.

SALMON MOUSSE
(Enough for eight)

8oz. and 4oz. tins pink salmon
½oz. powdered gelatine
5oz. carton double cream
½ pint white sauce—see page 24
salt and pepper
paprika
watercress

☐ Drain salmon and remove skin and bones. Flake fish finely.
☐ Put gelatine in a cup, add 3 tablespoons water, stand the cup in a pan of water and heat until the gelatine dissolves. Stir salmon and cream into sauce. Season again, if necessary, then stir in dissolved gelatine, pouring it from a height to cool it. Pour into 8 small dishes or into a 2lb. loaf tin. Leave to set.
☐ If you use a loaf tin, unmould mousse by dipping tin up to its rim in hot water. Count five. Turn mousse on to a plate, cut into 8 slices. Garnish with paprika and watercress.
☐ Serve with hot toast cut into fingers.

BAKED EGGS IN CREAM
(Enough for four)

1½oz. butter
two 5oz. cartons double cream
4 large eggs
1oz. grated Cheddar cheese
salt and pepper

☐ Butter a shallow, fireproof dish or 4 individual cocotte dishes with ½oz. butter. Pour the cream in and carefully break the eggs on top, making sure to keep the yolks intact. Sprinkle with grated cheese and a little salt and pepper. Cover with little dots of the remaining butter and bake for 12-15min., or until the eggs are just set and the top golden, in centre of oven, pre-heated to 325 deg. F. or Mark 3.
☐ Serve immediately.

CRAB MOUSSE
(Enough for four-six)

½oz. powdered gelatine
boiling water
2 level teaspoons tomato purée
4 level tablespoons mayonnaise—see page 26
8oz. fresh crab meat
5oz. carton double cream
2 tablespoons single cream
1 large egg white
¼ cucumber

☐ Put the gelatine in a bowl with 2 tablespoons cold water. Pour on ¼ pint boiling water; stir well. Leave to cool.
☐ Stir tomato purée into mayonnaise. Break up crab meat, removing all bony pieces and stir crab into mayonnaise mixture. Stir cold but liquid gelatine into mixture and leave until just beginning to set.
☐ Whisk creams. Whisk egg white stiffly. Fold cream then egg white into mixture. Pour into a 6in. soufflé dish. Leave in a cool place for at least 1 hour to set.
☐ Wash and thinly slice cucumber. Arrange round edge of mousse. Serve with brown bread and butter.

SPANISH OMELETTE
(Enough for three-four)

3oz. frozen runner beans
3oz. frozen peas
boiling water
salt and pepper
1 small onion
1 small green pepper
½oz. lard
4oz. tomatoes
6 large eggs

☐ Slice the beans if whole. Cook beans and peas separately in boiling salted water for 5min. Skin and finely slice the onion. Wash the pepper, cut in half and remove the core and seeds. Slice finely. Heat the lard in a large frying pan, add the onion and pepper, cover and cook slowly for 5min. Drop the tomatoes into boiling water, leave for 1min., then drain, skin and chop. Add tomatoes to pan, season with salt and pepper and cook for 2min. more.
☐ Beat the eggs. Add beans and peas then eggs to pan and cook gently for 3min. until the bottom is golden and the top is just set. Turn out, cut into portions and serve flat. Or make 3 or 4 separate small omelettes.

QUICHE LORRAINE
(Enough for four)

4oz. plain flour
salt and pepper
2oz. butter
4 standard eggs
8 rashers streaky bacon
½ pint double cream

☐ Sift flour and a pinch of salt into a
bowl. Rub in the butter until mixture
looks like breadcrumbs. Beat 1 egg
lightly. Make a well in the centre of
the flour and add the egg. Add 1
tablespoon cold water. Mix with your
fingers drawing the flour into the egg.
Add a few more drops cold water if
necessary to give a stiff dough. Knead
quickly into a ball. Wrap in greaseproof
paper and leave for 1 hour in a
refrigerator or cool place.
☐ Cut off the bacon rinds and cut the
bacon into 1in. strips. Fry bacon gently
for 2min. Remove from heat and drain
on kitchen paper. Beat remaining eggs
thoroughly. Season with pepper only.
Beat in the cream.
☐ Unwrap the pastry and roll out to fit
an 8in. flan ring, allowing an extra 1½in.
all round for the sides of the flan. Stand
the flan ring on a lightly greased baking
tray. Carefully line the ring with pastry,
lifting the pastry into the sides. Trim off
any excess pastry from the top. Prick the
base with a fork.
☐ Arrange bacon strips in the flan case
and pour on the cream and egg mixture.
Cook for 20min. just above centre of
oven, pre-heated to 400 deg. F. or Mark
6, then reduce heat to 350 deg. F. or
Mark 4 and cook for a further 10min.
until the filling has risen and is golden
brown. Slide off the baking tray. Let it
cool for a minute then remove the flan
ring carefully and serve.

FISH IN ASPIC
(Enough for eight)

¾ pint aspic jelly made from bought
crystals
boiling water
4 small lemon sole fillets
4oz. packet frozen prawns
salt and pepper
1 bay leaf
little tomato flesh
little lemon peel
cucumber slices

☐ Make up aspic jelly according to
packet instructions. Skin sole fillets—
see page 9.
☐ Reserve 8 prawns; chop rest. Season
with salt and pepper. Cut each sole fillet
in half lengthways. Place some chopped
prawns on each piece of fish. Roll up and
tie securely. Pour about 1in. cold water
into a saucepan, add bay leaf and bring
to simmering point.
☐ Place fish rolls in this and poach
gently for 5-7min. Remove from liquid
and leave on a plate until cold.
☐ While fish is cooking, pour a little
aspic jelly into each of 8 dariole moulds.
Leave to set in a cool place. Cut small
diamond shapes from tomato flesh and
lemon peel. Using a hat pin, dip the
shapes into liquid aspic jelly, place in
mould, best side down, put a prawn in
centre and leave to set. Then pour a
little more jelly over this. Leave to set.
☐ Trim the fish rolls so they will stand.
Place one in the centre of each dariole
mould. Pour a little jelly round, leave to
set. Top up with more jelly to rim of
mould. Leave to set.
☐ Turn out by holding mould in hot
water for 2 to 3 seconds. Invert mould
on a plate, shake gently, remove mould.
☐ Serve surrounded by slices of
cucumber. Heat the jelly very gently at
any time if it becomes too thick to pour.

TARAMASALATA
(Enough for six)

8oz. white bread and 3 slices white bread
8oz. smoked cod roe
1 clove of garlic
6 tablespoons olive oil
2 tablespoons strained lemon juice
pepper
lemon slices
2 level teaspoons chopped parsley

☐ Remove crusts from 8oz. white bread.
Crumble it into a bowl. Add 4
tablespoons cold water and leave to
soak. Skin roe, break it down with a
fork or wooden spoon. Skin and crush
clove of garlic. Squeeze out surplus
liquid from bread, mash and mix with
roe and garlic. Gradually add oil and
lemon juice alternately, beating until
smooth and creamy. Season with pepper.
Smoked cod roe is salty so do not add
salt.
☐ Spoon into a serving bowl. Cover and
chill. Meanwhile, toast remaining
bread on both sides. Serve Taramasalata
garnished with lemon slices, parsley and
triangles of toast.

BOLOGNAISE STARTER
(Enough for four)

1 small onion
1 small carrot
1 stick of celery
1 rasher of bacon
2oz. butter
½lb. raw minced beef
1 bay leaf
1 strip of lemon rind
3 level tablespoons tomato purée
1 beef stock cube
½ pint boiling water
salt and pepper
8oz. macaroni bows
Parmesan cheese

☐ Skin and chop onion finely. Peel and chop carrot and scrub and chop celery. Remove rind from bacon and cut rasher into small pieces. Melt 1oz. butter in a saucepan. Add chopped vegetables and bacon. Fry gently for 8min. or until tender but not brown. Remove from saucepan, leaving fat behind.
☐ Fry minced beef in remaining fat until well browned. Return vegetables and bacon to saucepan. Add bay leaf, lemon rind and tomato purée. Dissolve stock cube in boiling water. Mix into meat and vegetables until well blended. Season. Cover pan; simmer for 30min., or until tender.
☐ Twenty minutes before meat is ready, bring 3 pints salted water to the boil in a large pan. Add macaroni bows and cook for 12min. or until soft but not soggy. Drain. Toss in rest of butter and keep hot. Remove bay leaf and lemon rind from sauce.
☐ Spoon macaroni bows on to a hot serving plate; pour sauce in centre. Serve with grated Parmesan cheese.

LIVER TERRINE
(Enough for six)

1lb. pigs' liver
4oz. streaky bacon
2oz. butter
2oz. plain flour
½ pint milk
3 large eggs
1 clove of garlic—optional
pinch of dried thyme
salt and pepper

☐ Wash liver. Remove rinds from bacon. Put liver and bacon through a coarse mincer. Melt butter in a saucepan. Stir in flour and cook for 1min. over a gentle heat. Remove from heat. Gradually stir in the milk and bring to the boil, stirring all the time until thickened, then cook gently for 2min. Mix with liver and bacon in a large basin. Break eggs into a bowl. Beat thoroughly. Add to meat. Skin and crush clove of garlic if used. Add garlic, thyme, salt and pepper to mixture. Mix until smooth.
☐ Pour into a greased ovenproof dish. Cover, but not too closely as mixture rises. Stand in a dish containing cold water. Cook for 2 hours in centre of oven, pre-heated to 325 deg. F. or Mark 3. Remove from oven and leave until cold. Serve with slices of hot toast.

SCALLOPED FISH
(Enough for four)

1lb. potatoes
salt and pepper
1lb. cod
1 small onion
few parsley stalks
2 tablespoons white wine—optional
3 teaspoons strained lemon juice
1oz. butter
1oz. plain flour
milk
2 tablespoons single cream
2oz. grated Cheddar cheese
parsley sprigs

☐ Wash and peel potatoes. Cook in boiling, salted water for 20min. Wash fish. Skin and chop onion. Put fish, onion and parsley stalks in a pan. Add wine, if used, lemon juice and ¾ pint cold water. Simmer gently for 10-15min. Transfer fish to a plate; remove skin. Strain the liquid and discard onion and parsley.
☐ Make a white sauce—see page 24—using the butter, flour and ½ pint strained fish liquid instead of milk.
☐ Drain potatoes. Mash with a little milk until creamy. Spoon into a piping bag fitted with a large star pipe. Gradually heat sauce adding cream and seasoning to taste. Flake fish and divide evenly into 4 clean deep scallop shells or individual dishes.
☐ Pipe potato round edge. Pour sauce over fish only in centre. Sprinkle centre of each shell with grated Cheddar cheese.
☐ Place under a hot grill until potatoes are just turning golden brown. Garnish with parsley sprigs and serve.

AVOCADO PEARS AND BLACK OLIVES
(Enough for four)

2 avocado pears
1 tablespoon lemon juice
12 black olives
5oz. carton soured cream
salt and pepper
paprika

☐ Using a stainless steel knife, cut each pear lengthways through to the stone. Separate the two halves by carefully twisting them in opposite directions. Remove the stones, and sprinkle the pears with lemon juice to prevent them discolouring.
☐ Stone the olives and chop roughly. Pour the cream into a mixing bowl and add the olives. Season with salt and pepper. Arrange the avocados on small serving dishes and carefully spoon on the olive sauce. Sprinkle pears lightly with paprika.

EGG MAYONNAISE
(Enough for four)

4 hard-boiled eggs
1 small lettuce
¼ pint mayonnaise—see page 26
paprika

☐ Remove the shells from the eggs and cut the eggs in half lengthways.
☐ Wash the lettuce carefully and dry in a tea towel. Arrange on individual serving dishes. Place the eggs, cut side down, on the lettuce and carefully coat with the mayonnaise. Lightly sprinkle with paprika.

SWEET AND SOUR SPARE RIBS
(Enough for six)

2lb. pork spare ribs
salt and pepper
3 teaspoons soy sauce
4 tablespoons sherry
1 large egg
3 level tablespoons cornflour
3 tablespoons vegetable oil
3 level dessertspoons dark brown sugar
5 dessertspoons vinegar
1 level tablespoon tomato ketchup

☐ Ask the butcher for the ends of the ribs—not the fairly chunky chops we usually buy, but the kind the Chinese restaurants use for spare rib dishes.
☐ Wipe the meat with a damp, clean cloth and cut the bones apart by cutting through the meat in between each bone. Chop the bones and meat into 4in. lengths if very long. Mix together a pinch each of salt and pepper, the soy sauce and sherry. Soak the meat and bones in this mixture for 30min. Remove from the marinade and drain.
☐ Beat the egg well. Coat the ribs first in egg then in all but 3 level teaspoons of the cornflour. Fry the spare ribs quickly in the hot oil for 8–10min. Meanwhile, prepare the sweet and sour sauce by adding the remaining ingredients to the marinade together with 9 tablespoons cold water. Blend the remaining cornflour with 3 teaspoons water and stir into the marinade. Transfer to a pan and cook for 2min., stirring all the time until the sauce boils and thickens. Reduce heat and simmer for 2–3min. Remove and pour over the spare ribs and serve immediately.

PARMA HAM WITH MELON
(Enough for four)

1 small Honeydew melon
4 slices Parma ham

☐ Cut the melon into four slices. Cut the melon from the skin and slice down to the skin to make bite-sized wedges. Keep the melon positioned on the skin. Fold the slices of ham in two.
☐ To serve, place the melon on a serving dish and arrange a piece of ham over each slice of melon.

GNOCCHI
(Enough for four)

¾ pint milk
½lb. semolina
4oz. butter
3½oz. grated Parmesan cheese
2 large eggs
1 level teaspoon salt
¼ level teaspoon ground nutmeg

☐ Put the milk in a saucepan and bring nearly to boiling point. Sprinkle on the semolina gradually, stirring well to prevent lumpiness. When it is thick and smooth, add 2oz. butter and 2½oz. cheese. Remove from heat and add the eggs, one at a time, beating well after each addition.
☐ Pour the mixture into a shallow dish, about ½in. deep, and leave until quite cold. Cut the semolina into small pieces with a cold wet knife and roll into the size and shape of almonds. Melt remaining butter. Place gnocchi gently in a baking dish with the remaining cheese, salt, nutmeg and melted butter. Bake for 30-35min. in centre of oven, pre-heated to 350 deg. F. or Mark 4.

GRILLED GRAPEFRUIT
(Enough for four)

2 large grapefruit
2oz. Demerara sugar
4 glacé cherries

☐ Cut the grapefruit in half. Using a sharp knife, remove the pith between the segments. Cut between the flesh and the pith and draw the knife from the centre to the edge, between each segment. Sprinkle on the Demerara sugar and place the grapefruit under a hot grill for about 3min., or until golden brown. Serve hot with a cherry on each half.

MUSHROOMS IN BRANDY
(Enough for four)

1oz. butter
1 clove of garlic
½ small onion
1lb. mushrooms
little lemon juice
salt and pepper
pinch of caster sugar
2 tablespoons brandy
½ pint double cream
4 slices of bread
1 level tablespoon chopped parsley

☐ Melt the butter in a frying pan. Skin and finely chop the garlic and the onion and fry in the butter for 3-4min. Wash and finely chop the mushrooms and add to the pan. Add the lemon juice, salt and pepper. Cook for 2-3min. and then cook gently to steam off the water. Add a little sugar—to counteract the lemon juice.
☐ Add the brandy and light it. Pour in the cream when the flames have died down and cook gently until thick. Toast the bread and place the mushrooms on top. Sprinkle with parsley to serve.

GLOBE ARTICHOKES IN VINAIGRETTE DRESSING
(Enough for four)

4 medium-sized artichokes
boiling water
salt
vinaigrette dressing—see page 26

☐ Wash the artichokes well under running cold water before cooking so that they are thoroughly clean. Drain well. Trim the points off the leaves at the top. Cut off the stalk.
☐ Cook in a pan of boiling salted water for 30-40min., or until a leaf pulls off easily. Drain upside down on a rack.
☐ Place the artichokes on a serving dish and pour the vinaigrette dressing over the top. The dressing can also be served in little bowls so that each artichoke leaf can be dipped in separately.
☐ To eat, simply pull off a leaf at a time with your fingers and suck the fleshy part. Discard the rest. When you come to the centre, cut away and discard the choke—it looks like a frondy flower. Eat the artichoke bottom, which is considered the great delicacy, with a knife and fork.

OMELETTE AUX FINES HERBES
(Enough for two)

2 large eggs
salt and pepper
pinch of mixed dried herbs
½oz. butter

☐ Beat the eggs, a pinch each of salt and pepper and the herbs until blended.
☐ Place the butter in a frying pan and melt over a high heat. When it begins to foam and the butter begins to colour pour in the eggs.
☐ Let the eggs settle for a few seconds then mix round with a fork. Tilt the pan to let the egg flow into the spaces. Cook for a few more seconds then tilt the pan so that the omelette slides to one side of the pan. Slide the omelette out of the pan turning it in two as it reaches the serving plate.

CHEESE SOUFFLE
(Enough for four)

½oz. butter
½oz. plain flour
4 tablespoons milk
1½oz. finely grated Cheddar cheese
salt and pepper
2 large eggs

☐ Melt the butter in a saucepan, stir in the flour and cook gently for 2min., stirring occasionally. Gradually stir in the milk and bring to the boil, stirring all the time. Allow to cool slightly, then stir in the cheese and salt and pepper to taste.
☐ Separate the eggs and add the yolks to the mixture, beating well. Whisk the egg whites until stiff, then fold carefully into the mixture using a large metal spoon. Turn mixture into a greased 5in. soufflé dish and bake for 30min. or until well risen and golden brown, in centre of oven, pre-heated to 350 deg. F. or Mark 4. Serve immediately.

GUACAMOLE
(Enough for eight-twelve)

2 medium-sized onions
1 clove of garlic
4 medium-sized tomatoes
boiling water
1 small chilli pepper
4 avocado pears
1 teaspoon lime or lemon juice
salt and pepper

☐ Skin and chop the onions and clove of garlic. Put the tomatoes in boiling water; leave for 1min. Skin and chop roughly. Cut the top off the chilli pepper. Cut in half and remove the seeds. Wash and cut into small pieces. Put the onions, garlic, tomatoes and chilli pepper in a liquidiser and blend for 1min. You can do this well in advance.
☐ At the last moment, peel the avocado pears, cut in half and remove the stones. Cut into pieces. Add to tomato purée in the liquidiser with lime or lemon juice and salt and pepper to season and blend for 1min. Spoon into a large bowl and serve as a first course in individual bowls or as a dip at a party. Or you can just roughly chop all ingredients and serve as a salad.

CITRUS SALAD
(Enough for four)

2 large grapefruit
3 large oranges
1 lime
3 sprigs of mint
1oz. caster sugar

☐ Wash all the fruit and mint. Peel the grapefruit and oranges by cutting away peel and pith in one. Cut to centre by side of each segment skin and put flesh and juice in a bowl. Squeeze segment skins so no juice is wasted. Cut the lime, without peeling, into very thin slices; add to bowl.
☐ Pour ¼ pint water into a pan and add the sugar. Bring to boil and boil for 1min. Remove from heat, then add 2 sprigs of mint and cool.
☐ Strain liquid into fruit and stir well. Add mint leaves and chill.

Salads & Vegetables

We British make pretty dreary salads and we overcook our marvellous vegetables to a soggy mass. Vegetables can't be left to cook on their own, they need lots of care. Here are basic recipes for cooking vegetables plus some good filling dishes

POTATO SALAD
(Enough for six)

1lb. new potatoes
salt and pepper
1 tablespoon vinaigrette dressing—see page 26
4 spring onions
3 level tablespoons mayonnaise—see page 26

☐ Scrape the potatoes or leave their skins on. Cook gently in boiling salted water for 15-20min. until tender. Do not let them break up. Drain at once. Remove skins if necessary and cut potatoes into cubes while still warm.
☐ Put potatoes into a bowl. Pour over the vinaigrette dressing so that the potato absorbs it. Cut off roots and discoloured leaves of onions. Chop onions finely. Add to potatoes with mayonnaise. Stir well but gently.

YOGURT SALAD
(Enough for six)

½ large cucumber
1 clove of garlic
two 10oz. cartons plain yogurt
salt
paprika
6 mint leaves

☐ Peel the cucumber and cut into ¼in. dice. Skin and finely chop the garlic. Stir into the yogurt with salt to taste. Chill in the refrigerator and serve cold sprinkled with paprika. Chop the mint leaves roughly and add to the yogurt.

CHICKEN SALAD IN LEMON JELLY
(Enough for four-six)

2 packets lemon-flavoured jelly
1¼ pints boiling water
2 large lemons
¼ cucumber
4oz. black grapes
6oz. cooked chicken

☐ Dissolve the jellies in the boiling water. Squeeze out and strain the lemon juice. Stir into the jelly. Rinse a 9in. loaf tin with cold water. Pour ½in. liquid jelly into the base. Leave in the refrigerator or cool place until set. Cool remaining jelly but do not allow it to set.
☐ Wash and thinly slice the cucumber. Wash grapes. Cut in half and remove the pips. Cut chicken meat into ½in. dice. Pour some of the liquid jelly into a cup. Dip six slices of cucumber into the cup and arrange overlapping, down the centre of the set jelly. Dip 12 grape halves into the liquid jelly and arrange, cut side up, down either side of the cucumber. Leave until quite set. Pour jelly over the decorations to cover and leave to set.
☐ If the jelly for pouring begins to set, stand the bowl over a pan of hot water and leave until jelly is liquid again. But do remember to cool it again before use or the decorations will float to the surface. Mix two tablespoons jelly with the chicken and arrange it over the set jelly. Leave until set. Cover completely with liquid jelly and leave to set.
☐ Pour a little more jelly into a cup and repeat the first process of dipping and setting grapes and cucumber. Set as before. Cover with more jelly so that the tin is filled. Set overnight or for several hours in a cool place.
☐ Chop any remaining set jelly. To unmould the jelly, dip the tin in hot water and count up to three. Invert the mould on to a plate. Shake firmly. When you hear the jelly drop on to the plate, carefully ease off the tin. Garnish with the chopped jelly and serve with a salad.

RUSSIAN SALAD
(Enough for four-six)

8oz. carrots
1lb. new potatoes
8oz. peas
8oz. runner beans
salt and pepper
4 level tablespoons mayonnaise—see page 26

☐ Scrape the carrots. Scrape and rinse the potatoes. Shell the peas. Top and tail the beans, wash and drain. Dice the carrot and potatoes very neatly. Cut the beans into pieces. Put about 2in. water in a saucepan. Add a little salt and all the prepared vegetables. Bring to the boil and boil for 10min., or until the vegetables are just tender. Do not allow them to break up.
☐ Drain the vegetables well and rinse with cold water. Allow to become cold. Then mix into the mayonnaise and season to taste with salt and pepper.

COLESLAW SALAD
(Enough for four)

1 small white cabbage
salt and pepper
1 small onion
1 large red eating apple
juice of ½ small lemon
6 level tablespoons mayonnaise—see page 26

☐ Discard the outer leaves of the cabbage. Shred the rest and season it. Skin and finely chop the onion, and core and thinly slice the apple. Do not peel it. Coat with lemon juice to prevent the apple turning brown. Mix all the ingredients and serve.

Fruit and vegetables combined make
marvellous salads

TUNA SALAD
(Enough for four)

8oz. tin tuna fish
½ large green pepper
3 sticks of celery
12 small radishes
4 Cos lettuce leaves
2oz. red cabbage
½ small cucumber
few sprigs mustard and cress
vinaigrette dressing—see page 26
1 tablespoon lemon juice

☐ Drain the tuna fish and cut it into rough chunks. Wash the pepper and remove the white seeds. Cut into small dice. Wash and slice the celery into ⅓in. pieces. Wash the radishes, remove tops and tails and leave whole. Cut large radishes in half or quarters.
☐ Wash the lettuce and tear the leaves into small pieces. Shred the cabbage and cut long shreds in half. Wash and chop the cucumber into small dice. Wash the cress. Mix all the ingredients together in a bowl and stir gently to coat with the vinaigrette dressing and lemon juice.

CELERIAC SALAD
(Enough for four)

juice of ½ large lemon
2 medium-sized celeriacs
5oz. carton double cream
¼ pint mayonnaise—see page 26
1 level teaspoon made mustard

☐ Put the lemon juice in ½ pint cold water.
☐ Thickly peel the celeriac so that only the white part shows. Cut into very thin slices. Don't use the woody parts in the centre. Drop slices into lemon water.
☐ Whip the cream and add the mayonnaise and mustard. Drain celeriac and stir in. Chill for 2 hours.
☐ Serve on lettuce leaves.

AVOCADO SALAD
(Enough for four)

2 rashers lean green back bacon
2 large avocado pears
1 tablespoon lemon juice
12 small walnut halves
12 small stoned black olives
vinaigrette dressing—see page 26

☐ Remove the bacon rinds and fry the rinds gently until the fat runs. Cook the rashers until they are cooked but still soft. Chop the bacon in small pieces.
☐ Peel the avocado pears and cut the flesh in half. Remove the large stones and chop the flesh. Pour lemon juice over the avocado flesh so that it doesn't discolour. Roughly chop the walnuts.
☐ Mix all the ingredients in a bowl and carefully stir to coat everything well with the vinaigrette. Serve on a bed of crisp Cos lettuce leaves.

SPICED MIXED SALAD
(Enough for four)

1 large onion
4 large tomatoes
3in. piece of cucumber
¼ level teaspoon ground coriander
1½ level teaspoons finely chopped chilli
salt
2 slices of lemon

☐ Skin and finely chop the onion. Wash the tomatoes. Cut one in half and reserve half. Chop the rest. Wash cucumber and cut into very small dice. Mix all the chopped vegetables together with the coriander and green chilli, adding salt to taste.
☐ Slice the remaining tomato half. Serve the salad in a small bowl, garnished with the tomato and lemon slices.

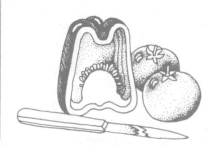

SAVOURY STRAWBERRY SALAD
(Enough for four)

2 sticks of celery
3 small spring onions
2 heads of chicory
8oz. firm strawberries
1lb. cottage cheese
salt and pepper

☐ Wash celery and remove leafy and discoloured parts. Slice 1 stick finely. Cut the other into 3 pieces, then into fine strips. Leave in iced water to curl. Wash onions. Cut off the root end and any discoloured parts. Slice thinly. Remove stalk end of chicory. Break off leaves. Wash in cold water and dry well. Wash and hull the strawberries. Reserve 5 for garnish and cut the rest into quarters.
☐ Stir sliced celery, onions and strawberries into cheese. Season to taste. Put chicory leaves on a plate with tips pointing out. Spoon the cheese mixture in the centre. Halve reserved strawberries. Arrange on cheese. Arrange drained celery curls between the strawberries.

CHINESE SALAD
(Enough for four)

4 level tablespoons bean sprouts
boiling water
2 standard eggs
4oz. cooked ham
1 large carrot
1 large tomato
¼ cucumber

☐ Remove any discoloured bean sprouts and drop the remainder into fast-boiling water. Leave off the heat for 3min. Drain, pour cold water over them and drain.
☐ Boil eggs for 12min. Cool then shell. Chop into small pieces. Cut ham into thin strips. Peel carrot and grate. Slice tomato and unpeeled cucumber.
☐ Mix bean sprouts, carrot, egg and ham strips together. Place in a serving dish. Garnish with cucumber and tomato slices.

SALAD NICOISE
(Enough for four-six)

1½lb. French beans
salt and pepper
1 clove of garlic—optional
small tin anchovy fillets
1lb. tomatoes
12 black olives
vinaigrette dressing—see page 26

☐ Cut tops and tails off beans. Wash beans and cut in half. Bring a pan of salted water to the boil. Add the beans and cook for 20min., or until tender. Drain well. Leave to become cold. Skin garlic clove—if used. Cut in half and rub round inside of salad bowl. Drain the anchovy fillets. Wash tomatoes, and cut in quarters. Put beans, tomatoes, anchovies and olives in bowl. Mix together with the vinaigrette.
☐ Flaked tuna fish can be added to the salad in place of the anchovies if liked, or small cold new potatoes.

WALDORF SALAD
(Enough for four)

2 medium-sized red eating apples
2 large sticks of celery
3 level tablespoons mayonnaise—see page 26
1 small lettuce
1½oz. walnut halves

☐ Wash apples; do not peel. Cut into quarters and remove core. Cut apples into ⅓in. dice. Scrub celery, remove leafy part. Cut into ⅓in. dice. Put apples and celery in a basin. Add enough mayonnaise to coat well.
☐ Wash lettuce leaves thoroughly. Dry on kitchen paper. Arrange on a large flat plate. Chop walnuts roughly. Mix into apples and celery. Pile mixture on the lettuce leaves and serve at once.

GREEN SALAD
(Enough for four)

1 medium-sized lettuce
¼ small cabbage
1 box mustard and cress
1 bunch watercress
1 head of chicory
4oz. white grapes
4 spring onions
vinaigrette dressing—see page 26
1 level teaspoon chopped parsley
1 level teaspoon chopped mint

☐ Wash the lettuce discarding damaged leaves. Shake well or dry in a clean tea towel. Discard discoloured leaves from the cabbage; wash and shred remainder coarsely.
☐ Trim the roots and stems off the mustard and cress and the watercress and wash under running water. Drain well. Trim off root end and outer leaves from the chicory and wash well. Tear leaves in half. Wash the grapes. Remove roots and tops of spring onions.
☐ Mix all the vegetables and grapes together in a large salad bowl. Toss with the vinaigrette dressing and sprinkle with parsley and mint.

TOMATO SALAD
(Enough for four)

1lb. medium-sized tomatoes
boiling water
1 small onion
1 heaped tablespoon finely chopped parsley
vinaigrette dressing—see page 26

☐ Put the tomatoes into a large mixing bowl and cover with boiling water. Leave for 1min. Drain off the water and skin and slice the tomatoes thinly. Skin and roughly chop the onion. Arrange the tomato slices on a plate and carefully place the onions in the centre. Sprinkle with the chopped parsley.
☐ Pour the vinaigrette dressing over the tomato salad and serve.

CUCUMBER SALAD
(Enough for four)

1 large cucumber
salt
vinaigrette dressing—see page 26

☐ Peel and cut the cucumber into very thin slices. Layer these slices in a dish with a good sprinkling of salt between. Cover the top layer with salt and leave to stand for 1 hour.
☐ Pour into a colander and rinse very well under the running cold tap. Drain well. Pour vinaigrette dressing over the cucumber slices, toss well and serve.

RICE SALAD
(Enough for four)

salt and pepper
8oz. Patna rice
2 rings of tinned pineapple
8oz. tin fruit cocktail
½ small green pepper
1 small eating apple
1 small onion
4oz. white grapes
6 level tablespoons mayonnaise—see page 26
1 level tablespoon chutney
2oz. chopped walnuts

☐ Bring a pan of salted water to the boil and add the rice. Boil for 12min., then drain. Rinse in plenty of running cold water and leave to cool.
☐ Dice the pineapple and drain the fruit cocktail—use the juice in some other recipe. Wash and chop the pepper, removing the seeds. Wash, core and chop the apple. Skin and roughly chop the onion. Wash the grapes.
☐ Mix all the ingredients together in a large bowl and season well.

CHEESE AND ONION FEAST
(Enough for four)

3 large onions
½ pint milk
4 slices white bread
1oz. butter
1oz. plain flour
4oz. grated Lancashire cheese
salt and pepper
1 large egg

☐ Skin and thinly slice the onions. Put in a pan with the milk and heat until almost boiling. Simmer for 20min., or until onions are tender. Toast bread and butter it.

☐ In a large basin, mix flour with a little cold water until smooth. Pour on a little hot milk, stirring, then return all to pan and stir well. Bring to the boil, stirring, and cook for 3min. Add cheese and stir until it melts. Season well with salt and pepper. Lightly beat the egg, and stir it into the mixture. Beat well over a low heat. Arrange the toast flat in a dish or frying pan then spoon the mixture on to the toast. Grill until the top is golden and serve at once.

SOMERSET RABBIT
(Enough for four)

¾lb. onions
10oz. grated Cheddar cheese
4oz. fresh white breadcrumbs

☐ Skin and finely chop the onions. Reserve 2oz. cheese and layer 8oz. cheese and the onions in a 9in. ovenproof dish. Mix the remaining cheese and breadcrumbs and sprinkle over the top. Bake for 30min. or until golden brown and cooked, in centre of oven, pre-heated to 350 deg. F. or Mark 4.

GLAZED CARROTS
(Enough for four)

1lb. new carrots
1oz. butter
½ level teaspoon caster sugar
salt and pepper
1 rounded teaspoon finely chopped mint

☐ Cut tops off the carrots and scrape the carrots. Leave whole. Melt the butter in a saucepan and add the carrots, caster sugar, salt and pepper to taste. Cover with water and bring to the boil. Simmer very slowly, shaking pan at times, for about 30min., or until the carrots are shiny and tender.

☐ Serve with some of the remaining liquid poured over the carrots. Sprinkle with mint.

PAN HAGGARTY
(Enough for two)

1lb. old potatoes
½lb. onions
1oz. dripping
4oz. grated Cheddar cheese
salt and pepper

☐ Peel potatoes and cut into very thin slices. Skin and thinly slice the onions. Melt the dripping in a heavy frying pan. When hot put in half the potatoes in a layer then the onions, 3oz. cheese and top with remaining potato slices, seasoning each layer with salt and pepper.

☐ Fry gently for about 10min. until nearly cooked through, then sprinkle with rest of cheese and brown the top for 5min. under a hot grill. Serve hot.

STUFFED CABBAGE
(Enough for four)

**3lb. hard white cabbage
4oz. Patna rice
6 pints boiling water
1 small onion
2oz. butter
8oz. tin peeled tomatoes
8oz. cooked ham
salt and pepper
mixed dried herbs
ground nutmeg**

☐ Wash the cabbage and remove the outer discoloured leaves; cut off the top. Remove the firm centre of the cabbage, leaving a 1in. thickness of outer leaves. Trim the base so that the cabbage will stand upright. Make a deep cut across the stalk. Place the cabbage shell in a bowl of cold salted water to soak. Shred the pieces of cabbage removed from the centre and the top piece.

☐ Cook the rice in 2 pints boiling salted water for 8min. or until soft. Rinse under cold water and drain well. Skin and roughly chop the onion. Melt 1oz. butter in a saucepan and lightly fry the onion until golden brown. Add the tomatoes and rice and stir well. Dice the ham and add to the rice with half the shredded cabbage. Season with salt and pepper and a pinch of mixed herbs. Cover and cook gently for 15min., stirring from time to time.

☐ Meanwhile, drain the cabbage shell and stand it on a triple-folded strip of foil. This makes it easier to lift in and out of the boiling water. Lower it carefully into a saucepan containing about 4 pints boiling salted water. Cover and cook gently for 15min., or until just tender. If it is over-cooked, it loses its shape.

☐ Melt the remaining butter in a small saucepan and add the rest of the shredded cabbage. Cover and simmer for 5min. Lift the cabbage shell into a colander and leave upside down for about 1min. to drain well. Place the cabbage in an ovenproof serving dish, and fill with the rice mixture.

☐ Sprinkle the cooked shredded cabbage with a little nutmeg and serve separately.

POTATO AND ONION SAVOURY
(Enough for four)

**1½lb. medium-sized old potatoes
1lb. medium-sized onions
8oz. grated Cheddar cheese
salt and pepper
1oz. butter**

☐ Wash, peel and thinly slice the potatoes. Skin and slice the onions. Layer the potatoes, onions and cheese into a greased 2½ pint casserole, seasoning well between each layer. Finish with a layer of potato. Dot with small pieces of the butter.

☐ Cover and cook for 1¾ hours in centre of oven, pre-heated to 350 deg. F. or Mark 4, then increase the heat to 400 deg. F. or Mark 6 and remove the casserole lid. Cook for a further 15min., until the potato is golden brown.

GREEN BEANS PORTUGUESE STYLE
(Enough for six)

1½lb. green beans
3½oz. unsalted pork fat
1 medium-sized onion
12oz. tomatoes
boiling water
salt and pepper
½ chicken stock cube
1 level dessertspoon chopped parsley

☐ Top and tail the beans. Cut the pork fat into small cubes. Skin and chop the onion. Place beans, fat and onion in a saucepan. Drop the tomatoes into boiling water; leave for 1min. then remove the skins. Chop the tomatoes and add to the saucepan with salt and pepper.
☐ Dissolve the stock cube in ½ pint boiling water and add to the saucepan. Cover and cook slowly for 20-30min., or until the beans are tender. Drain the beans and serve them sprinkled with chopped parsley.

MANGE TOUT IN BUTTER
(Enough for four)

1lb. mange tout
salt and pepper
1½oz. butter
2 level teaspoons chopped parsley

☐ Mange tout are undeveloped peas in their pods. They are very tender and sweet.
☐ Wash the mange tout and remove the stalks. Remove the stringy bit from along one side of the pod. Bring a pan a quarter full of salted water to the boil and add the mange tout. Boil for 3-4min., until they are cooked but still crisp. Drain thoroughly. Return them to the pan and toss the mange tout over the heat for 1min., or until they have dried a little
☐ Season with salt and pepper. Cut the butter into tiny pieces and add to the pan. Toss the mange tout in the butter until they are all coated evenly. Serve hot sprinkled with chopped parsley.

ROAST POTATOES ROUND THE JOINT
(Enough for four)

1½lb. old potatoes
salt

☐ Peel and quarter the potatoes. Bring to the boil in salted water and boil for 5min. Drain.
☐ One hour before the end of the cooking time for the meat, place the potatoes around the meat in the fat, and turn to coat on all sides. Cook for 1 hour or until crisp outside and soft and fluffy inside, turning the potatoes occasionally during cooking to brown all sides.

BEETROOT IN WHITE SAUCE
(Enough for four)

2 large beetroot
2oz. butter
salt
½ pint béchamel sauce—see page 24
1 level dessertspoon chopped parsley

☐ Wash the beetroot, trying not to break the skin, then dry. Do not cut off tops and roots. Wrap each one in foil. Bake them for 2 hours, or until they begin to give a little when pressed with a finger, in centre of oven, pre-heated to 375 deg. F. or Mark 5.
☐ Peel and cut the beetroot into fairly thick slices. Heat the butter and a pinch of salt in a frying pan and gently cook the beetroot for 8min., turning occasionally. Transfer the beetroot to a hot dish, cover with béchamel sauce and serve at once, sprinkled with parsley.

CHICK PEAS CURRY
(Enough for four)

8oz. chick peas
8oz. desiccated coconut
½ pint boiling water
1 medium-sized onion
1 clove of garlic
1½in. piece green root ginger
2 tablespoons olive oil
1½ level teaspoons ground turmeric
1½ level teaspoons cumin seeds
¼ level teaspoon finely chopped green chilli
1 level teaspoon salt

☐ Put the chick peas in a bowl and cover with cold water. Leave to soak for 24 hours. Put the coconut in a bowl and pour on the boiling water. Leave for 30min. Turn contents into a piece of muslin and wring out into another bowl to extract coconut liquid. Skin and finely chop the onion. Skin and crush the clove of garlic. Peel the root ginger until the green just shows through. Chop finely.
☐ Heat the oil in a saucepan, add the onion and fry for 5min. Stir in the garlic, ginger, spices, chilli and salt. Fry for 1-2min., stirring all the time. Pour in the coconut milk. Cover and simmer for 40min. Drain the chick peas and add to the curry with ¼ pint fresh cold water.
☐ Cover and simmer for 1½ hours more or until the chick peas are tender.

CREAMED SPINACH
(Enough for four)

2lb. fresh spinach
2 tablespoons single cream
salt and pepper

☐ Wash the spinach well in plenty of clean water and strip off the coarse stalks.
☐ Press the spinach into a saucepan with only the water on the leaves. Do not add any extra water. Cover and cook gently, turning the spinach occasionally for about 10-15min., or until soft. Drain thoroughly.
☐ Sieve the spinach and add the cream. Season well with salt and pepper. Heat gently before serving.

Green Peppers

Wash the peppers and cut in half. Remove the white inside ribs and seeds. Slice the flesh. Cook in butter or cooking oil for about 8min. with a chopped onion or tomato.
☐ If using oil, allow the mixture to cool and serve as a salad.

French Beans

Top and tail the beans, although there'll be no need to string them if they're fresh. Cook them whole for 7-15min. in boiling, salted water and serve with melted butter. Can also be sliced diagonally for cooking and served with a white sauce or cheese sauce.

Beetroot

Wash the beetroot trying not to break the skin as the purple juice will run. Cut off the leaves but leave the root. Cook in boiling water until tender—when the skin comes off. May take from 30min. to 2 hours depending on the age of the vegetable.

Carrots

Cut off tops and roots from carrots. Scrape if young and peel thinly when old. Cut into slices; leave whole if very tiny. Cook in boiling, salted water for 10min., or until tender. They can be served with a white sauce.

Leeks

Trim off discoloured tops of leaves and remove root. Wash very well, cutting in half almost to the root if you want to braise them whole. Cut into slices and cook in boiling, salted water for 30min. or until quite soft and tender.

Courgettes

Wash the courgettes and trim off any stalk. Do not peel; cut into slices. Simmer in a little boiling salted water for 10-15min. until tender. Do not overcook or they become mushy.

Sprouts

Cut off the stems and remove any discoloured outer leaves. Wash well. Cut a cross in the stalk. Cook for 5-7min. in a little boiling salted water until tender. Do not overcook.

Swedes

Cut off stems and roots from the vegetables. Peel thickly and cut into 1in. cubes. Cook for 20min. in boiling salted water. Mash with butter and pepper.

Turnips

Cut off stalks and roots from turnips. Peel thickly and cut into 1in. cubes. Cook for 20min. in boiling, salted water until tender. Mash into a purée if liked.

Tomatoes

Remove the calyx from the tomatoes. Wash tomatoes and slice. Fry in a half-and-half mixture of melted butter and oil for 5-10min., or until tender.

Chicory

Remove brown outside leaves from heads of chicory and trim off brown stems. Cut in half, wash carefully. Cook in 1 pint boiling water with a squeeze of lemon juice for 10-15min.
Chicory, which has a slightly bitter taste, can be chopped, raw, into very small pieces and mixed into salads.

Cabbage

Cut the cabbage into quarters. Remove outer damaged leaves. Wash well and shred coarsely. Wash again and put in pan with the water clinging. Cook for 5-7min. adding water only if cabbage sticks. Don't ever use bicarbonate of soda because it destroys the vitamin C content in cabbage.

Onions

Skin the onions and leave whole. Cook in just enough water to cover them. Cook for 45min.-1 hour in boiling, salted water.

Peas

Remove peas from their pods and cook for 15-20min. in a little boiling salted water. Drain and serve with chopped mint.

Mushrooms

Wash the mushrooms and peel only if ragged. Cut them in pieces if large, removing ends of stalks. Melt some butter in a frying pan and fry the mushrooms for 2-3min., or until tender.

Corn on the cob

Remove the leaves and silk threads from the cobs of corn. Cut off the stem. Cook in boiling, salted water for 8-10min. until tender. Serve with salt and melted butter.

Parsnips

Cut off the roots and stems. Thickly peel the parsnips and cut into 1in. cubes or thin slices. Cook in boiling salted water for 20min., or until tender.

Celery

Clean celery thoroughly. The tops and root can be eaten if washed well. Cut into 2in. pieces and cook in boiling, salted water for 20min. or until tender.

MUSHROOM FRITTERS
(Enough for four)

8 large or 16 small mushrooms
4oz. plain flour
pinch of salt
1 tablespoon cooking oil
¼ pint lukewarm water
1 standard egg white
oil for deep frying
little lemon juice

☐ Wash the mushrooms. Peel only if ragged. Dry them well.
☐ Sift the flour with a pinch of salt. Beat in the oil and lukewarm water until smooth. Heat the oil to the correct temperature—see page 15. Whisk the egg white until stiff. Fold it into the batter using a large metal spoon.
☐ Dip each mushroom in batter and deep-fry in batches in hot oil for about 2min. each batch, or until golden brown.
☐ Drain well and serve with a little lemon juice.

FRIED AUBERGINES
(Enough for four)

2 medium-sized aubergines
salt
cooking oil

☐ Trim off the stem and leaves from the top of the aubergines. Wash but do not peel. Cut into 1in. cubes or slice thinly. Sprinkle with salt. Cook slowly in oil until tender. This can take from 5-20min., depending on the age of the vegetables.

MIXED VEGETABLE CURRY
(Enough for four)

1 medium-sized onion
2oz. butter
1 level tablespoon curry paste
½ level teaspoon garam masala
½lb. leeks
½lb. ockra (ladies' fingers)
½ small cauliflower
½lb. tomatoes
½lb. potatoes
½lb. carrots
4oz. French beans
4oz. peas
½ pint hot water
salt

☐ Skin and roughly chop the onion. Heat the butter in a large pan. Add onion and fry until just beginning to turn golden brown. Stir in curry paste and garam masala.
☐ Cut the tops and roots from leeks. Wash well and cut into 1in. lengths. Wash the ockra and cut off stalks. Wash cauliflower and break into sprigs. Wash and chop the tomatoes. Peel the potatoes and cut into quarters. Peel and slice carrots; cut beans in half.
☐ Add all the vegetables, except tomatoes, to the pan with ½ pint hot water. Stir well and bring to the boil. Cover and simmer for 20min., adding tomatoes after 15min. cooking. The vegetables should be cooked but still firm and holding their shape.
☐ Season to taste with salt. Serve with plain boiled rice.

RATATOUILLE
(Enough for four)

1 large aubergine
1 large courgette
3 large tomatoes
boiling water
1 small green pepper
1 small onion
4 tablespoons olive oil
salt and pepper
1 small clove of garlic—optional

☐ Cut the stalks off the aubergine and courgette. Do not peel, but cut into ½in. slices and then into cubes. Put them in a colander and put a plate on top with a weight to press out the excess water. Leave for about 1 hour. Skin the tomatoes by putting them in boiling water for 1min. Chop roughly. Wash the pepper; cut in half and remove the seeds. Cut the flesh into small pieces. Skin and finely chop the onion.
☐ Heat the oil in a large frying pan and fry the onion until soft but not coloured. Add the aubergine, courgette, green pepper and tomatoes and fry gently for 30min., covering the pan. Season well with salt and pepper. If liked, skin and chop the clove of garlic and add it with the aubergine.

POTATO CROQUETTES
(Enough for four)

2lb. old potatoes
salt and pepper
1oz. butter
1 standard egg yolk and 1 standard egg
oil for deep frying
4oz. fresh white breadcrumbs

☐ Peel potatoes; rinse in cold water.
Cut into even-sized pieces. Place in a
large saucepan, cover with cold water
and add 1 level teaspoon salt. Bring to
the boil and cook for 20min., or until
soft. Drain off the water. Replace lid
and return pan to gentle heat to dry
potatoes. Push potatoes through a sieve
or mash very well. Season with a little
pepper and beat in the butter and egg
yolk. Leave to cool.
☐ Beat whole egg lightly on a large
plate. Heat oil to the correct
temperature—see page 15. Divide the
potato into 12 parts; form each into a
cylindrical shape. Brush shapes with
beaten egg, then roll them in
breadcrumbs. Fry 4 at a time in hot oil
for 3min., or until golden brown.
Drain well on crumpled kitchen paper.
Serve hot.

ASPARAGUS
(Enough for four)

1 bundle of asparagus
salt
2oz. butter

☐ Trim off any woody parts. Tie the
asparagus in a bundle; bring a deep pan
of water to the boil. Add a good pinch
of salt and the asparagus bundle, stems
downwards. The tips should be above the
water so that they are steamed. Boil
gently for about 15-20min., or until
asparagus is tender. Drain and untie.
Melt butter and pour over asparagus.

CAULIFLOWER CHEESE
(Enough for four)

1 medium-sized cauliflower
salt and pepper
½ pint cheese sauce—see page 24
1oz. grated Cheddar cheese

☐ Remove outer leaves from the
cauliflower and make a deep cut in the
stalk. Wash the cauliflower. Put it, stalk
down, in plenty of boiling salted water
and cook for 15min., or until tender but
still whole.
☐ Turn on the grill to full heat. Drain
the cauliflower and place in a fireproof
dish. Pour the sauce over the cauliflower,
sprinkle with the cheese and put under
the grill until the top is golden brown.

STUFFED TOMATOES
(Enough for eight)

1 small chicken joint
1oz. butter
8 large tomatoes
1 small onion
pinch of mixed dried herbs
2oz. cooked ham

☐ Wipe chicken joint. Put in a baking
tin with ½oz. butter and cook for 30min.
in centre of oven, pre-heated to 400 deg.
F. or Mark 6
☐ Cut tops off tomatoes, cutting them
in V-shapes if preferred. Scoop out a
little of the centres keeping tomato
intact. Put in oven, below chicken, for
10min.
☐ Skin and finely chop onion. Melt rest
of butter. Fry onion and herbs for
5min., or until onion is soft and golden.
Chop ham into small pieces. Remove
skin from chicken joint. Chop flesh into
small pieces. Stir ham, chicken and
tomato flesh into onion mixture. Remove
tomatoes from oven.
☐ Spoon stuffing in each one and
return to oven for 5-10min. to finish
cooking and to heat the ham.

CAULIFLOWER CAKE
(Enough for four)

1 small cauliflower
salt and pepper
½ pint milk
1oz. butter
4oz. fresh white breadcrumbs
2oz. grated Cheddar cheese
2 large eggs
toasted breadcrumbs

☐ Cut cauliflower into tiny sprigs. Boil in salted water for 3min. Heat the milk and stir in the butter. Add the white breadcrumbs and stir until they have swollen. Sprinkle in the cheese and season well.

☐ Separate eggs. Beat the yolks into the mixture. Cook gently for 2min., then add cauliflower. Whisk egg whites until very stiff; fold into mixture.

☐ Grease a round cake tin with a fixed base and sprinkle with toasted breadcrumbs. Add cauliflower mixture. Cook for 20-25min. or until firm, in centre of oven, pre-heated to 400 deg. F. or Mark 6.

SUGAR-BROWNED POTATOES
(Enough for four)

16 small new potatoes or
1lb. 4oz. tin potatoes
boiling water
salt
1oz. butter
1½oz. caster sugar

☐ Cook new potatoes in boiling salted water for 10-12min., or until just tender. Drain and skin. Drain tinned potatoes. Melt butter in a frying pan and when hot, stir in the sugar. Cook for 1-2min., stirring constantly until the sugar has browned.

☐ Add potatoes and reduce the heat to medium. Cook for 10min. or until browned on all sides, shaking the potatoes in the pan often. Don't allow them to burn. Sprinkle potatoes with 1 level teaspoon salt and serve with meat, or as part of a vegetable dish.

BRAISED CELERY
(Enough for four)

1 rasher of streaky bacon
1oz. lard
1 small onion
2 medium-sized heads of celery
1 chicken stock cube
½ pint boiling water
1 level teaspoon mixed dried herbs
good pinch of ground nutmeg
salt and pepper

☐ Cut up bacon roughly. Cook gently until fat runs freely. Add lard. Skin and chop onion roughly. Add onion and cook gently for 5min. Meanwhile, trim leaves and damaged parts from celery. Scrub well and cut into 4in. lengths. Drain fat from bacon and onions. Put them in a casserole. Add celery. Dissolve the stock cube in the boiling water. Pour into dish. Add herbs and nutmeg and some salt and pepper.

☐ Cover with lid or foil. Cook for 2 hours in centre of oven, pre-heated to 325 deg. F. or Mark 3. Drain and serve.

CHAMP
(Enough for four)

1½lb. old potatoes
salt and pepper
¼ pint and 3 tablespoons milk
1 level teaspoon finely chopped chives
1oz. butter

☐ Peel the potatoes and cut into equal-sized pieces. Put in a pan of cold water. Add a pinch of salt and boil for 20min.

☐ Drain and mash potatoes and season well with salt and pepper. Bring milk and chives to the boil and beat them into the potatoes until they're light and fluffy.

☐ Serve hot, piled on plates. Make a well in the centre of each and add a piece of butter.

FRIED COURGETTES
(Enough for four)

1lb. courgettes
salt and pepper
1oz. plain flour
1oz. butter
2 tablespoons cooking oil

☐ Wash the courgettes and cut them into 1in. lengths. Add a good pinch of salt and pepper to the flour and mix well. Toss the courgettes in this seasoned flour. Shake off excess. Heat the butter and oil in a shallow frying pan. Add the courgettes and fry for 6-8min., stirring them occasionally so that they become golden brown on all sides.

POMMES ANNA
(Enough for four)

1½lb. old potatoes
2½oz. butter
salt and pepper

☐ Thickly butter a round 6in. cake tin with a fixed base. Line the bottom with greased greaseproof paper.

☐ Peel the potatoes. Cut them into thin slices. Wash the slices and dry them well in a clean tea towel. Put a layer of potato slices in the prepared tin. Beat the butter lightly in a basin so that it spreads more easily. Season the potato layer with salt and pepper and spread with a little butter. Repeat the layer of potato spread with butter until all the potato and butter is used up. The top layer must be butter. Cover lightly with aluminium foil.

☐ Cook for 1 hour in centre of oven, pre-heated to 375 deg. F. or Mark 5. Add a little more butter if the potatoes begin to look dry. Turn out of the tin on to a plate to serve.

SPROUTS IN BATTER
(Enough for four)

1lb. sprouts
salt
2oz. plain flour
1 dessertspoon cooking oil
4 tablespoons lukewarm water
oil for deep frying
1 standard egg white

☐ Cook sprouts in boiling salted water until tender, but still crisp. Sift flour and pinch of salt into a basin. Add the dessertspoon of oil and lukewarm water and beat to a smooth paste, using a wooden spoon. Heat the oil to the correct temperature—see page 15.
☐ Whisk egg white in a basin until stiff and standing in peaks; fold this into the batter, using a large metal spoon. Dip the sprouts into the batter and fry in hot oil for 3-4min. or until golden. Drain well on crumpled kitchen paper.

COLCANNON
(Enough for four)

1lb. old potatoes
salt and pepper
¼lb. cabbage
boiling water
1 large onion
2 rashers fat bacon

☐ Peel potatoes, cut into equal-sized pieces and cook in salted water for 20min., or until soft enough to mash.
☐ Wash cabbage, shred and cook in boiling salted water for 5min. Drain and chop.
☐ Drain and mash the potatoes. Skin and chop onion finely. Fry bacon in a pan without adding any fat. Remove, leaving fat in pan. Fry onion in bacon fat. Chop bacon roughly.
☐ Mix potato, cabbage, onion and bacon and season well. Put in a pie dish and bake for 20min., in centre of oven, pre-heated to 375 deg. F. or Mark 5.

RED CABBAGE
(Enough for six)

1 medium-sized red cabbage
4 small cooking apples
1oz. butter
½ pint boiling water
salt
1 level tablespoon caster sugar
3 tablespoons vinegar

☐ Discard the outer leaves of the cabbage and shred the rest. Wash in cold water and drain well. Wash and slice the apples, removing the cores but not the peel. Melt the butter in a pan, add the cabbage and fry gently for 5min. Add the apple slices, the boiling water and ¼ teaspoon of salt. Cover with a lid and simmer very slowly for 1 hour.
☐ If the water has not all been absorbed by then, uncover the pan and simmer gently until all the liquid has been absorbed. Add the sugar and vinegar to the cabbage and stir well. Cover the pan and simmer for 10min. Serve the cabbage very hot.

PUREE OF PARSNIPS AND TURNIPS
(Enough for four)

1lb. parsnips
1lb. turnips
salt
2oz. butter
freshly ground black pepper

☐ Peel the parsnips and turnips thickly and boil in salted water for 30min. or until tender. Drain well. Push through a sieve or mash with a fork. Add the butter, salt and freshly ground black pepper, if you have a mill. Turn into a serving dish and serve immediately topped with a knob of butter.

BOXTY
(Enough for four)

2½lb. old potatoes
salt
2 level tablespoons plain flour
1 level teaspoon baking powder

☐ Peel potatoes. Reserve 2 large ones. Cut rest into small pieces and cook in salted water for 20min., or until soft enough to mash. Drain and mash well. Grate the raw potatoes and wring out the liquid with a cloth. Add grated potato to the mashed potatoes with 1 level teaspoon salt.
☐ Sift the flour with the baking powder and add to the potatoes. Roll out on a lightly floured board to a ½in. thick circle. Cut into quarters. Grease a griddle or heavy based frying pan with lard and add the Boxty. Cook gently for 30-40min. turning the pieces once. They should be nicely browned on both sides.

FRIED LEEKS
(Enough for four)

1½lb. leeks
4 tablespoons olive oil
1 clove of garlic
1 bay leaf
2 medium-sized tomatoes
boiling water
salt and pepper
1 teaspoon lemon juice

☐ Trim off the roots from the leeks and discard any discoloured leaves. Wash leeks well and cut into 1in. lengths. Heat the oil gently in a frying pan. Skin the clove of garlic and chop finely.
☐ Cook the leeks with the bay leaf and the garlic for 20min. covering the pan. Put the tomatoes in boiling water. Leave for 1min., then skin. Cut them in slices. Add the tomatoes to the leeks and cook for a further 5min. or until the leeks are very soft. Season well with salt and pepper and stir in the lemon juice. Serve immediately,

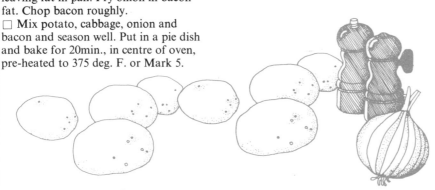

Food from the Sea

Fresh fish is really good and there are all kinds of ways in which you can prepare it for the family. Fish needn't be expensive either—the cheaper varieties such as coley, herrings and sprats can be as delicious as Dover sole, turbot and red mullet

CRAB LAYER
(Enough for three)

½oz. powdered gelatine
4 tablespoons boiling water
1 level teaspoon tomato purée
4 level tablespoons mayonnaise—see page 26
4oz. fresh crab meat
1 large cucumber
1 large onion
1 small green pepper
2 sticks of celery
1 large eating apple
5 tablespoons double cream
1 large egg white

☐ Soften the gelatine in 1 tablespoon cold water. Pour on the boiling water, stir well and leave to cool. Stir the tomato purée into the mayonnaise.
☐ Break up the crab meat and mix in the mayonnaise. Stir in the cold but still liquid gelatine. Leave until just beginning to set.
☐ Wash and thinly slice ¼ of the cucumber; coarsely chop the rest. Skin and finely chop the onion. Wash the pepper and celery. Chop pepper, removing white ribs and seeds. Chop the celery. Wash, core and dice the apple. Mix the chopped ingredients.
☐ Whip the cream until standing in soft peaks. Whisk the egg white stiffly. Fold the cream and then the egg white into the crab mixture. Place half the chopped ingredients at the bottom of a 6in. soufflé dish and add half the crab mixture. Allow to set, then repeat the layers finishing with the crab mixture. Heat the crab gently if it has set, then allow to cool. Leave the layer in a cool place until set. Arrange the slices of cucumber around the top.

PACIFIC PRAWN SALAD
(Enough for six)

10oz. Pacific prawns
boiling water
1 large lettuce
two 8oz. cartons plain cottage cheese
few fresh chives
4 small tomatoes
1 small green pepper
½ small tin red peppers
6 stuffed olives
1 level teaspoon curry powder
2 level tablespoons salad cream
salt and pepper

☐ Wash prawns. Plunge into boiling water. Leave for 1min. Drain and rinse with cold water.
☐ Wash lettuce well. Separate leaves and dry gently. Break up cottage cheese gently with a fork. Wash and chop chives very finely. Wash and quarter tomatoes. Wash green pepper; cut in half. Remove core and all white seeds. Cut pepper into 1in. pieces. Drain red pepper and cut into 1in. pieces. Slice olives into rings. Peel prawns and cut into ½in. chunks. Stir chives, tomatoes, peppers, olives, prawns, curry powder and salad cream lightly into cottage cheese, season with salt and plenty of pepper and stir well.
☐ Arrange lettuce leaves around edge of a serving dish. Spoon cheese mixture into centre and serve chilled.

LOBSTER PROVENCALE
(Enough for six)

1 large onion
1 small clove of garlic
1oz. butter
two 14oz. tins peeled tomatoes
1 bay leaf
1 sprig of thyme
1 sprig of rosemary
small piece lemon rind
salt and pepper
12oz. cooked lobster meat
1lb. Patna rice
1 level dessertspoon chopped chives
1 level dessertspoon chopped parsley

☐ Skin and finely chop onion. Skin and crush the clove of garlic.
☐ Melt butter in a medium-sized saucepan. Add onion and garlic. Cover and fry gently for 8min. until soft but not brown. Stir in tomatoes, bay leaf, thyme, rosemary and lemon rind. Season with salt and pepper. Cover and simmer for 30min.
☐ Cut lobster meat into large chunks. Fifteen minutes before sauce is ready, cook rice in 3-4 pints boiling, salted water for 12min. Drain and rinse in hot water.
☐ Remove herbs and lemon rind from sauce. Add lobster meat to sauce. Heat gently for 3min.
☐ Make a border of rice on a hot serving dish. Pour lobster and sauce into centre. Sprinkle with chives and parsley.

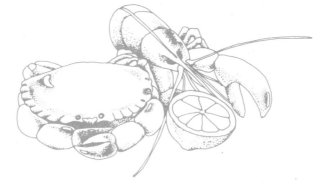

Left to right: Crab Layer, Pacific Prawn
Salad and Lobster Provencale recipes
on the opposite page.

BAKED STUFFED HADDOCK FILLET
(Enough for four)

2 large fillets of fresh haddock
4oz. packet of parsley, thyme and lemon stuffing
2 large tomatoes
boiling water
2oz. butter
1 level tablespoon chopped parsley

☐ Wipe the fish with a damp cloth. Make up the parsley stuffing as indicated on the packet.
☐ Place one fish fillet in a shallow, buttered ovenproof dish with the flesh side uppermost. Spread the stuffing over the fillet and place the other fillet on top, skin side up.
☐ Place the tomatoes in a basin and pour boiling water over them. Allow them to stand for about 1min. Drain off the water and skin the tomatoes. Cut into fairly thin slices and arrange the slices over the fish. Melt the butter and pour it over the fish.
☐ Bake for 1 hour or until the fish is cooked, in centre of oven, pre-heated to 350 deg. F. or Mark 4. Serve sprinkled with the parsley.

PRAWN FU YUNG
(Enough for four)

1lb. raw prawns
3 slices green root ginger
1 tablespoon sherry
1 teaspoon soy sauce
6 large egg whites
salt and pepper
2oz. lard
lemon slices
parsley sprigs

☐ Peel and wash the prawns. Drain well. Mix the ginger, sherry and soy sauce in a bowl. Add the prawns and leave to marinate for 10min.
☐ Whisk the egg whites until stiff. Drain prawns and add to egg whites. Add ¼ level teaspoon salt and mix well.
☐ Heat the lard in a pan until a faint haze rises. Pour in the prawn mixture and stir and toss over a high heat for 3-4min.
☐ Sprinkle with pepper and serve on a hot plate garnished with lemon slices and parsley sprigs.

LOBSTER MAYONNAISE
(Enough for two)

1½lb. cooked lobster
¼ pint mayonnaise—see page 26
1 large lemon
8 radishes
1in. piece of cucumber
2 level teaspoons paprika
parsley sprigs

☐ When buying a lobster, check that it doesn't feel heavier than it should—sometimes water in the shell will add weight. Don't buy a lobster if you hear water inside it. Ask for a hen lobster for its red coral.
☐ Wash the lobster and wipe dry. Twist off large claws and legs; reserve for garnish. Place lobster on a wooden board. Hold the head firmly with left hand. Using a large pointed knife, push the point through the shell at the top of the body to the board. Bring the blade down through the back of the shell to the tail, splitting it in two. There's a natural line on the shell to guide you. Pull halves apart gently. Remove black thread running along the back of the tail meat and the grey bag in each half of the head. The creamy coloured meat is edible and so is the coral. Lift out the meat from both shells and cut into bite-sized pieces. Crack the reserved large claws and remove meat. Wash the shell.
☐ Put meats into a bowl and mix with 2 level tablespoons mayonnaise.
☐ Wipe the outside of the shell with a little oil. Place shells on a large oval dish. Spoon lobster meat back into the two halves and level off. Coat meat with remaining mayonnaise.
☐ Wipe lemon and slice thinly. Wash radishes and trim off leafy parts. Slice 4 thinly. Wipe cucumber and cut into 6 slices. Arrange the legs at the sides of the shells. Halve 4 lemon slices and 4 cucumber slices. Arrange 4 overlapping halves of each down either half of the shell. Curl 1 lemon slice into each space where the tail curls round. Arrange overlapping radish slices round the tail. Put the paprika on a piece of paper; run the blade of a knife across the top, then lightly press the knife across the mayonnaise on the lobster to form a lattice pattern.
☐ Garnish with remaining whole radishes and sprigs of parsley. Twist a lemon slice at the tail end.

KEDGEREE
(Enough for four)

8oz. Patna rice
salt and pepper
2 large eggs
1lb. smoked haddock
3oz. butter
1 level teaspoon chopped parsley

☐ Cook the rice in boiling salted water for 12min., until tender. Hard-boil the eggs for 12min. Put the haddock in a pan. Add 1oz. butter, ¼ pint cold water and salt and pepper. Cook gently for 10min., or until fish flakes easily.
☐ Drain rice well. Shell eggs. Cut 4 slices from one egg for garnish. Chop rest. Drain haddock and flake into fairly small pieces.
☐ Melt rest of butter in a large saucepan. Add rice, chopped egg and fish. Heat gently, seasoning with salt and pepper to taste. Serve on a large plate, garnished with reserved egg slices and the parsley.

GRILLED RED MULLET
(Enough for four)

4 small red mullet
3 tablespoons oil
3 tablespoons white vinegar
1 small onion
8 peppercorns
1 bay leaf

☐ Wash the fish and wipe well. Put it into an ovenproof dish with the oil and vinegar. Skin and roughly chop the onion. Add the onion, peppercorns and bay leaf to the fish and leave to stand and marinate for about 2 hours. Turn the fish several times.
☐ Drain off the marinade and place the fish on a well-greased grill pan. Cook under a medium-hot grill for about 7min. each side basting occasionally with the marinade.

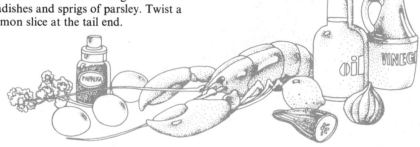

SOUSED MACKEREL
(Enough for four)

4 medium-sized mackerel
½ pint malt vinegar
4 peppercorns
1 small onion

☐ The mackerel should be very fresh. Remove the heads but not the tails. Split the fish down the belly and remove the insides. Split the backbone and remove it with as many of the small bones as possible. Rinse fish and pat dry. Roll mackerel from the head to the tail and secure with cocktail sticks, allowing the tails to stick up. Arrange in an ovenproof dish.
☐ Mix the vinegar with ½ pint cold water. Add the peppercorns and pour over the fish. Skin and thinly slice the onion. Separate into rings and add to the dish. Cook for 2 hours in centre of oven, pre-heated to 325 deg. F. or Mark 3. Serve them hot or cold.

FISH PUFFS
(Enough for four)

¼lb. cooked mashed potato
¼lb. cooked cod
1 level teaspoon finely chopped onion
salt and pepper
½oz. butter
1 large egg
oil for deep frying

☐ Mix all the ingredients together and mash well until completely smooth.
☐ Heat the oil to the correct temperature—see page 15. Drop about 6 or 8 teaspoons of the mixture at a time into the hot oil. Fry until golden brown, drain and repeat until the mixture is used up.
☐ Serve with quick tartare sauce made by adding 1 finely chopped gherkin, 4 or 5 chopped capers and a little finely chopped parsley to 4 tablespoons bottled mayonnaise or salad cream.

PRAWNS IN SOURED CREAM SAUCE
(Enough for four)

2oz. butter
3 teaspoons lemon juice
5oz. carton soured cream
2 medium-sized egg yolks
salt and pepper
12oz. peeled prawns
4 thick slices of white bread
paprika

☐ Melt the butter in a medium-sized saucepan, stir in the lemon juice, soured cream and egg yolks. Cook over a very low heat, stirring all the time, until the sauce thickens. Do not boil it. Season with salt and pepper. Add the prawns; leave for 5min. for prawns to heat through.
☐ Toast the bread and cut off the crusts. Spoon equal amounts of the prawn sauce on to each piece of toast and sprinkle with paprika.

PLAICE IN WINE SAUCE
(Enough for four)

4 large plaice fillets
salt and pepper
4oz. button mushrooms
1 shallot or 1 small onion
½oz. butter
1 level tablespoon chopped parsley
¼ pint dry white wine
½ pint white sauce—see page 24
5oz. carton single cream

☐ Skin the fillets—see page 9. Wipe fillets with a damp cloth. Wash and slice the mushrooms; skin and chop the shallot or onion. Melt the butter and fry the shallot or onion for 5min. Add fish to pan with mushrooms, parsley and wine and season with salt and pepper. Poach gently for 10-15min. until the fish is cooked. Drain the fish and vegetables and reserve the stock. Put the fish into a buttered ovenproof dish. Keep warm.
☐ Boil the wine rapidly to reduce it by half. Stir it into the white sauce with the cream. When the sauce is heated through pour it carefully over the fish. Place under a hot grill for 4-5min. until lightly golden brown. Serve immediately.

MOULES MARINIERE
(Enough for four)

2 quarts mussels
1 small onion
1oz. butter
¼ pint white wine
1 bay leaf
black pepper
few sprigs of thyme
1 level dessertspoon finely chopped parsley
grated rind of ½ small lemon

☐ Discard any of the mussels that are open. Sometimes if tapped sharply they will close. Use these. Discard any that float when you put them in a bowl of water. Scrub mussels very well to remove all grit and seaweed. Wash them in several changes of cold water.
☐ Skin and finely chop the onion. Melt the butter and fry the onion gently for 5min. or until transparent but not coloured. Add wine, bay leaf, a good sprinkling of black pepper, freshly ground if you have a mill, and the thyme sprigs. Add the mussels. Just cover with cold water. Bring to the boil; cover pan and simmer for 5min., or until the shells have opened. Strain liquid from the pan. Remove mussels. Discard half of each mussel shell. Pull out the tiny dark, weedy part from each mussel.
☐ Boil the mussel liquid until it is reduced by half. Arrange the mussels in their half shells on a serving plate. Pour over the liquid and sprinkle with parsley and lemon rind.
☐ Serve with lots of fresh crusty bread.

PRAWN CURRY
(Enough for four)

8oz. desiccated coconut
½ pint and 4 tablespoons boiling water
2 medium-sized cucumbers
1 small onion
1 clove of garlic
2oz. butter
1 level teaspoon ground turmeric
½ level teaspoon ground cumin
¼ level teaspoon finely chopped green chilli
½ level teaspoon ground ginger
4 cloves
½ level teaspoon ground cardamom
2in. stick of cinnamon
1 level teaspoon salt
10oz. peeled prawns

□ Put the coconut in a bowl and pour
on the boiling water. Leave to stand for
30min., then turn contents of bowl into
a piece of muslin and wring out over
another bowl to extract all the liquid.
□ Peel the cucumbers and cut them into
2in. pieces. Skin and finely chop the
onion. Skin and crush the clove of garlic.
Melt the butter in a saucepan and add
the onion, garlic, all the spices, and the
salt. Fry for 5min., stirring, until
everything is well browned.
□ Add the coconut liquid and cucumber
and bring to the boil. Simmer for 1-1½
hours or until thick and reduced.
□ Add the prawns and simmer for
10-15min. Serve with rice.

COLEY FISH CAKES
(Enough for four)

½lb. coley
salt and pepper
¾lb. potatoes
1oz. butter
2 level tablespoons chopped parsley
1 large egg
2oz. fresh white breadcrumbs
1oz. lard

□ Place the coley in a saucepan of cold
water with a good pinch of salt, and
bring to the boil. Reduce the heat and
simmer for about 10min. until the fish is
tender.
□ Peel and slice the potatoes and put in
a saucepan with cold water and a pinch
of salt. Bring to the boil and cook for
15-20min.
□ Drain the fish and allow to cool
slightly. Remove the bones and flake the
fish. Strain the potatoes and mash with
the butter.
□ Put the fish and mashed potatoes into
a large mixing bowl, with the chopped
parsley; season with salt and pepper.
Beat the egg; stir a little into the
mixture. Flour your hands and form the
fish mixture into 1in. thick cakes. Put the
breadcrumbs on a plate.
□ Coat the fish cakes in remaining egg
and breadcrumbs. Heat the lard in a
frying pan. Cook the fish cakes for about
6min. each side until golden brown.
Drain well and serve with a tomato
or parsley sauce.

TROUT WITH LEMON SAUCE
(Enough for four)

4 rainbow trout
1 small onion
1 small lemon
1 sprig of fennel—optional
1 large sprig of thyme
6 sprigs of parsley
1 bay leaf
6 peppercorns
salt and pepper
½oz. butter

□ Ask your fishmonger to clean the
trout. Remove fins and if preferred
remove the heads. Wash trout and lay
them in an oblong dish side by side.
□ Skin onion and slice thinly into rings.
Remove lemon peel, leaving all the white
pith on the lemon, and cut peel into
strips. Add onion, lemon peel, fennel,
thyme, 4 sprigs parsley, bay leaf and
peppercorns to fish. Squeeze out and
strain the lemon juice, then add to it
¼ pint water and pour over fish. Season
with a little salt and pepper. Cover with
a lid or aluminium foil and cook for
40min. in upper part of oven, pre-heated
to 350 deg. F. or Mark 4.
□ Strain off liquid, leaving onion, herbs
and lemon peel. Pour liquid into a pan.
Bring to the boil and boil rapidly for
2min. Add butter. Pour sauce over trout
and serve with the rest of the parsley.

EASTERN KEBABS
(Enough for four)

6oz. packet frozen cod steaks
1 large onion
1oz. lard
1 rounded tablespoon curry powder
1 level tablespoon plain flour
15oz. tin pineapple cubes
1 level tablespoon chutney
salt
4 medium-sized tomatoes
8 bay leaves
vegetable oil
8oz. Patna rice

☐ Allow fish to thaw for 30min. Skin and finely chop onion. Melt lard in a saucepan and fry the onion until golden. Stir in the curry powder and flour. Cook for 5min., stirring all the time.
☐ Drain the pineapple and make up the juice to ½ pint with water. Stir slowly into the onions with the chutney. Season with salt. Cover and cook for 30min., stirring from time to time.
☐ Wash tomatoes and cut into quarters. Cut the cod steaks into 16 cubes. Reserve half the pineapple. Divide the tomatoes, fish and remaining pineapple into 8 equal portions. Thread on to 8 skewers adding a bay leaf to each. Brush each with oil.
☐ Cook the rice in 3 pints boiling salted water for 12min.
☐ Meanwhile, cook the kebabs under a pre-heated grill for 10min., turning once. Chop reserved pineapple and stir it into the cooked rice.
☐ Pile the rice on to a serving dish and top with kebabs. Serve the curry sauce separately in a jug.

TURBOT AU GRATIN
(Enough for four)

1 small onion
4oz. button mushrooms
2 level tablespoons chopped parsley
4 medium-sized turbot steaks
salt and pepper
1 teaspoon lemon juice
¼ pint milk
4 tablespoons single cream
3oz. fresh white breadcrumbs
2oz. butter
lemon wedges
parsley sprigs

☐ Skin and finely chop the onion. Wash and chop the mushrooms. Arrange the onion and mushrooms in an ovenproof dish and sprinkle with the chopped parsley. Place the turbot on top and season with salt and pepper. Sprinkle on the lemon juice and pour over the milk and cream. Coat with the breadcrumbs. Dot with knobs of butter.
☐ Bake for 30-35min., until the fish is cooked and the breadcrumbs are a golden brown, in centre of oven, pre-heated to 375 deg. F. or Mark 5. Garnish with lemon wedges and parsley sprigs.

DEEP-FRIED WHITEBAIT
(Enough for four)

1lb. whitebait
2 heaped tablespoons plain flour
salt and pepper
oil for deep frying
parsley sprigs
Cayenne pepper
lemon wedges

☐ Whitebait are small enough to be eaten whole. Rinse the whitebait carefully and remove any pieces of weed. Drain well and dry with a tea towel. Water will cause the oil to spit.
☐ Mix the flour and ½ level teaspoon each of salt and pepper. Toss the whitebait in the seasoned flour.
☐ Heat the oil to the correct temperature —see page 15. Use a frying basket with a fine mesh and put a handful of whitebait in at a time. Never try to put in too many. Fry for 2-3min., until golden brown. Drain on kitchen paper and keep in a warm place. Fry the rest of the whitebait in the same way.
☐ Arrange cooked fish on a large ovenproof serving dish and garnish with sprigs of parsley, Cayenne pepper and lemon wedges.

PRAWN-STUFFED SOLE
(Enough for four)

½lb. fresh prawns or
4oz. frozen prawns
8 Dover sole fillets
1 small onion
little white wine—optional
1 small bay leaf
3 parsley sprigs
salt and pepper
12oz. Patna rice
4oz. packet frozen peas
little milk if necessary
1oz. butter
1oz. plain flour

☐ Peel prawns if fresh. Rinse and drain either kind. Wash the fillets. Reserve some prawns for the sauce and put a few of the remainder in the centre of each fillet. Fold each fillet in three.
☐ Skin and finely chop the onion. Put in an ovenproof dish with ½ pint cold water, the wine if used, bay leaf, parsley and a good sprinkling of salt and pepper. Add the fish fillets, folded sides down. Cover with greaseproof paper and cook gently for about 15min. in centre of oven, pre-heated to 350 deg. F. or Mark 4.
☐ While the fish cooks, boil the rice for 12min., or until tender. Add the peas for the last 4min. of cooking.
☐ Drain off the liquid from the cooked fish and make it up to ½ pint with milk if necessary. Keep fish hot.
☐ Melt the butter in a pan. Stir in the flour and cook gently for 1min. Stir in the fish liquid. Bring to the boil, stirring, and simmer for 3min. Stir the reserved prawns into the sauce and heat them gently for 1min.
☐ Drain the rice and peas. Arrange in a border round a hot serving dish. Arrange the fish in the centre.
☐ Pour sauce over the fish to coat it.

RIBBONS OF PLAICE
(Enough for four)

8 plaice fillets
salt and pepper
2oz. plain flour
1 large egg
8oz. fresh white breadcrumbs
oil for deep frying
1 gherkin
1 level teaspoon capers
4 tablespoons mayonnaise—see page 26
½ level teaspoon chopped parsley

☐ Wash the plaice fillets and skin them —see page 9. Cut each fillet into ribbons about 4in. long and ½in. wide. Mix a pinch of salt and pepper into the flour. Toss fish in flour. Beat the egg. Shake off surplus flour and coat the ribbons first with egg and then with breadcrumbs.
☐ Heat the oil to the correct temperature—see page 15. Fry the fish in batches for about 5min. each batch, or until golden brown.
☐ Finely chop the gherkin and roughly chop the capers. Stir them into the mayonnaise with the parsley. Drain the fish ribbons and serve them hot with this quick tartare sauce.

COD WITH LEMON SAUCE
(Enough for four)

4 cod steaks
1½oz. butter
10oz. packet frozen broccoli
1 large lemon
1 dessertspoon finely chopped parsley

☐ Wipe the cod steaks with a cloth. Melt ½oz. butter and brush steaks with butter. Grill for 8min., or until cooked and golden brown, turning once.
☐ Cook broccoli as directed on packet. Cut three slices from the lemon for garnish. Squeeze out and strain rest of the juice. Melt rest of butter.
☐ Stir in lemon juice and the parsley. Serve fish surrounded by broccoli with lemon sauce poured over.

TOMATO-BAKED HAKE
(Enough for four)

4 large hake steaks
salt and pepper
olive oil
juice of 1 lemon
pinch of dried basil or thyme
6oz. frozen peas
boiling water
12 mussels
1lb. tomatoes

☐ Wipe the fish steaks and season with salt and pepper. Arrange in an ovenproof dish. Sprinkle with 2 tablespoons olive oil, lemon juice and basil or thyme. Bake for 30min. in centre of oven, pre-heated to 350 deg. F. or Mark 4.
☐ Meanwhile, cook the peas in boiling salted water for 5min. Prepare the mussels as described in Moules Marinière—see page 59. Put mussels in a pan with a little water and shake over a high heat until the mussels open. Drain and remove mussels from shells, removing and discarding the dark weedy part from each one. Drop the tomatoes into boiling water; leave for 1min., then skin and chop roughly.
☐ Cover the hake with the tomatoes and scatter with peas and mussels. Sprinkle with a few drops of olive oil and return dish to oven for 10min.

WHITING QUENELLES
(Enough for four)

½lb. whiting
½ level teaspoon ground nutmeg
salt and pepper
2oz. choux pastry—see page 20
2 tablespoons double cream
½ pint white sauce—see page 24
2 level teaspoons capers

☐ Ask your fishmonger to bone the whiting. Mince the fish finely. Beat the whiting, ground nutmeg, ½ level teaspoon salt and a pinch of pepper into the choux pastry. Chill for about 3 hours.
☐ When the choux pastry has cooled beat in the double cream. Flour your hands and form the mixture into 4 egg shapes. Flatten slightly.
☐ Half fill a large saucepan with cold, salted water and bring to the boil. Carefully lower in the pastry mixture.
☐ Allow room for the pastry to expand. Poach very gently for 8-10min., until the pastry is cooked.
☐ While quenelles cook, make the white sauce and mix in the capers at the end. Lift out the quenelles and drain. Serve hot with the caper sauce.

CREAMED HALIBUT
(Enough for four)

1½lb. halibut
salt and pepper
1½oz. butter
1½oz. plain flour
milk
4 tablespoons single cream
2oz. grated Cheddar cheese

☐ Wash and trim the fish. Put it into a pan with enough cold water to cover and a good pinch of salt. Bring to the boil, remove from the heat and allow it to stand for about 5min., until the fish is tender.
☐ Drain off the liquid and reserve. Allow the fish to cool slightly then bone and flake it.
☐ Melt the butter and stir in the flour. Cook for about 2min. Measure off ½ pint of fish stock and make it up to ¾ pint with milk. Gradually add the liquid to the flour, stirring all the time. Bring to the boil and cook until the sauce thickens.
☐ Remove from the heat and add the flaked fish and cream. Add the cheese to the sauce. Season with salt and pepper. Heat through for 2min., but don't allow it to boil. Serve with boiled rice, lemon wedges and parsley.

DEEP-FRIED WHITING
(Enough for four)

4 small whiting
1 small egg
oil for deep frying
2oz. fresh white breadcrumbs

☐ Clean, wash and skin the whiting. Remove the eyes, but not the heads. Dry well in a cloth. Beat the egg.
☐ Heat the oil to the correct temperature—see page 15.
☐ Coat the fish with egg and breadcrumbs and fry for 5-10min. Handle them carefully as they break easily. Drain well and serve with parsley and lemon wedges.

SMOKED HADDOCK SOUFFLE
(Enough for four)

6oz. cooked smoked haddock
3 large eggs
¾ pint cheese sauce—see page 24
1 level teaspoon mustard powder
½ level teaspoon salt
½ teaspoon Worcester sauce

☐ Flake the haddock, removing skin and bones and put it into a mixing bowl.
☐ Separate the eggs and beat the yolks into the cool cheese sauce with the mustard, salt and Worcester sauce. Whisk the whites until they stand in peaks. Using a large metal spoon carefully fold them into the sauce.
☐ Pour the mixture into a well-greased 6in. soufflé dish. Cook for 45min., or until well risen and golden brown, in centre of oven, pre-heated to 375 deg. F. or Mark 5. Serve immediately the soufflé is cooked.

SKATE WITH BLACK BUTTER
(Enough for four)

2lb. skate
1 small onion
1 bay leaf
4 peppercorns
1 blade of mace
3oz. butter
1 tablespoon vinegar
2 level teaspoons capers
2 level teaspoons chopped parsley

☐ Put the skate in a saucepan with enough cold water to cover. Skin the onion and cut in half. Add half to the pan with the bay leaf, peppercorns and mace. Cover pan; bring to the boil and simmer for about 10min.
☐ Chop the remaining onion half. Heat the butter and rest of onion in a pan until slightly brown—"black" is the name given to this brown butter. Be careful not to burn it. Add the vinegar and capers. Cook for a further 2min. Drain off the fish stock, arrange the fish on an ovenproof serving dish and carefully pour the butter over. Sprinkle with chopped parsley and serve the skate immediately.

HERRINGS IN OATMEAL
(Enough for four)

4 large herrings
6oz. medium or fine oatmeal
salt
1oz. butter or dripping

☐ Cut off the heads and slit and clean the herrings. Place on a board, open side downwards, and press the thumbs along the backbones to loosen from the flesh. Turn the fish over, and beginning from the tail, lift the backbones away. Rinse and dry the fish.
☐ Season the oatmeal with a pinch of salt and dip the fish in the oatmeal to coat both sides. Fry in butter or dripping. Each side will take about 2-3min. until golden brown. Herrings are very fatty and little extra fat is required. Serve with brown bread and butter or fried potatoes.

SOLE MORNAY
(Enough for four)

1½lb. fillets of Dover sole
3 slices of lemon
2 sprigs of parsley
1 bay leaf
salt and pepper
½ pint milk
½ pint cheese sauce—see page 24
5oz. carton single cream
1oz. grated Cheddar cheese

☐ Wash the fish and skin—see page 9. Place fish in a shallow ovenproof dish with the lemon, parsley, bay leaf, salt and pepper and the milk. Cover with foil and bake for 20min., or until the fish is tender, in centre of oven, pre-heated to 350 deg. F. or Mark 4.
☐ Strain the liquid and reserve. Make the sauce using the ½ pint fish liquid (made up with milk if necessary). Stir in the cream. Pour the sauce over the fish and sprinkle on the grated cheese. Brown under a hot grill for 5-7min.

PAELLA
(Enough for four)

4 chicken joints
2oz. packet frozen prawns
salt and pepper
1 pork loin chop
8oz. pork chipolata sausages
olive oil
1 medium-sized onion
1 clove of garlic
1 fresh or 2oz. tin red pepper
12oz. tomatoes
boiling water
5½oz. jar prepared mussels
a pinch of saffron powder or saffron
colouring
1lb. Patna rice
8oz. packet frozen haricots verts
4oz. packet frozen peas

☐ Ask your butcher to joint a 2lb.
chicken for you and keep the giblets for
stock. This is preferable to buying fresh
or frozen pieces and using only water for
the rice. Allow the prawns (and the
chicken pieces if you have to use a frozen
bird) to thaw out. Wipe the chicken with
a clean cloth and sprinkle with a little
salt. Wash giblets (if you have them) and
put them in a saucepan with 1½ pints
cold water. Bring to the boil, remove any
white scum from the liquid, cover,
reduce heat and simmer for 30min.
Strain and keep hot.
☐ Cut the meat from the chop bone into
1in. cubes and slice the sausages into 2in.
lengths. Heat 4 tablespoons olive oil in a
large saucepan. Add the chicken pieces;
fry until pale golden, then add pork and
sausage pieces, cover and cook gently for
30min. Remove from heat and put to
one side.
☐ Skin and chop the onion and garlic,
Wash the fresh red pepper; cut off the
stalk end and remove seeds, and slice
into ⅛in. wide rings. (If you use tinned
red pepper drain off the liquid first).
☐ Put the tomatoes into a large basin,
cover with boiling water for 1min. then
drain and skin them and chop the flesh.
☐ Empty the mussels from the jar into a
sieve, rinse under cold water, drain and
put aside.
☐ Put the chicken, pork and
sausages back on the heat and add the
chopped onion and fresh red pepper (if
using tinned red pepper reserve this for
later in the recipe). Fry gently until the
onion turns pale golden. Add the
tomatoes. Mix saffron and chopped
garlic.
☐ While the chicken mixture is still
simmering, heat 3 tablespoons olive oil
in another large saucepan. Add the rice
and fry for 3min. Stir in the chicken
mixture, 1½ pints chicken stock or water,

saffron and garlic, haricots verts, peas
and the tinned red pepper. Bring to the
boil, then cover and simmer for 12min.
Remove from heat, stir in the drained,
prepared mussels and prawns and stand
for 5min. before serving to allow the
shellfish to heat through.

PLAICE WITH LEMON SAUCE
(Enough for four)

4 large plaice fillets
1 large egg
4oz. fresh white breadcrumbs
salt and pepper
3oz. butter
½oz. plain flour
¼ pint milk
2 large lemons
1 level tablespoon chopped parsley

☐ Wash the fillets and wipe dry. Beat the egg on a plate, and coat fish first with the egg and then with breadcrumbs seasoned with salt and pepper. Melt 2½oz. butter in a frying pan and fry the fish on both sides for 5min.
☐ Meanwhile, melt remaining butter in a saucepan, add flour and cook for 1min. Gradually add the milk, stirring all the time. Finely grate rind of 1 lemon; slice the other lemon. Add chopped parsley and most of lemon rind to sauce. Season and keep hot.
☐ Squeeze juice from grated lemon. Arrange fish on a hot serving dish. Strain butter from frying pan into a small pan and heat until it bubbles. Pour in lemon juice, and immediately pour over fish. Serve lemon and parsley sauce separately, sprinkled with remaining grated lemon rind. Garnish fish with lemon slices.

MIXED FRIED SEAFOOD
(Enough for four)

1lb. squid
24 small prawns
1lb. turbot
flour
oil for deep frying
1 large lemon
parsley sprigs

☐ To clean squid, remove the insides from the pocket-like part of the fish and pull out the transparent spine bone. Remove the purplish outer skin which comes off very easily in warm water. From each side of the head, remove the little ink bag and take out the eyes and the hard beak-like object in the centre of the tentacles. Rinse in running water and when clean squid should look milky white. Peel the prawns. Cut the turbot into bite-sized pieces removing the skin and bones. Boil the squid for about 1 hour or until tender. Drain.
☐ Cut squid into rings. Dust all fish lightly with flour, shaking off excess. Heat the oil to the correct temperature—see page 15—and add the turbot first and cook for 2-3min. Then add the prawns and squid and cook all for 3-4min. more. Drain well on kitchen paper and serve with lemon wedges and parsley.

ROLLMOPS
(Enough for six)

6 large herrings
¾ pint cider vinegar
3 juniper berries
3 cloves
6 peppercorns
1 small bay leaf
3 medium-sized onions
6 level teaspoons Dusseldorf prepared mustard
3 level teaspoons capers
2 dill-pickled cucumbers

☐ Clean and prepare the herrings as described in Herrings in Oatmeal—see page 63. Wash herrings and pat dry.
☐ Put the vinegar, ¾ pint cold water, juniper berries, cloves, peppercorns and bay leaf into a medium-sized saucepan. Bring to the boil, then simmer for 5min. Cool.
☐ Skin and slice the onions. Spread 1 teaspoon mustard evenly on flesh of each herring and add ½ teaspoon capers and a few onion rings. Cut each cucumber lengthways into three. Place a wedge of cucumber at the wide end of each herring and roll the herrings from head to tail. Secure with cocktail sticks.
☐ Place the rolls in an ovenproof glass dish. Add remaining onion rings to the herrings. Pour the marinade over the herrings, then cover the dish with foil and cook for 10-15min. in centre of oven, pre-heated to 350 deg. F. or Mark 4. Allow to cool, then put in the fridge for 2 days before serving.

FILLETS OF SOLE MEUNIERE
(Enough for four)

4 large fillets of Dover sole
1 level tablespoon plain flour
salt and pepper
4oz. butter
2 teaspoons lemon juice
lemon wedges
1 level teaspoon chopped parsley

☐ Wash and skin the fillets—see page 9. On a plate mix the flour with ½ level teaspoon salt and ½ level teaspoon pepper. Dip the fillets in the seasoned flour.
☐ Melt half the butter in a frying pan and fry the fillets until golden brown on both sides. Transfer the fillets on to a warm plate and keep in a warm place.
☐ Heat the remainder of the butter to a pale brown—don't burn it. Add the lemon juice and pour the sauce over the fillets. Garnish with lemon wedges and chopped parsley.

JELLIED EELS
(Enough for six)

2lb. eels
1 bay leaf
1 tablespoon vinegar
1 large onion
salt and pepper
whites and shells of 3 large eggs
2 level teaspoons powdered gelatine

☐ Ask your fishmonger to clean the eels, leaving them whole.
☐ Put into a saucepan with 1 pint cold water, the bay leaf and vinegar. Skin onion and add to pan. Season with salt and pepper.
☐ Simmer for 15min. until the eel is tender. Cut into pieces and remove the bones.
☐ Strain the liquid and return to the pan. Crush the egg shells and lightly whisk egg whites. Add to pan. Bring to the boil. Simmer for 2min. and strain. Soften the gelatine in 1 tablespoon cold water. Pour on hot stock and stir.
☐ Line a mould with eel, add the jelly and leave to set.

HERRINGS WITH GOOSEBERRY SAUCE
(Enough for four)

4 medium-sized herrings
salt and pepper
2oz. plain flour
1 large egg
6oz. medium oatmeal
2oz. butter
14oz. tin gooseberries
2 level teaspoons arrowroot
lemon wedges

☐ Clean and prepare the herrings as described in Herrings in Oatmeal—see page 63.
☐ Rinse the fish. Season inside.
☐ Coat the fish with flour. Beat the egg and brush it liberally over the fish. Coat with oatmeal pressing it on well. Melt 1oz. butter in a large frying pan; fry 2 herrings gently until brown, turning once. Keep hot. Fry the other herrings.
☐ Meanwhile, drain off the gooseberry juice and make up to ½ pint with water if necessary. Heat until almost boiling. Blend arrowroot with a little cold water. Add to syrup, stirring all the time. Bring to the boil, stirring until clear. Add gooseberries and heat through.
☐ Serve sauce with the herrings and garnish with lemon wedges.

MACKEREL WITH APPLE SAUCE
(Enough for four)

1lb. cooking apples
1 level tablespoon caster sugar
pinch of ground nutmeg
4 medium-sized mackerel
salt and pepper
oil

☐ Peel, core and slice the apples. Put them into a saucepan with the sugar and nutmeg and simmer gently for 10min., until pulpy. Cold water may be added but generally apples contain a lot of water in themselves. Push the apples through a nylon sieve. Keep hot.
☐ Clean the mackerel thoroughly and cut off the heads. Season the insides with salt and pepper and brush the fish with a little oil. Grill on both sides under a fairly hot grill for 7-8min. each side.
☐ Arrange the mackerel on an ovenproof serving dish and serve the sauce separately.

POTATO PASTRY FISH PIE
(Enough for four)

1lb. cooked cod
salt and pepper
5oz. packet frozen peas
4 tablespoons milk
½ pint mushroom sauce—see page 24
8oz. potato pastry—see page 19

☐ Bone and flake the cod and season with salt and pepper. Add the peas and milk to the mushroom sauce then gently stir in the fish. Put into an ovenproof dish.
☐ Roll out the potato pastry lightly and quickly to ¼in. thickness. Trim off ½in. strip to fit the rim of the dish. Grease the rim of the dish and lay the pastry strip round. Moisten the strip, then carefully place the pastry lid over the top. Press the edge to seal, trim and decorate it.
☐ Cook for 35-40min. until the pastry is golden brown, in centre of oven, pre-heated to 400 deg. F. or Mark 6.

MULLET PIE
(Enough for four)

3 medium-sized grey mullet
½oz. plain flour
salt and pepper
2 level teaspoons finely chopped parsley
milk
6oz. shortcrust pastry—see page 16
little egg yolk

☐ Wash and clean fish. Remove heads, fins and tails. Remove scales with the back of a knife. Remove backbones. Cut fish into 1½in. chunks.
☐ Toss in ½oz. flour, seasoned with salt and pepper. Put fish in a 9in. pie dish. Sprinkle with chopped parsley and just cover with milk.
☐ Roll pastry out to about 1in. larger than the pie dish. Cut off a ½in. strip. Grease edge of dish and press on strip of pastry. Moisten strip. Cover pie with large piece of pastry. Press edges to seal. Trim and decorate edges. Make 2 skewer holes at either end. Cut fish shapes from trimmings for decoration. Beat egg yolk and brush pie.
☐ Bake for 10-15min. in centre of oven, pre-heated to 425 deg. F. or Mark 7, reduce heat to 350 deg. F. or Mark 4; put decoration in place; brush with egg yolk, and cook for a further 30-35min.
☐ Serve hot garnished with parsley.

GEFÜLLTE FISH
(Enough for four)

1lb. mixed white fish
1 stick of celery
1 large onion
1 large carrot
1oz. medium matzo meal
salt and pepper
2 level teaspoons ground almonds
1 large egg

☐ Skin and fillet the fish—see page 9.
Place the trimmings in a saucepan.
Wash and cut the celery into large
pieces. Skin the onion; peel and slice
the carrot. Cut a ⅓ off each one.
☐ Add the celery, small piece of carrot
and onion to the pan. Cover with cold
water and simmer for 30min.
☐ Mince the fish and the remaining
onion. Add the matzo meal, seasoning
and ground almonds. Beat the egg and
add to the mixture. Mix well. Flour your
hands and shape the mixture into balls
about 2in. in diameter.
☐ Strain the stock, return it to the
saucepan and simmer. Add the remaining carrot and the fish dumplings.
Poach for 1-1½ hours.
☐ Arrange on a heated serving dish and
top each dumpling with a slice of carrot.
Pour a little stock around then cool.
Serve cold.

SQUID WITH RED WINE
(Enough for six)

2lb. squid
3 tablespoons olive oil
4 tablespoons red wine
1 level teaspoon caster sugar

☐ Prepare the squid as described in
Mixed Fried Seafood on page 65 but
leave the ink bag inside. Put the squid in
a heavy pan without any water and heat
gently until all the juices have run out
and evaporated, shaking the pan. Add
the olive oil, wine, sugar and 4
tablespoons cold water. Cook gently for
20min., then leave to cool in the pan.
☐ Eat cold but not chilled.

SOLE BONNE FEMME
(Enough for four)

1½lb. Dover sole
1 large onion
parsley stalks
3 peppercorns
salt and pepper
¼ pint white wine
2 teaspoons lemon juice
2oz. button mushrooms
1½oz. butter
¾oz. plain flour
4 tablespoons single cream

☐ Ask your fishmonger to fillet the fish.
Ask him for the bones. Put the bones in
a large saucepan. Just cover with cold
water. Skin the onion. Put onion in the
pan with the parsley stalks and
3 peppercorns. Bring to the boil and
simmer for 15min. Don't cook for
longer, as the fish stock becomes gluey.
☐ Wash and skin the fish—see page 9.
Rinse and dry the fillets and fold
them in three. Lay the fillets in a row in a
lightly buttered ovenproof dish. Pour
over the wine and add ¼ pint of the
strained fish stock. Add 1 teaspoon
lemon juice and cover dish with a
buttered paper.
☐ Cook the fish for 20min. in centre of
oven, pre-heated to 350 deg. F. or
Mark 4. Rinse the mushrooms and slice
them downwards, including the stalks.
Melt ½oz. butter in a pan. Add the
remaining lemon juice and mushrooms
and cook slowly for 5min. When fillets
are cooked, remove from the dish and
strain the liquid.
☐ Melt remaining butter in a saucepan;
stir in the flour and cook gently for
1min. Remove from the heat and
gradually add ¼ pint and 4 tablespoons
of the strained fish liquid. Return to
heat and bring to boil, stirring all the
time until thick. Stir in the cream and
season to taste.
☐ Arrange the fillets of sole on a hot
serving dish, spoon over the sauce made
from the fish liquid, and scatter the
mushrooms over each fillet.
Place under a hot grill until the top is
pale golden brown. Serve at once.

SCAMPI PROVENCALE
(Enough for four)

10oz. packet frozen scampi
1 medium-sized onion
1 clove of garlic
1oz. butter
1lb. medium-sized tomatoes
boiling water
pinch of dried thyme
3 tablespoons dry white wine
salt and pepper
1 level teaspoon caster sugar
1 level tablespoon chopped parsley

☐ Allow the frozen scampi to thaw at
room temperature for 1 hour.
☐ Skin and roughly chop the onion and
garlic. Melt the butter in a medium-sized
saucepan and lightly fry the onion and
garlic, but don't brown them. Drop the
tomatoes into the boiling water. Leave
for 1min. Skin and chop the tomatoes
and add them to the onions with the
thyme, wine, salt and pepper, sugar and
parsley. Mix well and bring to the boil.
Reduce the heat and simmer for 30min.
☐ Drain the scampi well and add them
to the sauce. Cook for a further 5min.
Carefully pour the sauce and scampi
into an ovenproof serving dish.
☐ Serve hot with plain boiled rice, or a
crusty French loaf.

BAKED SCALLOPS AU GRATIN
(Enough for four)

8 scallops
¼ pint white wine
1 small onion
1 small bay leaf
1 blade of mace
1oz. butter
1oz. plain flour
¼ pint milk
2oz. grated Cheddar cheese

☐ Remove the scallops from their shells
and remove and discard the beards.
Wash the scallops and slice the white
part. Place, with the red part, in an
ovenproof dish. Add the wine.
☐ Skin and chop the onion; add to pan
with the bay leaf and mace. Cover the
dish with greased paper or foil and cook
gently for about 10min., in centre of
oven, pre-heated to 350 deg. F. or Mark 4.
☐ Melt the butter in a saucepan and
stir in the flour. Cook gently for 1min.
Add the milk a little at a time, stirring.
Drain the stock from the scallops and
add ¼ pint to the sauce stirring. Cook
the sauce for 2min. then add 1oz. cheese.
☐ Pour a little of the sauce into 4 deep
scallop shells. Add the scallops and
remaining sauce. Add rest of cheese;
brown under grill.

How to Cook Meat

Meat is very expensive now so it is vital to get the most from even the smallest cut. Knowing how best to cook each piece of meat isn't difficult. All the recipes on these pages give you exact weights for each joint of meat and exact times for cooking

How to roast meat

Weigh the joint after you've added any stuffing and calculate the cooking time. You can roast meat at a high or low temperature depending on what you prefer. Low temperature roasting is done at 325 deg. F. or Mark 3, and high temperature roasting at 400 deg. F. or Mark 6.

Low temperature roasting

Allow 20min. per lb. for beef with bones, 25min. without bones. Lamb also needs 25min. per lb. and pork and veal need longer, about 30min. per lb. Allow 30-35min. per lb. for stuffed and rolled joints and in all cases add an extra 20min. if your joint is more than 6lb. And if it's huge—over 10lb.—deduct 20min.

Low temperature roasting has its advantages. It's very good for lean meat and small joints. Meat cooked this way is very juicy and tender and the outside is not dry. Also the smell of cooking isn't so noticeable and oven-splashing is cut down to a minimum.

High temperature roasting

Allow 15min. per lb. for beef with bones and 20min. without bones. Lamb also needs 20min. per lb. Pork, veal and stuffed or rolled joints require 25min. per lb. Allow 15min. over for joints up to 6lb. and deduct 15min. if the joint is over 10lb.

Don't use too large a meat tin because the fat becomes overheated if the tin isn't filled with meat and potatoes, and it splashes.

Heat 2-3oz. dripping in the tin while the oven is heating. Baste the meat with hot fat and season it well. No further basting is necessary.

Potatoes can be cooked round the meat, but they should be boiled first for 5min. Drain them well—water will make the fat splutter—baste with fat and allow about 1 hour to get them crisp on the outside and soft and fluffy inside.

STEAK AND KIDNEY PIE
(Enough for four)

8oz. packet frozen puff pastry
1lb. stewing steak
1 sheep's kidney or
2oz. ox kidney
1 level dessertspoon plain flour
1 level teaspoon salt
¼ level teaspoon pepper
¼ beef stock cube
¼ pint boiling water
little beaten egg

☐ Allow pastry to thaw at room temperature for at least 1 hour.
☐ Wipe meat and kidney. Cut meat into small chunks removing excess fat. Skin the kidney and cut into small pieces removing the core.
☐ Season the flour with salt and pepper and toss meat and kidney in the flour.
☐ Dissolve stock cube in the boiling water and add to meat. Pour into a 9in. pie dish.
☐ Roll pastry on a lightly floured board to ⅛in. thickness. Grease edge of pie dish. Cut off ½in. strip of pastry and press round edge of dish. Moisten pastry strip and cover pie with rest of pastry. Make a hole in centre of pie to allow steam to escape. Brush top with beaten egg and decorate round the hole with leaves of pastry.
☐ Bake for 15min. until the pastry is well risen and browned, in centre of oven, pre-heated to 450 deg. F. or Mark 8, then reduce heat to 325 deg. F. or Mark 3 and continue cooking for 2-2½ hours, or until meat is tender. Cover pie with greaseproof paper if it begins to brown too much. Push a skewer through the centre hole to check that the meat is cooked and tender.

ROAST BEEF AND YORKSHIRE PUDDING
(Enough for six)

3½lb. topside
3oz. dripping
4oz. plain flour
good pinch of salt
1 large egg
¼ pint water
¼ pint milk

☐ Wipe the meat with a clean cloth. Melt the dripping in a roasting tin in the oven, pre-heated to 325 deg. F. or Mark 3. When hot place the meat in the tin and baste it well with the dripping. Cook the meat for about 1½ hours—see Roasting Table on the left.
☐ Meanwhile, prepare the Yorkshire Pudding. Sift the flour and salt into a bowl. Make a well in the centre. Break in the egg. Mix the water and milk together and add half to the flour. Beat to make a thick smooth batter. Lightly beat in the rest of the milk. Leave the batter to stand for 30min. before using.
☐ Fifty minutes before the topside is cooked, pour about 2 tablespoons of fat from the meat into an 8in. square tin. When it is just about giving off a haze, stir the batter and pour it into the tin. Cook above the meat, in upper part of oven, for 45min., or until well-risen and very crisp.

Roast Beef
and Yorkshire Pudding

PORTUGUESE STEAK
(Enough for four)

4 fillet steaks
4 cloves of garlic
2½ teaspoons wine vinegar
salt and pepper
1oz. butter
3 dessertspoons olive oil
1 large bay leaf
8 thin slices lean smoked ham
3 tablespoons dry red wine
1 teaspoon fresh lemon juice
2 level teaspoons finely chopped parsley
lemon wedges for garnish

☐ Ask the butcher to cut the fillet steaks
¾in. thick. Skin the cloves of garlic.
Crush 2 cloves with the back of a spoon
and mash well with the vinegar, 1 level
teaspoon salt and a good pinch of pepper,
freshly ground pepper if you have a
mill. Rub the garlic paste into both
sides of the steaks.
☐ Melt the butter with the oil in a large
frying pan. Cut remaining cloves of
garlic in half lengthways and add to pan
with the crushed bay leaf. Cook for
1min., stirring all the time.
☐ Remove the garlic and bay leaf and
add the steaks. Cook for 2-3min. on
each side until brown on both sides but
still pink inside. Transfer steaks to
individual serving dishes and keep hot.
☐ Add the slices of ham to the frying
pan and cook for 1-2min., turning them
frequently. Arrange 2 slices of ham on
each steak. Pour off all but a little of the
fat left in the pan. Add the wine and
lemon juice and bring to the boil. Then
pour the sauce over the steaks and
sprinkle them with parsley. Garnish with
lemon wedges and serve.

PROVENCAL BEEF CASSEROLE
(Enough for six)

2 medium-sized onions
2 medium-sized carrots
2 large tomatoes
boiling water
2 cloves of garlic—optional
4oz. green bacon rashers
1 tablespoon olive oil
2lb. chuck steak
parsley stalks and 1 level tablespoon
chopped parsley
4in. piece of orange peel
1 bay leaf
2 sprigs or ½ level teaspoon dried thyme
4 tablespoons red wine
salt and pepper
2oz. stoned black olives

☐ Skin and slice the onions. Wash and
peel the carrots. Cut into 1in. slices. Skin
the tomatoes by plunging them into
boiling water. Leave for 1min. Remove
and carefully peel off the skins. Cut into
fairly thick slices. Skin the cloves of
garlic—if used. Crush one with the back
of a teaspoon, leave one whole. Cut the
rind from the bacon. Snip bacon into
1in. pieces. Put the bacon and the rinds
into a pan with the oil. Heat gently until
the bacon fat runs. Cook until pale
golden. Remove rinds.
☐ Put bacon into the base of a large
casserole dish. Add the onions and
carrots to the remaining fat in the pan.
Fry for 5-8min. until onions are
transparent but not brown.
☐ Meanwhile wipe the meat and trim off
excess fat. Slice into pieces about 3in.
square and ½in. thick. Put tomatoes and
vegetables into the casserole.
☐ Fry the meat for 5min. until it starts
to brown, adding more oil if necessary.
Arrange the slices overlapping on the
vegetables. Put the crushed garlic, if
used, 3 parsley stalks, the orange peel,
bay leaf and thyme into the centre.
☐ Pour the wine into the frying pan.
Heat until it boils. Set light to it with a
match and remove from heat. When the
flames die down, pour the wine over the
meat in the casserole. Add 4 tablespoons
cold water. Season with salt and pepper.
Cover the casserole with a piece of foil
and then the lid. Cook for 2½-3 hours
in lower part of oven, pre-heated to
300 deg. F. or Mark 2.
☐ Finely chop the remaining clove of
garlic, if used.
☐ Remove the casserole from the oven
and add the olives. Continue cooking for
a further 15min.
☐ Remove the bay leaf and sprigs of
thyme before serving. Sprinkle with the
chopped parsley and garlic.

GREEK BEEF CASSEROLE
(Enough for six-eight)

3lb. stewing steak
3 tablespoons olive oil
1lb. medium-sized onions or shallots
1 clove of garlic
1 level dessertspoon tomato purée
1 large bay leaf
2in. stick of cinnamon
pinch of ground cumin
4 tablespoons red wine
3 tablespoons wine vinegar
salt and pepper

☐ Cut the steak into portions, ready for
serving. Heat half the oil in a frying pan
and brown the pieces of meat on all
sides. Transfer meat to a large casserole.
Just cover with water and cook for 1
hour in centre of oven, pre-heated to
325 deg. F. or Mark 3.
☐ Skin the onions and cut them into
quarters, or skin shallots and leave
whole. Skin the clove of garlic. Put the
rest of the oil in a saucepan with the
onions or shallots, garlic, tomato purée,
bay leaf, cinnamon, cumin, wine and
wine vinegar and cook gently for 5min.
Add to casserole with salt and pepper.
Stir well, cover casserole and cook for
2 hours more.

FONDUE BOURGUIGNONNE
(Enough for four)

horseradish sauce
tomato ketchup
chutney
tartare sauce
1½lb. rump steak
oil for deep frying

☐ Spoon the sauces into small bowls.
Wipe meat. Trim off any fat. Cut into
bite-sized pieces. Place in dishes round
the burner or in individual dishes. Heat
the oil in the fondue pan and test the
temperature of the oil at the stove—see
page 15.
☐ Transfer the pan to the fondue
burner. The oil will stay at the right
temperature all through the meal and
will cook the meat perfectly. Spear a
cube of meat with a fork and lower it
into the hot oil. You can cook the meat
to your own taste. Then dip the meat
into one of the sauces. Other sauces to
include are brown table sauce, cold curry
sauce, mustard and piccalilli.

SAVOURY DUCKS
(Enough for four)

¾lb. stewing beef
¼lb. ox liver
1lb. onions
6oz. fresh white breadcrumbs
½ level teaspoon dried sage
salt and pepper
½oz. lard
½oz. plain flour

☐ Wipe the beef, remove excess fat and put beef in a large pan. Wash the liver and add to pan with 1 pint cold water. Bring slowly to the boil, skimming when necessary, then simmer for 2 hours.
☐ Drain meats and mince, reserving liquid. Boil liquid fast until you are left with about ¼ pint.
☐ Skin and mince the onions and add to the meat with the breadcrumbs, sage, salt, pepper and ¼ pint liquid. Beat until smooth.
☐ Melt the lard in a roasting tin. Divide meat mixture into 16 portions and shape each into a round cake. Coat lightly with flour and place in roasting tin. Bake for 50min., or until well browned, in upper part of oven, pre-heated to 375 deg. F. or Mark 5.

SAILORS STEW
(Enough for four)

1½lb. chuck steak
3 large onions
5oz. butter
½ pint beer
1 beef stock cube
1 pint boiling water
¼ level teaspoon salt
8 peppercorns
1 bay leaf
6 medium-sized potatoes
3 level dessertspoons finely chopped chives

☐ Wipe the meat and cut it into 1in. cubes. Skin and finely chop the onions. Melt 2oz. butter in a large pan and add meat and onions. Cook gently for about 5min. or until the onions are transparent but not brown. Stir frequently. Pour on the beer. Dissolve the stock cube in the boiling water and add to pan with the salt, peppercorns and bay leaf. The liquid should cover the meat. Simmer with the lid on the pan for 20min.
☐ Peel potatoes and cut into ½in. cubes. Add to pan and continue to simmer for 1½ hours or until the meat is tender and the potatoes have thickened the stew.
☐ Cut the remaining butter into 4 pats and shape each pat into a ball. Add butter to each serving of the stew, then sprinkle with chives.

PANCAKE BAKE
(Enough for four)

5oz. plain flour
salt and pepper
1 large egg
1 pint of milk
2oz. lard
1 small onion
8oz. raw minced beef
5oz. tin peeled tomatoes
1oz. butter
4oz. grated Cheddar cheese

☐ Sift 4oz. flour and a pinch of salt into a bowl. Make a well in the centre. Add the egg and a little of the milk and beat to make a thick smooth batter, drawing in the flour from the sides as you beat. Reserve ½ pint milk and lightly beat the rest into the batter. Melt a small piece of lard from 1oz. lard in a frying pan and when it begins to smoke pour in ⅛ of the batter. Cook over a moderate heat for about 1min., or until the pancake shakes loose from the pan. Turn or toss and cook the other side in the same way. Make 7 more pancakes like this.
☐ Skin and finely chop the onion. Melt the remaining lard in a saucepan and fry the onion until golden and cooked. Stir in the beef and fry until browned. Add the tomatoes; season and cook for about 20min., until some of the liquid has evaporated.
☐ Put 1 pancake in a deep ovenproof dish. Spoon on a ⅐ of the meat mixture. Add another pancake and continue in layers until the last pancake has been placed on top.
☐ Melt the butter in a saucepan. Stir in the remaining flour and cook for 1min. Remove from the heat and gradually stir in the reserved milk. Bring to boil, stirring all the time, then cook gently for 2min. Season well and stir in the cheese until melted.
☐ Pour this sauce over the pancake layers and bake for 20min. in centre of oven, pre-heated to 350 deg. F. or Mark 4. Serve hot.

STEAK TARTARE
(Enough for four)

1lb. good steak
3 small onions
4 level teaspoons capers
1 level tablespoon finely chopped parsley
½ level teaspoon finely chopped thyme
3 large eggs
Worcester sauce
mustard powder
salt and pepper
small tin anchovy fillets

☐ Use best quality steak such as rump. Trim off all pieces of fat. Mince meat finely. Skin onions. Chop 2 onions; thinly slice the other one. Roughly chop capers. Mix chopped onions and capers with steak. Add half the parsley and then the thyme to steak. Break eggs into steak. Mix thoroughly. Season with Worcester sauce, mustard powder, salt and pepper.
☐ Divide into 4 portions. Form into neat rounds. Arrange 3 anchovy fillets over top of each steak. Press back of knife into remaining parsley and then on to meat, between anchovies to form lines. Serve with salad, tomato wedges and onion rings.

BEEF STROGANOFF
(Enough for four)

1½lb. rump steak
1 large onion
8oz. button mushrooms
1oz. butter
salt and pepper
½oz. plain flour
½ beef stock cube
¼ pint boiling water
5oz. carton soured cream
2 level teaspoons finely chopped parsley

☐ Wipe the meat and cut it into strips 2in. by ½in. wide. Skin and finely chop the onion. Slice the mushrooms.
☐ Melt the butter and fry the onion gently for 5min. Add the steak and cook for 5min. more, stirring all the time. Add the mushrooms and season with salt and pepper. Continue stirring and cook for about 6min., or until steak is tender. Sprinkle in the flour and stir to mix well. Dissolve the stock cube in the boiling water. Add the stock, a little at a time, stirring well. Bring to the boil, stirring all the time until the stroganoff becomes thicker. Cook for 3min. then reduce the heat and stir in the soured cream. Heat through, but do not boil.
☐ Serve with plain boiled rice, sprinkling the stroganoff with parsley.

HAMBURGERS
(Enough for four)

1 small onion
1 large egg
¾lb. raw minced beef
salt and pepper
4oz. dripping
2 large tomatoes
4 lettuce leaves
4 large soft rolls
4 level tablespoons salad cream

☐ Skin and finely chop the onion.
Lightly beat the egg and add to the beef
with the onion and salt and pepper. Mix
well, then form into 4 flat cakes. Melt
the dripping in a frying pan and fry the
hamburgers for 7-10min. turning once
or twice.
☐ Cut each tomato into 8 slices. Tear
the lettuce leaves in half. Place one
hamburger in a split roll and top with 1
lettuce leaf, 2 tomato slices and 1
tablespoon salad cream; finally the other
half of the roll.
☐ Continue with the rest of the
ingredients to make 4 hamburgers.

SUKIYAKI
(Enough for four-five)

2oz. spring onions
3oz. mushrooms
1lb. 2oz. tin bamboo shoots
2 sticks of celery
1 small green pepper
3oz. blanched almonds
1½lb. rump steak
1oz. butter
3 tablespoons soy sauce
1oz. caster sugar
2 tablespoons beef stock made from a
stock cube

☐ Cut the roots and any damaged green
leaves off the spring onions. Cut the
onions, including the green parts, in half
lengthways, then into 2in. lengths. Rinse
mushrooms, peel only if ragged, and cut
into quarters. If small, simply rinse
and cut in half. Drain the bamboo shoots
and cut into thin slices. Wash and slice
celery lengthways into three. Cut into
2in. lengths. Wash green pepper, remove
core and seeds, and slice flesh into thin
strips. Slice half of the almonds into thin
strips. Cut the meat, across the grain,
into very thin strips.

☐ Melt the butter in a large frying pan.
Add the meat and fry until browned,
turning occasionally. Mix the soy sauce,
sugar and stock in a small bowl. Pour
over the meat, then add each of the
prepared vegetables, and the whole
almonds, keeping them separate during
cooking. Cover and cook gently for
12min.
☐ Arrange the meat and vegetables
separately on four or five hot plates. Top
with the sliced almonds and serve with
plain boiled rice.

CORNISH PASTIES
(Enough for four)

12oz. chuck steak
3 small potatoes
1 medium-sized onion
salt and pepper
12oz. shortcrust pastry—see page 16
milk

☐ Wipe meat and trim off excess fat. Cut into ½in. dice. Scrub potatoes and peel thinly. Cut into ½in. dice. Skin onion and chop fairly finely. Mix meat and vegetables. Season with salt and pepper and add 2 tablespoons cold water to moisten.

☐ Flour board; roll the pastry to a little less than a ¼in. thickness. Cut out 4 rounds using a saucer or the top of a cake tin as a guide.

☐ Put a quarter of the meat mixture on to each pastry round and moisten the edge of half the round. Bring the edges together and pinch well to seal. Knock up the edges again to seal. Make a hole through the sealed edge with a skewer to allow steam to escape. Brush with a little milk.

☐ Place on greased baking trays. Cook for 15min. in centre of oven, pre-heated to 400 deg. F. or Mark 6, then reduce heat to 350 deg. F. or Mark 4, and continue cooking for another 45min., or until golden brown. If the pastry browns too much, cover with a sheet of greaseproof paper. To test if the meat is cooked, push a skewer through the steam hole made in the edge. Serve hot or cold.

STEAK AND MUSHROOM PUDDING
(Enough for six)

1lb. good stewing steak
2oz. ox kidney
2 level teaspoons plain flour
salt and pepper
¼lb. mushroom stalks
8oz. suet crust pastry—see page 17
2 medium-sized onions
1 beef stock cube
¼ pint boiling water

☐ Wipe meat with a clean cloth. Cut into 1in. cubes. Cut kidney into pieces, removing white core and skin. Season flour with salt and pepper. Toss meat and kidney pieces in flour. Wash mushroom stalks; chop roughly.

☐ Roll the pastry into a ¼in. thick round to fit a 2 pint basin. Cut out a triangle-shaped quarter and reserve. Line basin with rest of round. Moisten cut edges and press together to seal. Roll out the remaining pastry to make a lid for top of pudding. Skin and finely chop onions. Put meat, kidney, mushroom stalks and onion in layers in the basin. Dissolve stock cube in water and pour into basin. Do not fill to top. Moisten edge of pastry in basin. Put pastry lid in position. Seal the pastry well using your thumb and forefinger.

☐ Cover pudding very loosely with greaseproof paper, then a clean cloth. Tie securely with string. Half fill the base of a steamer or saucepan. Bring to the boil. Put basin in steamer or pan. Steam or boil for 4 hours, replenishing pan with boiling—not hot—water as it evaporates. Serve the pudding from the basin.

BOILED SILVERSIDE AND CARROTS
(Enough for four)

2lb. salted silverside
2 medium-sized onions
4 cloves
2 sticks of celery
½lb. medium-sized carrots
4oz. self-raising flour
½ level teaspoon salt
1 level teaspoon baking powder
2oz. shredded suet

☐ Soak the beef in cold water overnight to remove the excess salt. Drain off the water and put the meat into a large saucepan. Cover with fresh cold water. Bring to the boil slowly and skim off any scum.
☐ Skin onions, leaving them whole. Press 2 cloves into each onion. Wash and chop the celery; peel and slice the carrots. Add celery and onions to the meat. Simmer, covered, for 1-1½ hours. Add the carrots and simmer for a further hour, until the meat is tender.
☐ Sift the flour, salt and baking powder into a large mixing bowl. Add the shredded suet and enough cold water to mix to a stiff dough. Allow the dough to rest. Then 15min. before the end of the cooking time, divide the suet mixture into 8 balls and lower them into the stew. Cover the pan and make sure the stew is boiling gently all the time the dumplings cook.
☐ Remove the silverside and put it on to an ovenproof serving dish. Arrange the sliced carrots, onions, celery and dumplings round it. Serve the gravy separately in a jug.

BEEF PUDDING COOKED IN PAPER
(Enough for four)

8oz. suet crust pastry—see page 17
1lb. stewing steak
1 shallot or onion
salt and pepper

☐ Roll out pastry on a lightly floured board to a large square, ¼in. thick. Lift the pastry on to a large sheet of greased greaseproof paper.
☐ Wipe the meat and cut it into ½in. pieces, removing excess fat. Skin and finely chop the shallot or onion. Put the meat and shallot or onion on the pastry and season well with salt and pepper. Add 1 tablespoon cold water.
☐ Roll the pastry like a Swiss roll and wrap quite loosely in the paper, then in a pudding cloth. Steam or boil pudding for 4 hours.

FORFAR BRIDIES
(Enough for three)

13oz. packet frozen puff pastry
1lb. rump steak
salt and pepper
1 medium-sized onion
3oz. shredded suet

☐ Let the pastry thaw for at least 1 hour, then roll it out to ¼in. thickness. Cut out three rounds using a tea plate as a guide.
☐ Beat the steak with your rolling pin, then cut the meat into ¾in. cubes. Season them with salt and pepper. Skin and finely chop the onion.
☐ Put a third of the seasoned meat in the centre of each pastry piece; sprinkle with a third of the suet and the onion. Moisten the edges and fold the pastry in two, nipping edges together with your fingers to seal and decorate. Take a tiny piece of pastry from the top centre of each pasty to allow steam to escape.
☐ Bake for 15min. in centre of oven, pre-heated to 450 deg. F. or Mark 8, then reduce heat to 350 deg. F. or Mark 4 and cook for 1 hour more or until the steak is tender. Test it by pushing a skewer through the hole in the top.

STEAK DIANE
(Enough for six)

1½lb. top rump steak
1 small onion
6oz. butter
1 large lemon
Worcester sauce
1 level tablespoon finely chopped parsley
2 tablespoons brandy

☐ This recipe should be made with fillet steak, but it's so expensive and top rump gives as good a result. Ask your butcher to cut the steak into 6 pieces and beat them until they are about ¼in. thick at the most.
☐ Skin and very finely chop the onion. Melt 2oz. butter and fry onion until soft but not coloured. Remove onion on to a plate, leaving the butter in the pan. Add 2 pieces of steak to pan and fry quickly for 1min. each side. Remove on to a hot plate and keep hot. Add 2oz. butter and fry 2 more steaks. Fry the last 2 in the rest of the butter.
☐ Finely grate the lemon rind and squeeze out and strain the juice. When all the steaks are cooked, return the onion to the pan and stir in lemon rind and juice. Add a few drops of Worcester sauce and the parsley. Stir and cook gently for a few minutes. Add the steaks, then pour in the brandy. Heat the brandy then set light to it. Serve immediately.

BEEF STEWED IN BEER
(Enough for four)

1½lb. skirt steak
2 level tablespoons plain flour
salt and pepper
2½oz. butter
1 large onion
4 medium-sized carrots
1 small turnip
½ pint beer

☐ Wipe the beef and cut into 1in. cubes.
Toss in the flour seasoned with salt and
pepper. Melt 1½oz. butter in a saucepan
and fry the meat until browned. Remove
the meat and put it on a plate.
☐ Skin and roughly chop the onion;
peel and slice the carrots. Peel the turnip
and dice.
☐ Add the remaining butter to the pan.
Fry the vegetables in the fat, for about
5min., until pale gold. Put the meat
back into the pan, add the beer and
¼ pint cold water. Bring slowly to the
boil then simmer for 1½-2 hours, until
tender. Serve with plain boiled rice.

POTTED HOUGH
(Enough for six–eight)

3lb. shin of beef
piece of marrow bone including the
knuckle end
salt and pepper
1 level teaspoon mixed dried herbs

☐ Wipe the meat and bone. Put into a
large saucepan and just cover with cold
water. Add 1 level teaspoon salt. Bring
slowly to the boil then simmer for 5
hours.
☐ Remove the meat and bone. Leave
until cool enough to handle.
☐ Strain the stock and return to the
rinsed pan. Discard the bones. Mince the
meat finely. Return to the pan with a
little more salt and freshly ground black
pepper, if you have a mill, or a pinch of
white pepper. Add the herbs.
☐ Bring quickly to the boil and boil for
10min. Leave until almost cold, then stir
and turn into wet basins or moulds.
☐ Unmould and serve with celery or
mixed salad.

BEEF AND POTATO PIE
(Enough for four)

8oz. onions
2oz. dripping
1lb. 4oz. stewing steak
1 beef stock cube
1 pint boiling water
salt and pepper
1lb. small potatoes
12oz. plain flour
2oz. lard
3oz. margarine

☐ Skin and slice the onions. Melt the
dripping in a large saucepan and add the
onions. Fry over a moderate heat for
10min. or until golden brown.
Meanwhile, remove pieces of skin and
large pieces of fat from the meat. Cut
meat into 1in. chunks. Remove the
onions leaving as much fat as possible
in the pan. Put the onions into a
casserole—if possible use one with a
round top and about 7in. across. Add
the meat to the fat in the pan and fry for
10min., or until well browned on all
sides. Put meat into the casserole.
Dissolve the stock cube in the boiling
water and add to the casserole. Season
with salt and pepper.
☐ Cover casserole and cook for 1½
hours in centre of oven, pre-heated to
325 deg. F. or Mark 3. Wash and peel
the potatoes. Cut any large ones into
quarters. Twenty minutes before the
casserole cooking time has finished,
increase heat to 425 deg. F. or Mark 7
and add the potatoes to the casserole.
☐ Sift the flour with a pinch of salt
into a mixing bowl. Rub the lard and
margarine into the flour until it looks
like fine breadcrumbs. Mix to a stiff
dough with cold water. Lightly flour a
clean working surface and roll the
pastry to a thick round, slightly larger
than the casserole. Make a hole in the
centre.
☐ Remove the casserole from the oven
and uncover. Lay the pastry over the top.
Do not cover again with lid. Return at
once to the oven and cook for a further
20-25min., or until pastry is golden.
Serve piping hot.

CLAVERSHAM RISSOLES
(Enough for four)

1lb. raw minced beef
salt and pepper
1oz. lard
1oz. plain flour
4oz. fresh white breadcrumbs
½ beef stock cube
¼ pint boiling water
1 level teaspoon finely chopped parsley
1 stick of celery
1 large egg
oil for deep frying

☐ Season the meat well with salt and
pepper. Melt the lard in a large frying
pan. Add the meat and fry until brown.
Add the flour and 2oz. breadcrumbs and
mix well. Dissolve the stock cube in
boiling water. Stir into meat with parsley.
☐ Wash celery and chop. Add to meat.
Return pan to heat and bring to boil,
stirring all the time until the mixture is
thick. Spread on a large plate and allow
it to cool. Beat the egg well. Toast
remaining breadcrumbs until golden.
☐ Divide the mixture into 8 parts and
shape each into a rissole. Coat each
rissole first with egg, then with toasted
breadcrumbs. Heat the oil to the correct
temperature—see page 15. Cook rissoles,
4 at a time, for 5min., or until golden
brown. Drain on kitchen paper and serve.

BEEF CASSEROLE WITH CRISPY OATMEAL SCONES
(Enough for six)

1½lb. chuck steak
1 large onion
1oz. dripping
¼ pint red wine
2 level tablespoons tomato purée
6oz. packet of sweetcorn kernels
salt and pepper
8oz. plain flour
4oz. medium oatmeal
3oz. margarine
2oz. lard

☐ Wipe and cut the meat into bite-sized
pieces. Skin and roughly chop the onion.
☐ Melt the dripping and lightly brown
the meat. Fry the onion for 5min.
☐ Put the meat, onion, red wine,
tomato purée and sweetcorn into a
casserole and season with salt and
pepper. Cook for 1½ hours, or until
tender, in lower part of oven, pre-heated
to 350 deg. F. or Mark 4.
☐ Meanwhile, sift the flour and a pinch
of salt. Stir in the oatmeal. Rub the
margarine and lard into the flour. Mix to
a stiff dough with cold water. Roll pastry
to ½in. thickness. Cut into 2in. rounds.
☐ Increase heat to 400 deg. F. or Mark 6.
Arrange the oatmeal scones over the
meat. Cook for a further 30min.

MADRAS BEEF CURRY
(Enough for four)

1½lb. chuck steak
1 large onion
1 clove of garlic
1 chilli
1oz. butter
1 level tablespoon curry paste
1 level dessertspoon tomato purée
salt and pepper

☐ Wipe meat and cut into bite-sized pieces. Skin and finely chop onion and clove of garlic. Chop chilli finely, removing seeds.
☐ Heat butter and fry onion, garlic and chilli for 4min., or until beginning to turn golden. Add meat and fry until browned. Stir in curry paste and fry for 2min.
☐ Stir in purée and ¾ pint cold water. Cover pan; bring to the boil and simmer very gently for about 2 hours or until beef is tender. Season to taste if necessary.

STEAK PIZZAIOLA
(Enough for two)

1½lb. ripe tomatoes
boiling water
1 clove of garlic
olive oil
salt and pepper
pinch of dried oregano or basil
1 level teaspoon chopped parsley
1lb. rump steak

☐ Drop the tomatoes in boiling water for 1min. Remove the skins and chop the tomatoes roughly. Skin and slice the clove of garlic.

☐ Heat 2 teaspoons olive oil in a small saucepan and add the tomatoes, salt and pepper and the garlic. Cover the pan and cook for 3-4min. Don't let the tomatoes turn to pulp—they should retain their fresh flavour. Add the oregano or basil and the parsley.
☐ Beat the steak and season with salt and pepper. Heat 1 tablespoon oil in a frying pan and cook the steak until brown on both sides. Spread the prepared sauce over the steak, cover the pan and cook for another 5min. Serve the steak covered with its sauce on a large hot dish. Cut in two to serve.

QUICK CANNELLONI
(Enough for four)

1 medium-sized onion
1 medium-sized carrot
2oz. butter
1lb. raw minced beef
3 level tablespoons tomato purée
1 bay leaf
pinch of ground nutmeg
pinch of mixed dried herbs
salt and pepper
8oz. lasagne squares
boiling water
1oz. plain flour
¾ pint milk
1½oz. grated Parmesan cheese

☐ Skin and chop the onion. Peel and grate the carrot. Melt 1oz. butter and fry the vegetables lightly for 10min. Stir in the beef and fry for 10min. more, or until browned. Mix tomato purée with 3 tablespoons cold water; add half to saucepan. Add herbs and seasoning. Cover and simmer for 20min., stirring occasionally.
☐ Cook the lasagne in 4 pints boiling salted water for 20min., or until tender.
☐ Meanwhile, melt remaining butter; stir in flour and cook for 2min. Remove from heat. Stir in the milk. Bring to boil and cook for 3min., stirring. Add 1oz. cheese. Season well. Keep hot.
☐ Drain lasagne. Place some meat mixture on each lasagne square and roll up like a Swiss roll. Lay rolls side by side in a greased ovenproof dish. Pour over cheese sauce. Pour rest of tomato mixture over and sprinkle with rest of cheese. Place under a moderately hot grill and cook for 15-20min., until it is golden brown on top. Serve at once.

BEEF CASSEROLE WITH DUMPLINGS
(Enough for four)

2 large leeks
2 medium-sized onions
½lb. small carrots
1oz. lard
2lb. shin of beef
2 level tablespoons tomato purée
1 pint boiling water
1 bay leaf
1 blade of mace
4 peppercorns
2 cloves
salt
4oz. self-raising flour
1 level teaspoon baking powder
2oz. shredded suet

☐ Cut off and discard roots and green leaves from the leeks. Leave in cold water. Skin and slice the onions. Peel carrots and leave whole. Melt lard in a saucepan, add onions and carrots. Slice leeks and add to the rest of the vegetables. Cover and fry gently for 10min.
☐ Remove any excess fat from the meat. Cut meat into 1in. cubes. Put the vegetables into a casserole and fry the meat in the remaining lard in saucepan. Stir the tomato purée into the boiling water. Tie herbs and spices in a small square of muslin. Put meat and juices on the vegetables. Add tomato liquid and the herbs. Add a good pinch of salt. Cover and cook for 2 hours in lower part of oven, pre-heated to 325 deg. F. or Mark 3.
☐ Sift the flour, baking powder and a pinch of salt into a bowl; add the suet. Make a well in the centre of the flour and add enough cold water to mix to a fairly stiff dough. Flour your hands and roll the mixture into 8 balls.
☐ Remove casserole from the oven. Increase heat to 375 deg. F. or Mark 5. Drop the dumplings into the liquid, cover casserole and replace in the oven for a further 20min. Remove the bag of herbs before serving.

LAMB CUTLETS IN ASPIC
(Enough for six)

6 lean lamb cutlets
salt and pepper
2 large firm tomatoes
¼ cucumber
1 bunch of radishes
1 pint aspic made from bought crystals

☐ Wipe cutlets with a clean cloth. Trim off excess fat. Trim meat near exposed bone so that it is neat. Season. Lay cutlets, on edge, side by side on a large sheet of aluminium foil. Seal foil tightly round cutlets to hold them together. Place on a baking tray. Bake for 1 hour or until meat is tender, in centre of oven, pre-heated to 400 deg. F. or Mark 6. Uncover and leave in a cool place until quite cold.
☐ Wash tomatoes. Cut in half and remove seeds. Cut flesh into 12 small diamond-shaped pieces. Wash cucumber. Peel off skin. Use peeled cucumber for a salad. Reserve ¼ of the skin and cut the remainder into 12 diamond shapes a little smaller than the tomato diamonds. Cut reserved cucumber skin in fine strips. Wash radishes. Slice thinly.
☐ Lay cutlets on a wire rack over a clean baking tray. Spoon a little cooled liquid aspic over cutlets. Leave to set.
☐ Dip diamonds of tomato and cucumber skin in aspic and arrange on 3 cutlets to form flowers. Dip radish circles in aspic and arrange on rest of cutlets to form flowers, with strips of cucumber peel, dipped in aspic, as stalks. Cover with a teaspoon of liquid aspic. Leave to set.
☐ When remaining aspic is thickening, but not set, spoon over cutlets. Leave until set. If aspic sets at any stage before it is required, heat gently over a pan of warm water until jelly liquifies.
☐ Decorate with cutlet frills.

LAMB KEBABS
(Enough for four)

½lb. very small onions
salt
8oz. Patna rice
1 small green pepper
2 large tomatoes
¼lb. button mushrooms
4 thick chump chops
8 bay leaves
cooking oil

☐ Skin the onions. Put into a saucepan containing about 1in. of boiling salted water. Reduce heat and simmer for 10min., or until tender. Drain. Cook the rice in boiling salted water for 12min.
☐ Wash the pepper, halve and remove seeds. Cut flesh into 1in. pieces. Wash tomatoes, cut into quarters. Wash mushrooms. Wipe the chops. Remove meat from bones and cut into bite-sized pieces.
☐ Thread onions, pepper, tomatoes, mushrooms, meat and bay leaves alternately on long skewers. Brush all sides with oil. Lay the skewers in the grill pan. Cook under a hot grill for 10-12min., turning skewers occasionally to cook the meat on all sides. Serve hot on a bed of rice.

LAMB CUTLETS IN PASTRY
(Enough for six)

6 lean lamb cutlets
salt and pepper
8oz. shortcrust pastry—see page 16
1 standard egg

☐ Wipe cutlets and trim off excess fat. Trim meat near exposed bone so that it is neat. Season with salt and pepper.
☐ Roll pastry thinly. Cut 6 circles, 5in. in diameter, using a saucer as a guide. Moisten edges of circles with water. Place a cutlet on each pastry circle— curved side nearest and to one side of pastry and fold pastry over. Pinch edges together and, using the back of a knife, knock the join so that it looks like flaky pastry. Roll out pastry trimmings and cut diamond shapes for leaf decoration. Moisten with water and press on to cutlets firmly. Lightly beat the egg. Brush each cutlet envelope with beaten egg. Place on a greased baking tray.
☐ Bake for 40min., or until golden brown, in upper part of oven, pre-heated to 400 deg. F. or Mark 6.
☐ Finish with cutlet frills and some salad ingredients. Serve hot or cold.

LAMB CURRY
(Enough for four)

1½lb. piece shoulder of lamb
1 large onion
1 clove of garlic
1 dry chilli or pinch of chilli powder
1 small cooking apple
1oz. butter
1 level tablespoon curry paste
1 level dessertspoon tomato purée
salt and pepper

☐ Wipe the meat and trim off any excess fat. Cut into bite-sized pieces. Skin and roughly chop the onion and clove of garlic. Remove the chilli seeds and cut chilli into strips. Peel, core and dice the apple.
☐ Heat the butter in a saucepan and lightly fry the onion, garlic, apple and chilli for about 4min., or until the onion is golden. Add the curry paste and stir well. Fry for a further 2min. Add the meat and fry until browned.
☐ Stir in the purée and ½ pint cold water. Bring to the boil. Reduce the heat and simmer gently for about 2 hours, until the meat is tender. Season with salt and pepper.

IRISH STEW
(Enough for four-six)

2lb. scrag neck of lamb
1lb. potatoes
2 large onions
salt and pepper

☐ Remove any excess fat from the meat and wipe meat well. Peel and thinly slice the potatoes. Skin and slice the onions. Put half the potatoes in a layer in a saucepan. Add a layer of half the onions, then meat; season meat well. Add the remaining onions in a layer. Then layer the remaining potatoes. Add 1 pint water.
☐ Cover pan with a tightly fitting lid and bring slowly to the boil, then simmer for 2½ hours or until the meat is cooked.

GUARD OF HONOUR
(Enough for eight)

**2 pieces best end neck of lamb each with
8 cutlets
2oz. lard
3lb. potatoes
salt and pepper
3oz. plain flour
2lb. very small onions
two 8oz. packets frozen sprouts
1lb. tomatoes
1oz. butter**

☐ Ask your butcher to chine joints and remove surplus skin and tissue for about 1in. from around bone ends. Tie together with the bones interlacing. Melt lard in a large meat tin in oven, pre-heated to 350 deg. F. or Mark 4. Put meat in tin, bones uppermost. Fold a large piece of aluminium foil over scraped bone ends so that they remain white during the cooking.

☐ Peel potatoes, cut in half if large. Boil in salted water for 5min. Drain and dry in a tea towel. Toss them in 2oz. flour. Add them to hot fat around the meat. Cook in centre of oven for about 1¼ hours.

☐ After meat has cooked for 25min., skin onions. Boil for 5min. in salted water. Drain and dry. Spoon a little hot fat from around meat into a small meat tin; add onions. Cook in oven for about 40min.

☐ Ten minutes before meat is ready to be served, boil a pan of salted water. Cook sprouts as directed on packet. Carefully take 1 tablespoon of hot fat from meat tin and pour into a saucepan. Stir in rest of flour and let it cook very slowly for about 10min. or until a rich brown colour. Don't let it burn. Gradually add ¾ pint cold water, stirring all the time. Bring gravy back to boil, stirring. Season and simmer gently until you're ready to serve.

☐ Wash and halve the tomatoes, season and dot with butter. Grill for 5min., or until soft but not squashy.

☐ Drain potatoes and onions. Drain meat and remove foil. Put a cutlet frill on each bone.

☐ Serve meat on a large hot serving dish with potatoes, onions and tomatoes round it. Drain sprouts and serve with a knob of butter. Stir gravy and serve separately in a gravy boat.

MIXED GRILL
(Enough for four)

**4 best end neck cutlets
4 lambs' kidneys
8 button mushrooms
4 medium-sized tomatoes
4 rashers back bacon
2oz. butter
4 small pork sausages**

☐ Wipe the cutlets and trim off any surplus fat. Wipe the kidneys and remove the outer skins. Wash mushrooms and tomatoes. Cut the rind off the bacon and snip one edge at 1in. intervals—this helps prevent the bacon from curling up when grilled. Melt the butter. Place the cutlets and kidneys in the grill pan and brush with a little melted butter.

☐ Grill for 4min. under a hot grill. Turn the cutlets and kidneys and add the sausages and mushrooms. Brush all ingredients with butter. Grill for 5min. Turn all the ingredients and add the tomatoes and bacon. Again, brush everything with melted butter. Grill for 4min.

☐ Serve on a large ovenproof dish.

NORWEGIAN LAMB AND CABBAGE
(Enough for four-six)

**2lb. lamb
1lb. white cabbage
2 sticks of celery
1½ level teaspoons salt
1oz. plain flour
1 chicken stock cube
1 pint boiling water
4 peppercorns
4 level tablespoons soured cream**

☐ This dish is the national dish of Norway. You can use any cut of lamb.

☐ Trim lamb of excess fat and cut meat into 2in. pieces. Remove outer damaged leaves from cabbage. Wash cabbage and cut into 1in. wedges. Wash celery and cut into dice. Put a layer of meat, fatty side down, in a large saucepan. Add a little cabbage, sprinkle with some celery, salt and flour. Continue in this way until you have at least 3 layers. Dissolve the stock cube in the boiling water and add to pan.

☐ Tie the peppercorns in a piece of muslin and add to the pan. Cover tightly with foil and then the lid and bring slowly to the boil. Cook over a very low heat for 2 hours, adding more stock if necessary. Remove the bag of peppercorns and stir in the soured cream. Serve lamb with boiled potatoes.

MOUSSAKA
(Enough for six)

**14oz. aubergines
salt and pepper
1 small onion
1½oz. butter
1¼lb. raw minced lamb
1 large tomato
boiling water
2 teaspoons finely chopped parsley
ground nutmeg
1 tablespoon red wine—optional
olive oil
1oz. plain flour
½ pint milk
1oz. grated Parmesan cheese
1 large egg**

☐ Wash aubergines. Slice fairly thinly. Sprinkle with 2 level teaspoons salt and leave for 30min.

☐ Meanwhile, skin and finely chop the onion. Melt ½oz. butter, add onion; fry for 3min. Stir in meat and cook for a further 5min. Drop tomato into boiling water; leave for 1min. Skin and chop tomato. Add tomato, parsley, a good pinch of nutmeg, salt and pepper to the meat. Stir in the wine if used. Cover and simmer for 20min.

☐ Rinse the aubergines well with cold water. Pat dry in kitchen paper. Heat 3 tablespoons olive oil, add a few aubergine slices and fry until golden, turning once. Drain on paper. Keep cooked slices warm while others are cooking.

☐ Melt remaining butter. Stir in the flour and cook for 2min. Add the milk a little at a time, stirring well after each addition. Bring to the boil and cook for 3min., stirring all the time. Stir 1 tablespoon of the sauce into the meat.

☐ Layer the aubergines and meat in a greased 9in. loaf tin, beginning and ending with a layer of aubergines. Sprinkle each layer of meat with a little Parmesan cheese. Beat the egg and stir into the cooled sauce. Add half of the remaining cheese, seasoning and a pinch of nutmeg. Pour over the aubergines. Sprinkle with remaining cheese.

☐ Cook for 45min. or until golden brown, in centre of oven, pre-heated to 350 deg. F. or Mark 4. Serve cut into large squares.

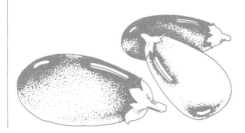

LANCASHIRE HOT POT
(Enough for six)

2lb. best end neck of lamb
salt and pepper
1lb. onions
3 lambs' kidneys
2lb. potatoes
1oz. butter

☐ Ask the butcher to divide the meat into neat cutlets. Trim off most of the fat. Cut off the ends of the bones. Put the fat, bones, ½ pint cold water and salt and pepper in a saucepan. Skin 1 small onion and add to the pan. Bring to boil and boil for 2 hours.
☐ Remove the skin from each kidney. Cut in half and remove the hard centre core. Cut kidneys into slices. Peel and slice the potatoes. Skin and finely chop remaining onions. Put a deep layer of sliced potatoes in a large casserole and add some cutlets, a few slices of kidney, and some onions. Season well. Continue in this way, finishing with overlapped potato slices.
☐ Strain the stock. Pour ½ pint down the side of the dish. Melt the butter and brush over top. Cover with a butter paper and cook for 3 hours in centre of oven, pre-heated to 300 deg. F. or Mark 2. Remove the butter paper for the last hour to allow the potatoes to brown. Serve from the cooking pot.

LAMB AND PEARL BARLEY STEW
(Enough for four-five)

2lb. middle neck of lamb
12 very small onions
1 large carrot
1 bay leaf
½ level teaspoon mixed dried herbs
salt and pepper
3oz. pearl barley
4oz. button mushrooms
5oz. packet frozen peas

☐ Ask your butcher to cut up the lamb. Discard excess fat from the meat. Skin onions; leave whole. Peel and slice the carrot. Put meat and the vegetables in a large saucepan. Add the bay leaf, herbs and a good pinch each of salt and pepper. Wash pearl barley; drain. Add to the saucepan with 1½ pints cold water. Wash mushrooms and add to pan. Cover.
☐ Bring pan of meat to the boil, then reduce the heat and simmer for 2 hours, or until the meat is tender. Remove pan from heat and cool. Leave in a refrigerator or very cold place overnight.
☐ Next day, using a metal spoon, remove the fat that has solidified on the stew. Return pan to the heat. Add the peas. Bring to boil; simmer for 15min., or until thoroughly hot. Check the seasoning. Serve with boiled potatoes.

LAMB LOAF
(Enough for four)

8oz. cooked lamb
1 small onion
½oz. butter
4oz. cooked mashed potato
1oz. fresh white breadcrumbs
1 large egg
salt and pepper
Worcester sauce
4 tablespoons stock made from a stock cube
parsley sprigs
tomato slices

☐ Mince lamb, removing excess fat and gristle. Skin and finely chop onion.
☐ Melt butter and fry onion until soft and golden. Stir in lamb, potato, breadcrumbs, egg, plenty of salt and pepper, Worcester sauce to taste and the stock. Mix well.
☐ Spoon into a greased 1lb. loaf tin. Bake for 1 hour in centre of oven, pre-heated to 350 deg. F. or Mark 4.
☐ Turn out of tin and garnish with parsley and tomato slices.

Lamb and Pearl Barley Stew

SHEPHERDS PIE
(Enough for four)

1lb. cooked lamb
1¾lb. potatoes
1 medium-sized onion
1 large carrot
8oz. tin peeled tomatoes
pinch of mixed dried herbs
salt and pepper
2 tablespoons milk
1oz. butter

☐ Mince the meat coarsely. Peel potatoes; cut into medium-sized pieces, and cook for 20min. in boiling, salted water. Skin and grate onion. Peel and grate carrot. Drain and reserve juice from tomatoes. Break up tomatoes with a fork and add with the grated onion and carrot to meat. Season with herbs and salt and pepper. Add enough tomato juice to moisten the meat. Spoon meat into an ovenproof dish and smooth the top.
☐ Drain potatoes and mash with milk and butter. Spread them over meat and fork into a pattern. Cook for 45min., or until golden, in centre of oven, pre-heated to 400 deg. F. or Mark 6. Serve hot.

LAMB AND TOMATO CASSEROLE
(Enough for four-six)

1 large onion
1oz. lard
6 pieces scrag end neck of lamb
15oz. tin peeled tomatoes
salt and pepper
dried marjoram

☐ Skin and finely chop the onion. Melt the lard in a frying pan and fry the onion until golden. Remove the onion from the fat and put it into a casserole. Add the pieces of lamb to the fat and cook quickly on both sides to brown. Put into the casserole with the fat from the pan. Pour over the tomatoes and their juice, and season well with salt and pepper. Add a good pinch of marjoram.
☐ Cook for 2 hours in centre of oven, pre-heated to 325 deg. F. or Mark 3.
☐ Serve with mashed potatoes.

LAMB AND APRICOT ROAST
(Enough for six)

4lb. leg of lamb
2oz. butter
1 small onion
3oz. fresh white breadcrumbs
½ level teaspoon dried thyme
salt and pepper
2oz. dried apricots
1 standard egg
1oz. dripping

☐ Ask your butcher to remove the bone from the lamb. Melt 1oz. butter in a saucepan. Skin and finely chop the onion; fry gently in the fat for 5min., or until tender but not browned. Add the breadcrumbs, thyme, a little salt and pepper and the rest of the butter. Wash and finely chop the apricots and add to pan. Beat the egg and add enough to bind. Mix the ingredients well.
☐ Put some stuffing in the pocket left by the bone. If necessary make the pocket a little deeper. Place the meat in a tin with the dripping and cook for 1½-2 hours in centre of oven, pre-heated to 350 deg. F. or Mark 4. To serve, cut into thick slices.

LITTLE MUTTON PIES
(Enough for four)

½lb. lean mutton
13oz. plain flour
salt and pepper
3oz. dripping
milk

☐ Cut the mutton into small pieces and roll in 1oz. flour seasoned with a little salt and pepper. Place in a casserole and add cold water to cover. Cover the casserole and cook gently for 1½ hours or until tender, in centre of oven, pre-heated to 325 deg. F. or Mark 3.
☐ Make Hot Water Crust pastry—see page 18—using the remaining flour, ½ level teaspoon salt, dripping and 12 tablespoons cold water. Set aside a quarter of the pastry and keep warm. Cut the remaining dough into four and roll each piece out to line 4 greased pie rings.
☐ Fill the cases with the meat mixture, adding a little of the stock. Moisten the edges of the pastry. Roll out remaining pastry and cover the pies. Seal and trim the edges and make a hole in the centre of each pie. Brush the pastry with milk.
☐ Bake pies for 40min., in centre of oven, pre-heated to 375 deg. F. or Mark 5. Remove the rings towards the end of the cooking time. Serve hot or cold.

BREAST OF LAMB WITH HERB STUFFING
(Enough for four)

2 lean breasts of lamb
4oz. pork sausagemeat
1oz. fresh white breadcrumbs
4 large sprigs of rosemary
small bunch of chives
grated rind of 1 small lemon
salt and pepper
1oz. lard

☐ Ask the butcher to bone the lamb for rolling. Remove any excess fat and wipe the meat with a clean cloth.
☐ Put sausagemeat into a bowl and add breadcrumbs. Wash herbs; reserve 2 sprigs of rosemary. Chop remaining rosemary and chives and add these to bowl. Add lemon rind. Season with salt and pepper and mix the stuffing well. Divide the mixture in half.
☐ Put the meat, skin side down, on a board and spread the stuffing over each piece. Roll up and secure at 1in. intervals with fine string. Sprinkle meat with a little salt. Tuck a sprig of rosemary under the string of each roll.
☐ Stand meat in a roasting tin and dot with lard. Cook for 1½ hours in centre of oven, pre-heated to 375 deg. F. or Mark 5. Baste occasionally. Remove string and slice meat thickly to serve.

BOILED MUTTON WITH CAPER SAUCE
(Enough for four)

3lb. leg of mutton or lamb
2 medium-sized onions
3 large carrots
1 medium-sized swede
1 small turnip
1 level teaspoon salt
2 level teaspoons capers
½ pint béchamel sauce—see page 24

☐ Wipe the meat and put into a large saucepan. Cover with cold water and bring slowly to the boil. Strain off the scum.
☐ Skin and thickly slice the onions, peel the carrots and cut each into 4 lengths. Thickly peel and dice the swede and turnip.
☐ Add the salt and vegetables to the mutton. Reduce the heat and cover the pan. Simmer for 1¾-2 hours, or until the meat is tender. Carefully lift the meat on to a large ovenproof serving dish. Arrange the vegetables round the meat.
☐ Chop capers and stir into the sauce. Heat through. Serve the meat and vegetables with boiled potatoes and caper sauce. The liquid makes a good stock for soup.

GREEK LAMB KEBABS
(Enough for four)

1½lb. lean lamb shoulder
1½ large lemons
2 tablespoons olive oil
2 tablespoons wine—optional
¾ level teaspoon dried oregano
salt and pepper
12oz. Patna rice
8 bay leaves

☐ Cut meat into 1in. cubes, removing all the fat. Squeeze out and strain the juice from the lemon half. Mix together the oil, wine if used, oregano and lemon juice. Season well with salt and freshly-ground black pepper if you have a mill. Put the meat into a bowl and pour over the marinade. Cover and leave overnight in the refrigerator or cool place.
☐ Just before serving the kebabs, cook the rice in 4 pints boiling salted water for 12min. Drain and rinse with hot water. Turn rice into a colander and keep hot.
☐ Thread the meat alternately with bay leaves on to 8 skewers. Cook kebabs for about 10min. or until browned on all sides, under a hot grill, turning them.
☐ Cut the whole lemon into 8 wedges. Spoon the rice on to a hot serving dish. Arrange kebabs on the top and garnish with lemon wedges. Serve immediately.

CROWN ROAST OF LAMB
(Enough for eight)

2 pieces best end neck of lamb
each with 8 cutlets
salt and pepper
3oz. lard
4oz. packet frozen peas
2 tablespoons oil
11oz. tin small new potatoes

☐ Tell your butcher that you want to make a crown roast. Ask him to scrape the meat from the top of each bone, leaving 1in. of bone clean. Bend the two pieces of meat to form a circle (fatty parts inside), tie securely with string. Season meat, put into a roasting tin with the scraped bones uppermost. Spread lard over joint using a palette knife. Cover scraped bones with foil during cooking to keep them white. You can use the meat trimmings to put in centre of joint if liked.
☐ Cook lamb for 30min., in centre of oven, pre-heated to 400 deg. F. or Mark 6, then reduce heat to 350 deg. F. or Mark 4 and cook for a further 50min. or until tender. Baste the meat occasionally. Towards the end of cooking, check that the meat will not overcook.
☐ Five minutes before the meat is due to come out of the oven, cook the peas in a little boiling salted water as directed on the packet and put the oil to heat in a frying pan. Fry the potatoes in the oil for about 6min., until golden on all sides. Remove the crown roast from the oven and replace the foil covers with cutlet frills. Drain the peas, and the potatoes on kitchen paper. Mix the peas and potatoes together and place in the cavity in the middle of the Crown Roast. Use any left to serve separately with a knob of butter.

APRICOT LAMB
(Enough for six)

3lb. piece shoulder of lamb
salt and pepper
1 small onion
3oz. dried apricots
1½oz. fresh white breadcrumbs
½ level teaspoon chopped parsley
½ level teaspoon mixed dried herbs
1 large egg
2oz. lard

☐ Ask your butcher to bone the shoulder of lamb. Wipe the meat with a clean cloth; season with salt and pepper. Skin and finely chop the onion. Wash and chop the apricots finely. Mix breadcrumbs with apricots, onion, parsley, herbs and a little salt and pepper. Beat the egg and add to mixture to bind. Spread this mixture on to the meat.
☐ Roll up the meat and secure with string. Place meat in a roasting tin and spread with lard. Cook for 30min. in centre of oven, pre-heated to 400 deg. F. or Mark 6, then reduce heat to 350 deg. F. or Mark 4 and continue cooking for 1 hour more, basting with lard. When cooked remove string and slice thickly to serve.

STUFFED SHOULDER OF LAMB
(Enough for six)

3lb. shoulder of lamb
2oz. shelled walnuts
1 large lemon
1 standard egg
1oz. margarine
3oz. fresh white breadcrumbs
salt and pepper
1oz. dripping

☐ Ask your butcher to bone the shoulder of lamb. Roughly chop the walnuts. Finely grate the rind from the lemon, and squeeze out the juice. Beat the egg. Melt the margarine in a saucepan and add the breadcrumbs, nuts, lemon juice and rind, egg, salt and pepper. Mix well together.
☐ Fill the pockets in the meat with the stuffing, and spread the remainder on the meat, keeping it well away from the edges. As you roll up the meat, the stuffing is pressed outwards to cover the edges. Tie securely with thin string. Season the meat and place it in a roasting tin with the dripping. Roast for 1½-2 hours in centre of oven, pre-heated to 350 deg. F. or Mark 4. Serve cut into thick slices.

CHINESE SWEET AND SOUR LAMB
(Enough for four)

2 tablespoons vegetable oil
1 medium-sized onion
1¼lb. piece leg of lamb
2 level tablespoons cornflour
½ chicken stock cube
½ pint boiling water
1 medium-sized green pepper
15oz. tin apricot halves
2oz. sultanas
1 level tablespoon honey
5 tablespoons wine vinegar
½ level teaspoon salt
½ level teaspoon ground ginger

☐ Heat the oil in a medium-sized saucepan for 1min. Reduce heat to low. Skin and grate the onion and add to pan. Fry for 5min., or until golden but not browned. Cut lamb into 1in. cubes and fry until browned on all sides. Blend cornflour with a little cold water. Dissolve stock cube in boiling water. Gradually blend stock and cornflour mixture into the pan and cook gently, stirring from time to time until sauce thickens.
☐ Wash the pepper and cut into strips, discarding the core and seeds. Reserve ¼ of the pepper strips. Drain the apricots and reserve the juice, and 4 apricot halves for garnish. Coarsely chop remaining apricot halves. Add rest of the pepper strips and the apricot halves to the meat in the pan together with 5 tablespoons apricot juice, the sultanas, honey, vinegar, salt and ginger.
☐ Cover pan with a lid and simmer very gently for about 40min.-1 hour, or until meat is tender. Transfer meat and sauce on to a hot serving dish, and garnish with the uncooked pepper and apricot halves. Serve with freshly cooked flat noodles tossed in butter, and a crisp green salad.

LAMB PUDDING
(Enough for six)

1lb. plain flour
salt and pepper
6oz. shredded suet
½ pint milk or water
2lb. boned loin of lamb
1 large onion

☐ Sift the flour with a pinch of salt. Stir in the suet. Mix to a smooth dough with the milk or water. Knead lightly until smooth. Wipe the meat. Slice the meat thinly and season the slices with salt and pepper. Skin and finely slice the onion. Grease a 2 pint pudding basin.
☐ Roll the pastry into a large round. Cut out a quarter section for the lid. Line the basin with the large piece; moisten cut edges and press well to seal. Fill with the slices of meat and onion, and add enough water to come to within 1in. of the top. Roll out the remainder of the pastry into a round and moisten the edge. Place it on the top; press the edges to seal. Cover with a large piece of greased greaseproof paper and aluminium foil, leaving some room for the pudding to rise a little. Steam or boil for about 4 hours, replenishing pan with more boiling water as it evaporates.

LAMB TIKA KEBABS
(Enough for four)

1¼lb. lean lamb shoulder
5oz. carton plain yogurt
¼ level teaspoon ground coriander
¼ level teaspoon ground cumin
½ level teaspoon finely chopped green chilli
1 clove of garlic
1in. piece green root ginger
1 level teaspoon salt
juice of ½ lemon

☐ Cut the lamb into serving pieces. Mix the yogurt, coriander, cumin and green chilli. Skin and crush the clove of garlic into the yogurt. Peel ginger until green part just shows. Roughly chop the ginger. Add to yogurt with the salt and lemon. Stir in the lamb pieces and leave to marinate for 30min.
☐ Remove meat from marinade and thread on to 4 skewers. Grill under a hot grill for 5-8min., or until tender, turning from time to time.
☐ Serve with plain boiled rice.

FRICASSEE OF LAMB
(Enough for four-six)

1½lb. piece shoulder of lamb
1 medium-sized onion
1oz. butter
1 bay leaf
2 cloves
6 peppercorns
1 chicken stock cube
1 pint boiling water
salt and pepper
1½oz. plain flour
3 tablespoons single cream
1 level dessertspoon capers

☐ Wipe the lamb and trim off any excess fat. Cut into 1in. cubes. Skin and slice the onion. Melt the butter in a large saucepan. Put the meat into the saucepan and add the onion. Fry gently for 5min. Tie the bay leaf, cloves and peppercorns in a piece of muslin.
☐ Dissolve the stock cube in boiling water and pour over the meat and onion. Add the bag of herbs and salt and pepper. Bring to the boil slowly and cover. Reduce the heat and simmer gently for about 1½ hours, or until the meat is tender.
☐ Mix the flour to a smooth paste with a small quantity of cold water. Remove the meat from the saucepan and put it on a plate. Strain the liquid. Pour a little from 1 pint over the blended flour; stir well and mix with the rest of the pint of liquid. Pour into a pan. Add the meat to the pan. Bring to the boil. Simmer for a further 10min. Stir in the cream.
☐ Make a border of mashed potato and carefully put the lamb in the centre. Pour over the sauce and sprinkle with capers.

CASSEROLE RABBIT
(Enough for four)

2½lb. rabbit
2oz. fine oatmeal
salt and pepper
1 medium-sized onion
2 medium-sized carrots
1 stick of celery
2 rashers of streaky bacon
2oz. lard
¼ pint dry cider
2 small sprigs of rosemary or
1 level teaspoon dried rosemary
1 small sprig of thyme or
pinch of dried thyme
1 small bay leaf

☐ Ask your butcher to joint the rabbit
and reserve the heart, kidneys and liver.
Cover the pieces of rabbit with cold
water and leave to soak for 2 hours.
☐ Put the offal into a small saucepan.
Add 1 pint cold water and bring slowly
to the boil; cover and simmer for
30min.
☐ Meanwhile, dry the pieces of rabbit.
Season the oatmeal with salt and pepper.
Coat each joint with oatmeal, pressing
it on well. Shake off the excess and
reserve. Skin and slice the onion, peel
and slice the carrots. Scrub and chop the
celery. Chop the bacon.
☐ Melt 1½oz. lard in a frying pan and
add the bacon and rabbit joints. Lightly
fry the rabbit joints on all sides. Remove
on to a plate and keep hot. Add the
onion and carrot to the pan and fry for
10min., or until just golden. Add the
celery and transfer the vegetables to a
large casserole leaving behind as much
fat as possible. Add the remaining fat to
the pan and melt gently. Transfer the
rabbit and bacon to the casserole.
☐ Stir in the rest of the oatmeal and
cook over the lowest heat until just
golden; do not allow to burn as this
gives a bitter flavour. Strain the stock
from the offal and stir a little into the
oatmeal; add the rest of the stock,
stirring slowly all the time. Bring to the
boil, add the cider and pour over the
ingredients in the casserole. Season with
salt and pepper and add the herbs.
☐ Cover and cook for 2½ hours or until
tender, in lower part of oven, pre-heated
to 325 deg. F. or Mark 3. If the sauce is
too thick, stir in a little more cider.
Remove the bay leaf, thyme and
rosemary sprigs before serving.

RABBIT PIE
(Enough for four-five)

2lb. rabbit
4 prunes—optional
1 large onion
2oz. carrots
2oz. bacon
1½oz. dripping
2oz. plain flour
salt and pepper
1 chicken stock cube
1 pint boiling water
pinch of mixed dried herbs
13oz. packet frozen puff pastry
3oz. button mushrooms
milk

☐ Ask your butcher to joint the rabbit.
Soak rabbit for 1 hour in cold water.
Cover prunes with cold water and leave
for 1 hour. Skin and slice onion. Peel
and slice carrots. Remove bacon rinds
and snip bacon into small pieces. Put
bacon and dripping in a large pan and
heat. Add onion and carrot and fry for
7-8min. Remove on to a plate, leaving
behind as much fat as possible. Drain
rabbit well. Season the flour with salt
and pepper and toss rabbit in the flour
to coat. Add to pan and fry for 10min.
until golden brown. Dissolve the stock
cube in the boiling water. Gradually stir
stock into pan. Add herbs to pan and
prunes, if used. Add ingredients from
the plate. Cover and simmer gently for 1
hour.
☐ Meanwhile, allow pastry to thaw at
room temperature for 1 hour. Check
seasoning of meat, adding salt and
pepper if necessary. Turn meat and
stock into a large pie dish. Wash
mushrooms and add to pie. Leave until
cool (otherwise pastry softens and is
spoiled). Flour a clean working surface
and roll pastry to 1in. larger than dish.
Grease edge of pie dish. Cut ½in.
border and lay round edge. Moisten
pastry border and lay pastry top over.
Press edges to seal. Trim off pastry using
a sharp knife. Knock up edges and
decorate. Use any pastry scraps to make
leaves for the top. Brush pastry with
milk—decorate with leaves.
☐ Bake for 30min. in centre of oven,
pre-heated to 450 deg. F. or Mark 8,
then reduce heat to 375 deg. F. or Mark
5 and continue cooking for another
30min., or until pastry is well risen, crisp
and golden. Serve hot with vegetables.

DURHAM POT PIE
(Enough for four)

8oz. suet crust pastry—see page 17
4 large rabbit joints
2oz. dripping
3 medium-sized carrots
2 large leeks
salt and pepper

☐ Roll pastry out on a lightly floured
board to 4in. larger than the top of a
2½ pint pudding basin. Cut off a 2in.
border all round. Grease the top of the
basin and press the band of suet crust
inside the top edge of the basin, to make
a 2in. deep lining.
☐ Wipe the rabbit. Cut the joints into
small pieces. Melt the dripping in a
frying pan and fry the rabbit joints until
browned on all sides. Peel and slice the
carrots. Trim off roots and damaged
leaves from leeks. Cut leeks in half
downwards and wash well. Cut into ½in.
slices. Put the rabbit and vegetables into
the basin; season well. Add ¼ pint water.
☐ Moisten the edge of the suet crust
band in the basin and cover the pudding
with the round, pressing the edges well
to seal. Cover with a piece of foil or
greaseproof paper allowing room for the
pudding to rise a little. Boil or steam
for 3½ hours, adding more boiling water
as it evaporates from the pan.

ROMAN RABBIT
(Enough for four)

4 rabbit joints
salt and pepper
½lb. onions
½lb. carrots
½ chicken stock cube
¼ pint boiling water
¼ pint milk
1oz. butter
1oz. plain flour
4oz. grated Cheddar cheese

☐ Put the rabbit in a pan. Cover with
cold water and bring to the boil. Drain.
Season the rabbit. Skin and thinly slice
the onions. Peel and cut the carrots into
¼in. dice. Arrange the rabbit, onions and
carrots in a casserole. Dissolve the stock
cube in the boiling water and pour over
the rabbit. Cover dish and cook for
1 hour or until tender, in centre of oven,
pre-heated to 350 deg. F. or Mark 4.
☐ Drain stock from rabbit; use to make
milk up to ½ pint. Melt the butter in a
small pan. Stir in the flour and cook
gently for 2min. Gradually stir in the
milk mixture and bring to the boil,
stirring all the time. Cook gently for
2min. Season well and add 3oz. cheese.
☐ Pour sauce over the rabbit; sprinkle
top with remaining cheese and return to
oven to cook for 1 hour more.

SAVOURY KIDNEY SUPPER
(Enough for two)

1 medium-sized onion
1oz. butter
6 lambs' kidneys
2oz. button mushrooms
1 level teaspoon cornflour
1 level teaspoon tomato purée
2 tablespoons port
salt and pepper
2 thick slices of white bread
oil for deep frying
2 level teaspoons chopped parsley

☐ Skin the onion, halve and slice thinly.
Melt butter in a pan, add the onion,
cover and cook gently for 5min.
Remove fat from kidneys, cut each in
half, peel off the outer skins and remove
the white cores, and slice. Wash the
mushrooms and slice thinly. Add the
kidneys and mushrooms to the saucepan
and cook gently for 2min. Blend
cornflour, purée, port and 2 tablespoons
cold water. Pour this into the saucepan
and stir gently until the sauce begins to
boil. Season with salt and pepper, reduce
heat, cover and simmer gently for 7min.,
or until the kidneys are tender.
☐ Remove crusts from bread, cut into
4 squares, then cut each square in half to
make triangles. Heat the oil to the
correct temperature—see page 15. Fry
the triangles for 1-2min., or until golden.
☐ Serve the kidneys in individual dishes
garnished with triangles of bread and
sprinkled with the parsley.

TRIPE AND ONIONS
(Enough for two)

1lb. tripe
1 large onion
½ pint milk
salt and pepper
½oz. cornflour

☐ Wash the tripe well and cut into
square pieces. Put in a pan; cover with
cold water and bring to the boil. Skin
and roughly chop the onion. Drain the
water from the tripe; pour on milk and
½ pint cold water. Add the onion and
salt and pepper to season. Bring to the
boil, cover pan, then simmer for 3 hours.
☐ Blend the cornflour with a little cold
water. Pour on a little hot liquid and stir
well. Return to pan and stir well all the
time. Bring to the boil and cook gently
for 3min. Serve immediately.

OXTAIL CASSEROLE
(Enough for six)

2 small oxtails
3oz. margarine or lard
2 medium-sized onions
2oz. plain flour
1½ beef stock cubes
1½ pints boiling water
salt and pepper
1 level teaspoon dried sage
1 level teaspoon dried rosemary
6 cloves
juice of ½ lemon

☐ Wash the tail joints carefully. Trim off
any excess fat. Melt the margarine or
lard in a large saucepan and lightly fry
the joints until golden brown. Remove
them, leaving the fat in the pan. Skin
and roughly chop the onions and fry
them lightly in the fat. Stir in the flour
and cook for about 2min.
☐ Dissolve the stock cubes in the boiling
water and add to the pan. Bring to the
boil, stirring all the time. Add salt and
pepper, sage, rosemary, cloves and the
lemon juice.
☐ Transfer the contents of the pan and
the pieces of oxtail to a casserole. Cover
and cook for 3-4 hours in centre of oven,
pre-heated to 300 deg. F. or Mark 2.
Serve hot with croûtons, if liked.

LOVE IN DISGUISE
(Enough for four)

3oz. vermicelli
salt and pepper
4 medium-sized calves' hearts
10oz. fresh white breadcrumbs
1 level teaspoon dried marjoram
2 level teaspoons finely chopped parsley
1 level teaspoon grated lemon rind
3oz. shredded suet
3oz. ham
1 large egg
milk
4 rashers of fat bacon

☐ Break up the vermicelli and cook it in
boiling salted water for 3min. Cool.
Remove all the pipes from the hearts.
Wash and soak in cold water for 30min.
☐ Reserve 2oz. breadcrumbs. Mix rest
of breadcrumbs with the herbs, salt and
pepper, lemon rind and suet. Finely chop
the ham and add to bowl. Beat the egg
and add half to the bowl. Mix well with
enough milk to bind.
☐ Dry the hearts and fill with stuffing.
Stretch the bacon rashers; wrap one
round each heart. Fasten with small
skewers or cocktail sticks. Wrap in butter
papers. Arrange in a roasting tin and
bake for 1½ hours in centre of oven, pre-
heated to 350 deg. F. or Mark 4. Remove
the papers and brush the hearts with rest
of egg.
☐ Mix the remaining breadcrumbs and
vermicelli and roll each heart in this
mixture to coat well. Put back in the
baking tin and bake for 20min., or until
nicely browned.

CRUBEENS (PIGS TROTTERS)
(Enough for two)

6 pigs' trotters
1 large onion
4 cloves
1 large carrot
1 sprig of parsley
1 bay leaf
12 peppercorns
salt
pinch of dried thyme

☐ The front trotters of the pig are the true crubeens with succulent meat between the bones.
☐ Wash trotters well. Skin onion, and stick it with cloves. Peel carrot. Wash parsley. Put all ingredients in a large pan. Cover with cold water. Bring slowly to the boil, then simmer for 3 hours. Drain the trotters. Eat crubeens hot or cold with your fingers.

CATALAN TRIPE
(Enough for four)

2lb. tripe
4oz. onions
6oz. tomatoes
boiling water
1 tablespoon olive oil
¼ pint white wine
1lb. potatoes
1 small clove of garlic
1 level dessertspoon chopped parsley
salt and pepper

☐ Wash the tripe well. Put in a pan; cover with cold water. Bring to the boil and boil for 10min. Drain.
☐ Skin and finely chop the onions. Drop the tomatoes into boiling water; leave for 1min., then drain and skin. Chop roughly. Heat the oil in a frying pan; add the onions and tomatoes and fry gently for 5min. Drain the tripe and cut it into serving pieces.
☐ Add tripe to frying pan and cook gently for 5min. Pour in the wine, add ½ pint cold water, cover pan and simmer gently for 1 hour.
☐ Peel and slice the potatoes. Add potatoes to pan. Skin and chop garlic. Pound garlic and parsley together. Add to pan. Season with salt and pepper and simmer for 1 hour more. Serve hot.

CALVES SWEETBREADS
(Enough for four-six)

3 calves' sweetbreads
salt and pepper
1 pint boiling water
1 medium-sized egg
4oz. toasted breadcrumbs
3oz. butter
1 tablespoon oil

☐ Soak the sweetbreads in lukewarm salt water for about 1 hour. Plunge them into boiling salted water for a few seconds and then rinse them under cold water. Trim off any fat and place the sweetbreads under a heavy chopping board or between two plates until cold.
☐ Cut each sweetbread in half and season with salt and pepper. Break the egg on a flat plate and whisk lightly.
☐ Coat the sweetbreads in egg and breadcrumbs. Melt the butter and the oil in a frying pan and fry the sweetbreads for about 15min., or until they are golden and cooked.

KIDNEY IN THE OVEN
(Enough for four)

4 large onions
4 lambs' kidneys
salt and pepper
1 beef stock cube
½ pint boiling water
2 tablespoons rum

☐ Skin onions carefully keeping them whole. Slice off the top of each to form a lid. Hollow out the onions until 1 kidney will fit exactly in each. Chop the pieces hollowed out of the onion; put in a casserole. Skin the kidneys; remove the cores, and put one kidney in each onion case. Season well. Place the lid on top and arrange carefully in the casserole.
☐ Dissolve the stock cube in the boiling water and add to the casserole to halfway up the onions. Add more boiling water if necessary.
☐ Bake for 2-2½ hours in centre of oven, pre-heated to 325 deg. F. or Mark 3. Twenty minutes before they are ready, uncover the dish and pour ½ tablespoon rum over each kidney. The onions and kidneys should be well cooked and the kidneys soft enough to be eaten with a spoon.

BOILED OX TONGUE
(Enough for eight)

4lb. fresh ox tongue
1 large carrot
1 large onion
1 small turnip
3 peppercorns
1 bay leaf
3 parsley stalks
1 sprig of thyme

☐ Rinse the ox tongue then skewer it into a good shape. Place in a large saucepan and cover with cold water. Bring to the boil gradually then drain.
☐ Peel the carrot, skin the onion and thickly peel the turnip. Add to the pan. Tie the peppercorns, bay leaf, parsley and thyme in a piece of muslin and add to pan. Cover tongue with fresh cold water. Bring to the boil and simmer for 4–5 hours or until tender. Skim from time to time.
☐ Plunge the tongue into cold water. Skin the tongue as soon as it's cool enough to handle, removing any bones or gristle.
☐ Curl the tongue in a 7in. cake tin with a fixed base. Add a little of the cooking liquid and place a plate on top of the tongue. Add a weight from your scales. Leave to set. Turn out and serve with salad.

LIVER ROLL
(Enough for six)

1 medium-sized potato
salt and pepper
1 large onion
3oz. dripping
1½lb. pigs' liver
¼ pint milk

☐ Peel the potato and cut into pieces. Cook in boiling, salted water for 20min., or until soft enough to mash. Drain and mash well. Skin and slice the onion. Melt 2oz. dripping in a frying pan. Fry the liver slices until cooked, turning them once or twice. Remove and drain on kitchen paper. Add the onion and fry until brown. Drain on kitchen paper. Mince liver and onion finely. Add the milk, potato and plenty of salt and pepper and mix well.
☐ Spread mixture on a piece of greased foil. Dot with rest of dripping. Put into a roasting tin and form mixture into a roll with the aid of the foil. Remove foil. Bake for 45min. in centre of oven, pre-heated to 375 deg. F. or Mark 5. Cut into slices to serve.

BROCHETTES OF PORK
(Enough for four)

1½lb. lean pork
4 bay leaves
1 tablespoon Madeira or brown sherry
salt and pepper
2 large onions
1oz. plain flour
oil for deep frying

☐ Wipe the meat and cut it into 1in. squares. Tear the bay leaves into small pieces.
☐ Skewer the meat alternately with small pieces of bay leaf allowing a little space between the meat cubes. Put in a dish and sprinkle with the Madeira or sherry. Leave for 1 hour. Season.
☐ Slice the onions thinly, separate into rings. Toss in the flour to coat. Heat the oil to the correct temperature—see page 15. Fry the onion rings until golden.
☐ Grill the brochettes for 10min., or until well-cooked, turning several times.
☐ Serve the brochettes on a bed of plain rice garnished with the fried onion rings.

BELLY OF PORK CASSEROLE
(Enough for four)

1½lb. belly of pork
2 large onions
1 large cooking apple
½ chicken stock cube
½ pint boiling water
salt and pepper
2 level tablespoons plain flour
2 large carrots

☐ Wipe the pork and cut it into 8 pieces, trimming off any excess fat.
☐ Skin and slice the onions, and place them in a casserole. Peel, core and slice the apple and lay over the onions. Overlap the slices of pork on top. Dissolve the stock cube in the boiling water, pour over the meat. Season well with salt and pepper. Cover and cook for 2 hours in centre of oven, pre-heated to 325 deg. F. or Mark 3.
☐ Skim off any excess fat. Blend the flour with 2 tablespoons cold water. Stir in ¼ pint liquid from the casserole and return it to the casserole.
☐ Peel and slice the carrots. Add to casserole. Cover and cook for 1 hour more. Serve hot.

STUFFED PORK WITH APPLE RINGS
(Enough for six)

3lb. loin of pork
4oz. fresh white breadcrumbs
2oz. shredded suet
2 level tablespoons chopped parsley
1 level tablespoon chopped chives, spring onions, or grated onion
6 small cooking apples
salt and pepper
1 large egg
2oz. lard

☐ Ask your butcher to bone the loin or remove bones carefully to leave a flat piece of meat. Wipe the meat. Mix the breadcrumbs, suet, parsley and chives or onions. Peel, core and chop 1 apple and add this to the ingredients. Season with salt and pepper. Beat the egg and add enough to the mixture to bind. Mix well.
☐ Spread the mixture over the meat carefully and roll the meat. Tie with thin string. Brush the scored fat with melted lard and sprinkle lightly with salt.
☐ Cook for 1½ hours, or until the crackling is crisp and the meat is tender, in centre of oven, pre-heated to 400 deg. F. or Mark 6.

☐ Core the apples and slice thickly. Place in the tin 20min. before the end of cooking. Remove the meat on to a hot dish when cooked. Pour off surplus fat, leaving just 1 tablespoon in roasting tin and use this as a base for gravy—see page 8. Surround the meat with the sliced apples and serve the gravy separately.

ROLLED PORK WITH PEPPER STUFFING
(Enough for six-eight)

4lb. lean belly of pork
$\frac{1}{4}$ small red pepper
$\frac{1}{4}$ small green pepper
boiling water
4oz. fresh white breadcrumbs
pinch of dried thyme
pinch of dried sage
salt and pepper
1 standard egg
oil
parsley

☐ Ask your butcher to bone pork ready for rolling and score the skin. Trim off any excess fat. Wash peppers, discard seeds and white cores. Cover with boiling water and leave for 5min.

☐ Drain off water and cut peppers into $\frac{1}{4}$in. dice. Add to breadcrumbs with herbs, salt and pepper. Beat egg, stir enough into breadcrumbs to make a fairly dry mixture.

☐ Lay pork flat, skin side down and spoon stuffing along centre of pork. Bring the two long edges together. Tie with fine string at 1in. intervals. Brush skin with a little oil and sprinkle with salt for crisp crackling.

☐ Place in roasting tin and cook for $2\frac{1}{2}$ hours, in lower part of oven, pre-heated to 350 deg. F. or Mark 4. If the skin becomes too brown, cover loosely with foil and reduce heat to 325 deg. F. or Mark 3. Garnish with parsley.

PORK CONES
(Enough for four)

4 prunes
4 lettuce leaves
1 small orange
butter
4 slices of rye bread
4 slices of cold roast pork
4 level tablespoons pickled red cabbage

☐ Cover prunes with cold water. Leave overnight. Drain off water; remove the stones.
☐ Wash lettuce, shake dry. Wash and slice the orange. Thickly butter each slice of bread.
☐ Place a small lettuce leaf on each slice. Add a slice of meat and top with a tablespoon of red cabbage. Cut into the centre of 4 orange slices. Twist each one to make a cone shape. Arrange on the top of the cabbage and place a prune in the centre.

PORK CHEESE
(Enough for eight)

4lb. hock of salt pork
1 small onion
1 stick of celery
1 sprig of sage
1 sprig of thyme
4 peppercorns
2 blades of mace
½ bay leaf
pepper

☐ Put the pork in a bowl. Cover with cold water and leave to stand for 12 hours or overnight. Drain and put in a pan. Cover with cold water. Bring to the boil and boil for 3-3½ hours or until the meat just comes off the bone. Cool for 1 hour.
☐ Remove pork from pan and take out the bones. Put bones back in the pan. Skin the onion. Wash the celery and cut in half. Add onion and celery to pan with sage, thyme, peppercorns, mace and bay leaf. Bring to the boil and simmer for 2 hours or until you have ½ pint of stock. Rub a little pepper into the meat and cut meat very finely. Strain the stock over the meat and pour into a wetted basin or mould. Leave to set then unmould.

EPPING SAUSAGES
(Enough for four)

1lb. belly of pork
1lb. butchers' suet
salt and pepper
pinch of dried sage
pinch of dried thyme
pinch of ground nutmeg
grated rind of 1 large lemon
1 large egg

☐ Wipe pork and mince twice. Grate suet. Mix meat with all but 1oz. of suet. Season meat with salt, pepper, sage, thyme and nutmeg. Add lemon rind to meat. Beat egg; mix into meat. Divide the mixture into 8 pieces and form each into a sausage.
☐ Melt the remaining suet in a frying pan. Remove any tissues, then fry sausages gently for 20-30min., turning frequently. Serve hot or cold.

BOILED BACON
(Enough for ten)

5lb. piece middle gammon
1 large onion
1 bay leaf
6 peppercorns
4oz. fresh white breadcrumbs

☐ Put bacon in a bowl and cover with cold water. Leave to soak for not more than 2 hours.
☐ Drain bacon. Skin onion. Put bacon in a large pan, cover with fresh cold water and add the onion, bay leaf and peppercorns. Bring to boil, then simmer for 2 hours.
☐ Toast breadcrumbs until golden, turning all the time. Remove skin from bacon and cover the fat with toasted breadcrumbs, pressing them on well.
☐ Serve bacon thickly sliced.

MEDLEY PIE
(Enough for four)

10oz. plain flour
salt and pepper
5oz. dripping
8oz. back bacon
1 large cooking apple
3 medium-sized onions
1 level teaspoon dried sage
1 large egg yolk

☐ Sift the flour and a pinch of salt into a bowl. Rub in the dripping until the mixture looks like fine breadcrumbs. Mix to a stiff dough with cold water. Turn on to a lightly floured board and roll out to ¼in. thickness. Line a 9in. pie dish with half the pastry.
☐ Cut rinds from the bacon. Peel, core and slice the apple. Skin and slice the onions. Layer the bacon, apples and onions in the dish, sprinkling each layer with sage and salt and pepper. Add ¼ pint water.
☐ Cover pie with rest of pastry, pinching edges well to seal. Trim edges and decorate. Prick top in a pattern with a fork to allow steam to escape. Lightly beat egg yolk, and brush over pie. Bake for 40min. in centre of oven, pre-heated to 350 deg. F. or Mark 4, then reduce heat to 300 deg. F. or Mark 2 and bake for 40min. more.

BACON TWO-CRUST PIE
(Enough for six)

8oz. shortcrust pastry—see page 16
12oz. thin streaky bacon
6 standard eggs
2 medium-sized tomatoes
salt and pepper

☐ Roll out half of the shortcrust pastry to fit a 10in. pie plate. Put on plate. Cut rinds from bacon. Cut rashers into 1in. pieces. Spread bacon pieces over pastry on plate. Break eggs on to bacon. Wash and slice tomatoes. Arrange on eggs. Season with salt and pepper.
☐ Roll out rest of pastry to a round slightly larger than the pie plate. Moisten edge of pastry on plate and cover pie with remaining pastry. Press edges to seal. Trim edges of pastry. Decorate with trimmings if liked. Cook for 20min., in centre of oven, pre-heated to 425 deg. F. or Mark 7, then reduce heat to 375 deg. F. or Mark 5 and continue cooking for a further 25–30min., or until the pastry is crisp and golden and the bacon cooked.
☐ Serve pie hot or cold with salad.

MOCK GOOSE
(Enough for ten)

6lb. leg of pork
3 large onions
1 large carrot
½ small turnip
6 peppercorns
2 blades of mace
1oz. butter
4oz. fresh white breadcrumbs
2 level teaspoons dried sage
salt and pepper
2oz. lard

☐ Wipe the leg of pork and put in a large pan. Cover with cold water. Skin 1 onion and leave whole. Peel carrot. Thickly peel turnip. Add to pan with peppercorns and mace. Bring to the boil and simmer for 1¼ hours, removing white scum as soon as it rises.

☐ Skin and finely chop the remaining onions. Melt the butter. Mix the breadcrumbs, sage, onion and butter to make a stuffing. Season well with salt and pepper. Drain pork.

☐ Remove the skin from the pork and using a very sharp small knife, remove the bone, easing back the meat with the knife and keeping the leg of pork whole. Push the stuffing into the hole left by the bone. Tie the meat carefully with string, pushing the leg into the shape of a goose. Roast in the lard for 1½-2 hours, or until tender, in centre of oven, pre-heated to 400 deg. F. or Mark 6. Turn and baste during cooking.

☐ Serve with apple sauce and brown onion gravy.

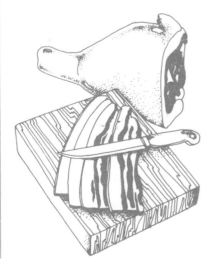

PORK SAUSAGES
(Makes fourteen sausages)

1½lb. fat and lean pork
6oz. fresh white breadcrumbs
salt and pepper
½ level teaspoon dried marjoram
1oz. lard

☐ Ask your butcher if he sells 4oz. sausage skins ready-cleaned. They only need washing well in cold water and they are ready for filling. If you can't obtain skins, shape sausages into small pats.

☐ Cut off pork skin and mince pork coarsely. Put the breadcrumbs in a bowl and cover with cold water. Leave to soak for 30min. Squeeze out water, but leave crumbs still very wet. Mix wet bread into the pork using your hands. Add salt and pepper and the marjoram. Fill skins, or make into 14 pats.

☐ To cook, melt the lard and fry sausages for 20min., on both sides until golden brown and cooked through.

PORK VINDALOO
(Enough for four)

2lb. thick belly of pork
1 large onion
1 clove of garlic
3oz. butter
2 tablespoons cooking oil
2 level tablespoons vindaloo paste
salt

☐ Wipe the pork and cut into good-sized chunks including some of the fat. Skin and roughly chop the onion and garlic.

☐ Heat the butter and oil in a large pan and cook the onion and the garlic until soft and just beginning to turn golden brown. Remove the onion and garlic and leave fat in pan. Fry the meat until brown on all sides. Remove meat, leaving fat in pan.

☐ Stir in the vindaloo paste and cook gently for 3min. over a very gentle heat, stirring all the time. Take care that this mixture does not burn. Return onion, garlic and pork to pan. Stir in 4 tablespoons water and mix well. Cover the pan with a tight-fitting lid and cook for 2 hours or until the pork is really tender. But remember this dish burns easily if cooked too fast.

☐ When cooked, uncover pan and, if necessary, simmer until you have a thick gravy. Add salt to taste.

FRIED PORK RIBBONS WITH LEEKS
(Enough for four)

3 young leeks
1lb. lean shoulder of pork
1 large egg
½ level tablespoon cornflour
2 tablespoons vegetable oil
3 dessertspoons soy sauce
2 tablespoons chicken stock made from a stock cube
1 level teaspoon caster sugar

☐ Cut off roots and any damaged green leaves from leeks. Cut into ½in. pieces and wash thoroughly. Cut the pork against the grain into 1½in. lengths, no more than ¼in. wide. Beat the egg. Dip pork ribbons in the egg and then the cornflour.

☐ Heat the oil and fry the pork and leeks quickly for 7-8min. turning all the time, so they don't burn on any side. Add the soy sauce and stock and fry for a further 3min. Add the sugar and cook for 2min. more.

☐ Serve immediately on a hot plate with bean shoots.

BACON PUDDING
(Enough for four-six)

1lb. suet crust pastry—see page 17
8oz. fat bacon
2 medium-sized onions
1 level teaspoon dried sage
salt and pepper

☐ Turn pastry on to a floured board and roll out to a ½in. thick square.

☐ Cut off bacon rinds and cut bacon into pieces. Spread over pastry. Skin and roughly chop onions and sprinkle over bacon with the sage and salt and pepper. Roll up the dough and seal by pinching the ends together.

☐ Wrap the roll in a large piece of clean floured muslin and tie the ends with string. Put into boiling water. Boil gently for 2 hours, adding more boiling water as it evaporates. Remove cloth to serve and slice the roll.

FIDGET PIE
(Enough for four-six)

1lb. potatoes
1lb. cooking apples
½lb. onions
½lb. lean bacon or ham
little caster sugar
salt and pepper
½ ham stock cube
½ pint boiling water
8oz. shortcrust pastry—see page 16

☐ Peel and slice potatoes. Peel, core and slice the apples. Skin and chop the onions. Cut the bacon or ham into small pieces.

☐ Place a layer of potatoes in a 3 pint ovenproof dish, then bacon or ham, then apples, adding a little sugar if sour. Repeat until the dish is full, seasoning each layer and sprinkling with the onions. Dissolve the stock cube in the boiling water; pour into the dish.

☐ Roll the pastry thinly to 1in. larger than the dish. Cut off a ½in. strip all round. Grease the edge of the pie dish and place the strip of pastry around the edge. Moisten the pastry and cover dish with the large piece. Press edges well to seal, trim and decorate. Make a small hole in the centre.

☐ Bake for 30min. in centre of oven, pre-heated to 350 deg. F. or Mark 4, then reduce heat to 300 deg. F. or Mark 2 and cook for 1 hour more.

SPARERIBS WITH PICKLED GHERKIN SAUCE
(Enough for four)

2lb. sparerib of pork
1 level teaspoon salt
black pepper
4oz. onions
1oz. lard
¼ level teaspoon ground allspice
¼ level teaspoon ground cloves
1 small bay leaf
½oz. plain flour
1½ level tablespoons tomato purée
9½oz. jar dill-pickled gherkins

☐ Cut the spareribs into serving-sized pieces. Sprinkle on both sides with the salt and pepper, freshly ground if you have a mill. Skin and finely chop the onions. Heat the lard in a large frying pan until a faint haze rises. Add the spareribs and brown them on both sides without burning them. Remove on to a plate and keep the chops hot.

☐ Add the onions to the pan, with the allspice, cloves and bay leaf. Stir in the flour and tomato purée, using a wooden spoon. Drain the gherkins and cut into small dice. Add to pan with ¾ pint cold water. Bring to the boil, stirring all the time until thickened.

☐ Add spareribs to the pan. Baste well with the sauce. Cover pan and simmer for 1-1½ hours, basting at times, until ribs are tender. Remove bay leaf. Taste for seasoning.

☐ Serve the spareribs with the sauce poured over them.

MELTON MOWBRAY PORK PIE
(Enough for six)

2 veal knuckles
12oz. hot water crust pastry—see page 18
1¼lb. lean shoulder of pork
salt and pepper

☐ Rinse the veal knuckles and put in a large pan. Cover with cold water, and simmer for 2 hours.

☐ Make the hot water crust pastry using 12oz. plain flour, 1 level teaspoon salt, 4oz. lard and ¼ pint mixed milk and water—see page 18. Cut off a third of the pastry for the lid of the pie.

☐ Flour a 2lb. jam jar. Put the dough on top and using your hands, mould the dough down the sides keeping it about ⅓in. thick. Keep remainder of dough warm. Leave to set for 10min., then remove from the mould.

☐ Wipe the pork, remove all excess fat and skin. Mince the meat coarsely. Season. Mix in 2 tablespoons cold water and press meat into the pie crust to within ¾in. of the top, pushing it into the corners.

☐ Roll out reserved third of pastry for the lid. Put in place and press edges to seal. Trim edge. Decorate edge and make a hole in centre. Decorate top of pie

with the trimmings cut into leaf shapes.

☐ Cut a length of greaseproof paper about 1in. higher than pie and wind it round, making sure it goes right to base of the pie. Fix with clear adhesive tape.

☐ Stand pie on a sandwich tin and bake for 1 hour in centre of oven, pre-heated to 350 deg. F. or Mark 4 then reduce heat to 300 deg. F. or Mark 2 and cook for 45min. more. Allow pie to become nearly cold.

☐ While pie cooks, strain stock from veal knuckles and season well. Remove pie from oven. Pour stock into the pie through the hole in the centre and then leave to set.

BAKED HAM IN A CRUST
(Enough for ten)

4lb. middle cut ham
1½lb. plain flour

☐ Put the ham in a bowl and cover with cold water. Leave to soak for no more than 2 hours. Drain ham.
☐ Make a stiff paste of the flour and ½ pint cold water and spread this over the ham to completely cover it, making sure there are no holes.
☐ Bake for 20min. in centre of oven, pre-heated to 425 deg. F. or Mark 7, then reduce heat to 350 deg. F. or Mark 4 and cook for 2 hours more. Remove and discard the crust to serve.
☐ This old-fashioned way of baking keeps in all the flavour and juices and is particularly good for very small joints of bacon because it prevents them drying.

SAUSAGEMEAT BALLS
(Enough for four)

¾lb. pork sausagemeat
2 level tablespoons tomato ketchup
salt and pepper
1 large egg
4oz. fresh white breadcrumbs
oil for deep frying

☐ Break the sausagemeat down with a fork; add ketchup and salt and pepper to season. Lightly beat the egg and add half to the sausagemeat with 2oz. breadcrumbs. Mix well. Form into 12 small balls. Brush with remaining egg and coat with the rest of the breadcrumbs.
☐ Heat the oil to the correct temperature —see page 15—and cook sausagemeat balls for 15min., or until cooked and golden brown. Drain well.
☐ Serve with baked beans and tomato halves. Garnish with a sprig of parsley or with a little watercress.

SPANISH RICE
(Enough for four)

1 fish head, skin and bones
2 medium-sized onions
2 cloves of garlic
salt and pepper
1 bay leaf
¼ level teaspoon dried thyme
¼ level teaspoon finely chopped parsley
12oz. tomatoes
3 tablespoons olive oil
½ level teaspoon caster sugar
1lb. Patna rice
2½oz. butter
½lb. lean loin of pork
4 chicken livers
1½oz. plain flour
¾ pint milk
1 large egg yolk

☐ Wash the fish trimmings and put in a large pan. Skin and slice 1 onion. Skin 1 clove of garlic and leave whole. Add to pan with salt, pepper and herbs. Add 2 pints cold water, cover and bring to the boil. Simmer for 15min. Strain and discard fish and vegetables.
☐ Skin and chop remaining onion. Skin and crush remaining clove of garlic. Wash and chop the tomatoes. Heat 1 tablespoon oil in a small pan. Fry onion for 5min., or until tender. Add garlic and tomatoes, sugar and 2 tablespoons water. Cover and simmer for 10min. Season with salt and pepper. Remove from heat.
☐ Heat rest of oil in a large pan. Add rice and fry for 5min., stirring all the time. Pour in 1½ pints fish stock. Simmer for 25min., or until rice is tender and all liquid has been absorbed, stirring in more stock if necessary.
☐ Melt 1oz. butter in a small pan. Cut the pork into small pieces. Wash livers. Gently fry pork and livers for 10min. Turn on to a plate and roughly slice the livers.
☐ Add remaining butter to the small pan and heat. Stir in flour and cook gently for 2min. Remove from heat. Gradually add the milk, stirring all the time. Bring to the boil and cook for 3min., stirring all the time. Stir in the pork and livers and cook for 5min. Taste for seasoning. Allow to cool a little.
☐ Mix egg yolk with a little cold water and stir into pork and livers. Cover and keep hot, but do not allow sauce to boil or it will curdle.
☐ Butter a large ring mould well and light press in the cooked rice to give it shape. Place in oven to heat through for 5min. Strain tomato sauce and reheat. Turn rice on to a large hot serving plate, cover with the tomato sauce and fill centre with meat sauce. Serve at once.

SPARERIB PIE
(Enough for six)

6oz. shortcrust pastry—see page 16
2lb. sparerib of pork
¼oz. plain flour
salt and pepper
½ level teaspoon finely chopped parsley
½ level teaspoon finely chopped sage
1 chicken stock cube
1 pint boiling water

☐ Roll out pastry on a lightly floured board to ¼in. thickness.
☐ Cut the pork into 1½in. pieces; toss in the flour and put into a deep ovenproof pie dish. Season with salt, pepper and the chopped herbs.
☐ Dissolve the stock cube in the boiling water and pour into the dish to half fill. Grease the edge of the dish. Cut a ½in. wide strip off the pastry and press it on the edge of the dish. Moisten strip and cover pie with the large piece of pastry, pressing edges well to seal. Trim and decorate.
☐ Cook for 10min. in centre of oven, pre-heated to 425 deg. F. or Mark 7, then reduce heat to 350 deg. F. or Mark 4 and cook for 45min. more. Serve hot.

FILLET OF PORK DUMPLING
(Enough for four)

8oz. suet crust pastry—see page 17
1lb. pork fillet
1 packet sage and onion stuffing
salt and pepper

☐ Roll pastry out on a lightly floured board to a large square ¼in. thick. Flour a large pudding cloth and carefully place pastry on it.
☐ Cut the fillet of pork into small pieces, removing fat. Spread over the pastry. Make up the stuffing as directed on the packet and dot pieces over the pastry. Season well with salt and pepper. Gather the corners of the pastry together (like a swag bag) and gather the corners of the cloth and tie tightly to hold the pudding in a good shape. Place in boiling water and simmer pudding for 4 hours, replenishing with boiling water as it evaporates. This is good eaten hot or cold with apple sauce.

STUFFED CHINE
(Enough for six)

3½lb. neck chine of bacon
½ small lettuce
6 small spring onions
1 level tablespoon finely chopped parsley
1 level teaspoon dried thyme
1 level teaspoon dried marjoram
3oz. lard

☐ Put the bacon in a bowl; cover with cold water and leave to soak for not more than 2 hours.
☐ Remove any damaged lettuce leaves. Cut off roots and tops of spring onions. Chop very finely and mix with the herbs. Include some young raspberry or blackcurrant leaves if liked.
☐ Deeply score the bacon all over with a small sharp knife. Rub herb mixture into the cuts, pushing it well down into the meat. Cover the bacon with foil. Melt the lard in a roasting tin, add the bacon and cook for 1½ hours in centre of oven, pre-heated to 350 deg. F. or Mark 4.

PORK WITH SPICY LEMON SAUCE
(Enough for two)

1lb. shoulder of pork
1 clove of garlic
½oz. lard
8 tablespoons dry white wine
2 level teaspoons ground cumin
salt and pepper
3 thin slices of lemon
1 level teaspoon ground coriander

☐ Cut the meat into 1in. cubes and pat them dry with kitchen paper. Skin and crush the clove of garlic or chop it very finely. Heat the lard in a large frying pan until a faint haze rises.
☐ Add the pork and brown the meat, turning it frequently. Don't let meat burn. Stir in 6 tablespoons wine, the cumin, garlic, ½ level teaspoon salt and a good pinch of pepper, freshly ground if you have a mill. Bring to the boil, then simmer for 55min., or until the pork is tender. Add the remaining wine.
☐ Cut the lemon slices into quarters and add to the pan. Cook, stirring, until the sauce thickens slightly. Stir in the coriander and serve at once.

FRIKADELLER
(Enough for four)

1lb. lean pork
1 small onion
salt and pepper
2 level tablespoons plain flour
pinch of dried basil
1 large egg
2 tablespoons milk
oil for deep frying

☐ Wipe the meat and cut into 1in. cubes. Skin and quarter the onion. Mince the two together twice.
☐ Add 1 level teaspoon salt and a good pinch of pepper. Stir in the flour and basil. Beat the egg and milk; use to bind the pork mixture. The mixture should be soft. Flour your hands and roll into small balls.
☐ Heat the oil to the correct temperature—see page 15. Cook the meat balls for 6min., or until brown. Drain on kitchen paper and serve with tomato sauce.

BACON AND EGG PIE
(Enough for six)

8oz. shortcrust pastry—see page 16
4 rashers of streaky bacon
2 large tomatoes
4 large eggs
5 tablespoons milk
salt and pepper

☐ Roll out the pastry on a lightly floured board and use half to line a 7in. pie plate.
☐ Cut off the bacon rinds and chop the rashers. Sprinkle over the pastry. Wash and thinly slice the tomatoes and add to pie. Whisk the eggs and 4 tablespoons milk together and season with salt and pepper. Pour over the bacon.
☐ Moisten the edge of the pastry on the plate and cover with the remaining pastry. Press the edges to seal. Decorate the edge of the pastry. Brush with the remaining milk.
☐ Bake for 10min., in centre of oven, pre-heated to 425 deg. F. or Mark 7, then reduce heat to 350 deg. F. or Mark 4 and cook for a further 30min. Serve hot or cold.

SWEET AND SOUR PORK
(Enough for four)

3oz. and 1 level tablespoon self-raising flour
1 standard egg
peanut oil
1 small carrot
1½in. piece cucumber
1 level tablespoon pickled cabbage—optional
salt and pepper
brown malt vinegar
6oz. lean leg of pork
Ve-Tsin
½ teaspoon sesame oil
1 level dessertspoon caster sugar
½ teaspoon soy sauce
1 level teaspoon tomato ketchup
1 level teaspoon cornflour

☐ Sift 3oz. flour into a basin. Make a well in the centre; add half the egg and gradually beat in with ¼ pint cold water. When well mixed stir in ½ teaspoon peanut oil. Leave to stand for 20min.
☐ Meanwhile, peel carrot. Cut carrot, unpeeled cucumber and pickled cabbage, if used, into matchstick like strips. Sprinkle with a pinch of salt and leave for 5min. Press out liquid. Sprinkle with a pinch of salt and 2 teaspoons vinegar.
☐ Wipe pork and cut into ½in. cubes, removing all fat. Put into a bowl. Add a pinch of salt, pepper and Ve-Tsin and sesame oil and work them well into the meat. Toss pork in rest of flour. Turn meat into a sieve; shake to remove surplus flour. Drop meat into batter.
☐ Mix sugar, a tiny pinch of salt, pepper, and Ve-Tsin, 3 dessertspoons vinegar, soy sauce and tomato ketchup with 6 tablespoons cold water. Bring to boil. Blend cornflour with 1 dessertspoon cold water and stir into sauce in pan. Cook for 1½min. Remove and keep hot.
☐ Heat some peanut oil in a deep pan to the correct temperature—see page 15. Remove meat from batter and allow excess to drip off. Drop carefully into hot oil. Cook for 8min. until pork is cooked through and a warm golden colour. Drain on absorbent paper. Turn pork into a heated dish, add vegetables and pour over the sauce.

PORK PANCAKE ROLLS
(Enough for four)

4oz. plain flour
salt and pepper
2 large eggs
½ pint milk
2oz. lard
½ packet sage and onion stuffing
6oz. cooked pork
4oz. fresh white breadcrumbs
1 small onion
1lb. 13oz. tin peeled tomatoes
oil for deep frying

☐ Sift the flour and a pinch of salt into
a basin. Make a well in the centre. Add
1 egg and a little milk and beat until
smooth. Beat in remaining milk. Melt a
little lard from 1oz. in a frying pan and
when hot pour in ⅛ of the batter.
Cook for 1min. until golden brown
underneath. Turn and cook other side.
Make 7 more pancakes the same way.
☐ Make up the sage and onion stuffing
and add salt and pepper to season. Cut
the pork into small pieces. Fill each
pancake with a little pork and stuffing.
Turn in the sides and roll the pancakes.
Beat the remaining egg. Brush each
pancake roll with egg then coat with
breadcrumbs.
☐ Skin and very finely chop the onion.
Melt 1oz. lard and fry onion until soft
and golden. Add the tomatoes and juice
and cook for 10min. Sieve the mixture.
Return to pan; season and keep hot.
☐ Heat the oil to the correct temperature
—see page 15—and deep-fry the rolls for
5min. or until golden. Drain and serve
with the tomato sauce.

PORK CHOPS WITH APPLE RINGS
(Enough for four)

4 pork loin chops
pepper
6 fresh sage leaves
2 cooking apples
1oz. butter
2 tablespoons cooking oil
sprigs of parsley

☐ Trim excess fat from chops and wipe
with a clean cloth. Season with pepper.
Wash and finely chop sage, press on to
chops. Cook chops under a hot grill for
20min., turning them occasionally.
☐ Meanwhile, wash apples but do not
peel. Remove cores. Cut into ½in. rings.
☐ Heat butter and oil. Add apple rings,
a few at a time, and fry gently for
2-3min., until just tender, turning once.
☐ Wash parsley. Serve chops on a large
dish, garnished with apple and parsley.

GAMMON IN PASTRY
(Enough for six)

4lb. piece gammon hock
1 bay leaf
6 peppercorns
1 blade of mace
¼ small onion
2 large oranges
two 8oz. packets frozen puff pastry
1 large egg
½lb. fresh or 8oz. tin black cherries
watercress

☐ When buying the gammon, ask your grocer for a nice lean one. It may be more economical to buy the piece without the knuckle bone, but of course the shape of the finished dish will not be the same, and will be more difficult to carve. Ask the grocer to bone the joint—leaving only the end bone in. Soak the gammon for no more than 2 hours in enough cold water to cover it. Rinse and put into a large saucepan. Cover with fresh cold water and add the bay leaf, peppercorns and mace. Skin the piece of onion, and add it to the saucepan. Wash and thinly peel one of the oranges, but be careful to remove only the rind, because the pith is bitter. Put the rind into the saucepan. Bring to the boil, reduce the heat, cover and simmer for 2 hours, or 25min. to the pound plus 20min. over if you have used a smaller or larger piece. Remove from the heat and leave the gammon in the water to become cold overnight.
☐ Allow the pastry to thaw for at least 1 hour at room temperature.
☐ Lightly flour a working surface and roll the pastry thinly, or until large enough to enclose the gammon.
☐ Remove the gammon from the liquid and carefully pull off the rind. Pat dry with a clean cloth. Place the gammon upside down on the pastry. Lightly beat the egg, and brush a little along one pastry edge. Press the edges together to enclose the gammon, and knock up with the back of a knife blade. Turn the right way up and seal both ends in the same way. If using a joint with the bone in it, don't cover the bone with pastry but pleat it round the start of the bone, and then cover the bone with a piece of foil during cooking to prevent it from browning. Use trimmings of pastry to make diamond-shaped leaves for decoration, and attach each one firmly with beaten egg.
☐ Lift carefully on to a greased baking tray and brush the pastry thoroughly with the rest of the beaten egg.
☐ Cook for 20min. in centre of oven, pre-heated to 450 deg. F. or Mark 8, then reduce heat to 350 deg. F. or Mark 4, and cover the joint with a piece of

greaseproof paper or foil. Continue cooking for a further 30min.
☐ Meanwhile, remove the rind and pith from both the oranges, leaving the fruit whole; cut into thick slices. Wash the cherries if fresh, strain off the juice if using tinned cherries. Use the cherry juice in a fruit salad. Wash watercress. Serve the gammon hot or cold, garnished with the fruit and watercress.

BLANQUETTE OF VEAL
(Enough for four)

1½lb. shoulder of veal
2 medium-sized onions
2 medium-sized carrots
1 teaspoon lemon juice
¼ level teaspoon mixed dried herbs
salt and pepper
1½oz. butter
1½oz. plain flour
1 large egg yolk
3 tablespoons single cream
lemon wedges

☐ Wipe the veal and cut into small pieces. Put it in a large saucepan. Skin and roughly chop the onions; peel and slice the carrots. Add the onions and carrots, lemon juice, herbs and salt and pepper to the veal. Add enough cold water to cover. Cover and bring to the boil. Reduce the heat and simmer for about 1½ hours, or until tender.
☐ Strain the meat and measure off 1 pint of the stock. Put the veal and vegetables in a warm place.
☐ Melt the butter in a medium-sized saucepan and stir in the flour. Cook for 2min. Remove pan from heat and gradually stir in the stock. Bring to the boil. Cook for about 2min. Season with salt and pepper. Stir in the veal and vegetables. Remove from the heat and allow the sauce to cool.
☐ Beat in the egg yolk—if the sauce is too hot the egg will scramble. Add the cream. Reheat gently, but do not allow to boil. Place the veal on a hot serving dish and garnish with lemon wedges.

ROAST VEAL WITH ORANGE
(Enough for eight)

4lb. leg of veal
3oz. fresh white breadcrumbs
1½oz. shredded suet
1½oz. currants
1½oz. stoned raisins
salt and pepper
ground nutmeg
1 large orange
1 large egg yolk
¾oz. plain flour
caster sugar
3 tablespoons claret

☐ Ask your butcher to bone the leg of veal.
☐ Mix breadcrumbs, suet, dried fruit and a pinch each of salt and nutmeg. Finely grate the orange rind. Add to mixture. Bind together with egg yolk, adding a little of the white if necessary.
☐ Stuff the veal where bone was removed. Hold together with skewers. Place in a roasting tin. Cover tightly with foil and roast for 1 hour 50min. in centre of oven, pre-heated to 400 deg. F. or Mark 6.
☐ When cooked, remove meat on to a hot dish. Cover and keep hot. Skim off all fat from juices left in pan.
☐ Heat some of juice in a small pan. Blend flour with rest of juice, then pour hot juice on to flour. Stir well and return to pan; strain if necessary. Bring to the boil, stirring all the time. Season, adding a little sugar, a pinch of nutmeg and the claret. Remove all peel and pith from orange. Chop flesh and add to sauce. Heat for 5min. Serve with the veal.
☐ An orange and green salad would go well with this dish.

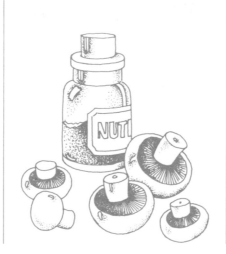

CURRIED VEAL
(Enough for four)

1lb. shoulder of veal
1 level tablespoon plain flour
salt and pepper
2oz. butter
2 large onions
1 level tablespoon curry powder
1 chicken stock cube
1 pint boiling water
2 level tablespoons chutney
1 teaspoon lemon juice

☐ Wipe the veal and cut it into bite-sized pieces. Season the flour with salt and pepper and toss in the veal pieces to coat them well. Melt the butter in a pan and fry the veal for 5min. or until browned on all sides, stirring all the time. Remove from the pan.
☐ Skin and chop the onions. Add to fat in pan and fry for 5min., or until soft but not browned. Stir in the curry powder and cook gently for 2min.
☐ Dissolve the stock cube in the boiling water and stir it gradually into the pan. Bring to the boil, stirring, then add the meat. Cover and cook over a low heat for 2 hours or until the veal is tender. Uncover the pan for the last 30min.
☐ Stir in the chutney and lemon juice and serve the curry on plain boiled rice.

VEAL FRICASSEE
(Enough for six)

1½lb. lean pie veal
1 medium-sized onion
4 peppercorns
1 bay leaf
2 sprigs of parsley
salt
2oz. button mushrooms
1½oz. butter
1½oz. plain flour
¼ pint milk
1 teaspoon lemon juice

☐ Wipe the meat and cut up. Place in a saucepan. Cover with ¾ pint water. Skin and slice the onion, and add to pan with peppercorns and bay leaf. Wash parsley and add 2 sprigs to pan with some salt. Bring to the boil, then reduce heat, and simmer for 1 hour with the lid on the pan. Strain and reserve the liquid and the meat. Wash the mushrooms and put with the veal on a hot plate.
☐ Melt the butter in a saucepan; stir in the flour. Cook gently for 2min. Remove from the heat then gradually stir in ½ pint of the reserved liquid and the milk. Season to taste then bring to the boil, stirring until thickened. Cook gently for 2min. Add lemon juice and cook for 1min. Add meat and mushrooms to sauce and heat thoroughly.

BREAST OF VEAL
(Enough for four)

4lb. lean breast of veal
boiling water
1 bay leaf
6 peppercorns
pinch of dried thyme
salt and pepper
2 large egg whites
5oz. fine fresh white breadcrumbs
2oz. butter
3 level dessertspoons finely chopped
parsley
½ large lemon

☐ Ask your butcher to chop the meat
into large chunks. Put meat and bones in
a large saucepan and cover with boiling
water. Add the bay leaf, peppercorns
and thyme and a good pinch of salt.
Bring to the boil, skimming as often as
necessary, then simmer for 1 hour or
until the meat is tender.
☐ Take out meat and dry with kitchen
paper. Cut meat from the bones into
2in. pieces, removing the fat. Strain and
reserve the cooking liquid. Lightly beat
the egg whites. Combine the breadcrumbs
with a good pinch each of salt
and pepper. Dip the meat first into the
egg whites and then coat with the
crumbs, patting them on well.
☐ Heat butter in a frying pan and fry the
meat for 5-10min., or until crisp and
golden. Transfer to a hot serving dish,
leaving excess crumbs in the pan. Keep
meat hot. Sprinkle the parsley into the
pan and add ½ pint reserved cooking
liquid. Heat, stirring to blend with the
crumbs. Squeeze out and strain the
lemon juice into the pan. Bring to the
boil and cook for 10min. Strain sauce
and serve separately.

VEAL KNUCKLE STEW
(Enough for four)

2 veal knuckles
3 medium-sized onions
3 large carrots
3 sticks of celery
1oz. plain flour
1oz. butter
1 chicken stock cube
¾ pint boiling water
¼ pint red wine
salt and pepper
2 level tablespoons tomato purée
1 bay leaf
pinch of dried thyme
½oz. cornflour
1 large lemon
1 level tablespoon finely chopped parsley

☐ If the veal knuckles have plenty of
meat on them, two will be sufficient. If
not, buy some pie veal to make up the
amounts. Ask your butcher to cut the
knuckles into pieces ready for serving.
☐ Skin and grate the onions. Peel and
grate the carrots. Thinly slice the celery.
Toss meat in the flour. Melt the butter
in a large saucepan and add the
vegetables. Fry for 5min. Add the meat
to the pan and cook over a moderate
heat until the meat is pale golden brown,
turning the bones frequently.
☐ Dissolve the stock cube in the boiling
water and add to the pan with the wine
and salt and pepper to taste. Bring to the
boil, then stir in the tomato purée, bay
leaf and thyme. Simmer for 1 hour,
adding a little more stock if necessary.
(If the knuckles are big they will absorb
more stock.)
☐ Remove meat from pan and strain the
liquid. Keep meat hot. If the liquid is too
thin, blend ½oz. cornflour with a little
cold water. Pour on some hot stock,
stirring well, then pour cornflour into the
stock. Bring to the boil, stirring all the
time until thickened. Cook gently for
3min.
☐ Finely grate the lemon rind and
squeeze out and strain the juice. Add 2
tablespoons juice to the sauce. Place
meat on a large hot dish and pour over
the sauce. Sprinkle over the lemon rind
and parsley.

VEAL CASSEROLE
(Enough for four)

1 large aubergine
salt and pepper
1½lb. pie veal
1oz. butter
1 chicken stock cube
boiling water
8 large tomatoes
1 large green pepper
pinch of marjoram
1 level teaspoon cornflour

☐ Wash and slice the aubergine. Layer
the slices in a bowl and sprinkle each
layer with salt. Leave to stand for
1 hour. Strain off the liquid and rinse
the aubergines until they're free of salt.
☐ Wipe the meat and cut it into bite-
sized pieces. Heat the butter in a pan and
fry the meat until browned on all sides,
stirring frequently. Remove into a
casserole, leaving behind as much fat as
possible.
☐ Dissolve the stock cube in 1 pint
boiling water. Drop the tomatoes into
boiling water, leave for 1min., then skin
and chop. Wash and chop the green
pepper, removing the white ribs and
seeds. Add tomatoes, aubergine and
pepper to the fat in the pan and fry for
5min., stirring occasionally. Cover the
veal with this mixture and season well
with salt and pepper and the marjoram.
☐ Pour on the stock and cook the
casserole for 2 hours or until the meat
is tender, in centre of oven, pre-heated to
325 deg. F. or Mark 3.
☐ Blend the cornflour with 1 tablespoon
cold water. Pour on a little hot stock
from the casserole and stir well. Return
this to the casserole, stir well and cook
for 30min. more.

RAVIOLI
(Enough for four)

1lb. plain flour
3 large eggs
1 large egg yolk
2 tablespoons olive oil
pinch of salt
warm water
6oz. raw breast of chicken
6oz. raw veal
2oz. sweetbreads
1 level tablespoon frozen spinach
½ clove of garlic
2oz. butter
1 slice white bread
3 tablespoons milk
½ bay leaf
1½ chicken stock cubes
1½ pints boiling water
1 level tablespoon grated Parmesan cheese
¼oz. cornflour

☐ Pile the flour in a mound on a smooth surface. Make a well in the centre and add 2 eggs and the yolk, oil and salt and 2 tablespoons warm water to begin with. Fold the flour over the well with your fingers, and turn gently until all the liquid is absorbed. Add more warm water if necessary, then knead the dough to a smooth ball. It shouldn't stick to your hands if you've added the right amount of water.

☐ Flour your hands and knead the dough well for 20min. Cut the dough in two and roll each half into a large square. Knead and roll again and repeat this 3 more times. Leave both pieces for 1 hour then roll each into a 17in. wafer-thin square. By this time you should have rolled each piece 6 times. Leave on the table for 30min., covered with a cloth.

☐ Mince the chicken and veal. Chop the sweetbreads and spinach. Skin and chop the garlic. Melt butter in a small pan; add the meats, spinach and garlic and fry gently for 5min.

☐ Remove crusts from bread and crumble slice into the milk. Add the bay leaf. Dissolve the stock cubes in the boiling water and add 2 tablespoons stock to the bread. When bread has absorbed the liquid add to pan and simmer altogether for 30min., or until the mixture is dry. Break up mixture with a fork, add half the cheese and mix with a little of the remaining egg to bind the mixture.

☐ Place ½ teaspoons of the stuffing on 1 large square leaving ½in. space at the edge and 1in. space between each stuffing piece. Brush round stuffing with water. Cover with other large square, pressing both pieces together at edges and round the stuffing. Using a

pastry wheel, cut between the stuffing to make 2in., square cushions.

☐ Bring remainder of the stock to the boil and cook the ravioli squares for 20min. Remove and drain. Mix the cornflour with a little cold water until smooth. Pour on ½ pint hot stock, stirring well. You don't need the rest of the stock for this recipe.

☐ Bring the ½ pint stock to the boil, stirring all the time, until the sauce is thick. Add rest of cheese and serve with the ravioli.

VEAL ESCALOPES
(Enough for four)

4 veal escalopes
1 large egg
4oz. fresh white breadcrumbs
1 large lemon
1 stuffed green olive
4 gherkins
1oz. butter
3 tablespoons cooking oil
sprigs of parsley

☐ Ask your butcher to beat the escalopes until wafer thin or you can do it yourself using a wooden rolling pin.

☐ Beat egg lightly. Brush escalopes with egg. Coat with breadcrumbs, pressing them on until evenly coated. Slice the lemon and the olive. Cut the gherkins into fan shapes. Heat the butter and oil in a frying pan. Lay 2 escalopes in the pan and fry for 3-4min. Turn carefully and fry for 3-4 min. more or until veal is tender and golden brown. Keep hot. Cook the other 2 in the same way.

☐ Garnish the escalopes with lemon slices, olive slices, gherkin fans and parsley. Serve immediately.

VEAL IN MARSALA
(Enough for four)

12oz. or 2 large veal escalopes
1oz. plain flour
salt and pepper
1½oz. butter
½ beef stock cube
¼ pint boiling water
1 bay leaf
4 cloves
4 tablespoons Marsala

☐ Ask your butcher to beat the meat until it is wafer thin. Put the flour on a plate and add a good pinch of salt. Coat the meat with the flour shaking off excess.
☐ Heat the butter but do not allow it to brown. Fry veal gently, turning it once or twice. Dissolve the stock cube in the boiling water and add slowly to the pan as the veal begins to brown. Bring to the boil, then lower the heat.
☐ Cover the pan and simmer for 20min., turning the veal at least once during cooking. Add bay leaf, cloves, Marsala and a little pepper. Bring quickly to the boil and serve immediately.

MEATBALLS
(Enough for four)

1½lb. lean pie veal
1 small onion
4oz. fresh white breadcrumbs
1 large egg
1 level tablespoon finely chopped parsley
1 level teaspoon finely chopped mint
½ level teaspoon dried oregano
1 small clove of garlic
olive oil
2 teaspoons wine vinegar
hot water
salt and pepper
little flour

☐ Mince the veal. Skin and grate the onion finely. Put into a bowl with the breadcrumbs and knead well with your hands. Break in the egg and knead until well mixed. Add the herbs. Skin and finely chop the garlic and add to bowl with 3 dessertspoons olive oil. Add the vinegar and mix well, adding a little hot water to moisten if necessary. Season to taste and leave for at least 1 hour before cooking.
☐ Flour your hands and shape the mixture into balls the size of small eggs. Toss balls lightly in flour. Heat ¼in. olive oil in a large frying pan and fry the meatballs slowly until well browned. Serve with a salad.

ROLLED VEAL WITH APPLE
(Enough for four)

2lb. loin of veal
1oz. streaky bacon
½oz. butter
1 large onion
1 stick of celery
5 medium-sized cooking apples
2oz. fresh white breadcrumbs
1 level tablespoon chopped parsley
salt and pepper

☐ Ask your butcher to bone the loin and prepare it ready for rolling. Cut off bacon rinds and chop bacon. Melt the butter in a frying pan and fry bacon for 3-4min. Remove from pan. Skin and chop the onions; scrub and chop the celery. Add the onions and celery to the pan and fry for 5min. Remove from pan.
☐ Peel, core and chop 2 apples; add to the pan. Fry for 2-3min., until soft. Mix bacon, onions, celery and apple with the breadcrumbs and parsley. Season well. Stuff and roll the loin.
☐ Cook the meat for 1 hour 30min., basting frequently, in centre of oven, pre-heated to 375 deg. F. or Mark 5.
☐ Peel and core remaining apples. Slice into fairly thick rings. Thirty minutes before the end of the cooking time add the apple rings to the fat around the meat turning once.

VEAL LOAF
(Enough for four)

1½oz. butter
2oz. plain flour
salt and pepper
¾lb. raw minced veal
2 large eggs
2 large carrots
parsley sprigs

☐ Melt the butter in a pan. Stir in 1½oz. flour and cook for 1min. Gradually stir in ¼ pint and 4 tablespoons water and bring to the boil. Cook for 2min., stirring. Season with salt and pepper. Allow to cool.
☐ Beat the veal into the mixture. Beat the eggs and add, beating well after each addition. Season well. Spoon into a small ovenproof dish. Cover with foil and steam for about 1–1½ hours, or until firm to the touch, replenishing the pan with boiling water as it evaporates.
☐ Peel the carrots and cut into slices. Cook in boiling salted water for 20min., or until tender. Drain and toss in ½oz. butter.
☐ Turn veal loaf on to a hot dish. Garnish with parsley sprigs and carrot slices and serve with tomato sauce—see Pork Pancake Rolls on page 96.

RAISED VEAL AND HAM PIE
(Enough for eight)

8oz. hot water crust pastry—see page 18
¾lb. pie veal
¼lb. ham
1 level tablespoon chopped parsley
1 large lemon
1 chicken stock cube
¾ pint boiling water
salt and pepper
2 large eggs
2 level teaspoons powdered gelatine

☐ Make a pie case using the hot water crust pastry as described in Melton Mowbray Pork Pie on page 93.
☐ Cut the veal and ham into ½in. cubes and mix them together with the parsley. Grate the rind from the lemon, squeeze out and strain the juice. Add both to the veal mixture. Dissolve the stock cube in the boiling water, reserve ½ pint. Season and moisten the veal with stock. Hard-boil 1 egg and shell.
☐ Fill the case with the meat mixture and push the egg into the centre. Cover and decorate the pie. Make a hole in centre. Beat remaining egg and brush top of pie. Tie a band of greaseproof paper round the pie and bake for 15-20min., in centre of oven, pre-heated to 425 deg. F. or Mark 7, then reduce heat to 350 deg. F. or Mark 4 and continue cooking for a further 1½ hours, or until meat is tender. Remove paper 30min. before the end of cooking time, brush pie with remaining beaten egg and return to oven.
☐ Sprinkle the gelatine on to the reserved stock and heat it very gently until the gelatine has dissolved. Pour into the pie and leave to cool.

VEAL IN CREAM
(Enough for four)

4 veal escalopes
salt and pepper
1½oz. butter
6 button mushrooms
3 tablespoons brandy
4 tablespoons double cream
1 tablespoon lemon juice
1 level tablespoon chopped parsley

☐ Beat the escalopes with a rolling pin to flatten and season with salt and pepper.
☐ Melt 1oz. butter in a frying pan and fry the escalopes until brown on both sides. Remove from the pan, leaving fat in pan. Keep veal hot.
☐ Rinse and slice the mushrooms caps and slice stalks separately. Add stalks to the pan and cook for 3min. Add 2 tablespoons brandy and set alight. When the flames have died down, pour in the cream and lemon juice. Stir well and cook until thickened, stirring. Season and strain over the escalopes.
☐ Melt the rest of the butter and fry rest of mushrooms for 5min. Add the remaining brandy and set alight.
☐ Garnish the escalopes with the mushroom slices and with parsley.

WIENER SCHNITZEL
(Enough for four)

4 slices of veal fillet
1oz. plain flour
1 large egg yolk
salt and pepper
2oz. fine fresh white breadcrumbs
4oz. butter
1 large lemon
4 anchovy fillets
4 olives
parsley sprigs

☐ Ask your butcher to beat the veal until it is wafer thin. Coat the veal with flour, shaking off the excess. Beat the egg yolk with salt and pepper to season. Dip meat in the egg yolk mixture, then in the breadcrumbs. Pat the breadcrumbs on well.
☐ Heat the butter in a large pan, but do not let it brown. Cook the veal for about 4min. or until golden brown on both sides, turning it once.
☐ While veal cooks, slice the lemon. Curl 1 anchovy fillet round each olive. Serve veal on a hot plate immediately it is cooked. Add a garnish of a lemon slice to each fillet and top with anchovy olives and parsley sprigs.

VEAL MARENGO
(Enough for four)

1lb. veal fillet
2 large onions
1 dessertspoon oil
2oz. butter
6 tablespoons dry white wine
1 clove of garlic
½ chicken stock cube
boiling water
1 bay leaf
3 parsley stalks
4 peppercorns
1 sprig of thyme
salt and pepper
½lb. tomatoes
4oz. button mushrooms
croûtons
1 level teaspoon chopped parsley

☐ Wipe the veal and cut it into large squares. Skin and slice the onions. Heat the oil and 1oz. butter in a pan and add the onions. Cook for 2min. then add the veal and cook, stirring until brown on all sides. Add the wine. Skin and crush the clove of garlic into the pan. Dissolve the stock cube in ½ pint boiling water and add to pan. Tie the bay leaf, parsley stalks, peppercorns, and thyme in a piece of muslin and add to pan. Season with salt and pepper.
☐ Drop the tomatoes in boiling water; skin and chop. Cut into thick slices. Add to pan, and bring the veal to the boil. Simmer for 30-40min., or until tender.
☐ Rinse mushrooms. Heat remaining butter and cook the mushrooms for 5min. Drain well.
☐ Remove veal from the pan using a perforated spoon and keep hot. Remove the herbs and boil the liquid fast to reduce by half. Spoon over the meat and garnish with the mushrooms. Surround with croûtons and parsley.

VEAL AND HAM PLATE PIE
(Enough for six)

1lb. pie veal
4oz. ham or bacon
½ chicken stock cube
¼ pint boiling water
3 large eggs
8oz. shortcrust pastry—see page 16
2 level tablespoons chopped parsley
grated rind of ½ lemon
1 tablespoon lemon juice
salt and pepper

☐ Wipe the meats and cut into bite-sized pieces. Place the veal and ham or bacon in a saucepan. Dissolve stock cube in boiling water. Add ¼ pint of the stock and bring to the boil. Simmer for 1½ hours. Hard-boil 2 eggs.
☐ Roll out the pastry on a lightly-floured board and use half to line an 8in. pie plate. Slice the hard-boiled eggs. Drain the meat and stir in the parsley lemon rind and juice and salt and pepper. Spoon meat on to the pastry. Add the eggs to the pie, and a little stock.
☐ Moisten edges of pastry on plate and cover with rest of pastry. Seal the edges and decorate. Beat remaining egg and brush over pie. Cook for 15min., in centre of oven, pre-heated to 400 deg. F. or Mark 6, then reduce heat to 350 deg. F. or Mark 4 and cook for 30-35min.

VEAL PAPRIKA
(Enough for six)

2lb. lean pie veal
2 medium-sized onions
1oz. butter
½ chicken stock cube
½ pint boiling water
½ level teaspoon salt
1 level tablespoon paprika
1 level tablespoon tomato purée
6oz. button mushrooms
5oz. carton soured cream
1 teaspoon lemon juice

☐ Cut the veal into 1in. cubes. Skin and roughly chop the onions. Melt the butter in a frying pan and brown the veal cubes over a high heat, turning frequently so that they brown on all sides. Add the onions and cook gently for 5min., or until they are soft.
☐ Dissolve the stock cube in the boiling water and add to the pan with the salt, paprika and tomato purée. Cover and cook over a low heat for 1 hour or until the meat is tender.
☐ Wash mushrooms. Peel if ragged and cut large ones into quarters; leave whole if small. Add to pan and cook for 30min. more.
☐ Just before serving, stir in the cream and a few drops of lemon juice.

How to Cook Poultry

Poultry nowadays makes a much cheaper meal than meat. Ducks like chickens are produced in large quantities and you buy them oven ready. Here are recipes for making meals from duck, chicken, turkey, goose and from poultry pieces

When you're buying fresh poultry for roasting, remember that the skin should have a good creamy colour and there should be no unpleasant smell. Young birds have smooth legs and feet and they shouldn't be limp. Also the end of the breast should be soft and pliable.

If you order a frozen bird, do bring it home in plenty of time for it to thaw properly. Cooking them while even still slightly frozen makes the bird very tough. Allow 36 hours for a 6-10lb. bird, 48 hours for 11-18lb. birds and 56 hours for a really large turkey, weighing 19-26lb.

Take it out of its box but not out of the bag and leave it at room temperature for the required time. Best way is to slightly tilt it on a wire rack so that the liquid runs away. Take out the bag of giblets. Once thawed, cook within 24 hours if you haven't got a refrigerator, 72 hours if you have.

All birds whether fresh or frozen should be washed before cooking. Make sure that all the giblets have been removed. Run cold water right through the bird. Drain and dry well using a clean cloth. Stuffing a bird not only provides another tasty flavour but it helps the meat to go further. Don't stuff a bird too tightly as the stuffing expands in cooking. You can stuff the body of all poultry, but it's usual to stuff the breast of chicken to plump it out, the tail end of duck and goose and both ends of turkey.

Roasting by the conventional method— that is the bird sitting on its back— usually means breast flesh is overdone while you make sure the legs are cooked through. I find the following method is better. Once you've calculated how long the bird will take to roast, and you've got your oven and tin of fat to the required temperature, cover the breast with a butter paper making sure it goes under the breast nearest the bottom of the roasting tin. Put the chicken on one side of the breast and baste thoroughly. After a third of the cooking time, turn it on to the other side keeping the butter paper on and baste again. Cook for another third of the time. Finally turn it on its back for the remainder of the cooking time, baste it thoroughly and remove the butter paper to brown the skin 30min. before the end of the cooking time.

Times for roasting

Chicken: Allow 20min. to the lb. for quick roasting at 400 deg. F. or Mark 6 and 25-30min. to the lb. for slow roasting at 325 deg. F. or Mark 3. Allow 15min. over for birds up to 6lb. and deduct 15min. from the time for birds of 10lb. and over.

Turkey: Cook for 20min. to the lb. at 400 deg. F. or Mark 6 and 30min. to the lb. at 325 deg. F. or Mark 3. If you've got a bird larger than 8lb., deduct about an hour off the calculated cooking time, and check from this point.

Duck: Cook for 20min. per lb. at 400 deg. F. or Mark 6.

Goose: Cook for 15min. to the lb. plus 15min. over at 375 deg. F. or Mark 5. For the slow roasting method, allow 25-30min. to the lb. at 325 deg. F. or Mark 3.

Remember to remove the bacon and papers from the birds towards the end of the cooking time to allow the skin to brown.

TURKEY WITH CRANBERRY SAUCE
(Enough for eight-ten)

14lb. turkey
1lb. chestnuts
boiling water
milk
2 rashers of streaky bacon
8oz. fine fresh white breadcrumbs
1 large lemon
1 large egg
2 level tablespoons finely chopped parsley
salt and pepper
2lb. pork sausagemeat
2 level teaspoons mixed dried herbs
lard

☐ If the turkey is frozen allow it to thaw completely—see this page. Remove the giblets and wipe the bird inside and out.
☐ Cover chestnuts with boiling water and simmer for 3min. Drain off water and carefully peel chestnuts while still hot. Replace in saucepan and just cover with milk. Cover pan and simmer for 45min., or until tender. Drain and reserve milk; sieve chestnuts.
☐ Cut off bacon rinds and chop rashers. Fry gently until crisp. Stir in the chestnut purée and 4oz. breadcrumbs. Finely grate lemon rind, squeeze out and strain the juice. Beat egg. Mix lemon juice, 1 level teaspoon lemon rind, 1 level tablespoon parsley and the egg into the chestnuts. Season with salt and pepper.
☐ Use to stuff neck end of turkey, then fold the flap of skin over and tuck it under the wings. Put sausagemeat in a bowl; add remaining breadcrumbs, lemon rind, parsley, mixed herbs and seasoning. Use to stuff carcass.
☐ Place in a roasting tin and spread with lard. Cook for 5½-7 hours on lowest shelf of oven, pre-heated to 325 deg. F. or Mark 3. Cover with foil if the bird is browning too much. To test if done, push a skewer into the thickest part of the leg. If pink juices run, cook longer.
☐ Serve turkey on a large hot dish. Serve cranberry sauce separately.

Roast Turkey

CHICKEN BLANQUETTE
(Enough for five)

4lb. chicken
salt and pepper
3 large carrots
3 large onions
1½oz. butter
1½oz. plain flour
1 large egg yolk
5oz. carton single cream
1 level teaspoon dried tarragon

☐ Ask your butcher to cut the chicken into small pieces. Remove skin and place the chicken in a saucepan. Cover with 3½ pints cold water. Add 1 level teaspoon salt. Bring to the boil and skim off any scum as it rises.
☐ Peel the carrots and slice fairly thinly. Skin and quarter the onions. Add the vegetables to the pan and cover. Simmer for 30min., or until the chicken is tender. Strain off stock.
☐ Melt the butter in a small saucepan and add the flour. Stir well, then add 1½ pints of the hot chicken stock gradually, stirring all the time. Bring to boil stirring and cook for 2-3min. Season well. Beat the egg yolk with the cream and stir this into the sauce. Add the tarragon.
☐ Place the chicken on a heated serving dish and cover with the sauce.

LEMON CHICKEN
(Enough for four-six)

2½lb. chicken
2oz. very small onions
1 clove of garlic
2 small lemons
¼ level teaspoon dried thyme
2 tablespoons olive oil
salt and pepper
1oz. butter
glacé cherries
1 level teaspoon chopped parsley

☐ Allow chicken to thaw out completely if frozen—see page 104.
☐ Cut into 4 or 6 joints and place in a shallow dish. Skin onions and leave whole. Skin and chop garlic. Add to the chicken. Finally grate rind from 1 lemon and squeeze out juice. Pour over chicken with thyme and oil. Season well. Marinate for 2 hours.
☐ Remove from marinade and put in a baking tin. Dot with butter and cook for 45min., or until tender, near top of oven, pre-heated to 375 deg. F. or Mark 5.
☐ Slice remaining lemon and fold slices into cone shapes. Place a cherry in centre of each cone and secure with a wooden cocktail stick.
☐ Sprinkle chicken with parsley and arrange lemon cones on the chicken.

DEVILLED TURKEY
(Enough for six)

2-3lb. cooked turkey
½ pint double cream
½ pint single cream
1 level tablespoon cornflour
2 teaspoons anchovy essence
3 tablespoons Worcester sauce
2 level teaspoons mustard powder
1 level teaspoon French mustard
½ level teaspoon curry powder
dash Cayenne pepper
½ teaspoon salt
3 level tablespoons chutney

☐ Dice the turkey meat and place in a shallow greased baking dish. Whisk the creams together until standing in peaks. Gradually whisk in the remaining ingredients, except the chutney, keeping the sauce thick. Fold in the chutney.
☐ Pour the sauce over the turkey and cook for about 20-30min., in centre of oven, pre-heated to 350 deg. F. or Mark 4.

HASHED GOOSE
(Enough for four)

12oz. cooked goose
1 large onion
2oz. butter
1 pint left-over gravy or stock
1 level dessertspoon cornflour
2 tablespoons port
2 level tablespoons tomato ketchup
salt and pepper

☐ Dice the cooked goose. Skin and slice the onion. Melt the butter in a saucepan and fry the onion for 5min. or until golden. Add any left-over stuffing, and small trimmings from the meat and the gravy or stock to the pan. Cook gently for 45min.
☐ Blend the flour with a little cold water. Pour into the stock and cook gently for 2min. Add the port and the ketchup. Season to taste with salt and pepper. Add the diced goose meat to the pan and heat through slowly. Serve with slices of toast.

TURKEY A LA KING
(Enough for four)

1 medium-sized green pepper
2½oz. butter
¼lb. button mushrooms
1½oz. plain flour
¾ pint turkey stock
¼ pint milk
¾lb. cooked turkey
4 tablespoons single cream
2 large egg yolks
1 tablespoon dry sherry or lemon juice
salt and pepper

☐ Wash the green pepper; remove seeds and white ribs, and chop flesh. Heat butter and gently fry pepper for 10min., or until soft. Slice mushrooms including stalks and add these to the pan. Fry gently for 5min. Remove from pan.
☐ Stir flour into the remaining butter and cook for 2min. without browning. Gradually blend in the stock and milk. Cook, stirring, until the sauce boils, and thickens. Lower the heat and add the pepper and mushrooms mixture.
☐ Cut turkey into bite-sized pieces, then add to pan. Heat through gently for 10min. Beat cream with egg yolks and add sherry or lemon juice. Add to the turkey mixture and cook for a further 2-3min. without boiling. Season to taste with salt and pepper. Serve with rice.

MOGLAI CHICKEN
(Enough for four-six)

3lb. chicken
2in. piece green root ginger
1 clove of garlic
pinch of salt
½ level teaspoon saffron powder
¼ level teaspoon ground turmeric
4oz. blanched almonds
2oz. hazelnuts
2 large onions
1 tablespoon single cream
three 5oz. cartons plain yogurt
3 tablespoons oil

☐ Wash the chicken and cut into neat joints, discarding the rib cage. Peel ginger until green part just shows. Roughly chop the ginger. Skin and crush the clove of garlic. Pound the ginger, garlic, salt, saffron and turmeric to a paste.
☐ Put the almonds and hazelnuts on a piece of foil on the grill pan and toast until golden brown, turning frequently. Skin and roughly grate the onions.
☐ Stir onion, cream and yogurt into the spices. Heat the oil in a pan. Add chicken pieces and fry for 5min., turning occasionally. Add yogurt mixture and toasted nuts. Cover and simmer for 1-1½ hours or until tender. Serve hot, garnished with nuts.

CHICKEN AND ALMONDS
(Enough for four)

2 breast of chicken joints
1oz. whole almonds
peanut oil
1oz. tinned bamboo shoot
4 tinned water chestnuts
1½in. piece cucumber
1 small onion
1 chicken stock cube
¼ pint boiling water
½ teaspoon sherry
salt
caster sugar
½ teaspoon soy sauce
½ level teaspoon cornflour

☐ Cut chicken off the bones and cut meat into bite-sized pieces. Bring almonds to the boil in a little water. Drain and skin. Dry almonds and toss in 1 dessertspoon peanut oil to coat. Put almonds on a baking tray and bake for 30min. or until golden brown, in centre of oven, pre-heated to 400 deg. F. or Mark 6.

☐ Thinly slice bamboo shoot and thickly slice water chestnuts. Cut unpeeled cucumber into small dice. Skin and roughly chop the onion. Heat 2 tablespoons peanut oil and fry onion for 1min. Add chicken pieces and cook for 2min. over a high heat. Add bamboo shoot, water chestnuts and cucumber and cook for 2min.

☐ Dissolve the stock cube in boiling water. Add to pan with almonds, sherry, a pinch each of salt and sugar and the soy sauce. Cook for 1min. Blend cornflour with 1 dessertspoon of water and stir in. Bring to boil and cook for 1½min. Serve at once.

GOOSE BIGARRADE
(Enough for eight)

6lb. goose
1lb. cooking apples
1 small onion
1oz. shelled walnuts
¼ level teaspoon dried sage
5oz. fresh white breadcrumbs
salt and pepper
1 large egg
2oz. butter
1 teaspoon olive oil
1oz. ham or bacon
½ small carrot
½ small stick of celery
1oz. mushroom stalks
1oz. plain flour
½ beef stock cube
½ pint boiling water
1 level dessertspoon tomato purée
1 bay leaf
2 sprigs of parsley
1 small lemon
1 large orange—Seville if available
2 tablespoons dry red wine

☐ Wash the goose inside and out. Wipe dry with a clean cloth. Peel, core and coarsely chop the apples. Skin onion and grate half. Finely chop the walnuts. Mix the sage, breadcrumbs, walnuts, grated onion and the apple together. Season to taste with salt and pepper. Beat the egg. Melt 1oz. butter and use this and the beaten egg to bind the mixture together.

☐ Stuff carcass of the goose. Stand the goose on a grid in the roasting tin and prick the skin all over with a fork. Sprinkle well with salt. Roast for 2½ hours in centre of oven, pre-heated to 325 deg. F. or Mark 3. Do not baste or cover.

☐ While goose cooks, put rest of butter and the olive oil into a pan. Heat for 2min. Chop the ham or bacon and add to pan. Chop the rest of the onion; peel and slice the carrot. Wash and chop celery and mushrooms stalks. Add all vegetables to pan. Fry gently for 12-15 min., or until golden. Add the flour and cook over a low heat for about 25min., stirring from time to time until it turns golden brown. Do not allow to burn. Dissolve the stock cube in the boiling water and add this gradually to the pan. Cook, stirring until the sauce comes to the boil and thickens. Add the purée, bay leaf and parsley. Cover pan and simmer gently for 30min.

☐ Strain the sauce and season to taste with salt and pepper. Squeeze out and strain the juice from the lemon and orange. Stir in the orange and lemon juice and the red wine. Reheat before serving. Transfer the cooked goose to a carving dish and carve. Coat the sliced goose with the sauce and serve.

CHICKEN WITH PEACHES AND ALMONDS
(Enough for four)

2 tablespoons soy sauce
1 tablespoon oil
1 tablespoon sherry
1 dessertspoon lemon juice
3lb. chicken
1 large onion
1 small green pepper
4oz. button mushrooms
1½oz. butter
8oz. tin peach slices
2 level dessertspoons cornflour
1 chicken stock cube
¼ pint boiling water
salt and pepper
1½oz. blanched almonds

☐ Mix together the soy sauce, oil, sherry and lemon juice. Cut the chicken into fairly small pieces removing the skin and bones. Add to the marinade. Leave for 30min.

☐ Skin and roughly chop the onion. Wash and cut pepper into small dice removing white ribs and seeds. Wash and quarter mushrooms. Drain chicken pieces—keeping marinade for sauce.

☐ Heat 1oz. butter in a heavy pan. Add chicken pieces and cook gently for 3-4 min. Remove chicken. Add onion to pan and cook for 1min.; add green pepper and cook for 1min. more. Finally add mushrooms and chicken; cook for 2min.

☐ Drain juice from peaches. Blend cornflour with the juice. Dissolve the stock cube in boiling water. Stir into vegetables with the marinade, peach juice and seasoning to taste. Stir until boiling; cover and simmer for 3-4min. Add peach slices and heat for 1min. Fry the almonds in rest of butter until golden. Serve chicken scattered with fried almonds.

POULTRY PIE
(Enough for four)

10oz. cooked poultry
1 medium-sized onion
1 large leek
2 medium-sized carrots
1oz. butter
½oz. plain flour
1 chicken stock cube
¾ pint boiling water
2oz. peas
pinch of mixed dried herbs
salt and pepper
8oz. rough puff pastry—see page 21
beaten egg or milk

☐ Cut poultry into bite-sized pieces.
Skin and chop onion. Trim off roots and
discoloured leaves from leek. Cut into
slices. Wash and peel carrots, slice
thinly. Melt butter. Add vegetables,
cover and fry gently for 10min. Stir in
flour and cook for 2min. Dissolve stock
cube in boiling water. Remove pan from
heat and gradually stir in the stock.
Bring to the boil, stirring all the time;
add poultry, peas, herbs, salt and pepper.
Pour into pie dish.
☐ Roll pastry to 1in. larger than dish.
Cut off ½in. strip. Grease edges of pie
dish and lay the strip round; moisten the
edges. Lay pastry lid over and press
edges to seal. Trim off excess pastry.
Knock up edges with back of knife.
☐ Roll remaining pastry into a strip 1in.
wide. Cut off 8 diamond pastry leaves
and 4 flowers using a special cutter if
liked. Brush pie and decorations with
beaten egg or milk. Arrange decorations
round the top of the pie. Make 2 holes
with a skewer at either end of pie. Cook
for 20min. in centre of oven, pre-heated
to 425 deg. F. or Mark 7, then reduce
heat to 350 deg. F. or Mark 4 and cook
for 40min. more or until pastry is crisp
and golden.

ROAST CHICKEN
(Enough for four-six)

6lb. chicken
4oz. dried apricots
8oz. pork sausagemeat
5oz. fresh white breadcrumbs
½ level teaspoon mixed dried herbs
½ large lemon
salt and pepper
2oz. butter
2 level teaspoons chopped parsley
1 standard egg
½ pint bread sauce—see page 26
4 rashers streaky bacon
2 packets potato crisps

☐ Allow chicken to thaw if frozen—see
page 104. Remove giblets and thoroughly
wipe out carcass. Soak apricots in cold
water overnight.
☐ Mix the sausagemeat, 1oz.
breadcrumbs and the herbs. Finely grate
the lemon rind and squeeze out the
juice. Add grated rind to sausagemeat
and season with salt and pepper. Reserve
half for sausagemeat balls and use the
remainder to stuff the breast of the
chicken. Fold the flap of skin over the
stuffing and tuck under the wings. Drain
and roughly chop apricots.

☐ Melt butter. Put remaining
breadcrumbs, the apricots, parsley and
half the butter into a bowl; stir in the
lemon juice and enough beaten egg to
bind ingredients together. Season with
salt and pepper. Use the mixture to stuff
the chicken carcass. Sew the skin
together with strong cotton and tie legs
together if this has not already been
done.
☐ Put the chicken into a large roasting
tin. Brush with the remaining butter and
sprinkle with salt and pepper. Cook for
2½ hours in lower part of oven,
pre-heated to 400 deg. F. or Mark 6. If
at any time the chicken browns too
much, cover loosely with foil or butter
papers.
☐ Roll the reserved stuffing into small
balls. Gently heat the bread sauce. Cut
off rinds and stretch the bacon with the
back of a knife. Cut rashers in half and
roll up. Put stuffing balls and bacon rolls
on to a baking tray and cook on the
shelf above the chicken for the last
20min.
☐ Spread the potato crisps on a baking
tray and heat for 2-3min. Put chicken on
to a serving plate, garnish with stuffing
balls, bacon rolls, crisps and parsley.
Serve bread sauce separately.

CREAMED POULTRY ON RICE
(Enough for four)

12oz. cooked poultry
1 small onion
1oz. butter
½oz. plain flour
½ chicken stock cube
boiling water
¼ pint milk
2oz. peas
1 bay leaf
salt and pepper
8oz. Patna rice
¼ small red pepper
1oz. flaked almonds
½ large lemon
4 tablespoons single cream

☐ Cut poultry into bite-sized pieces. Skin and chop onion. Melt butter in a medium-sized saucepan, add onion, cover and fry for 5min. Stir in the flour and cook for 2min. Dissolve stock cube in ½ pint boiling water. Remove pan from heat and gradually stir in stock and milk. Return to heat and bring to the boil, and add the poultry, peas, bay leaf, salt and pepper. Cover and simmer for 15min.
☐ Meanwhile, cook the rice for 12min., in plenty of boiling salted water. Drain well and keep in a warm place.
☐ Cover the pepper with boiling water and leave for about 3min. Drain off water and cut pepper into thin strips. Toast the almonds until golden. Peel off the lemon rind leaving behind all the white pith. Cut the rind into thin strips.
☐ Remove the bay leaf from the poultry and stir in the cream. Spoon the rice on to a serving dish and carefully pour the poultry mixture into the centre. Garnish with almonds, lemon rind and pepper.

DUCK WITH SAVOURY RICE
(Enough for six)

6lb. duck
1 clove of garlic
salt and pepper
1 large lemon
7oz. Patna rice
1 medium-sized carrot
1 medium-sized onion
4oz. lean smoked ham
4oz. garlic-seasoned smoked pork sausage
½oz. lard
4 level tablespoons finely chopped parsley

☐ Allow the duck to thaw completely if frozen—see page 104. Wipe duck inside and out. Skin garlic and cut in half. Rub over duck. Season inside. Remove lemon rind; put inside duck. Close opening with skewers. Cut lemon in half and rub cut sides over duck. Squeeze out and strain lemon juice. Cook duck for 2 hours in centre of oven, pre-heated to 400 deg. F. or Mark 6.
☐ Boil rice for 12min. Drain well. Peel and chop carrot. Skin and chop onion. Slice ham into fine strips. Cut sausage into ⅛in. rounds.
☐ Heat lard; add sausage, ham and vegetables and cook gently for 8min. Stir in rice, lemon juice and 3 tablespoons parsley. Season; keep hot. Carve duck.

☐ Skim off fat from roasting tin. Add ¼ pint water to juices left and boil until reduced by half. Season.
☐ Spread rice on a hot dish. Add duck and spoon over gravy. Sprinkle with rest of parsley; garnish with lemon wedges.

ROAST DUCK WITH APPLES AND PRUNES
(Enough for six)

¾lb. dried prunes
6lb. prepared duck
½ large lemon
salt and pepper
6 large cooking apples
2 tablespoons port
½oz. butter
½oz. plain flour
2 level tablespoons redcurrant jelly

□ Put the prunes in a bowl. Cover with cold water and leave to soak for 1 hour.
□ Remove all excess fat from the duck—most of it is around the openings. Rub the duck inside and out with the lemon half and salt and pepper. Peel and core 3 apples. Cut into ¼in. dice. Stone and chop all but 6 prunes. Mix chopped prunes with the apple and use to stuff the duck. Close the openings with skewers or by sewing. Rub duck with a little of its own fat and prick skin all over to allow excess fat to escape during roasting.
□ Place duck on a grid in a roasting tin. Put duck in centre of oven, pre-heated to 400 deg. F. or Mark 6, then reduce heat to 350 deg. F. or Mark 4 and roast for 2½ hours or until tender.
□ Peel and core rest of apples. Cut in half. Stand on a baking tray. Put in oven for 10-15min., or until soft but not breaking.
□ Stone remaining prunes and soak in the port.
□ Remove duck on to a large hot plate. Keep hot. Pour off all fat from roasting tin. Add enough water to remaining juices to make ½ pint. Bring to boil. Cream the butter and flour together, then stir small pieces into the hot liquid, stirring all the time, until the butter has melted, the flour cooked and the sauce thickened. Remove prunes from the port. Stir port and redcurrant jelly into the sauce.
□ Garnish duck with the apple halves, stuffed with the prunes. Serve sauce separately.

DUCK IN RED WINE
(Enough for six)

6lb. duck
½ clove of garlic
¾lb. onions
¾lb. medium-sized carrots
2oz. plain flour
2oz. button mushrooms
¾ pint red wine
1 bay leaf
4 parsley sprigs
½ level teaspoon dried thyme
1 level teaspoon salt

□ Cut the duck into joints, or ask your butcher to do this, reserving the carcass. Remove the skin and fat from the duck and put them with giblets and carcass in a saucepan with enough cold water to cover. Bring to the boil. Reduce the heat and simmer for 1 hour. Strain off the fat and allow the stock to cool.
□ Heat 2 tablespoons of the duck fat in a pan and brown the joints evenly. Remove them from the pan and put them into a large casserole. Skin the garlic and cut into small pieces. Skin and slice the onions. Peel and slice the carrots; fry in the fat for about 10min. Add the flour and stir well; cook for 2min. Wash the mushrooms. Add the wine, mushrooms, herbs, ½ pint duck stock and salt to the pan. Bring slowly to the boil, stirring all the time until the sauce thickens.
□ Put the vegetables and sauce into the casserole. Cover and cook for 1½ hours or until the meat is tender, in centre of oven, pre-heated to 350 deg. F. or Mark 4. Remove parsley to serve.

BRAISED DUCK
(Enough for four)

4lb. duck
1 large onion
2 large carrots
½ small turnip
1oz. streaky bacon
1oz. butter
2 medium-sized oranges
1 small lemon
1 bay leaf
pinch of dried sage
salt and pepper
¼ pint red wine or port
1 level tablespoon redcurrant jelly
2 level teaspoons arrowroot

□ Allow the duck to thaw completely if frozen—see page 104. Remove giblets. Clean and put in a pan. Cover with water and bring to the boil. Simmer for 1 hour.
□ Skin onion and peel carrots. Thickly peel turnip and cut vegetables into large pieces. Roughly chop bacon.
□ Heat butter in a fireproof pan large enough to hold the duck. Add vegetables and bacon and fry lightly for 10min. Finely grate the rind from 1 orange. Peel rind from second orange leaving bitter white pith on orange. Cut peel into fine strips. Squeeze out and strain juice from both oranges and the lemon. Add grated orange rind, bay leaf and sage to pan. Strain the giblet stock over the vegetables to just cover. Season well with salt and pepper and put the trussed duck on the vegetables. Cover with greaseproof paper and a lid. Cook for 2-2½ hours in centre of oven, pre-heated to 375 deg. F. or Mark 5. Add wine or port and fruit juices to pan, then cook for another 30min.
□ Remove duck from pan and joint it for serving, removing the breast skin and taking the breast meat off in whole pieces. Skim surplus fat from the stock. This is essential as there will be about ½ pint. Strain stock and discard vegetables. Add jelly to stock.
□ Blend the arrowroot with a little cold water. Heat the stock in a pan. Pour a little on to the arrowroot, stir well then pour back into the stock, stirring all the time. Cook for 3min. or until thickened, stirring. Arrange the pieces of duck on a hot serving dish. Pour the sauce over and garnish with the orange rind strips.

DUCK AND HAM LOAF
(Enough for four-six)

1 small onion
6oz. cooked duck
6oz. lean ham
4oz. fresh white breadcrumbs
½ level teaspoon finely grated orange rind
3oz. mushrooms
½ level teaspoon dried sage
2 tablespoons finely chopped parsley
2 large eggs
¼ pint milk
salt and pepper

☐ Skin the onion and chop roughly. Mince the duck, ham and onion. Add the breadcrumbs and orange rind. Wash and slice the mushrooms and add to mixture. Add the sage and parsley. Beat the eggs and milk; add to mixture. Season to taste with salt and pepper. Mix well.
☐ Grease a 2lb. loaf tin and add the mixture to this. Smooth the top with a knife. Bake for 1½ hours or until firm to the touch, in centre of oven, pre-heated to 350 deg. F. or Mark 4. Leave in the tin for 5min. before turning out on to a serving dish. Serve hot or cold.

DUCK A L'ORANGE
(Enough for four)

4lb. duck
salt and pepper
½oz. butter
2 medium-sized oranges
2 sugar lumps
1 tablespoon wine vinegar
4 tablespoons dry white wine
1 tablespoon lemon juice

☐ Wipe the duck with a clean cloth; season with salt and pepper. Place the duck in a roasting tin and dot with knobs of butter. Roast for 1 hour 20min., or until cooked, in centre of oven, pre-heated to 400 deg. F. or Mark 6.
☐ Meanwhile, wash the oranges and peel one thinly. Cut the rind into thin strips and place in a small pan. Cover with cold water; bring to the boil and drain. Put the sugar lumps and the vinegar in another saucepan with 1 tablespoon cold water and heat together for about 10min. until golden. Boil the wine in a small saucepan to reduce it a little. Squeeze out and strain the juice of the peeled orange and add to the wine with the lemon juice. Bring to the boil. Add sugar mixture and rind. Slice remaining orange very thinly.
☐ Place the cooked duck on a serving dish; add the sauce and orange slices.

DUCK WITH CIDER AND ALMONDS
(Enough for six)

5lb. duck
2oz. streaky bacon
1 medium-sized onion
2 sticks of celery
1oz. butter
2 medium-sized cooking apples
6oz. fresh white breadcrumbs
1 level tablespoon chopped parsley
1 level teaspoon dried sage
salt and pepper
2 tablespoons cooking oil
4oz. blanched whole almonds
1 pint dry cider
8oz. shallots

☐ Allow the duck to thaw completely if frozen—see page 104. Wipe duck inside and out. Remove rinds from bacon. Cut rashers into small pieces. Put the pieces and the rinds into a saucepan and heat gently. Increase the heat and fry the bacon for 3min., or until pale golden. Remove bacon; discard rinds.
☐ Skin and roughly chop the onion. Wash celery and slice thinly. Add the butter to the bacon fat and fry the chopped onion and celery for 7-8min.
☐ Wash, peel and core the apples. Dice and add to the vegetables in the pan. Fry for a further 3-4min. Remove from the heat and stir in the breadcrumbs, parsley, sage and bacon. Season well with salt and pepper. Use this to stuff the carcase of the duck. Sew up.
☐ Pour the oil into a large meat tin. Stand this over a moderate heat and place the duck in the tin. Fry for 25min., turning frequently so that the duck is golden on all sides. Remove the duck and place in a fairly deep ovenproof dish or roaster. Pour the fat in which the duck was fried into a saucepan, add the almonds and fry for 5min., or until pale golden. Drain well leaving the fat in the pan. Add the almonds to the duck.
☐ Pour ½ pint cider over the duck. Cover with the lid of the dish or a large piece of foil. Cook for 1 hour in lower part of oven, pre-heated to 375 deg. F. or Mark 5. Meanwhile, skin the shallots and fry gently in the remaining fat until golden. Drain well.
☐ Remove duck from oven. Skim off all the fat from the liquid surrounding the duck—this will probably be a thick layer about ½in. deep. Add the shallots and rest of cider. Cover dish again and cook for a further 20min. Uncover duck and cook for a further 30min.
☐ When cooked, remove duck from oven and place on a heated serving dish. Surround with the shallots and almonds.
☐ Skim off and discard any remaining fat from the cider and serve the cider separately in a sauce boat.

OVEN-COOKED CHICKEN
(Enough for four)

5oz. carton plain yogurt
¼ level teaspoon ground cumin
¼ level teaspoon ground coriander
½ level teaspoon finely chopped green chilli
1 clove of garlic
1in. piece green root ginger
1 level teaspoon salt
1 large lemon
4 large chicken joints

☐ Mix the yogurt, cumin, coriander and chilli together. Skin and crush the clove of garlic into the yogurt. Peel ginger until green part just shows. Roughly chop the ginger and add to yogurt with the salt. Finely grate the lemon rind and squeeze out and strain the juice. Add rind and juice to yogurt with the chicken pieces and leave to marinate for 1 hour.
☐ Remove from marinade and put in an ovenproof dish. Cover with foil and bake for 45min.-1 hour, or until tender, in centre of oven, pre-heated to 375 deg. F. or Mark 5.

POULTRY VOL-AU-VENT
(Enough for four)

1lb. puff pastry—see page 18
milk
6oz. cooked poultry
2oz. ham or tongue
3oz. button mushrooms
½ pint white sauce—see page 24
salt and pepper
½ level teaspoon ground nutmeg

☐ Roll pastry out to 1in. thickness; cut into 2 ovals using a 6in. fluted oval cutter. Place the cases on wet baking trays. Cut an inner ring on the pastry cases using a 4in. fluted oval cutter and taking care only to cut half way through. These will form lids. Brush the top of each case with a little milk.
☐ Bake for 20-25min. until well risen, firm to touch and golden, in centre of oven, pre-heated to 450 deg. F. or Mark 8. Dice the poultry and ham or tongue and wash and slice the mushrooms. Add to the sauce; season well with salt, pepper and nutmeg. Heat sauce gently.
☐ When the vol-au-vent have cooled slightly, remove the centres carefully and keep for the lids. Scrape out any soft dough which hasn't cooked. Carefully spoon the sauce into the cases and replace the lids. Serve immediately.

CHICKEN AND PORK DISH
(Enough for six)

8oz. desiccated coconut
½ pint and 4 tablespoons boiling water
3lb. chicken
1½lb. lean pork
2 level teaspoons salt
½ level teaspoon black pepper
¼ pint cider vinegar
1 bay leaf
2 cloves of garlic
2 tablespoons oil
yellow vegetable colouring

☐ Put the coconut in a bowl and pour on the boiling water. Leave to stand for 30min., then turn contents of bowl into a piece of muslin and wring out over another bowl to extract all liquid.

☐ Ask your butcher to chop the chicken into 2in. pieces, bones and all. Discard any sharp piece of bone on its own. Cut the pork into 1½in. pieces. Mix together the salt, pepper, freshly ground if you have a mill, vinegar and bay leaf. Skin and crush the garlic cloves and add to vinegar. Pour over pork and chicken and leave to stand for 30min. Drain meat well, reserving the marinade.

☐ Heat the oil in a heavy saucepan. Add chicken and pork and fry for 10-15min., or until browned. Add the marinade and ½ pint cold water. Cover partially and cook over a medium heat for 40min., or until tender and almost all of the liquid has evaporated.

☐ Stir coconut liquid into the saucepan with a few drops of colouring. Cook gently for 5min., check for seasoning, then serve.

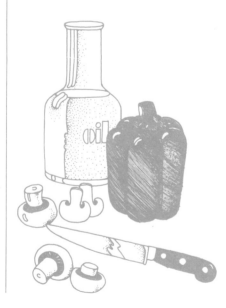

PANCAKE LAYER
(Enough for four)

10oz. cooked poultry
½ small onion
½ small green pepper
boiling water
3 medium-sized tomatoes
½oz. butter
½oz. plain flour
½ pint and 2 tablespoons milk
pinch of dried thyme
salt and pepper
1oz. lard
½ pint pancake batter—see page 9
parsley sprigs

☐ Cut poultry into small pieces. Skin and chop onion. Discard seeds and white core from pepper. Cover with boiling water and leave for 3min. Drain and chop roughly. Wash and roughly chop 1 tomato. Melt butter in a small pan. Add onion and pepper, cover and fry gently for 5min. Stir in the flour and cook for 2min. Remove from heat and stir in the milk gradually. Bring to the boil, stirring all the time. Add poultry, chopped tomato, thyme, salt and pepper. Cover and simmer for 15min.

☐ Put ⅓ of the lard in a large pancake pan. Heat and pour in ⅕ of the batter. Cook for 1min., then turn and cook for 1min. more. Make 5 in all. Keep each one warm, as it is cooked.

☐ Slice remaining tomatoes. Layer up the pancakes and poultry mixture, starting and finishing with a pancake.

☐ Arrange tomato slices and sprigs of parsley on the top. Serve hot.

ROAST SPRING CHICKENS
(Enough for four)

4 baby chickens, each weighing about
$\frac{3}{4}$lb. when dressed
2 large lemons
salt and pepper
3oz. butter

☐ Wash and dry the chickens. Wash the lemons and cut in half. Push half a lemon into the body cavity of each chicken. Season chickens well with salt and pepper. Soften 2oz. of the butter and spread it over the chicken breasts. Put remainder in a roasting tin and melt.

☐ Put chickens in tin and cook for 45min., or until golden brown, in centre of oven, pre-heated to 400 deg. F. or Mark 6.

☐ Serve one to each person garnished with a little watercress.

CHICKEN IN RED WINE
(Enough for four-six)

3lb. chicken
3 rashers of streaky bacon
10 very small onions or 1 large onion
$\frac{1}{4}$lb. button mushrooms
1oz. butter
2 tablespoons oil
1 clove of garlic
1 bay leaf
1 sprig of thyme
salt and pepper
2oz. plain flour
2 tablespoons brandy
$\frac{1}{2}$ bottle red wine

☐ Allow chicken to thaw if frozen—see page 104. Rinse under running water, then wipe out body cavity with a clean cloth. Remove rind from bacon and cut rashers into $\frac{1}{2}$in. strips. Skin small onions but leave whole, or skin and roughly chop large onion. Wash mushrooms and leave whole; if large cut into quarters.

☐ Melt butter with oil in a large frying pan; add bacon and onions and fry for 5min., or until onions are transparent. Add mushrooms, cover and fry for 5min. more. Remove and keep warm in a large casserole.

☐ Skin and finely chop garlic and add to casserole with herbs, salt and pepper.

Coat chicken with flour, seasoned with salt and pepper, shaking off excess. Fry chicken in the remaining butter and oil, turning occasionally until golden brown.

☐ Pour brandy over chicken and set alight when hot. Then add the wine. Turn into the casserole and cook for 3 hours, just below centre of oven, pre-heated to 300 deg. F. or Mark 2.

ROAST GOOSE
(Enough for seven-eight)

10lb. goose
3 large onions
10 fresh sage leaves or
1 heaped teaspoon dried sage
1½oz. butter
8oz. fresh white breadcrumbs
salt and pepper
10 medium-sized cooking apples
16oz. tin cranberry sauce
watercress

☐ Ask your butcher to prepare the bird ready for stuffing. Tuck the neck skin under the trussing string or wings. Skin and finely chop the onions. Chop the sage leaves if fresh. Melt the butter, add the onions, cover and fry gently for 10min., or until soft. Remove from heat and stir in breadcrumbs and sage. Season to taste. Use stuffing to stuff the carcass of the goose. Fold the flap of skin over and sew with strong cotton. Tie the two legs together with string. Prick goose all over with a fork. Stand the bird on a wire rack in a roasting tin and cover with butter papers. Cook for 2½-3 hours in lower part of oven, pre-heated to 375 deg. F. or Mark 5. Reduce the heat if the bird appears to be cooking too quickly and remove the butter papers after 2 hours to allow skin to crisp.
☐ Wipe the apples and make a shallow cut through the skin round the middle of each. Core the apples and stand them in an ovenproof dish, or on a baking tray. Cook for 30min., or until soft, in centre of oven above the goose. When they are cooked, remove the skin from the top of each apple and fill the holes left by coring with some of the cranberry sauce.
☐ When the goose is cooked lift it out carefully as a lot of fat will have run into the baking tin. Serve the goose on a large meat dish and arrange the baked apples round the bird. Wash the watercress and garnish the goose. Serve the rest of the cranberry sauce separately.

BAKED CHICKEN
(Enough for four)

4 medium-sized chicken joints
milk
5 level tablespoons plain flour
salt and pepper
6 level tablespoons toasted breadcrumbs
3oz. butter
1 tablespoon olive oil

☐ Wash the chicken joints and wipe dry. Dip in milk. Season flour with salt and pepper. Toss chicken in flour to coat. Leave to dry for 30min. Dip in milk again and then coat with breadcrumbs. Shake off surplus crumbs.
☐ Put the butter and oil into a roasting tin and heat for 10min. in centre of oven, pre-heated to 375 deg. F. or Mark 5. Add the chicken joints and baste with the hot butter and oil. Return to the oven and cook for 30min., or until tender. Drain on kitchen paper.

TURKEY FLAN
(Enough for four)

4oz. plain flour
salt and pepper
2oz. butter
1½oz. walnuts
6oz. cream cheese
2oz. grated Cheddar cheese
½ clove of garlic—optional
5 tablespoons milk
6oz. cooked turkey
1 large tomato

☐ Sift the flour and salt into a bowl. Add the butter and rub in until the mixture looks like fine breadcrumbs. Finely chop the nuts and add to the mixture. Mix to a soft dough with cold water. Roll out pastry and line a 6in. flan ring. Prick well with a fork. Cover pastry with a piece of greaseproof paper. Fill with baking beans. Bake for 15min., in centre of oven, pre-heated to 425 deg. F. or Mark 7. Remove paper and beans and cook for 7-10min. more. Cool.
☐ Mash the cream cheese and the Cheddar cheese. Skin and crush clove of garlic—if used—and add to cheeses. Gradually beat in the milk and season.
☐ Chop the turkey into bite-sized pieces. Stir into cheese dressing and then spoon into the pastry case. Slice the tomato and use to garnish the flan.

DEEP-FRIED PANCAKES
(Enough for four)

4oz. plain flour
salt and pepper
2 large eggs
½ pint milk and water mixed
1oz. lard
1 large lemon
½ packet parsley and thyme stuffing
small piece tinned red pepper
1 large cooked chicken joint
4oz. fresh white breadcrumbs
oil for deep frying

☐ Sift the flour and a pinch of salt into a bowl. Make a well in the centre. Break in 1 egg, add half the milk and water, and beat well until the mixture is smooth. Add the remaining liquid gradually, beating well all the time.
☐ Melt a little of the lard in an 8in. frying pan, running it round the pan to coat the base and sides well. Pour in just enough batter to cover the base thinly, tilting the pan as you pour to get a thin and even pancake. Cook quickly until golden brown underneath, then turn or toss, and cook the other side until golden brown. Make 7 more pancakes.
☐ Finely grate the lemon rind. Squeeze out and strain the lemon juice. Make up the parsley and thyme stuffing, using the lemon juice in place of some of the hot water and stirring in the lemon rind and salt and pepper to season. Chop the red pepper into rough pieces. Remove the chicken from the bones, discarding the skin. Cut chicken into small pieces.
☐ Fill each pancake with a little chicken, pepper and stuffing. Fold sides of pancakes over the stuffing into the centre then roll the pancakes. Beat the remaining egg. Brush each pancake roll with egg, then coat with breadcrumbs. Heat the oil to the correct temperature —see page 15—and deep-fry the rolls for 5min. or until golden brown. Drain well and serve.

CHICKEN LOAF
(Enough for four)

2 large chicken joints
1 bay leaf
4 peppercorns
salt
½oz. powdered gelatine
2oz. cooked ham
1 hard-boiled egg
3 level dessertspoons aspic jelly powder
¼ pint hot water
little tomato flesh
small piece of green pepper

☐ Place the chicken, bay leaf, peppercorns and a good pinch of salt in a pan. Cover with cold water, then bring to the boil. Simmer for 1 hour. Strain the liquid and make this up to ½ pint with water, if necessary. Sprinkle the gelatine on to the liquid and leave to dissolve.
☐ Skin the chicken and mince chicken and ham. Turn into a bowl. Add the gelatine. Rinse a 1lb. loaf tin with cold water and then spoon in the meat. Shell the egg and push this gently into the centre of the meat, covering it with a layer of meat. Leave to set in a cold place. Unmould the loaf by dipping the tin quickly in hot water—up to the edge of the tin—then turn out on a serving dish.
☐ Dissolve the aspic powder in hot water; leave until almost set. Meanwhile, cut tiny circles from the tomato flesh and stalks from the pepper. Use these to make flower decorations on the mould. Spoon on the jelly and leave to set.

DEVILLED CHICKEN
(Enough for four)

4 medium-sized joints of chicken
2oz. butter
1 tablespoon lemon juice
1 level teaspoon paprika
½ level teaspoon mustard powder
2 tablespoons Worcester sauce
¼ level teaspoon Cayenne pepper
¼ level teaspoon mixed dried herbs

☐ Wipe the chicken joints. Melt the butter and brush the joints with a little of it. Place them in the grill pan, and grill for 15min. under a medium grill; turn and grill other side for a further 15min., or until tender.
☐ Put the rest of the melted butter into a mixing bowl with the lemon juice, paprika, mustard, Worcester sauce, Cayenne pepper and herbs.
☐ Brush the chicken with the devil sauce and grill for a further 5min. Serve hot.
☐ Small joints of turkey can be prepared and cooked in the same way.

CHICKEN SOUFFLE
(Enough for four)

2oz. butter
2oz. plain flour
½ pint milk
½ level teaspoon salt
4oz. cooked chicken
1 level tablespoon finely chopped parsley
¼ teaspoon Worcester sauce
3 large eggs
1 large egg white

☐ Melt the butter in a saucepan. Stir in the flour and cook for 2min. without browning, stirring all the time. Gradually add the milk to the pan, stirring all the time. Stir continually until the sauce comes gently to the boil and thickens. Add the salt. Remove from the heat and cool slightly.
☐ Mince the chicken. Add the parsley to the pan with the chicken and Worcester sauce. Separate the whole eggs. Beat the yolks into the chicken mixture. Whisk the whites until stiff and standing in peaks. Gently fold the egg whites into the mixture.
☐ Butter a 2½ pint soufflé dish and add the soufflé mixture to this. Bake for 45min. in centre of oven, pre-heated to 375 deg. F. or Mark 5. The soufflé should be well-risen and golden.

CURRIED CHICKEN SALAD
(Enough for six)

3lb. cooked chicken
1 small onion
1 tablespoon olive oil
1 level tablespoon curry powder
1 chicken stock cube
¼ pint boiling water
1 level teaspoon tomato purée
½ large lemon
2 rounded tablespoons chutney
½ pint mayonnaise—see page 26
3 tablespoons single cream
4oz. Patna rice
salt
5 tablespoons vinaigrette dressing—see page 26
2 pineapple rings
1 small green pepper
3 spring onions
1oz. stoned raisins

☐ Cut the chicken off the bones and slice, or cut into chunks. Skin and finely chop the onion. Heat the oil in a saucepan and gently fry the onion for 5min. Stir in the curry powder and cook for 3min. Dissolve the stock cube in the boiling water and stir into the pan with the tomato purée. Squeeze out and strain the juice from ½ lemon and add to pan, together with the chutney. Simmer for 5min. Strain and cool. When cool, stir in the mayonnaise and cream.
☐ Cook the rice in boiling salted water for 12min., then drain. Stir in the vinaigrette dressing. Chop the pineapple rings. Wash and finely chop the pepper, removing seeds and white ribs. Chop spring onions. Add to the rice with the raisins. Allow to cool.
☐ Arrange the rice round a serving dish. Arrange the chicken in the centre and spoon over the sauce.

CURRIED CHICKEN AND PINEAPPLE FLAN
(Enough for four)

6oz. shortcrust pastry—see page 16
1½ level teaspoons powdered gelatine
¼ pint boiling water
1 level teaspoon curry powder
8½oz. tin pineapple rings
2in. piece cucumber
2oz. black grapes
6oz. cold cooked chicken
3 level tablespoons mayonnaise or salad cream

☐ Roll pastry to fit an 8in. fluted flan ring. Line the ring carefully, pushing pastry well down into the corners. Trim off excess pastry. Prick pastry well. Put greaseproof paper in the flan and cover with baking beans or crusts of dry bread. Cook for 15min. towards the top of oven, pre-heated to 425 deg. F. or Mark 7, then reduce heat to 375 deg. F. or Mark 5, remove paper and beans, and cook for a further 10min. Remove and cool on a wire rack.
☐ Meanwhile, soften the powdered gelatine in 2 tablespoons cold water. Pour on the boiling water and add curry powder. Leave until cold.
☐ Drain the tin of pineapple rings. Cut them in half. Wash cucumber and slice thinly. Wash grapes. Cut in half and remove seeds. Cut chicken into small pieces and arrange over base of cold flan. Stir mayonnaise or salad cream into the cold but liquid gelatine. Pour over the chicken and leave for 30min. in a cold place to set.
☐ Before serving, arrange the crescents of pineapple round the edge and rings of cucumber in the centre. Arrange the grapes in the spaces between the pineapple crescents.

ROAST DUCK
(Enough for six)

6lb. duck
1 large onion
1oz. butter
4oz. fresh white breadcrumbs
2 level teaspoons dried sage
1 level tablespoon chopped parsley
salt and pepper
milk
1 large lettuce
1 bunch watercress
¼ small cucumber
3 large oranges

☐ Allow bird to thaw if frozen—see page 104. Rinse under running cold water then wipe out body cavity and the skin, with a clean cloth.
☐ Skin and chop the onion. Melt butter in a saucepan, add onion; cover and fry gently for 7min. Remove from heat and stir in breadcrumbs, sage, parsley and seasonings. A little milk may be used to bind the ingredients together. Use this to stuff the tail end only. Sprinkle the skin with salt and pepper.
☐ Place duck in a roasting tin and cook for 2 hours, in centre of oven, pre-heated to 400 deg. F. or Mark 6.
☐ Wash lettuce and watercress. Dry carefully and reserve a little watercress to garnish duck. Wipe cucumber and

slice thinly. Remove peel and all white pith from 2 of the oranges. Slice into rings. Wash, but do not peel, the remaining orange. Slice thinly and cut each slice in half. Cut almost through each half and open out halves to form butterflies.
☐ Arrange lettuce, watercress and most of the cucumber on a plate. Alternate slices of peeled orange and cucumber on the lettuce.
☐ Remove duck from oven and place on a hot dish. Garnish duck with orange butterflies or halves and remaining watercress. Serve with thin gravy.

CHICKEN KIEV
(Enough for four)

4 breast of chicken joints
4oz. butter
1 clove of garlic
1 level dessertspoon finely chopped parsley
salt and pepper
1 large egg
6oz. fresh white breadcrumbs
oil for deep frying

☐ Ask your butcher to remove the wing bones from the chicken breasts. Normally these are left in so that you can tell it's chicken breast and not leg! They're easier to manage without the bones.
☐ Put the butter in a bowl; beat until soft. Skin and crush the garlic. Mix parsley, butter and garlic with salt and pepper. Flour your hands; form butter mixture into a roll. Wrap in greaseproof paper. Leave to harden for about 30min. in the refrigerator.
☐ Using a rolling pin, lightly beat each chicken piece until fairly thin. Remove butter mixture from paper. Cut into 4 pieces lengthways. Place a piece of butter in the centre of each piece of chicken. Wrap chicken round closely, forming a neat parcel. Tie firmly with cotton. Beat the egg. Coat each chicken parcel with

egg then breadcrumbs, pressing them on firmly.
☐ Heat some oil to the correct temperature—see page 15.
☐ Carefully lower 2 parcels into the pan. Don't use a wire basket or the chicken will have an imprint of the mesh when cooked. Fry for 5-7min., until chicken is tender and golden brown. Cook remainder in the same way. Remove cotton. Drain well.
☐ Serve with tomato and lemon wedges.

Fine breadcrumbs

CHICKEN CHAUDFROID
(Enough for four)

4lb. chicken
1 bay leaf
1 small onion
1 medium-sized carrot
1 level teaspoon dried thyme
½ pint aspic jelly made from packet crystals
2 level teaspoons powdered gelatine
½ pint béchamel sauce—see page 24
¼ small cucumber
2 small tomatoes

☐ Wash and wipe the chicken. Place in a large saucepan with enough cold water to cover. Add the bay leaf. Skin and roughly chop the onion; peel and slice the carrot. Add the vegetables and thyme to the chicken. Bring to the boil slowly. Cover and reduce the heat; simmer for 1½-2 hours until the chicken is cooked. Carefully lift the chicken out of the stock and drain. Leave to cool.
☐ Make up the aspic jelly as directed on the packet and add the powdered gelatine. Allow it to stand until it has almost set. Add half the aspic to the béchamel sauce and stir it in well. Allow it to thicken but not set. Keep the remaining aspic in a bowl over hot water to prevent it from setting.
☐ Carefully skin the chicken and stand it on a cake rack with a large plate underneath. Pour the béchamel sauce evenly over the chicken allowing the excess to run off. Leave to set.
☐ Peel off the cucumber skin thinly and cut some thin strips. These will form the stalks. Cut the rest of the skin into diamond-shaped pieces. Cut tomatoes in half and scoop out the insides. Cut the flesh into diamond-shaped pieces. Dip each piece of decoration in aspic using a hat pin. Arrange the strips of cucumber carefully on the breast of the chicken. Arrange the diamond-shaped pieces of tomato and cucumber in a circle.
☐ Spoon over the rest of the aspic jelly and leave to set for about 10min.

Flour the chicken before coating with egg

TURKEY CROQUETTES
(Enough for four)

12oz. cooked turkey
3 shallots or 1 small onion
3oz. butter
2oz. and 1 level teaspoon plain flour
salt and pepper
ground mace—optional
½ level teaspoon caster sugar
½ pint milk
1 large egg and 2 large egg yolks
4oz. fresh white breadcrumbs
oil for deep frying

☐ Mince the turkey. Skin the shallots or onion and chop roughly. Melt 1oz. butter and gently fry the shallot or onion. Add the turkey, 1 level teaspoon flour and season to taste with salt and pepper, mace if used, and the sugar. Melt remaining butter in a pan; stir in rest of flour and cook for 2min. Remove from heat and stir in the milk. Bring to boil and cook for 2min. Stir the white sauce into the turkey. Stir in egg yolks.
☐ Beat whole egg on a shallow plate. Flour your hands and form the turkey mixture into balls. Dip the balls into beaten egg and then in the breadcrumbs. Heat the oil to the correct temperature—see page 15—and fry the croquettes for 8min., or until nicely browned.

DEEP-FRIED CHICKEN PASTIES
(Enough for six)

8oz. shortcrust pastry—see page 16
1 large cooked chicken joint
1 heaped teaspoon mayonnaise—see page 26
salt and pepper
few drops Worcester sauce
oil for deep frying

☐ Roll out the pastry until it is the thickness of a penny. Cut the chicken from the bones and cut the meat into small pieces. Mix with the mayonnaise, adding enough salt and pepper and Worcester sauce to taste.
☐ Using a 4in. plain cutter, cut rounds from the pastry. Moisten the edge of each round. Put some chicken mixture in the centre of each round then fold over the pastry to make little pasty shapes. Decorate the edges and seal them by pressing the back of a fork all round the join.
☐ Heat the oil to the correct temperature—see page 15—and lower in 3 pasties at a time. Cook for 5-10min. or until puffy and golden brown. Drain well on kitchen paper.

TURKEY PATTIES
(Enough for eight)

13oz. packet frozen puff pastry
9oz. cooked turkey
grated rind of 1 small lemon
pinch of ground nutmeg
salt and pepper
1oz. butter
6 tablespoons double cream

☐ Allow the pastry to thaw for at least 1 hour at room temperature. Roll out the pastry. Cut out rounds using a 4in. plain cutter. Place half the rounds on a greased baking tray, keeping other half for lids. Mince the turkey and season with lemon rind, nutmeg, salt and pepper. Melt the butter and add to mixture with cream. Mix until filling binds together.
☐ Fill the pastry rounds with turkey, then moisten the edges of pastry. Place the lids on top, press edges to seal and decorate with a fork. Bake for 20min., or until pastry is golden and well-risen, in centre of oven, pre-heated to 450 deg. F. or Mark 8. Serve hot or cold.

BUTTERED CHICKEN
(Enough for six-eight)

8oz. cooked chicken joint
2oz. cooked ham
2oz. butter
pinch of ground nutmeg
salt and pepper

☐ Skin the chicken and cut the flesh from the bones. Mince the chicken and ham twice. Soften the butter and gradually beat in until the mixture is smooth. Season to taste with the nutmeg and some salt and pepper.
☐ Serve with buttered toast.

CHICKEN RICE SALAD
(Enough for six)

12oz. Patna rice
boiling water
salt and pepper
1 small cauliflower
1 red eating apple
2 tablespoons lemon juice
1 small green pepper
2lb. cooked chicken
¼ pint mayonnaise—see page 26
5oz. carton single cream
1 level tablespoon curry powder

☐ Cook the rice in boiling salted water for 12min. Drain and rinse under cold water. Leave to cool completely.
☐ Trim off outer leaves and stalk from cauliflower. Break head into small florets cutting off a little stalk from each. Soak in cold water for 10min.
☐ Wash but do not peel the apple. Cut into quarters; remove core and cut apple into ¼in. dice. Put into a small bowl and sprinkle with lemon juice. Wash pepper. Cut it in half and remove the seeds. Cut into ¼in. wide strips. Put into a bowl and cover with boiling water. Leave for 2min. then drain under cold water.
☐ Remove meat from chicken bones and cut into large bite-sized pieces.
☐ Mix mayonnaise, cream, ¼ level teaspoon salt and curry powder together. Mix chicken, cauliflower, apple and lemon juice, green pepper and rice. Mix into the creamy mayonnaise until all ingredients are lightly coated. Season and if liked add more curry powder.

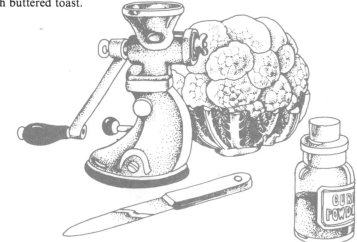

SPICED CHICKEN FRICASSEE
(*Enough for six*)

3½lb. chicken
2 level teaspoons ground coriander
1 level teaspoon ground aniseed
½ level teaspoon ground cumin
1½ level teaspoons ground cinnamon
⅛ level teaspoon ground cardamom
¼ level teaspoon ground nutmeg
1 level teaspoon freshly ground black pepper
⅛ level teaspoon ground cloves
2 level teaspoons salt
12 small onions
2 cloves of garlic
2oz. butter
4 rounded tablespoons desiccated coconut
2 level teaspoons grated lemon rind
¼ pint fresh coconut liquid—see Chicken and Pork Dish, page 112

□ Cut the chicken into 12 pieces and put in a large bowl. Mix the spices with the salt. Mix into the chicken and leave to stand for 1 hour.
□ Skin the onions and garlic. Chop 6 onions and cut the rest in half. Chop the garlic very finely.
□ Melt the butter in a large pan. Add the chicken, coconut, chopped onion and garlic. Fry gently until brown all over. Add the halved onions, lemon rind, coconut liquid and any spices left in the bowl. Bring to the boil, cover and simmer very gently for 35min. or until the chicken is tender. There should be very little liquid left when the dish is cooked. Serve with rice.

CHICKEN FRIED WITH WALNUTS
(*Enough for six*)

¼lb. walnut halves
½ large young chicken
2oz. mushrooms
4 tablespoons vegetable oil
½ level tablespoon cornflour
1 level teaspoon caster sugar
1 tablespoon sherry
2 tablespoons soy sauce
1 level teaspoon salt

□ Chop the walnuts roughly. Cut the chicken from the bones and cut the meat into small dice. Rinse mushrooms and cut into dice the same size as the chicken. Peel only if ragged.
□ Heat 1 tablespoon oil, testing the temperature with one nut. It should become golden brown. Fry the walnuts until golden brown, then remove and drain on thick kitchen paper.
□ Mix the cornflour, sugar, sherry, soy sauce and salt together. Put remaining oil in a pan and fry the chicken quickly, turning all the time. Stir for 1min. Add the cornflour mixture and diced mushrooms. Fry and stir for a further 3min. Stir in walnuts. Serve immediately on a hot plate, with noodles if liked.

TURKEY FRITTERS
(*Enough for four*)

3oz. plain flour
salt and pepper
½oz. butter
¼ pint lukewarm water
1 level teaspoon curry powder
½lb. cooked turkey
1 level teaspoon grated lemon rind
2 large egg whites
oil for deep frying
2oz. grated Wensleydale cheese

□ Sift flour and ½ level teaspoon salt into a bowl. Add a pinch of pepper. Melt the butter. Gradually add to flour with the water, to make a thick, smooth batter. Stir the curry powder into the batter. Mince the turkey. Add turkey and lemon rind to batter. Season well. Whisk egg whites to stiff peaks. Fold in the egg whites.
□ Heat oil to the correct temperature—see page 15. Drop dessertspoons of mixture into the hot oil and fry for 5min., or until well puffed and golden. Remove from the pan and drain on crumpled kitchen paper. Transfer to a serving dish and sprinkle with the cheese.

GOOSE CASSOULET
(*Enough for five-six*)

4oz. haricot beans
2 ham stock cubes
2 pints boiling water
2 level teaspoons brown sugar
salt and pepper
2oz. lard
3 large onions
pinch of dried thyme
1 blade of mace
1 bay leaf
2lb. cooked goose meat
3 large Frankfurter sausages

□ Soak the haricot beans overnight in cold water to cover; drain off the water and put the beans into a saucepan. Dissolve the stock cubes in the boiling water and add half the stock to the pan with the sugar, salt and pepper. Add a little extra water to cover the beans if necessary. Simmer for about 2 hours.
□ Meanwhile, heat the lard in a large saucepan. Skin and slice the onions and add to pan. Fry for 5min., until golden, but not brown. Pour in the rest of the ham stock and bring to the boil. Add the herbs tied in a muslin bag. Cut the goose meat into ½in. cubes. Put in the pieces of goose. Strain haricot beans and reserve the liquid. Add beans to the goose. Simmer very gently for 30min.
□ Towards the end of the cooking time, if necessary, add a little more of the stock used in cooking the beans. Slice the sausages and add to the pan 10min. before serving. Season well. Serve with green salad or vegetables.

Puddings of all kinds

Puddings to a Northerner means all the varieties which are called sweets or desserts in the south. So in this chapter you'll find recipes for steamed puddings, all the old favourites such as bread pudding, as well as the fancier concoctions for parties

CARAMEL SURPRISE
(Enough for four)

8oz. tin gooseberries
1 packet cream caramel mix
1 pint milk
5oz. carton double cream

☐ Drain the gooseberries. Spoon the fruit into 4 sundae glasses. Make up the custard from the cream caramel mix with the milk. Pour into the glasses and leave to set.
☐ Whip the cream until standing in soft peaks. Spoon into a piping bag fitted with a medium-sized plain pipe. Pipe cream on top of each sundae. Top with the caramel from the cream caramel mix.

CHOCOLATE CRISP LAYER
(Enough for eight)

6oz. plain chocolate
3oz. cornflakes
1lb. 4oz. tin pear halves
½ pint double cream
2oz. packet chocolate dessert whirl
¾ pint milk

☐ Break the chocolate into a large basin. Melt it over a pan of boiling water. Stir in the cornflakes until well coated with the chocolate. Spoon into two well-buttered 7in. sandwich tins with loose bases. Smooth the tops but don't press down. Mark one chocolate layer into 8 sections. Leave to set.
☐ Drain the pears. Put the whole chocolate layer on a serving plate. Cut the other into the 8 marked sections. Whip the cream until standing in peaks. Spread half the cream on the whole layer. Arrange the pears on the cream, cut sides down. Spread with the rest of the cream. Put the 8 sections on top.
☐ Serve with creamy chocolate sauce made by whisking the chocolate dessert whirl with the milk. Serve within 1 hour.

SPECIAL TRIFLE
(Enough for eight)

2 jam Swiss rolls
8oz. tin raspberries
1 packet red jelly
8oz. tin creamed rice
5oz. carton double cream
glacé cherries

☐ Cut the Swiss rolls into 1in. slices. Arrange round the bottom and sides of a glass dish. Drain the raspberries. Make up the juice to ¾ pint with cold water. Heat this liquid and dissolve the jelly in it. Pour into the dish on top of the sponges and leave to set. Spoon the raspberries on top, then spoon on the creamed rice.
☐ Whip the cream until standing in soft peaks and spread ¾ of it over the rice, making a pattern with a knife. Put the rest in a piping bag fitted with a large star pipe and pipe a border all round the trifle. Decorate with pieces of glacé cherries. Chill in the refrigerator before serving for 2 hours.

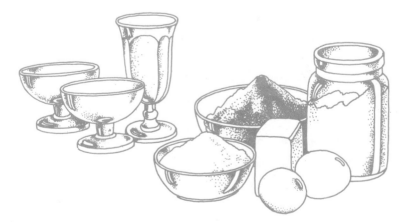

Caramel Surprise,
Chocolate Crisp Layer
and Special Trifle

CHARLOTTE CREAM
(Enough for six)

1 packet lemon jelly
¼ pint boiling water
1 glacé cherry
small piece of orange rind
little angelica
1 level tablespoon custard powder
½ pint milk
1 level tablespoon caster sugar
¾oz. powdered gelatine
¼ pint double cream
8oz. packet chocolate finger biscuits

☐ Divide jelly into cubes, add boiling water and stir well to dissolve. Add ½ pint cold water. Rinse a round 6in. cake tin with a fixed base with cold water. Pour in 4 tablespoons liquid jelly. Leave in a cold place to set.
☐ Cut cherry in half. Cut any white pith off orange rind and cut four diamond shapes. Cut four diamonds from the angelica. Dip half cherry, orange rind and angelica in liquid jelly and place on set jelly, best sides down to form a pattern. Leave to set.
☐ Pour on ¼ pint jelly; heat if necessary to liquify. Leave again until firm. Leave remaining jelly to cool, but don't let it set.
☐ Blend custard powder with a little of the milk. Bring the rest to the boil. Pour on to custard powder. Stir, adding sugar and return to saucepan. Bring back to boil, stirring continuously. Cook gently for 2-3min. Remove from heat. Leave to cool, stirring occasionally, to prevent a skin forming.
☐ Put gelatine and 3 tablespoons cold water into a small cup. Stand in pan of hot water. Leave to dissolve over gentle heat.
☐ Whip cream until it stands in soft peaks. Stir cream into cooled custard with the remaining jelly and the gelatine. Carefully pour cold custard over the set jelly in tin. The custard must be cold or the jelly will melt. Leave in the refrigerator to set.
☐ To unmould, dip tin up to its rim in hot water for 5sec. Put a serving plate over the mould, invert it and shake until you feel the jelly fall on to the plate. Arrange chocolate fingers round the side, pressing on to make them stick. Tie a ribbon round the biscuits.

ALMOND PUDDING
(Enough for four)

5oz. carton single cream
1 tablespoon milk
2oz. fresh white breadcrumbs
1oz. caster sugar
2oz. ground almonds
1 large egg
orange flower water
½oz. butter

☐ Mix the cream with the milk and pour over the breadcrumbs. Stir in sugar and almonds. Beat the egg and add gradually to the mixture. Flavour with 6 teaspoons orange flower water and put into a greased 1 pint pie dish. Dot with butter and cook for 40min. in centre of oven, pre-heated to 350 deg. F. or Mark 4. Serve hot.

CHESTER PUDDING
(Enough for six)

4oz. self-raising flour
4oz. fresh white breadcrumbs
4oz. shredded suet
2oz. caster sugar
6oz. blackcurrant jam
5 tablespoons milk
1 level teaspoon bicarbonate of soda
pinch of salt

☐ Mix flour, breadcrumbs, suet and sugar in a bowl. Make a well in the centre and add 4oz. jam. Warm the milk but do not let it boil. Stir in the bicarbonate of soda and the salt. Pour into the mixing bowl and stir well. The mixture becomes a rather odd blue at this stage but browns during cooking.
☐ Turn the mixture into a well greased 2 pint pudding basin and cover with a piece of pleated foil. Steam or boil for 3 hours. Turn out of basin to serve.
☐ Heat remaining jam with 2 tablespoons cold water and pour over pudding or serve separately.

CHRISTMAS PUDDING
(Enough for eight)

½lb. dried prunes
1 small orange
1 small lemon
2oz. dried apricots
½lb. stoned raisins
¼lb. sultanas
3oz. chopped mixed peel
1oz. ground almonds
3oz. plain flour
pinch of salt
1 level teaspoon ground mixed spice
4oz. soft brown sugar
1oz. fresh white breadcrumbs
5oz. shredded suet
2 large eggs
3 tablespoons rum, whisky or brandy

☐ Wash prunes. Put in a basin and cover with cold water; soak overnight.
☐ Next day, drain and put in a saucepan with ½ pint cold water. Bring to boil; cook for 15min. Drain and reserve 2 tablespoons juice. Stone and roughly chop prunes. Finely grate orange and lemon rind. Squeeze out and strain the juices. Chop the apricots. Put all ingredients except prune juice, orange and lemon juice, eggs and spirit in a large bowl. Mix well. Beat eggs lightly; add to ingredients in bowl together with fruit juices and spirit. Stir well with a wooden spoon.
☐ Put into a greased 3 pint pudding basin. Cover with pleated greaseproof paper and foil or a pudding cloth. Steam or boil for 4 hours, replacing boiling water as it evaporates. Lift pudding out of saucepan. Leave to cool in basin. Replace coverings with fresh ones. Store in a cool, dry place until required. The pudding will require a further 2 hours boiling on the day it is to be served.

CREPES SUZETTE
(Enough for six)

4oz. plain flour
pinch of salt
1oz. caster sugar
2 large eggs
½ pint and 4 tablespoons milk
4oz. butter
3 tablespoons brandy
1 large orange
4 sugar lumps
3oz. granulated sugar
2 tablespoons orange Curaçao
1oz. lard

☐ Sift the flour and salt into a basin. Stir in the caster sugar. Make a well in the centre and drop in the eggs. Add the milk a third at a time, beating well after each addition. Melt ½oz. butter; allow to cool for 4min., then stir into the batter with 1 tablespoon brandy. Leave to stand for 1 hour.
☐ Wipe the orange. Rub the sugar lumps over the skin until all sides of sugar have absorbed the oil. Finely grate the orange rind. Squeeze out and strain the orange juice. Cream the remaining butter until soft. Crush the sugar lumps and beat them into the butter with the grated rind and 1½oz. granulated sugar. Beat in the orange juice until the mixture is light and fluffy and the juice is well mixed in. Stir in 1 tablespoon orange Curaçao. Leave in the fridge until required.
☐ Melt a little of the lard in a pancake pan, and pour in a sixth of the batter. Allow it to run round the pan to coat it evenly. Cook over a high heat until brown on the underside, then turn and brown the other side. Repeat with the remaining batter, making six pancakes in all and lightly greasing the pan with lard each time.
☐ Melt the orange butter in a large omelette or non-stick pan, making sure it is free of all savoury smells and tastes. Dip both sides of one pancake in melted butter, then fold it into quarters with the best side outside. Push pancake to one side of the pan.
☐ Repeat with the rest of the pancakes until they have all been dipped and folded. Sprinkle the pancakes with the remaining granulated sugar; pour over the remaining orange Curaçao and brandy. Light the liqueurs with a match. Shake the pan gently backwards and forwards over the flame and spoon the flaming liqueurs over the pancakes until the flames die down. Serve at once.

CROFTERS PLUM PUDDING
(Enough for six)

1lb. plain flour
pinch of salt
8oz. shredded suet
8oz. stoned raisins
1 large egg
brown ale to mix
½ level teaspoon bicarbonate of soda

☐ Sift the flour and salt into a large bowl. Stir in the suet. Chop the raisins and add to the bowl. Beat the egg until smooth and add to the mixture with enough ale to give a very stiff dropping consistency.
☐ Dissolve the bicarbonate of soda in 1 tablespoon ale, add to the bowl and mix well.
☐ Put mixture into a well-greased 2 pint pudding basin. Cover with greaseproof paper then with foil allowing room for the pudding to rise. Steam or boil pudding for 3 hours, adding more boiling water as it evaporates. Remove papers and turn pudding on to a hot dish. Serve immediately with custard.

APPLE TANSIE
(Enough for four-six)

½ pint double cream
¼ level teaspoon ground nutmeg
pinch of ground mixed spice
3 boudoir biscuits
½oz. fresh white breadcrumbs
2 large eggs and 2 large egg yolks
2oz. caster sugar
1 large cooking apple
1oz. butter
1 tablespoon lemon juice

☐ Pour cream into a pan. Stir in nutmeg and mixed spice. Crumble in the biscuits with the breadcrumbs and heat gently until warm, stirring all the time. Add the whole eggs and egg yolks to the cream with 1oz. sugar. Cook over a very low heat for 5min., but do not allow to boil. Remove from heat.
☐ Peel and core the apple. Cut into rings. Melt butter in a frying pan. Add apple rings and fry gently for 3min. Pour in cream mixture, reduce heat and cook gently for 10-15min. Turn on to a plate and slide back into the pan with the cooked side uppermost. Fry gently for a further 10-15min.
☐ Turn on to a hot serving dish, sprinkle with lemon juice and rest of sugar and serve.

MERINGUE LAYER
(Enough for eight)

4 large egg whites
8oz. caster sugar
two 11oz. tins mandarin oranges
11oz. tin black cherries
little angelica
½ pint double cream

☐ Whisk egg whites until they form very stiff peaks. Whisk in 4oz. sugar, whisking until stiff again. Using a metal spoon, fold in remaining sugar. Do this quickly or meringue loses its bulk. If you have an electric mixer, an easier method is to put the unwhisked whites and sugar into the mixer bowl and whisk together until very thick. This takes 4-5min., but this method produces a meringue which is easier to pipe and remains firmer. Spoon into a piping bag fitted with a large star pipe.
☐ Draw a 7in. circle on 3 pieces of greaseproof paper. Grease 3 flat baking trays and line with paper, pencilled sides to tin. Grease paper lightly. Pipe meringue on to paper starting from the centre of the circles. Leave to dry for 3-4 hours in centre of oven, pre-heated to 225 deg. F. or Mark ¼, or your lowest setting. Keep checking to see that the meringue is not browning. If it is, turn off oven and let the meringue dry in the remaining heat.
☐ It is possible to dry overnight by pre-heating the oven and then turning it off once the meringue is in the oven. This way the meringue stays white and dries slowly. When dry, gently peel off greaseproof paper.
☐ Drain fruit. Cut strips of angelica into diamond shapes. Whisk cream until thick. Spread ⅔ of the cream on 2 meringue layers. Arrange ¼ of the mandarin oranges on each layer. Put the top layer in place.
☐ Arrange mandarins and cherries on top. Spoon remaining cream into a piping bag fitted with a large star pipe. Pipe stars round the border. Decorate with angelica pieces.
☐ Serve within an hour or meringue softens. Do not put in refrigerator.

RHUBARB FLUFF
(Enough for four)

1lb. rhubarb
½oz. powdered gelatine
3 tablespoons boiling water
3oz. caster sugar
pinch of ground ginger
2 large eggs

☐ Wash rhubarb, trim and cut into ½in. pieces. Cook, covered, over a low heat for 15min., or until soft.
☐ Meanwhile, soften gelatine in 2 tablespoons cold water; pour on boiling water and leave to dissolve. Sweeten rhubarb with the sugar and add the ginger.
☐ Separate the eggs. Stir the yolks into the rhubarb with the cooled gelatine. Leave for about 1 hour to cool and thicken. Whisk the egg whites stiffly and fold them into the rhubarb. Spoon into serving dishes.

STRAWBERRY SHORTCAKE
(Enough for eight)

9oz. plain flour
1½ level teaspoons baking powder
¼ level teaspoon salt
4oz. butter
4oz. caster sugar
¼ pint milk
1¼lb. strawberries
½ pint double cream

☐ Sift the flour, baking powder and salt into a bowl. Rub in the butter until the mixture looks like fine breadcrumbs. Stir in 2oz. sugar. Stir in the milk, using a fork, to give a soft dough. Form into a smooth ball. Lightly roll the dough to fit a 7½in. sandwich tin. Carefully lay in the tin. Prick the surface.
☐ Bake for 15-20min., or until pale golden, in centre of oven, pre-heated to 400 deg. F. or Mark 6.
☐ Meanwhile, wash and hull the strawberries. Pick out the best ones and reserve for the top. Thickly slice remaining berries and sprinkle with 1½oz. sugar.
☐ Whip the cream until standing in soft peaks. Remove cake from oven. Turn on to a wire rack and leave to cool.
☐ Cut cake in half across to make two layers. Spread half the cream over the bottom half. Cover with the sliced berries. Sandwich with the top half. Spread rest of cream on top. Arrange whole berries on the cream. Sprinkle with remaining sugar.

MANCHESTER PUDDING
(Enough for six)

4oz. shortcrust pastry—see page 16
½ pint milk
rind of 1 large lemon
2oz. fresh white breadcrumbs
2 large eggs
2oz. butter
4oz. caster sugar
1 tablespoon brandy
3 level tablespoons jam

☐ Roll out pastry to ¼in. thickness. Line an 8in. pie dish; trim edges.
☐ Boil the milk and lemon rind together. Leave to stand for 5min., then remove the lemon rind. Pour milk over the breadcrumbs. Separate the eggs and beat the yolks into the breadcrumb mixture with the butter, 1oz. sugar and the brandy. Spread jam over pastry, then cover with breadcrumb mixture. Bake for 45min. in centre of oven, pre-heated to 350 deg. F. or Mark 4.
☐ Whisk the egg whites until standing in stiff peaks. Whisk in half the remaining sugar, then gently fold in the remainder of the sugar. Swirl on top of the breadcrumb mixture. Return the pudding for 5-10min., or until meringue is golden, to centre of oven, pre-heated to 400 deg. F. or Mark 6. Serve cold.

BREAD PUDDING
(Makes about nine squares)

1lb. stale white bread
3oz. currants
3oz. sultanas
2oz. stoned raisins
3oz. shredded suet
½ level teaspoon salt
2oz. chopped mixed peel
1 level teaspoon ground cinnamon
½ level teaspoon ground nutmeg
3oz. soft brown sugar
1 large egg
2 tablespoons milk

☐ Weigh the bread after removing the crusts, then tear bread into small pieces. Put in bowl, cover with 1 pint cold water and leave to soak for 40min. Wash the currants, sultanas and raisins and drain well.
☐ Squeeze bread very dry; put into a clean bowl. Add rest of ingredients and mix well. Put into a greased 8in. square cake tin. Smooth the top.
☐ Cook for 2-2½ hours or until the top is crisp and golden brown, in centre of oven, pre-heated to 375 deg. F. or Mark 5. Leave in the tin until cold.
☐ Turn out, cut into squares and sprinkle with caster sugar.

BREAD AND BUTTER PUDDING
(Enough for four)

8 thin slices white bread
3oz. butter
3oz. currants
2oz. Demerara sugar
1 level teaspoon ground cinnamon
1 level tablespoon custard powder
1 level tablespoon caster sugar
1 pint milk

☐ Remove the crusts from the bread. Spread the slices with butter. Cut 4 slices in half diagonally. Cut the rest into 1½in. wide fingers. Arrange the diagonally cut slices round the edges of an ovenproof dish. Cover the base of the dish with the fingers of bread.
☐ Sprinkle half of the currants over the bread. Sprinkle with 1oz. Demerara sugar and cinnamon. Cover with the remaining bread. Sprinkle with the rest of the currants.
☐ Blend the custard powder and caster sugar with 4 tablespoons milk. Boil rest of milk and pour into custard powder, stirring. Return to pan, bring to boil, stirring all the time until thick. Cook for 2min. Pour custard over the bread; sprinkle with remaining Demerara sugar. Cook for 1 hour or until golden brown, in centre of oven, pre-heated to 375 deg. F. or Mark 5. Serve hot or cold.

ZABAGLIONE
(Enough for four-five)

3 large eggs
3 level tablespoons icing sugar
4 tablespoons Marsala

☐ Put eggs and sugar into the top of a double boiler. Place over boiling water and beat constantly for 10min., or until mixture is almost white and very fluffy.
☐ Add the wine and blend thoroughly, beating the mixture until it is very stiff. Pour into glasses and serve warm with boudoir biscuits.

CHINESE FRUIT SALAD
(Enough for four)

12 tinned lychees
12 Maraschino cherries
2 slices of fresh pineapple
1 large red eating apple
12 tinned cumquats

☐ Drain syrup from lychees and place a cherry in each one. Cut pineapple slices into sections. Core apple and cut into ½in. cubes. Drain cumquats.
☐ Arrange all fruit in a bowl and push a cocktail stick into each piece of fruit. Stand the bowl of fruit on crushed ice to serve.

LENT PIE
(Enough for six-eight)

3 large eggs
¾lb. cooking apples
¼lb. stoned raisins
¼lb. currants
¼lb. soft brown sugar
1½ level teaspoons ground cinnamon
1½ level teaspoons ground nutmeg
½ level teaspoon ground ginger
juice of 2 lemons
3oz. chopped mixed peel
3 tablespoons brandy or rosewater
¼ pint white wine
8oz. shortcrust pastry—see page 16

☐ Hard-boil the eggs for 12min. Shell and chop finely. Peel, core and finely dice the apples. Mix eggs, apples, dried fruit, sugar, spices, lemon juice, mixed peel, brandy or rosewater and wine.
☐ Roll out pastry on a lightly floured board. Line a 9in. pie dish with half the pastry. Fill with the fruit mixture. Moisten edge of pastry in dish and cover with remaining pastry. Press edges to seal, trim and decorate. Cook for 15min. in centre of oven, pre-heated to 425 deg. F. or Mark 7, then reduce heat to 350 deg. F. or Mark 4 and cook for 45-50min. more. Serve hot or cold.

TREACLE TART
(Enough for six)

12oz. shortcrust pastry—see page 16
2oz. fresh white breadcrumbs
6oz. golden syrup
½ level teaspoon ground ginger
juice of ½ lemon
1oz. caster sugar

☐ Roll out pastry on a lightly floured board and use half to line a 7in. fluted flan ring standing on a baking tray.
☐ Sprinkle pastry with half the breadcrumbs, then spoon on the syrup. Sprinkle with ginger and lemon juice, then add remainder of the crumbs. Moisten edge of pastry in flan ring and cover with the remaining pastry. Press edges to seal, trim and decorate.
☐ Bake for 50min. in centre of oven, pre-heated to 400 deg. F. or Mark 6. Sprinkle with sugar while still hot.

SNOWDON PUDDING
(Enough for four)

2oz. stoned raisins
4oz. shredded suet
pinch of salt
1oz. cornflour
3oz. soft brown sugar
4oz. fresh white breadcrumbs
1 large lemon
3oz. lemon marmalade
3 large eggs
1½oz. caster sugar
¼ pint sherry or Madeira

☐ Butter a 1½ pint pudding basin and strew ⅓ of the raisins round the sides and base. Mix suet, salt, ¾oz. cornflour, brown sugar and breadcrumbs with remaining raisins. Peel off half the lemon rind without removing any of the pith. Finely grate remaining rind. Add grated rind and marmalade to suet mixture. Beat the eggs and add to mixture to make a stiff consistency.
☐ Spoon mixture into prepared basin and cover with foil or greaseproof paper, pleating it to allow the pudding to rise. Steam for 2½ hours, adding more boiling water to the pan as it evaporates.
☐ Put the caster sugar and peeled lemon rind in a saucepan with 4 tablespoons cold water. Bring slowly to the boil, stirring until the sugar has melted, then boil for 5min., or until syrupy. Remove the lemon peel. Mix remaining cornflour with a little cold water. Pour on a little hot syrup, mix well and return to the pan, stirring all the time. Cook for 1min., or until thickened. Add the sherry or Madeira and stir well.
☐ Turn out the pudding and serve with the wine sauce.

NORFOLK DUMPLINGS
(Makes about ten dumplings)

8oz. self-raising flour
1 level teaspoon salt

☐ Sift the flour and salt. Mix with about ¼ pint and 4 tablespoons cold water to make a dough. Lightly roll pieces of the dough into balls, flouring your hands each time. Steam for 20min. but do not remove the lid during the cooking time.
☐ Serve immediately with heated jam or golden syrup as a sauce.

CHURROS
(Enough for three-four)

1 large egg
5oz. plain flour
6 tablespoons milk
finely grated rind of ½ lemon
olive oil for deep frying
caster sugar

☐ Beat the egg. Sift the flour and gradually fold into the egg. Gradually add the milk and stir to a smooth paste. Stir in the lemon rind. Heat oil to correct temperature—see page 15. Spoon mixture into a piping bag fitted with a large star pipe. Pipe mixture in the shape of a wide spiral starting at the edge and going into the centre into plenty of hot deep oil. Fry until golden. Drain on kitchen paper. Cut to required lengths, sprinkle with sugar and serve at once.

APPLE PUDDING
(Enough for four-six)

8oz. packet frozen puff pastry
1½lb. cooking apples
pinch of ground cloves
pinch of ground nutmeg
pinch of ground cinnamon
3oz. butter
1 large egg and 1 large egg yolk
2oz. Demerara sugar
juice of ½ lemon

☐ Allow the pastry to thaw for at least 1 hour. Peel, core and slice the apples. Stew in 1 tablespoon cold water over a very low heat until soft. Stir in cloves, nutmeg and cinnamon. Push apples through a nylon sieve to make a purée. Stir the butter, egg yolk, whole egg, sugar and lemon juice into the apples and mix well.
☐ Roll the pastry on a lightly floured board to ¼in. thickness. Line a 9in. pie dish with the pastry, trim edges and decorate. Pour in the mixture and bake for 1 hour until filling is set and the pastry is cooked, in centre of oven, pre-heated to 325 deg. F. or Mark 3. Serve hot or cold.

FRIARS OMELETTE
(Enough for four)

4 large cooking apples
3½oz. butter
2oz. caster sugar
1 level teaspoon finely grated lemon rind
ground nutmeg
4oz. fresh white breadcrumbs
1 large egg

☐ Wipe apples. Put in a large pie dish and bake whole for 1 hour in centre of oven, pre-heated to 375 deg. F. or Mark 5. Scoop out apple flesh when cooked. Cool.
☐ Cream 3oz. butter and the sugar until light and fluffy. Add lemon rind, apple purée and nutmeg to taste.
☐ Sprinkle a greased 9in. pie dish with a few breadcrumbs. Beat egg into apple mixture and pour into prepared dish. Cover with rest of breadcrumbs and dot with rest of butter.
☐ Bake for 1½ hours in centre of oven, pre-heated to 375 deg. F. or Mark 5. Serve hot.

YORKSHIRE CHEESECAKE
(Enough for six-eight)

6oz. shortcrust pastry—see page 16
8oz. curd cheese
2 large eggs
1 small lemon
5oz. carton double cream
2oz. caster sugar
vanilla essence

☐ Roll out pastry on a lightly floured board to ¼in. thickness. Line a shallow 8in. pie dish, trim edges and decorate. Prick the pastry, cover with a piece of greaseproof paper and fill with baking beans. Bake for 10min. in centre of oven, pre-heated to 400 deg. F. or Mark 6, then remove beans and paper and bake for 5min. more until golden and crisp. Remove and cool.
☐ Push the curd cheese through a sieve. Separate the eggs and beat in the yolks. Finely grate the lemon rind and squeeze out and strain the lemon juice. Beat into the cheese mixture with the cream, sugar and vanilla essence. Whisk the egg whites until stiff and carefully fold into the mixture. Spread evenly over the pie crust and bake for 30min. or until golden brown, in centre of oven, pre-heated to 350 deg. F. or Mark 4.

CHOCOLATE SURPRISE FLAN
(Enough for six)

5oz. plain chocolate
2oz. butter
2 level tablespoons instant coffee
4oz. digestive biscuits
1½oz. caster sugar
6 tablespoons boiling water
2 level teaspoons powdered gelatine
1 large egg
5oz. carton double cream

☐ Melt 2oz. chocolate, butter and 2 level teaspoons instant coffee. Crush biscuits finely. Stir chocolate and butter until blended. Add biscuits, mix well. Press into a lightly greased 7½in. flan tin with a loose base. Leave in refrigerator or cold place overnight until set.
☐ Carefully ease up the base and slide the case on to a plate. Dissolve remaining coffee and sugar in boiling water. Soften gelatine in 2 tablespoons cold water. Pour on hot coffee liquid. Stand bowl in pan of hot water. Leave until gelatine has dissolved. Reserve 3 tablespoons coffee mixture. Add 4 tablespoons cold water to rest. Remove bowl from pan; leave to cool. Pour into flan case; leave to set.
☐ Melt remaining chocolate with 1 tablespoon cold water. Remove and cool for 5min. Separate egg. Beat yolk into chocolate. Stir in reserved coffee. Leave in cool place for about 20min. or until beginning to thicken.
☐ Whisk egg white stiffly. Fold into setting chocolate mixture. Spoon over layer of set coffee jelly. Leave in cool place for 2 hours or until set.
☐ Whip the cream. Pipe large swirls round the top of the flan.

LEMON CREAM
(Enough for three-four)

½ pint double cream
4 tablespoons single cream
1 large lemon
2oz. caster sugar

☐ Put the creams in a pan and warm to blood heat, stirring all the time. Squeeze out and strain the juice from the lemon. Add sugar to lemon and leave for 10min. Add lemon juice. Stir well.
☐ Rub a piece of lemon peel around three or four glasses or custard cups and pour in the mixture. Chill for 2 hours.

VANILLA ICE CREAM
(Enough for eight-ten)

1 pint single cream
2in. piece of vanilla pod
8 standard egg yolks
10oz. caster sugar
½ pint double cream

☐ Bring a saucepan of water to the boil. Pour single cream into a large bowl; add vanilla pod and stand bowl over hot water. Bring cream almost to the boil.
☐ Meanwhile, whisk yolks and sugar for 5min., or until pale and thick enough to hold a trail of mixture. Discard vanilla pod from the cream and pour the hot cream slowly into the yolk mixture, beating gently all the time.
☐ Pour mixture back into the bowl and cook over hot water until the mixture thickens. Stir all the time using a wooden spoon and don't allow the mixture to boil. Stir in the double cream. Strain through a fine nylon sieve and allow to cool to room temperature.
☐ Pour into an 8in. cake tin with a fixed base and put the tin in your freezer or in the freezer box of the fridge. Allow to freeze, removing ice cream every 30min. and whisking it well. Serve it in glasses with wafers.

IRISH PANCAKES
(Enough for four)

4 tablespoons double cream
2 large eggs and 2 large egg yolks
2½oz. butter
3oz. plain flour
ground nutmeg
caster sugar

☐ Warm the cream until lukewarm. Whisk the whole eggs with the yolks until frothy. Melt 1½oz. butter.
☐ Stir the cream into the eggs then the melted butter. Sift in the flour a little at a time and mix to a smooth batter, adding nutmeg to taste.
☐ Melt a little of the remaining butter in a frying pan. Don't have the pan too hot or the mixture cooks before it spreads. Add a thin layer of batter and fry until golden on one side. Turn and fry the other side. Keep hot while you make the rest.
☐ Roll each pancake, sprinkle with caster sugar and serve hot in a dish.

POOR KNIGHTS OF WINDSOR
(Enough for four)

eight ½in. thick slices of white bread
¼ pint milk
2oz. caster sugar
1 large egg
2oz. butter
5 level tablespoons raspberry jam

☐ Cut the crusts from the bread. Put the milk and sugar in a dish. Beat in the egg. Dip in the bread quickly on each side to moisten it. It shouldn't be soggy.
☐ Melt the butter in a large frying pan and fry the bread until golden brown and crisp on each side. Spread with the jam. Cut into fingers if liked and serve immediately.

STRAWBERRY CHEESECAKE
(Enough for eight-ten)

1½oz. plain semi-sweet biscuits
pinch of ground cinnamon
½oz. butter
4 large eggs
7oz. caster sugar
1lb. soft cream cheese
1½oz. plain flour
2 tablespoons lemon juice
two 5oz. cartons soured cream
1lb. strawberries
4 level tablespoons strawberry jam
4 level teaspoons arrowroot

☐ Crush the biscuits with a rolling pin. Add cinnamon. Melt butter and liberally brush the sides and base of a 7½in. cake tin with a loose base. Dust the biscuit crumbs over the butter. Shake out excess crumbs. Separate eggs, putting yolks into a large bowl. Whisk yolks until thick. Add sugar and beat with a wooden spoon until light and thick. Break up the cheese with a fork. Add to yolks and beat until smooth. Beat in the flour, then the lemon juice and soured cream. Whisk egg whites until stiff but not dry. Fold into the cheese mixture. Pour into the prepared tin. Cook for 1½ hours in centre of oven, pre-heated to 250 deg. F. or Mark ½. Turn off the oven and leave the cake for 2 hours without opening the oven door. Remove and cool in tin.
☐ Push the base and cake up, free of the tin. Cut into two layers. Slide the bottom layer on to a plate.
☐ Wash, hull and halve the strawberries. Arrange over both layers. Gently heat the jam and ¼ pint cold water until the jam has melted. Blend the arrowroot with 1 tablespoon cold water. Strain the hot jam on to the arrowroot, stirring. Return to pan and bring to the boil, stirring, and cook for 2min., or until thick and clear. Cool for 5-10min. but don't let the glaze set.
☐ Spoon glaze over both lots of strawberries. Carefully lift the top layer on to the bottom layer and leave for 30min. to set.

LEMON MERINGUE PIE
(Enough for four)

4oz. shortcrust pastry—see page 16
2 large lemons
1½oz. cornflour
2 large eggs
7½oz. caster sugar

☐ Roll out pastry on a lightly floured board to fit a 7in. flan ring.
☐ Prick the base with a fork and line the pastry with greaseproof paper. Fill with baking beans to prevent it rising. Cook for 15min., just above centre of oven, pre-heated to 425 deg. F. or Mark 7. Remove the paper, beans and flan ring and cook for a further 5-10min. Remove and cool on a wire rack.
☐ Thinly peel the rind from 1 lemon, cut into narrow 2in. lengths and reserve for decoration. Grate the rind from the other lemon, and squeeze the juice from both. Blend the cornflour and half of the lemon juice. Put remaining juice and ¼ pint water into a saucepan; bring to the boil. Pour into the cornflour, stirring all the time. Pour back into the saucepan, bring to the boil and cook for 3min., or until the mixture thickens, stirring all the time.
☐ Remove from the heat and cool for a few minutes. Separate the eggs and beat the yolks lightly. Add the yolks a little at a time to the lemon mixture. Stir in 3½oz. sugar. Put flan case on an ovenproof dish, and pour lemon mixture into the case.
☐ Whisk egg whites until standing in stiff peaks, and reserve 1 tablespoonful. Quickly whisk 3½oz. caster sugar into the remaining egg whites and pile on the top of the flan. Cook for 7-10min., until the meringue is golden, in centre of oven, pre-heated to 425 deg. F. or Mark 7.
☐ Meanwhile, dip the strips of lemon peel in the reserved egg white and sprinkle with the remaining caster sugar. Cook for 2min. below the pie. Serve the pie decorated with the lemon curls.

STRAWBERRY LIQUEUR ICE CREAM
(Enough for four)

8oz. strawberries
1 miniature bottle Cointreau
5oz. carton double cream
2½oz. caster sugar

☐ Wash and hull the berries. Put into a bowl and sprinkle with the Cointreau. Leave for 1 hour.
☐ Mash strawberries well until smooth. Put into a freezing tray and freeze for 1-1½ hours or until slushy. Whip the cream until thick. Stir in the sugar. Turn the half-frozen strawberries into a bowl and fold in the cream. Put back into the tray and freeze for 1½ hours or until half frozen. Turn into a bowl, beat for a minute until smooth and return to the tray. Freeze again until firm. The second beating ensures the mixture freezes evenly and does not form large ice crystals.
☐ Spoon into sundae glasses and serve at once with crisp fan wafers.

REDCURRANT SORBET
(Enough for four)

8oz. granulated sugar
1lb. redcurrants
2 large egg whites
½oz. caster sugar

☐ Put the granulated sugar and ½ pint cold water into a saucepan. Heat gently until the sugar has dissolved. Bring to the boil; boil for 10-15min. until syrupy.
☐ Meanwhile, wash the currants. Reserve 4 small bunches. Strip the rest from the stalks. Put into a pan and add 3 tablespoons water. Heat gently until the currants split. Push through a nylon sieve; discard the seeds. Mix together the syrup and redcurrant purée. Leave until cold. Pour into a freezing tray and freeze for 1½ hours or until half frozen.
☐ Whip the egg whites stiffly. Turn the redcurrant ice into a bowl and fold in all but 1 tablespoon egg white. Mix until smooth. Return to the tray and freeze for 2-3 hours or until firm but not hard. It is best to do the final freezing in the freezer set at the normal temperature.
☐ Dip the reserved currants into the egg white then into the caster sugar. Leave to dry.
☐ Serve the sorbet at once in sundae glasses and decorate with frosted berries.

GOOSEBERRY FOOL
(Enough for four)

1lb. gooseberries
2oz. granulated sugar
½ level tablespoon custard powder
½ level tablespoon caster sugar
¼ pint milk
5oz. carton double cream
finely chopped walnuts

☐ Stew the fruit in a little water and granulated sugar until tender. Sieve the fruit or liquidise.
☐ Mix the custard powder and caster sugar to a smooth paste with about 1 tablespoon of the milk. Put the rest of the milk on to boil. When nearly boiling pour the milk on to the custard mixture and mix well. Return to heat and bring to boil again. Leave to cool, putting a piece of wet greaseproof paper on the custard surface to prevent a skin forming.
☐ Whip the cream. Stir into the custard. Fold in the sieved fruit. Turn into 4 sundae glasses and decorate with the chopped nuts. Serve with shortbread fingers or plain biscuits.

YORKSHIRE SECRET CAKE
(Enough for four)

13oz. packet frozen puff pastry
2oz. chopped candied lemon peel
1 tablespoon brandy
½lb. currants
½oz. caster sugar

☐ Allow the pastry to thaw for at least 1 hour. Steep the candied lemon peel in the brandy and let it stand for 1 hour.
☐ Roll out the pastry on a lightly floured board to ¼in. thickness. Cut out two 7½in. rounds using a fluted cutter or a fluted flan tin. Place 1 round on a lightly greased baking tray. Mix the candied peel, brandy and currants together, and pile in the centre of the pastry. Moisten the edge of the pastry and cover with the second piece. Press edges well to seal and decorate. Cut the cake into quarters, but leave them pushed close together.
☐ Bake for 15min. in centre of oven, pre-heated to 450 deg. F. or Mark 8, then reduce heat to 425 deg. F. or Mark 7 and cook for 30min. more or until the top is golden brown and the pastry is flaky. Cover the top with a piece of foil if it gets too brown. Sprinkle with caster sugar while still warm.

CHOUX GATEAU
(Enough for eight)

4oz. shortcrust pastry—see page 16
2oz. choux pastry—see page 20
5oz. carton double cream
5oz. carton single cream
8oz. granulated sugar

☐ Flour a clean board. Roll out the shortcrust pastry, then cut a 6in. circle, using a large tea plate. Place on greased baking tray. Prick with a fork. Spoon choux pastry into a piping bag, fitted with a plain ½in. pipe. Pipe a circle of small buns—a little smaller than a walnut—round the edge of the pastry circle, leaving a ½in. space between each one. If you do not have a piping bag, use a teaspoon. Pipe the remaining choux pastry in the same size buns on to another greased baking tray.
☐ Bake the shortcrust circle and choux buns for 15min. on 2 shelves above centre of oven, pre-heated to 425 deg. F. or Mark 7, then reduce heat to 375 deg. F. or Mark 5; reverse the positions of baking trays and bake for another 15-20min. Remove and cool.
☐ Whip creams together; spread half over the shortcrust pastry base. Put rest in piping bag fitted with a small star pipe. Make small slits in choux buns, pipe a little cream in the centre of each bun leaving a little for decoration.
☐ Put the sugar and ¼ pint water into a saucepan. Dissolve sugar over a very low heat. Increase heat, simmer without stirring until the temperature reaches 300 deg. F. or a little syrup when dropped in cold water forms brittle threads. Carefully dip the choux buns into the caramel, being careful not to burn your fingers. Place each one on the pastry base and build into a pyramid. This must be done quickly or caramel sets—if this happens, place caramel over low heat, do not stir, and heat for a few minutes. For a special finish—though it's tricky—dip a fork into remaining caramel, pull out strands and spin them round gâteau. Pipe remaining cream between the buns.

VANILLA JELLY
(Enough for four)

1 pint milk
2 large eggs
2oz. caster sugar
vanilla essence
½oz. powdered gelatine
3 tablespoons hot water

☐ Warm the milk. Separate the eggs and beat the yolks with the sugar and a few drops of vanilla essence to flavour. Add to milk and stir mixture over a low heat until creamy but not thick. Do not boil. Pour into a basin. Dissolve the gelatine in the hot water. Add to milk mixture. Whisk the egg whites until stiff. Fold egg whites carefully into bowl. Pour into a wetted mould and leave in a cold place to set. Turn out and serve cold.

APPLE CRISP
(Enough for six)

¼lb. plain flour
¼lb. caster sugar
½ level teaspoon baking powder
1 large egg
4 medium-sized cooking apples
2½ teaspoons dried mint leaves
2½ level teaspoons ground cinnamon

☐ Butter the base and sides of a shallow 8in. square baking dish.
☐ Mix the flour, sugar and baking powder and sift them into a mixing bowl. Make a well in the centre and drop in the egg. Mix together until the flour has absorbed the egg.
☐ Peel, core and slice apples. Stir the mint leaves and cinnamon together. Add the apples and toss with a wooden spoon until the slices are evenly coated all over. Arrange the slices in the baking dish and scatter the flour mixture over the apples to completely cover them.
☐ Bake for 45min. or until the topping is crusty, in centre of oven, pre-heated to 350 deg. F. or Mark 4. Remove the dish from the oven and cover it tightly with a lid or foil and set aside to cool.
☐ Serve cold, with whipped cream.

GOOSEBERRY CONDE
(Enough for four)

12oz. gooseberries
2oz. caster sugar
15½oz. tin creamed rice
5oz. carton double cream

☐ Wash the gooseberries, then top and tail them. Put gooseberries into a saucepan with the sugar. Cover with a lid and cook very gently for 10min., or until tender but not mashed. Leave until cold.

☐ Put the rice into a large bowl. Whip the cream until standing in soft peaks. Stir cold gooseberries into the rice, then fold in the whipped cream. Spoon into 4 glasses to serve. You can add a little vegetable colouring to tint the condé a delicate green shade, or use raspberries instead of gooseberries.

SUMMER PUDDING
(Enough for six)

¼lb. raspberries
¼lb. blackcurrants
¼lb. redcurrants
3oz. caster sugar
8 slices white bread

☐ Wash and pick over fruit. Put fruit into saucepan with sugar; cover and cook gently for 5min., until soft but not pulpy. Allow fruit to cool.

☐ Pour off juice into a separate bowl. Cut crusts off bread. Soak 6 slices in the juice and use to line a 1½lb. pudding basin. Spoon fruit into lined basin. Soak remainder of bread for the top, then pour remaining juice over fruit. Cover top of pudding with rest of bread. On top of the pudding, place a plate, small enough to sit inside the basin to press the pudding. Add a weight from your scales and leave overnight in a cool place.

☐ Turn out the following day and serve decorated with plenty of whipped cream.

SPONGE RING
(Enough for six-eight)

4oz. plain flour
1 level teaspoon baking powder
4oz. butter
4oz. caster sugar
2 large eggs
1 large lemon
1 large orange
1 large red apple
1 large banana
4oz. white grapes
3 level tablespoons golden syrup
1 tablespoon rum or a few drops rum essence

☐ Sift flour and baking powder into a bowl. Cream butter and sugar together until fluffy. Lightly beat eggs together, then add gradually to the creamed mixture beating all the time. If mixture looks as if it might curdle, beat in 1 tablespoon flour. Then continue beating in egg. Fold in flour using a large metal tablespoon. Spoon into greased and floured 7in. ring tin. Bake for 25-30min., until risen and firm to the touch, in centre of oven, pre-heated to 375 deg. F. or Mark 5. Invert tin on to a wire rack and leave to cool. The sponge will drop out as it cools.

☐ Squeeze out and strain the lemon juice. Peel orange, removing all white pith, and cut segments from their skins using a very sharp knife. Wash the apple. Core but do not peel. Slice. Skin and cut banana into ¼in. slices. Toss apple and banana in lemon juice to prevent them turning brown. Wash the grapes, halve them and remove pips. Put syrup and 2 tablespoons cold water into a saucepan. Heat gently to melt. Add the rum or essence. Put all the fruit and lemon juice into pan; coat with syrup. Remove and drain.

☐ Put a large plate beneath wire rack holding sponge. Pour rest of syrup over sponge to soak in. Pour over any that collects on the plate.

☐ Transfer sponge to a serving plate and pile the fruit in the centre. You could make and soak sponge the day before you want it. In fact, the longer it soaks, the better it is.

STEAMED BATTER PUDDING
(Enough for four)

3 level tablespoons flour
1 pint milk
1oz. butter
½ level teaspoon salt
3 large eggs

☐ Mix the flour in a large bowl with a little milk until it is smooth. Add remainder of the milk, stirring all the time to make sure the mixture is free of lumps. Melt the butter and add to the flour mixture with salt. Beat in the eggs and mix well.

☐ Pour mixture into a well-greased 2 pint pudding basin. Cover with aluminium foil and seal tightly. Put the basin into a large pan of boiling water and move the basin about for the first minute to prevent the flour settling to the bottom of the pudding. Boil for 1 hour 35min. Turn out and serve with a fruit, jam or wine sauce.

PEASANT GIRL WITH A VEIL
(Enough for four-six)

1½ packets dry pumpernickel or very dark rye bread
1½oz. butter
1oz. caster sugar
2½lb. cooking apples
5oz. carton double cream
2 level tablespoons raspberry jam

☐ Rub the dry bread into fine crumbs, or grate finely. Melt the butter in a frying pan; add breadcrumbs and sugar and cook over a very low heat for about 5min., or until the breadcrumbs are very crisp. Stir all the time. Leave to cool.

☐ Peel, core and thinly slice the apples. Put in a pan with 1 tablespoon water and cook over a very low heat until soft. Stir well to make a purée.

☐ Butter a 6in. soufflé dish and place alternate layers of breadcrumbs and apple purée in the dish, beginning and ending with breadcrumbs. Whip the cream until very stiff and spread over the top of the pudding. Decorate centre with small spoonsful of jam. Chill for 2 hours.

LIQUEUR ORANGES
(Enough for four)

8 medium-sized oranges
4oz. caster sugar
2 tablespoons Grand Marnier

☐ Cut off the top and bottom of each orange so that it will stand. Using a sharp knife, cut downwards on to the board, cutting away the peel and pith together. A little of the flesh will be cut away at the same time but this cannot be helped. Work all round the orange until all the peel and pith has gone. Peel the others in the same way.
☐ Cut the white pith off the peel of 2 oranges and cut the peel into very fine shreds. Dissolve the sugar in 1 pint cold water over a very gentle heat. Bring to the boil, add the orange peel shreds and simmer for 5min., or until soft. Add the Grand Marnier. Arrange the oranges in a glass bowl and pour the sugar syrup and orange peel over.
☐ Allow to cool, and chill in summer.

CHOCOLATE MOUSSE
(Enough for four)

8oz. plain chocolate
½oz. butter
3 large eggs

☐ Using the largest side of your grater, grate long pieces of chocolate. Keep these for decoration. Put the rest of the chocolate in a small pan with 4 tablespoons cold water. Dissolve chocolate over a gentle heat then cook for about 5min., stirring occasionally, until mixture becomes thick and creamy. Remove from heat. Stir in the butter until melted. Separate the eggs. Whisk the whites until stiff. Beat the egg yolks into the slightly cooled chocolate mixture. Fold in the egg whites quickly. Pour the mixture into four small glass dishes and leave overnight.
☐ Decorate with rest of the chocolate.

BILBERRY PIE
(Enough for six-eight)

1lb. bilberries
8oz. shortcrust pastry—see page 16
3oz. caster sugar
1 standard egg

☐ Wash and pick over bilberries. Leave to drain.
☐ Cut off just over a half of the pastry and reserve for top of pie and decoration. Roll out smaller piece to ¼in. thickness. Lift it into a lightly greased 7½in. ovenproof pie plate. Trim edge.
☐ Put the bilberries in pie; sprinkle with sugar. Roll out remainder of pastry. Moisten edge of pastry in the plate, and cover with pastry lid. Press edges well to seal; trim with a sharp knife. Knead all trimmings lightly and roll out. Using a thimble or very small cutter, cut out lots of small rounds. Beat egg lightly. Brush pastry lid with egg; press rounds in place to form a pattern. Brush rounds carefully with egg.
☐ Bake for 15min. in centre of oven, pre-heated to 400 deg. F. or Mark 6, then reduce heat to 350 deg. F. or Mark 4 and cook for 15-20min. more.

RICH PANCAKES
(Makes ten pancakes)

9oz. plain flour
2 large eggs
½ pint less 4 tablespoons milk
6 tablespoons mild beer
pinch of caster sugar
pinch of salt
1oz. butter
5 level tablespoons jam
icing sugar

☐ Sift the flour. Separate the eggs and beat the yolks well. Gradually beat in the milk, beer, sugar and salt. Add the flour and beat until smooth.
☐ Whisk egg whites until stiff and standing in peaks and fold them into the batter using a large metal spoon.
☐ Lightly grease a 6in. frying pan with butter. Put 2 tablespoons batter into the pan and tilt the pan to spread the batter evenly. Cook over medium heat until golden brown; turn and brown on the other side. Keep hot while you make the rest of the pancakes.
☐ Serve hot spread with strawberry or raspberry jam, and sprinkled with icing sugar. Or you can fill with ice cream, fold the pancakes in three, and dust with icing sugar.

BAKEWELL TART
(Enough for six)

8oz. packet frozen puff pastry
2 level tablespoons raspberry jam
4oz. butter
4oz. caster sugar
3 large eggs
4oz. ground almonds

☐ Allow the pastry to thaw for at least 1 hour. Roll pastry on a lightly floured board to fit a shallow 9in. pie dish. Line dish with pastry. Trim edges and decorate. Spread the jam over the pastry.
☐ Cream butter and sugar until light and fluffy. Beat eggs lightly. Add to mixture a little at a time, beating after each addition. Stir in almonds. Spread over the jam.
☐ Bake for 5min. in centre of oven, pre-heated to 450 deg. F. or Mark 8, then reduce heat to 300 deg. F. or Mark 2 and cook for 40-45min. longer until set.

CLIPPING-TIME PUDDING
(Enough for four)

8oz. Carolina rice
pinch of salt
1¼ pints milk
½ level teaspoon ground cinnamon
3oz. caster sugar
1 large egg
4oz. currants
4oz. stoned raisins
1½oz. beef marrow

☐ Put the rice and salt in a pan. Cover with cold water and bring to the boil. Drain and add rice to the milk. Add cinnamon and sugar. Bring to the boil and simmer for 20min. or until the rice is tender. Beat the egg and add to rice with currants and raisins and stir well together. Cut the marrow into small pieces and stir in.
☐ Turn into a pie dish and bake for 20min. in centre of oven, pre-heated to 350 deg. F. or Mark 4.

DEVONSHIRE JUNKET
(Enough for four)

1 pint milk
2oz. caster sugar
1 teaspoon rennet
whole nutmeg

☐ Warm the milk to blood heat. Remove from the heat and stir in the sugar until it has dissolved. Stir in the rennet and pour the mixture into a 1 pint serving bowl. Leave in a warm place for about 1 hour to set. Don't put it in the fridge to set or disturb it once set because it will separate.
☐ When the junket has set, grate a little nutmeg over the top. In Devon, junket is covered with a layer of scalded cream. Try a layer of thickly whipped cream, if liked, for a very rich sweet.

BANBURY APPLE PIE
(Enough for six-eight)

5 large cooking apples
2oz. chopped mixed peel
4oz. currants
1oz. butter
3oz. Demerara sugar
pinch of ground ginger
pinch of ground cinnamon
6oz. shortcrust pastry—see page 16

☐ Peel, core and slice the apples. Put half the apples in a greased 9in. pie dish and sprinkle with half the peel and half the currants. Melt the butter and pour half over the apples. Add apples, peel, currants and butter as before.
☐ Dissolve the Demerara sugar in 3 tablespoons water and pour over the apples. Sprinkle with the spices.
☐ Roll out the pastry on a lightly floured board to ⅛in. thickness. Cut off a ½in. border all round. Grease the edge of the pie dish and press the border of pastry in place. Moisten pastry border and cover with remaining round. Press edges to seal, trim and decorate.
☐ Bake for 30min. or until pastry is golden brown, in centre of oven, pre-heated to 400 deg. F. or Mark 6. Sprinkle with caster sugar while warm. Serve hot or cold.

MERINGUE BASKETS
(Enough for eight)

2 large egg whites
4oz. caster sugar
5oz. carton double cream
1 tablespoon orange Curaçao
½lb. raspberries
1oz. granulated sugar

☐ Whisk the egg whites until stiff and standing in peaks. Add half the caster sugar and beat until the meringue is shiny and stands in peaks again. Gradually add the remaining caster sugar, beating until the meringue is stiff. Put into a piping bag and pipe small rounds on a well greased baking tray covered with two thicknesses of greased greaseproof paper. Pipe a circle on the edge of each round to make a basket.
☐ Bake for 1½-2 hours in centre of oven, pre-heated to 225 deg. F. or Mark ¼. Remove on to a cooling rack, turn off oven and return meringues to dry for 45-60min. Allow to cool.
☐ Whip the cream until stiff. Stir in the Curaçao. Wash the raspberries and allow to drain. Spoon cream into each basket, fill with raspberries and sprinkle each basket with granulated sugar.

APPLE FLORENTINE PIE
(Enough for four-eight)

6oz. shortcrust pastry—see page 16
5 large cooking apples
1 large lemon
3 level tablespoons caster sugar or golden syrup
1 pint light ale
pinch of ground nutmeg
pinch of ground cinnamon
1 clove

☐ Roll out pastry on a lightly floured board to ⅛in. thickness.
☐ Wash, peel, core and cut the apples into 1in. thick rings. Arrange in a 9in. pie dish. Finely grate lemon rind and sprinkle rind and 2 tablespoons sugar or syrup over apples. Grease edge of dish. Cut off a ½in. strip round pastry and press on to edge of dish. Moisten strip and cover pie with large round. Press edges to seal, trim and decorate.
☐ Bake for 10min. in centre of oven, pre-heated to 425 deg. F. or Mark 7, then reduce heat to 350 deg. F. or Mark 4 and cook for 20min. more.
☐ Heat the ale with the spices and rest of sugar or syrup until hot but not boiling. When pie is cooked, carefully remove the crust and pour the hot spiced ale over the apples. Cut pastry into required number of pieces and replace.

CUMBERLAND SWEET PIE
(Enough for four)

4oz. shortcrust pastry—see page 16
2oz. stoned raisins
2 large eggs
1oz. caster sugar
½ pint milk
2oz. desiccated coconut
pinch of ground nutmeg

☐ Roll out pastry on a lightly floured board to a ⅛in. thickness and line a 7½in. sandwich tin, pressing the pastry well into the corners. Trim the edge and decorate.
☐ Sprinkle the raisins over the base of the pie. Beat the eggs and stir in the sugar. Bring the milk to the boil, then pour on to the eggs, stirring. Pour into the pastry case. Sprinkle most of the coconut on top with the nutmeg.
☐ Bake for 10min. in centre of oven, pre-heated to 425 deg. F. or Mark 7, then reduce heat to 325 deg. F. or Mark 3 and cook for 30min. more. Sprinkle rest of coconut on top to serve.

HUNTINGDON PUDDING
(Enough for four-six)

8oz. plain flour
2 level teaspoons baking powder
5oz. shredded suet
3oz. caster sugar
12oz. gooseberries
1 large egg
¼ pint milk

☐ Sift the flour and baking powder into a bowl. Stir in the suet and sugar. Top and tail the gooseberries and add to the mixture. Stir well. Beat the egg and milk together and gradually stir into the gooseberry mixture.
☐ Turn into a greased 2½ pint pudding basin. Cover with greaseproof paper and foil allowing room for the pudding to rise. Steam for 3 hours, then turn out and serve with hot golden syrup.

MINCEMEAT PUDDING
(Enough for four-six)

6oz. fresh white breadcrumbs
3oz. shredded suet
3oz. soft brown sugar
4 heaped tablespoons mincemeat
1 large egg
3 tablespoons milk

☐ Mix the breadcrumbs, suet, sugar and mincemeat together. Lightly beat the egg and add to the ingredients together with the milk.

☐ Press mixture into a greased 1½ pint pudding basin. Cover with greased foil or a double piece of greaseproof paper and steam for 2½ hours, replenishing the steamer with boiling water when necessary.

☐ Turn out and serve hot with syrup.

SYLLABUB
(Enough for four)

1 large lemon
4oz. sugar lumps
4 tablespoons sherry
2 tablespoons brandy
½ pint double cream

☐ Wash the lemon. Rub the sugar lumps over the skin until the sugar has absorbed the oil. Put the sugar in a bowl with the sherry and brandy. Leave for 15min. to dissolve.

☐ Squeeze out and strain the lemon juice. Add to bowl. Pour on the cream and whisk gently until the mixture thickens. Pour into 4 glasses.

☐ Serve with plain biscuits.

SWEDISH LEMON CREAM
(Enough for four)

4oz. caster sugar
¼ pint white wine
1 large lemon
6 large egg yolks

☐ Mix the sugar and wine in a saucepan. Finely grate the lemon rind and squeeze out and strain the juice. Add rind and juice to the pan with the egg yolks. Heat very gently, stirring all the time until the cream begins to thicken. Don't let it boil. Remove pan from heat and continue to stir until the cream is cool.

☐ Pour into a serving dish and leave in the fridge or a cool place for 3 hours or until set.

THREE DECKERS
(Enough for six)

8oz. shortcrust pastry—see page 16
1½lb. fruit for cooking
4oz. Demerara sugar
milk
caster sugar

☐ Roll out pastry on a lightly floured board to ¼in. thickness. Cut out 1 round 1in. larger than a deep 9in. pie dish. Cut out 2 more rounds, one the same size as the base of the dish and one a little larger. Put the smallest round in the base of the pie dish.

☐ Prepare the fruit. You can use all one kind or a mixture of fruits. Put half the fruit in the dish and sprinkle with half the Demerara sugar.

☐ Cover with next largest round of pastry and add remaining fruit and sugar. Grease edge of pie dish. Cut a ½in. strip from round remaining pastry. Press on to edge of dish. Moisten strip and cover pie with remaining round of pastry. Press edges of pastry to seal. Decorate edges. Brush pie with milk.

☐ Cook for 15min. in centre of oven, pre-heated to 425 deg. F. or Mark 7, then reduce heat to 350 deg. F. or Mark 4 and cook for a further 40min., or until pastry is cooked. Remove from oven and sprinkle with caster sugar while still hot.

PEARS IN RED WINE
(Enough for four)

¼ pint red wine
4oz. caster sugar
1 clove
4 firm well shaped eating pears
1 large lemon
1 heaped teaspoon arrowroot
1oz. flaked almonds

☐ Pour wine and ¼ pint cold water into a saucepan. Add sugar and clove. Heat gently to dissolve sugar, then bring to the boil. Boil for 10-15min., or until slightly syrupy.

☐ Peel pears, leaving stalks in place. Using a teaspoon, carefully remove cores from base, keeping pears intact. Place pears in the syrup and spoon it over them. Cover pan and simmer gently for 10min., or until tender, coating them with syrup occasionally.

☐ While pears cook, peel rind from lemon in one long thin strip, being careful not to cut off any white pith. Leave peel to soak in a little cold water for 30min.

☐ Blend arrowroot with a little cold water. Remove pears from the syrup and stand upright in serving dish. Pour hot syrup on to arrowroot, stir well and return to pan. Bring to the boil, stirring all the time until thickened and transparent. Pour syrup over the pears. Leave to chill for 4 hours.

☐ Just before serving, put almonds on a sheet of foil on the grill pan. Grill until golden brown. Decorate each pear with a spiral of lemon peel and sprinkle with the browned almonds.

EGG YOLK SWEET
(Enough for three)

5oz. caster sugar
5 large egg yolks

☐ Put the sugar and 2 tablespoons cold water into a small pan. Stir over a very low heat until the sugar has dissolved. When the syrup begins to simmer and becomes translucent, remove from the heat and allow to cool at room temperature.
☐ Meanwhile, beat the yolks with a whisk until thick. Pour in the syrup in a thin stream, beating all the time. Put the bowl over a pan of hot water and cook, stirring all the time with a wooden spoon, for 10min., or until the mixture is smooth and thick enough to coat the spoon heavily. Don't let the mixture come to the boil or it will curdle. Strain through a fine nylon sieve and allow it to cool, when it will become thicker.
☐ Serve as a sweet in glasses or use as a cake icing.

MARBLE PUDDING
(Enough for six-eight)

6oz. self-raising flour
6oz. margarine
6oz. caster sugar
3 large eggs
milk
1oz. cocoa
¼ level teaspoon baking powder
15oz. tin chocolate dessert

☐ Sift the flour on to a piece of paper. Cream the margarine and sugar until light and fluffy. Beat the eggs and add them gradually to the creamed mixture, beating after each addition. If the mixture looks like curdling, fold in 1 tablespoon flour.
☐ Gradually fold in the flour and mix to a soft dropping consistency with milk, if necessary. Divide the mixture in half and fold the cocoa and baking powder into one half.
☐ Using a large spoon, put the chocolate mixture and plain mixture alternately into a greased 2 pint pudding basin. Cover with a piece of foil pleated in the centre to allow the pudding to rise. Steam or boil the pudding for 2 hours, replenishing the pan with boiling water whenever necessary.

☐ Turn the chocolate dessert into a pan. Add 1 tablespoon milk and heat gently. Turn out the pudding and pour on the hot sauce; serve immediately.

STAFFORDSHIRE SYLLABUB
(Enough for four-six)

1 medium-sized lemon
¼ pint medium-sweet cider
1 tablespoon brandy—optional
2 tablespoons sweet sherry
3oz. caster sugar
½ pint double cream

☐ Wipe the lemon. Finely grate lemon rind. Cut the lemon in half and squeeze out 2 tablespoons of juice. Put the lemon juice and most of the rind—keep a little for decoration—into a bowl. Add the cider, brandy, if used, and the sherry. Stir in the sugar and leave sugar to dissolve.
☐ Pour in the cream and whisk for about 5min., or until the mixture thickens and forms soft peaks. Whisk slowly as it starts to thicken.
Spoon into serving glasses.
☐ Leave at least 1 hour before serving. Sprinkle with the remaining lemon rind.

LEMON SOUFFLE
(Enough for eight)

3 large eggs
4½oz. caster sugar
1 large lemon
½oz. powdered gelatine
boiling water
5oz. carton double cream
5oz. carton single cream
2oz. almonds nibs
angelica

☐ Cut a piece of greaseproof paper long enough to go round a 5in soufflé dish and wide enough to stand 2in. higher than the dish. Grease the paper lightly with butter and secure round dish with transparent adhesive tape.
☐ Separate the eggs. Put the yolks and sugar in a large bowl. Finely grate lemon rind into bowl. Squeeze out and strain lemon juice into bowl. Put gelatine in a basin, add 2 tablespoons cold water to soften the gelatine, then add 4 tablespoons boiling water and leave gelatine to dissolve.
☐ Stand bowl of egg yolks, sugar and lemon over a pan of hot water, making sure bowl does not touch the water, and whisk for 10-15min. or until light and fluffy and thick enough to hold a trail of mixture for 5sec. Remove from heat and whisk until mixture cools. Trickle in

dissolved gelatine, beating all the time.
☐ Whip creams together until they form soft peaks. Whisk egg whites stiffly. When lemon mixture is just beginning to set, fold in the cream and then the egg whites. Pour into prepared soufflé dish and leave to set. It is best left in a cool place—but not the refrigerator.
☐ When set, carefully remove the paper using a palette knife dipped in hot water held against the soufflé itself. Dip knife frequently. Grill the nuts until golden brown. Allow to cool. Press them against the sides of the soufflé with a knife, until well coated.
☐ Decorate with some extra whipped cream and angelica.

RASPBERRY LIQUEUR GATEAU
(Enough for eight)

2 bought Victoria sponges
1 miniature bottle Cointreau
12oz. raspberries
5oz. carton double cream
1 tablespoon milk
1oz. caster sugar
1½oz. toasted flaked almonds

☐ Cut each Victoria sandwich into 2 layers. Sprinkle each layer with a little of the Cointreau, leaving about 1 teaspoonful in the bottle. Reserve ¼lb. raspberries and break up the others using a fork, but do not mash.
☐ Spread half of the raspberries on one sponge layer. Whip the cream and milk until standing in fairly stiff peaks. Fold in the sugar and rest of the Cointreau. Add a layer of sponge and spread it with about a third of the cream. Cover with another sponge layer and spread with the remaining raspberries. Top with the last layer.
☐ Spread the sides of the cake with some of the cream. Roll the sides lightly in the toasted almond flakes. Spoon remaining cream into a piping bag, fitted with a large star pipe. Pipe a border round the top. Put the whole raspberries in the centre and serve.

EVE'S PUDDING
(Enough for four-six)

1lb. cooking apples
3oz. Demerara sugar
grated rind of 1 large lemon
3oz. butter
3oz. caster sugar
1 large egg
4oz. self-raising flour

☐ Peel, core and slice the apples thinly. Arrange them in a greased ovenproof dish and sprinkle with the sugar, lemon rind and 1 tablespoon cold water.
☐ Cream the butter and caster sugar until light and fluffy. Beat the egg and beat it into the creamed mixture a little at a time. Sift the flour and fold it in using a metal spoon.
☐ Spread the sponge mixture over the apples and bake for 40-45min., or until sponge is well risen and golden brown, in centre of oven, pre-heated to 350 deg. F. or Mark 4.

COFFEE CREAMS
(Enough for six)

3 level teaspoons powdered gelatine
4 level teaspoons instant coffee
1 tablespoon hot water
1 large egg white
3oz. caster sugar
5oz. carton double cream
½ pint single cream
1 tablespoon brandy
12oz. toasted almonds

☐ Put the gelatine into a small bowl and add 4 tablespoons cold water. Stand the bowl in a saucepan of hot water and heat gently until the gelatine has dissolved.
☐ Dissolve the coffee in the hot water. Remove the bowl of dissolved gelatine and stir in the coffee. Leave to cool.
☐ Meanwhile, put the egg white and the caster sugar in a bowl and whisk until thick and glossy—this takes about 10min. by hand. Reserve 2 tablespoons of the double cream and the same amount of single cream and whisk the remainder until standing in soft peaks. Whisk the creams into the egg white and sugar and add the brandy. Whisk for a few minutes until smooth and fairly thick. Whisk in the cooled but still liquid gelatine.
☐ Pour into 6 small glasses or into 1 large dish. Leave for 1 hour in a cool place to set. Just before serving whisk the reserved creams together until standing in soft peaks. Spoon into a piping bag fitted with a large star pipe. Pipe swirls on top of the coffee creams. Place 2 toasted almonds in the cream.

APPLE DUMPLINGS
(Enough for four)

8oz. shortcrust pastry—see page 16
4 large cooking apples
2oz. Demerara sugar
1oz. sultanas
1oz. chopped mixed peel
milk
1oz. caster sugar

☐ Roll out the pastry to a round and cut out 4 rounds large enough to enclose the apples. Peel the apples and remove the cores keeping the apples whole. Mix the Demerara sugar with the sultanas and peel and stuff this mixture into the cores of the apples.
☐ Moisten the edge of the pastry rounds and gather the edges to the top and press well to seal. Turn apples over. Brush with milk.
☐ Place on a greased baking tray and bake for 10min., towards top of oven, pre-heated to 425 deg. F. or Mark 7, then reduce heat to 325 deg. F. or Mark 3 and cook for 35min., or until the apples are soft.
☐ Dredge with the caster sugar and serve hot or cold with custard or cream.

RICE PUDDING
(Enough for four)

1½oz. Carolina rice
1oz. caster sugar
1 pint milk
½oz. butter
ground nutmeg

☐ Wash the rice and put it into a greased ovenproof dish with the sugar. Pour on the milk. Cut the butter into shavings and add to the milk with some ground nutmeg sprinkled on top.
☐ Bake for 2 hours in lower part of oven, pre-heated to 300 deg. F. or Mark 2. Stir the pudding once after 30min.

BAKED ALASKA
(Enough for four)

1 bought sponge
11oz. tin strawberries
3 large egg whites
6oz. caster sugar
1 family block vanilla ice cream

☐ Place the sponge on a flat ovenproof dish and spoon the fruit and some of the juice over it. Add only enough juice to just moisten the sponge.
☐ Whisk the egg whites until standing in stiff peaks. Whisk in half the sugar until the meringue is stiff again and then gently fold in the remaining sugar.
☐ Put the block of ice cream on the sponge, making sure it's frozen solid. Cover immediately with meringue, making sure there are no holes in the covering. Peak the meringue.
☐ Bake for 2-3min., or until the meringue peaks become golden brown, in centre of oven, pre-heated to 450 deg. F. or Mark 8. Serve at once.

FIGS IN PORT
(Enough for four)

1 medium-sized lemon
1lb. 14oz. tin green figs
2 tablespoons port

☐ Wash the lemon. Thinly peel off rind, leaving behind the white pith. Squeeze out and strain the juice. Put the figs and lemon rind into a saucepan.
☐ Heat gently for 10min., until the juice is just starting to boil. Add the lemon juice and turn into a serving dish. Stir in the port and leave until cold. Remove the lemon rind before serving.

PLUM CRUMBLE
(Enough for four)

1lb. 4oz. tin Victoria plums
6oz. plain flour
3oz. butter
3oz. caster sugar

☐ Turn the plums and juice out of their tin into an ovenproof dish. Sift the flour and rub in the butter until the mixture looks like fine breadcrumbs. Stir in the sugar.
☐ Cover the fruit with this mixture, sprinkling it all over. Bake for 30-40min. in centre of oven, pre-heated to 375 deg. F. or Mark 5.

CUSTARD TART
(Enough for four)

6oz. shortcrust pastry—see page 16
3 large eggs
1½oz. caster sugar
½ pint milk
ground nutmeg

☐ Roll out the pastry and use to line a deep 8in. pie plate. Trim and decorate the edge.
☐ Whisk the eggs with the sugar. Warm the milk until it's lukewarm and pour it on to the egg mixture, stirring. Strain the custard into the pastry case. Stand the pie plate on a baking tray and sprinkle the custard with nutmeg.
☐ Bake for 10min., in centre of oven, pre-heated to 425 deg. F. or Mark 7, then reduce heat to 350 deg. F. or Mark 4 and cook for 20min., or until the custard is set and the pastry golden brown and cooked. Allow to cool and serve cold.

CINNAMON ORANGE PUDDING
(Enough for four)

5oz. soft brown sugar
11oz. tin mandarin oranges
4oz. margarine
2 large eggs
4oz. wholemeal flour
½ level teaspoon baking powder
1 level teaspoon ground cinnamon
pinch of salt
½ level teaspoon arrowroot

☐ Grease a 9in. pie dish and coat the inside with 1oz. of the sugar. Drain the mandarins. Put half the fruit in dish. Cream the margarine and rest of sugar.
☐ Beat the eggs and add a little at a time to the creamed mixture, beating after each addition. Sift the flour, baking powder, cinnamon and salt. Fold into the creamed mixture. Add 1-2 tablespoons of the mandarin syrup to mix.
☐ Spread mixture over the fruit. Bake for 45min., in centre of oven, pre-heated to 350 deg. F. or Mark 4.
☐ Meanwhile blend the arrowroot with 2 tablespoons mandarin syrup. Bring remainder to the boil, then pour on to the arrowroot, stirring. Return to the pan and bring to the boil, stirring until thick and clear. Cook gently for 2min., stirring. Arrange rest of mandarins on pudding and serve with the hot sauce.

JAM ROLY-POLY
(Enough for six)

6oz. suet crust pastry—see page 17
8 level tablespoons raspberry jam
milk

☐ Roll out the pastry to a large oblong about 8in. by 10in. Spread with the jam leaving a ¼in. border all round. Brush the edges with milk and roll the pastry evenly starting at one short end. Place the roll on a large piece of foil and wrap the foil loosely round the roll to allow it to rise.
☐ Steam for 1½-2 hours over fast boiling water, replenishing the pan with more boiling water as it evaporates. Serve hot with custard.

MELON BASKET
(Enough for four)

1 medium-sized melon
11oz. tin mandarin oranges
8oz. packet frozen strawberries
a little brandy—optional
sugar for dredging

☐ Cut the top off the melon and take out the flesh and pips. Chop the flesh into cubes and put in a large mixing bowl. Add the mandarin oranges and strawberries. A tablespoon of brandy may be added, if liked. Return the fruit to the melon shell and sprinkle with caster sugar. Chill before serving.

Perfect Cakes

Making a batch of cakes to last the whole week isn't possible for most of us these days and cake-making seems to be confined purely to occasions. Here are lots of super recipes from the grand to the everyday to tempt you back to the kitchen

GATEAU TIA MARIA

6oz. plain flour
½ level teaspoon salt
2 level teaspoons baking powder
5oz. Demerara sugar
2 large eggs
6 tablespoons salad oil
3 level tablespoons instant coffee
1 tablespoon boiling water
4 tablespoons milk
1½oz. shelled walnuts
4oz. granulated sugar
3 tablespoons Tia Maria or brandy—
optional
2oz. flaked almonds
5oz. carton double cream

☐ Sift flour, salt and baking powder into a mixing bowl. Stir in Demerara sugar. Separate eggs. Add oil to yolks. Dissolve 2 level tablespoons coffee in boiling water. Add milk then pour into egg mixture. Finely chop 1oz. walnuts. Whisk coffee and egg liquid until well mixed.
☐ Make a well in centre of dry ingredients. Pour in liquid. Add chopped walnuts; beat well until smooth. Whisk egg whites stiffly. Fold into mixture.
☐ Pour into a lightly greased, round 7½in. cake tin. Cook for 30min. in centre of oven, pre-heated to 375 deg. F. or Mark 5, then reduce heat to 350 deg. F. or Mark 4 and continue cooking for a further 15min., until firm to the touch. Leave to cool in tin for 30min. Turn out and finish cooling on a wire rack.
☐ Dissolve granulated sugar in ¼ pint water over a low heat. Bring to boil and boil for 5min. Remove from heat. Blend remaining coffee with 2 tablespoons Tia Maria, brandy or water. Pour on hot syrup. Leave to cool.
☐ When cake is cold, return it to cake tin. Make a few holes in cake with a skewer. Pour coffee syrup over cake. Cover with a plate, so that it is not touching cake, and leave overnight or for several hours in a cool place.

☐ Lightly toast almonds under a moderately hot grill. Leave to cool.
☐ Just before serving, whip cream. Stir in remaining Tia Maria, or brandy, if liked. Spread a third of cream round sides of cake. Press toasted nuts round sides of cake. Place cake on serving plate. Spoon remaining cream into a piping bag fitted with a large star pipe. Decorate top edge by piping on a border of cream. Arrange rest of walnuts on cream. Once cake has been decorated, it must be eaten within a day.

COFFEE LAYER

5½oz. plain flour
3 level tablespoons cocoa
1½oz. margarine
1½oz. lard
3½oz. caster sugar
½oz. blanched almonds
1 large egg and 1 large egg yolk
2oz. butter
1½oz. self-raising flour
2 teaspoons coffee essence
2 teaspoons milk
1oz. ground almonds
6 level tablespoons raspberry jam
5oz. carton double cream
6 sweet coffee beans

☐ Sift the plain flour and 3 level dessertspoons cocoa into a bowl. Rub in the margarine and lard until the mixture looks like fine breadcrumbs. Stir in 1½oz. caster sugar. Finely chop the almonds and stir into the flour and sugar. Make a well in the centre and add the egg yolk and 2 teaspoons cold water. Mix to a stiff dough adding a little more water if necessary. Wrap pastry in a piece of greaseproof paper and leave in a cool place.
☐ Cream the butter and remaining caster sugar until light and fluffy. Beat the egg and gradually beat it into the

creamed mixture. Sift the self-raising flour and rest of the cocoa and fold in. Mix the coffee essence and milk. Fold the ground almonds and then the coffee liquid into the creamed mixture.
☐ Lightly flour a working surface and roll the pastry to 1½in. larger than an 8in. fluted flan ring. Stand the flan ring on a baking tray. Carefully line the flan ring with the pastry, pushing it well down into the corners. Trim off excess pastry by pushing a rolling pin over the top.
☐ Spread the jam in the base of the flan. Spoon the filling into the flan and smooth the top. Bake for 15min., in centre of oven, pre-heated to 400 deg. F. or Mark 6 then reduce heat to 350 deg. F. or Mark 4 and cook for 15-20min. more until well risen and firm to the touch. Remove and leave to cool on the tray for 10min. Whip the cream and spoon it into a piping bag fitted with a large star pipe. Decorate the cake with swirls of whipped cream topped with sweet coffee beans.

Above: Gâteau Tia Maria, right: Coffee Layer Flan

BLACK BUN

2lb. plain flour
salt
¼lb. butter
7 large eggs
6oz. whole blanched almonds
1lb. stoned raisins
1 heaped teaspoon ground cinnamon
1 heaped teaspoon ground ginger
1 level teaspoon ground allspice
½ level teaspoon ground black pepper
1 heaped teaspoon cream of tartar
1 level teaspoon bicarbonate of soda
2lb. currants
¼lb. chopped mixed peel
¼lb. light brown sugar
1 tablespoon brandy
1 tablespoon rum
¼ pint buttermilk or ordinary milk

☐ Sift 1lb. flour with a pinch of salt. Rub in the butter until the mixture looks like breadcrumbs. Beat 4 eggs and stir enough into the mixture to make a stiff dough. Grease a round 9in. cake tin with a loose base. Roll out the dough on a floured board to ¼in. thickness. Cut a strip as deep as the tin and long enough to go round it. Fit this strip inside the tin; moisten the short ends and mould them smoothly together. Cut a round to fit the top of the tin and reserve it. Roll pastry trimmings to a round to fit bottom of tin. Moisten edge and fit into tin; then mould the round to the pastry strip. Prick the bottom well.
☐ Chop almonds roughly. Chop the raisins. Sift the rest of the flour, a pinch of salt, the cinnamon, ginger, allspice, black pepper, cream of tartar and bicarbonate of soda into a large bowl. Stir in almonds, raisins, currants, peel, brown sugar, brandy and rum.
☐ Beat the rest of eggs with the buttermilk or ordinary milk. Save a little for brushing the top of the cake. Add remainder to mixture to thoroughly moisten. Pack this mixture into the pastry lined tin and flatten it.
☐ Moisten the edge of the reserved pastry round and put in place. Pinch edges together to seal. Make 4 holes of equal distance apart by pushing a skewer right down to the bottom of the tin. Brush top lightly with the rest of the egg and milk mixture. Prick the pastry.
☐ Bake for 3 hours in centre of oven, pre-heated to 350 deg. F. or Mark 4. Test by pushing a skewer into one of the holes. If the skewer is clean when withdrawn, the cake is cooked.
☐ Leave to cool in the tin, then remove on to a wire rack to cool thoroughly.
☐ Tradition says you should keep this cake for 10 days before cutting it.

QUICK CHOCOLATE LOG

1 bought chocolate Swiss roll
5½oz. icing sugar
a little egg white
5oz. plain chocolate
1oz. bought marzipan
green and red food colourings

☐ Cut a 2½in. slice from one end of the roll. Sift 3oz. sugar into a bowl. Add a teaspoon of the egg white and mix the icing until fairly stiff. Put a teaspoon of the icing on one side of the log and press on the slice. Spread a little icing on a cake board and place the roll on the icing.
☐ Break the chocolate into a bowl and stand it over a pan of hot water to melt. Sift the remaining sugar. Stir the sugar into the melted chocolate and quickly spread it over the roll, not forgetting the ends.
☐ Put the remaining icing into a small piping bag fitted with a small plain pipe. Pipe rings at either end of the log and on the end of the small slice. Colour ⅔ of the marzipan green and the rest red. Make holly leaves and berries. Arrange these by the top slice. Decorate with a toy robin.

VICTORIA SANDWICH

4oz. self-raising flour
pinch of salt
4oz. margarine
5oz. caster sugar
2 large eggs
4 heaped tablespoons raspberry jam
5oz. carton double cream

☐ Sift the flour and salt. Cream together margarine and 4oz. sugar until light and fluffy. Lightly beat the eggs and gradually beat into the creamed mixture. If it begins to curdle, add 1 tablespoon flour. Carefully fold in half the flour, using a large metal spoon. Fold in the remaining flour.
☐ Divide the mixture between 2 greased 6in. sandwich tins and spread lightly. Bake for 20-30min. in centre of oven, pre-heated to 350 deg. F. or Mark 4.
☐ Spread one cake with the jam. Whip the cream; spread over the jam and sandwich with the second cake. Dredge remaining caster sugar over top.

HIGHLAND SLIM CAKES
(Makes fifteen cakes)

8oz. self-raising flour
pinch of salt
2oz. butter
1 large egg
milk to mix
1oz. lard

☐ Sift the flour and salt into a bowl. Rub in the butter. Lightly beat the egg and add to flour with enough milk to make a stiff dough. Roll out on a lightly floured board to ¼in. thickness. Cut into rounds using a 2in. plain cutter.
☐ Heat a griddle or heavy frying pan and grease with lard. Cook the Slim Cakes in batches for 2-3min. each side or until golden. Serve hot.

BUTTERMILK CAKE

1lb. plain flour
¼ level teaspoon salt
8oz. butter
8oz. soft brown sugar
8oz. sultanas
4oz. glacé cherries
4oz. currants
1½ level teaspoons ground mixed spice
1 level teaspoon bicarbonate of soda
1 level tablespoon black treacle
½ pint buttermilk

☐ Sift the flour and salt into a mixing bowl. Rub in the butter until the mixture looks like fine breadcrumbs. Stir in the sugar and sultanas. Chop the cherries and add to the mixture, together with the currants, mixed spice and bicarbonate of soda. Mix in the treacle and buttermilk.
☐ Turn into a greased and lined 8in. cake tin. Level off top. Bake for 2½ hours in centre of oven, pre-heated to 375 deg. F. or Mark 5.

RICH FRUIT CAKE

4oz. whole blanched almonds
4oz. glacé cherries
1lb. plain flour
pinch of salt
12oz. butter
12oz. Demerara sugar
6 large eggs
1lb. sultanas
1lb. currants
6oz. stoned raisins
4oz. chopped mixed peel
½ level teaspoon ground mixed spice
2 level tablespoons black treacle
4 tablespoons brandy

☐ Chop almonds fairly finely. Chop the cherries. Sift the flour and salt together.
☐ Cream the butter until light and fluffy. Gradually beat in the sugar until mixture is light in colour again. Beat the eggs together, then add to the creamed mixture beating all the time and adding a little flour with the last of the egg. Fold in the remaining flour.
☐ Stir in the dried fruit, almonds, cherries, peel, spice, treacle and brandy. Mix well—the mixture should be stiff. Turn mixture into a round 9in. cake tin which has been greased and lined with a double thickness of greaseproof paper. The paper should be greased well. Smooth the top and make a hollow in the centre. Tie a double thickness of brown paper round the outside of the tin.
☐ Cover the cake with a piece of brown paper, laying it over the whole tin so it does not touch the mixture. Bake for 6 hours in centre of oven, pre-heated to 275 deg. F. or Mark 1.
☐ When the cake is nearing the end of its cooking time, push a skewer through the centre of the cake to the bottom. If the skewer is clean when withdrawn, the cake is cooked.
☐ Leave the cake overnight in its tin to cool completely. Then wrap in clean greaseproof paper and store in a tin, or wrap in aluminium foil and store on a shelf where it is cool, until you want to eat it. This cake may be iced if liked.

CELEBRATION CAKE

double Victoria Sandwich mixture—see page 142
8oz. butter
16oz. icing sugar
1oz. green grapes
two 11oz. tins mandarin oranges
3oz. flaked almonds
4oz. glacé cherries
¼ pint arrowroot glaze—see page 27

☐ Cook the double quantity of Victoria Sandwich—see page 142—in a round 8in. cake tin for 45-50min., or until golden brown, in centre of oven, pre-heated to 350 deg. F. or Mark 4.
☐ Cream the butter in a large bowl. Sift in the icing sugar a little at a time and beat well until fluffy.
☐ Wash the grapes, halve them and remove the pips. Drain and reserve juice from the oranges. Reserve one tin of oranges and roughly chop remainder. Toast the almonds until golden.
☐ When the sponge has cooled cut it into three layers. Sandwich them together with butter cream and sprinkle the chopped orange segments between each layer. Leave the top layer plain. Spread the sides of the cake with butter cream and roll the cake in the toasted almonds, pressing them on. Using the whole orange segments, start ½in. in from the top edge and arrange a circle of orange segments. Make an inner circle of glacé cherries, and a circle of grape halves. Arrange 6 orange segments in the centre and top with a cherry. Spoon the remaining butter cream into a piping bag fitted with a large star pipe. Pipe stars round the edge.
☐ Make arrowroot glaze using ¼ pint reserved mandarin juice. Cool for 5min., and carefully spoon over the fruit. Leave for 30min. to set.

JAM TURNOVERS
(Makes four turnovers)

13oz. packet frozen puff pastry
8 level tablespoons raspberry jam
1 small egg white
caster sugar

☐ Allow pastry to thaw for at least 1 hour. Lightly flour a working surface. Roll the pastry to a 13in. square. Trim off the edges. Divide the pastry into 4 squares. Put 2 tablespoons jam into the centre of each square. Moisten two edges with water and fold over to make a triangle. Seal the edges with a fork.
☐ Lightly beat the egg white. Brush this over the puffs and sprinkle with caster sugar. Place on a lightly greased baking tray and cook for 20min. towards top of oven, pre-heated to 425 deg. F. or Mark 7, then reduce heat to 375 deg. F. or Mark 5 and cook for a further 5-10min. or until well risen and golden brown. Cool on a wire rack.

HONIED BOWS
(Makes twelve bows)

8oz. plain flour
1 level teaspoon baking powder
¼ level teaspoon salt
5 tablespoons olive oil
3 large eggs
finely grated rind of 1 small orange or lemon
oil for deep frying
4 level tablespoons honey
2oz. walnuts
ground cinnamon

☐ Sift the flour twice with the baking powder and salt. Mix with 5 tablespoons olive oil. Beat the eggs, and add gradually to the flour mixture with the orange or lemon rind and mix to a soft but not sticky dough. Leave in the fridge for 1 hour.
☐ Heat the oil to the correct temperature—see page 15.
☐ Roll out on a lightly floured board to ⅛in. thick and cut into 12in. strips, each 1in. wide, using a pastry wheel or a very sharp knife. Carefully tie in bows and fry two at a time in deep hot oil until puffed and golden. Drain on kitchen paper. Then pile on a serving dish.
☐ Warm the honey until runny. Chop the nuts. Pour honey over the bows. Sprinkle with cinnamon and nuts.

BRANDY SNAPS
(Makes ten snaps)

2oz. granulated sugar
2 level tablespoons golden syrup
2oz. butter
2oz. plain flour
pinch of salt
1½ level teaspoons ground ginger
1 tablespoon lemon juice
5oz. carton double cream
1 tablespoon brandy—optional

☐ Put the sugar, syrup and butter into a small saucepan. Heat gently until the butter and sugar have melted. Sift the flour, salt and ginger together. Stir into the melted ingredients, together with the lemon juice. Mix well, using a wooden spoon. Drop teaspoons of the mixture, 4in. apart to allow for spreading, on to greased baking trays. Do not cook more than 4 at a time. Cook for 10min., or until dark golden brown, in centre of oven, pre-heated to 350 deg. F. or Mark 4. Leave to cool on the baking trays for 1min.
☐ Slide brandy snaps off the trays using a palette knife, and immediately roll round the handle of a wooden spoon. They must be rolled when still hot. Leave on the handle to harden, then slide off carefully as they are brittle when cold. If snaps become too brittle to roll, put the tray back in the oven until they soften again. Repeat the cooking and rolling process until all the brandy snaps are ready for filling.
☐ Whip the cream stiffly and stir in the brandy, if used. Pipe or spoon the cream into each end of the brandy snaps. Once filled, serve the brandy snaps within 1 hour, as they become soft with the cream filling. Unfilled brandy snaps can be stored in an airtight tin for a week or more. If any break, crush them into rough pieces and sprinkle over ice cream for a sweet.

FRUIT LOAF

2oz. glacé cherries
1lb. plain flour
2 heaped teaspoons baking powder
8oz. margarine
8oz. caster sugar
2 large eggs
8oz. currants
8oz. sultanas
2oz. chopped mixed peel
ground nutmeg
milk

☐ Chop the glacé cherries roughly. Sift flour and baking powder into a bowl. Cream margarine and sugar until fluffy. Beat eggs and add gradually to creamed mixture beating well. Fold in flour using a large metal spoon. Then fold in fruit and peel and add nutmeg to flavour. Add milk if necessary to give a fairly stiff dropping consistency.
☐ Turn into a 2lb. loaf tin, greased and lined with greased greaseproof paper. Cook for 2½-3 hours in centre of oven, pre-heated to 325 deg. F. or Mark 3.

TRUFFLE CAKES
(Makes ten truffles)

8oz. sponge cake crumbs
½oz. cocoa
1oz. ground almonds
6 level tablespoons apricot jam
1 teaspoon rum or brandy—optional
chocolate vermicelli

☐ Mix crumbs, cocoa and almonds. Heat jam. Pour into crumbs, together with rum or brandy, if used.
☐ Form into 10 balls, then toss in the chocolate vermicelli.

CHOCOLATE BOXES AND FINGERS
(Makes twelve boxes, ten fingers)

6oz. butter or margarine
4oz. caster sugar
2 large eggs
3oz. self-raising flour
1½oz. cocoa
milk to mix
6oz. plain chocolate
11oz. icing sugar
2 rounded tablespoons raspberry jam
walnut halves

☐ Cream 4oz. butter or margarine with the caster sugar until fluffy. Beat eggs lightly. Add a little at a time to creamed mixture, beating well after each addition. Sift flour and 1oz. cocoa. Fold in flour and cocoa using a tablespoon. A little milk may be added to give a soft dropping consistency. Spoon into a greased and lined baking tin, 11in. by 7in. Smooth into corners.
☐ Cook for 15-20min., or until well risen and firm to touch, just above centre of oven, pre-heated to 375 deg. F. or Mark 5. Turn out and cool on a wire rack.
☐ Cut in half and trim ½in. off the outside edges from one half. Cut cake into twelve 1½in. squares.
☐ Break chocolate on to a plate. Stand over a pan of hot water to melt. Mark a rectangle about 1½ times the size of the baking tin, on a sheet of greaseproof paper. Spread melted chocolate to size of rectangle. As it begins to set, mark into 1¾in. squares. Leave to set.
☐ Cream remaining butter or margarine and 5oz. icing sugar until smooth. Spoon into piping bag fitted with a small fluted pipe.
☐ Melt the jam then spread the sides of the cake squares with jam. Press chocolate squares round the cakes to form boxes. Pipe butter cream lines over the top of each cake. Put the remaining chocolate squares on the top of cakes. Sift remaining icing sugar and cocoa into a small basin; add enough water to mix to thick coating consistency. Spread icing over remaining sponge cake. Cut into fingers and decorate each with a walnut.

MADELEINES
(Makes ten cakes)

4oz. self-raising flour
pinch of salt
4oz. margarine
4oz. caster sugar
2 large eggs
2 level tablespoons red jam
5 glacé cherries
angelica
2oz. desiccated coconut

☐ Sift flour and salt. Cream margarine and sugar until light and fluffy. Lightly beat eggs; add gradually to creamed mixture, beating all the time. Add 1 tablespoon flour if it looks like curdling. Sift half flour into mixture; fold it in carefully, using a large metal spoon. Repeat with remaining flour until it is all folded in.
☐ Half-fill 10 greased dariole moulds with the mixture. Cook for 15-20min. towards top of oven, pre-heated to 375 deg. F. or Mark 5. Turn out and cool on a wire rack.
☐ Melt jam. Cut cherries in half. Cut 10 pieces of angelica. Push a skewer through base of cake to hold while brushing. Brush sides with hot jam and roll each cake in coconut. Decorate each with ½ cherry and a piece of angelica.

CHOCOLATE BUTTERFLIES
(Makes twelve butterflies)

3oz. self-raising flour
pinch of salt
1oz. cocoa
pinch of baking powder
6oz. butter
4oz. caster sugar
2 large eggs
4½oz. icing sugar

☐ Sift flour, salt, cocoa and baking powder together.
☐ Cream 4oz. butter and caster sugar until light and fluffy. Lightly beat the eggs then gradually add to the creamed mixture, beating all the time. Fold in the flour mixture gradually. Spoon into 12 paper baking cases standing on a baking tray.
☐ Bake for 12-15min., towards top of oven, pre-heated to 375 deg. F. or Mark 5. Remove and cool.
☐ Cream rest of butter and 4oz. icing sugar until smooth. Spoon mixture into a piping bag fitted with a small star pipe. Cut the tops off the cakes and cut these in half. Sift on rest of icing sugar. Pipe butter cream on top of each cake; stick the two top halves in to form wings. Pipe cream down the centre.

ROSE CAKES AND CAULIFLOWERS
(Makes eight roses, seven cauliflowers)

Victoria Sandwich mixture—see page 142
5oz. bought marzipan
red and green vegetable colouring
4 level tablespoons red jam
2oz. almond nibs
1½oz. butter
3oz. icing sugar

☐ Put cake mixture into an 11in. by 7in. tin. Cook for 15-20min. just above centre of oven, pre-heated to 375 deg. F. or Mark 5.
☐ Cut off 1½oz. marzipan; colour it pink. Colour remainder green. Roll marzipan thinly. Cut out 56 pink circles using a ½in. plain cutter and 21 green circles using a 2½in. plain cutter. Cut a third off each green circle.
☐ Heat jam until boiling, then sieve. Cut cooled sponge into 2½in. circles using a plain cutter. Brush top and sides of each cake with jam. Coat sides of 8 pieces with almonds. Mould 3 green leaves round each remaining cake, straight edges to base. Arrange 7 pink circles on top of each nutty cake to form a rose. Put a little jam in centre. Cream butter and sugar until smooth. Fill a piping bag fitted with a small star pipe. Pipe stars on cauliflowers and on edge of roses.

145

ALMOND CHEESECAKES
(Makes twenty-four cakes)

8oz. packet frozen puff pastry
3oz. sweet almonds
3 bitter almonds
boiling water
1oz. butter
½ large lemon
2 large eggs
2oz. caster sugar
1 teaspoon rosewater

☐ Allow pastry to thaw for at least 1 hour. Roll out on a lightly floured board until it is ¼in. thick. Cut out 24 rounds using a 3in. plain cutter. Line 24 patty tins. Leave in a cool place until required.
☐ Drop sweet and bitter almonds into boiling water. Leave for 1min. Drain and skin. Chop very finely. Melt butter. Finely grate lemon rind and squeeze out and strain juice.
☐ Beat the eggs for 5min. until frothy. Add cooled butter, lemon rind and juice, sugar, rosewater and eggs to almonds.
☐ Divide mixture between the lined patty tins. Bake for 5min. on 2 shelves towards top of oven, pre-heated to 450 deg. F. or Mark 8, then reduce heat to 400 deg. F. or Mark 6 and cook for a further 12min. or until risen and golden. Change tins over after 4min.

PALMIERS
(Makes ten palmiers)

13oz. packet frozen puff pastry
4oz. caster sugar
5oz. carton double cream

☐ Allow the pastry to thaw for at least 1 hour. Roll to a 16in. square using caster sugar rather than flour to prevent the pastry sticking. Trim off a border all the way round to give a good square. Sprinkle the pastry generously with caster sugar. Fold the sides of the pastry to the centre. Press lightly with a rolling pin. Sprinkle with sugar again. Repeat the folding of the sides to centre, and then fold one side on top of the other. Press again with a rolling pin. Dredge with caster sugar.
☐ Cut the pastry roll into ½in. slices, using a sharp knife. Place on a wet baking tray, cut sides down, leaving 3in. space between them to allow for spreading. Cook for 10min., or until golden, in upper part of oven, pre-heated to 425 deg. F. or Mark 7. Turn the pastries over and cook for a further 10-15min., until golden and crisp. Remove on to cooling racks.
☐ Whip the double cream until standing in peaks and place a spoonful on half of the palmiers. Use the others to make sandwiches.

POPE LADY CAKE

6oz. butter
8oz. caster sugar
8 large egg whites
8oz. plain flour
1oz. cornflour
½ level teaspoon baking powder
lemon or almond essence or rosewater

☐ Cream the butter and sugar with 4 egg whites until light and fluffy. Sift flour, cornflour and baking powder together and fold into the mixture. Whisk the remaining egg whites until very stiff and fold gently into the mixture with lemon or almond essence or rosewater to flavour.
☐ Turn the mixture into a greased, round 7½in. cake tin lined with greased, greaseproof paper. Bake for 1½ hours in centre of oven, pre-heated to 300 deg. F. or Mark 2. Cool on a wire rack.

CHOUX BUNS
(Makes eight buns)

2oz. choux pastry—see page 20
5oz. carton double cream
2 level teaspoons caster sugar
icing sugar

☐ Spoon pastry into a piping bag fitted with a ½in. plain pipe. Pipe 8 blobs about 1in. high and 3in. apart on to wet baking trays. Cover with deep roasting tins.
☐ Cook for 40min., or until buns are golden brown, in centre of oven, pre-heated to 400 deg. F. or Mark 6. Do not uncover during cooking. Cool.
☐ Whisk cream until it stands in soft peaks. Fold in caster sugar. Spoon cream into piping bag with ½in. plain pipe. Split cold buns and remove any uncooked mixture. Pipe or spoon in the cream. Dust with icing sugar.

WHITBY YULE CAKE

1lb. plain flour
8oz. butter
6oz. soft brown sugar
¼oz. ground cinnamon
2 level teaspoons ground nutmeg
6oz. stoned raisins
6oz. currants
2oz. candied lemon peel
2oz. blanched almonds
2 large eggs
2 tablespoons brandy
6 tablespoons single cream

☐ Sift the flour into a bowl. Rub in the butter until the mixture looks like fine breadcrumbs. Stir in the sugar, cinnamon, nutmeg, raisins and currants. Chop the peel and almonds and stir in. Beat the eggs with the brandy and add to the bowl. Mix with the cream to make a stiff dough.
☐ Press the mixture into a greased, 13½in. by 9½in. Swiss roll tin lined with greased greaseproof paper. Bake for 1 hour in centre of oven, pre-heated to 350 deg. F. or Mark 4. Turn on to a wire rack to cool and break or cut into rough pieces when cold.

CREAM HORNS
(Makes twelve cream horns)

8oz. flaky pastry—see page 20
1oz. butter
milk
caster sugar
12 level teaspoons raspberry jam
½ pint double cream
icing sugar

☐ Roll out pastry thinly, then cut twelve 1in. wide strips—each about 12in. long. Melt the butter. Brush 12 cream horn tins with the butter. Moisten one side of each strip of pastry with water. Starting at the pointed end of each tin, wind pastry strip round, making sure that the moistened side faces inwards and that the strip overlaps by about ¼in. Transfer the cream horns to a baking tray. Stand in a cool place for 30min.
☐ Bake for 10min. in upper part of oven, pre-heated to 450 deg. F. or Mark 8. Remove from the oven; brush with milk and dust with caster sugar. Transfer to a cooling rack and cool for about 5min. Carefully remove the tins. Leave the cream horns to cool.
☐ Place a teaspoon of jam in the bottom of each horn. Whip the cream until standing in peaks. Stir in icing sugar to sweeten to taste. Fill horns with cream.

OVINGTON FRUIT CAKE

8oz. plain flour
1 level teaspoon baking powder
8oz. ground rice or semolina
8oz. butter
8oz. caster sugar
3 large eggs
2oz. chopped mixed peel
12oz. currants
milk to mix

☐ Sift the flour, baking powder and ground rice or semolina into a bowl. Cream together the butter and sugar until light and fluffy. Beat in the eggs one at a time.
☐ Mix the peel with the currants. Add to the creamed mixture alternately with the flour. Mix in about 1 tablespoon milk to give a fairly stiff mixture.
☐ Turn mixture in a greased 7in. cake tin, lined with greased greaseproof paper. Bake for 2 hours in centre of oven, pre-heated to 350 deg. F. or Mark 4. Insert a skewer into the cake to test if it is cooked. If the skewer is hot and clean when removed the cake is done. Let the cake cool in tin.
☐ This cake improves with keeping a few days before cutting.

DUNDEE CAKE

10oz. plain flour
8oz. butter
8oz. caster sugar
5 standard eggs
4oz. currants
4oz. sultanas
4oz. stoned raisins
4oz. chopped mixed peel
3oz. ground almonds
pinch of salt
1 level teaspoon bicarbonate of soda
1 dessertspoon milk
3oz. whole blanched almonds

☐ Sift the flour into a bowl. Cream butter and sugar until light and fluffy. Beat eggs lightly. Add egg gradually, beating all the time. Fold in the flour. Stir in the dried fruit, peel, ground almonds and salt. Dissolve bicarbonate of soda in the milk, stir into the mixture. Turn into a greased round 8in. cake tin lined with greased greaseproof paper. Make a hollow in the centre. Cover the top with the almonds.
☐ Bake for 2 hours in centre of oven, pre-heated to 325 deg. F. or Mark 3.
☐ Insert a skewer to see if cooked. It should be clean when withdrawn. Allow cake to cool in tin.

YORKSHIRE PARKIN

4oz. self-raising flour
1 level teaspoon ground ginger
8oz. medium oatmeal
4oz. soft brown sugar
4oz. golden syrup
3 tablespoons milk
2oz. butter
1 large egg

☐ Sift flour and ginger into a bowl. Mix in oatmeal and sugar. Heat syrup, milk and butter in a pan, stirring until melted. Cool a little. Beat egg lightly. Stir into syrup mixture and add to dry ingredients and mix well.
☐ Spread mixture in a greased 9in. square tin. Bake for 1 hour in centre of oven, pre-heated to 325 deg. F. or Mark 3. Allow to cool in tin, then cut into large pieces and store in an airtight tin.
☐ Parkin is better for the keeping.

SULTANA CAKE

8oz. self-raising flour
salt
4oz. margarine
4oz. granulated sugar
6oz. sultanas
grated rind of 1 large lemon
1 large egg
milk

☐ Sift flour and salt into a bowl. Rub in margarine until the mixture looks like breadcrumbs. Stir in sugar, sultanas and the lemon rind. Beat egg lightly. Add egg to dry ingredients and mix well with a wooden spoon, adding just enough milk to make the mixture moist but not wet. The mixture should just drop from a spoon.
☐ Turn into a greased, round 6in. cake tin, lined with greased greaseproof paper. Bake for 1¼ hours in centre of oven, pre-heated to 375 deg. F. or Mark 5. Turn out and cool on a wire rack.

FLUFFY CAKES
(Makes fourteen cakes)

3oz. butter
2oz. plain flour
2oz. cornflour
½ level teaspoon baking powder
2oz. caster sugar
1 large egg
2 teaspoons lemon juice

☐ Cream the butter until soft. Sift the flours and baking powder. Add gradually to the butter with the sugar. Lightly beat the egg with the lemon juice and stir into the mixture. Beat for 1min. until smooth.
☐ Place teaspoons of the mixture into 14 greased patty tins. Cook for 10min. or until risen and pale golden, towards top of oven, pre-heated to 400 deg. F. or Mark 6. Cool on wire racks.

STANHOPE NUT AND DATE CAKE

4oz. shelled walnuts
4oz. stoned dates
5oz. stoned raisins
5oz. sultanas
14oz. plain flour
1 level teaspoon baking powder
8oz. butter
8oz. caster sugar
3 large eggs
1 level tablespoon black treacle
¼ pint milk

☐ Put the walnuts in a pan, cover with cold water. Bring to the boil, drain and run cold water over them. Dry well. Chop nuts and all fruit finely. Sift the flour and baking powder.
☐ Cream the butter and sugar until light and fluffy. Add the eggs to the creamed mixture one at a time, beating well after each one. Stir in the treacle, nuts and fruit. Fold in the flour and mix to a stiff dropping consistency with the milk. Turn into a greased round 7in. cake tin.
☐ Bake for 10min. in centre of oven, pre-heated to 350 deg. F. or Mark 4, then reduce heat to 325 deg. F. or Mark 3 and cook for 1 hour 40min.-2 hours more. Keep cake in an airtight tin for 2 days before cutting.

ROSE WEDDING CAKE

1lb. stoned raisins
1lb. 10oz. currants
1lb. sultanas
11oz. glacé cherries
6oz. whole blanched almonds
1lb. 12oz. plain flour
$\frac{1}{2}$ level teaspoon salt
$2\frac{1}{2}$ level teaspoons ground mixed spice
$2\frac{1}{2}$ level teaspoons ground cinnamon
1lb. 7oz. butter
1lb. 7oz. soft dark brown sugar
12 large eggs
grated rind of 1 large lemon
6oz. chopped mixed peel
brandy—optional

☐ Roughly chop the raisins if very large. Mix raisins, currants and sultanas together. Rinse cherries in warm water to remove the sugar. Cut into quarters. Roughly chop almonds.
☐ Sift together 1lb. 6oz. plain flour and $\frac{1}{4}$ teaspoon salt, 1 rounded teaspoon mixed spice and 1 rounded teaspoon cinnamon. Cream 1lb. 2oz. butter with 1lb. 2oz. sugar until fluffy and light in colour. Break 9 eggs into a jug and beat lightly. Add eggs to creamed mixture a little at a time, beating well after each addition. Beat in $\frac{2}{3}$ of the lemon rind. Mix together the flour, 2lb. 10oz. of the mixed fruit, 9oz. glacé cherries, 5oz. chopped almonds and 5oz. mixed peel. Add half to creamed mixture and fold in using a large metal spoon. Fold in remaining half. Add 1 tablespoon of brandy if liked.
☐ Spoon this mixture into a greased and double lined, round 10in. cake tin. Push mixture well down and smooth it from the centre to the outside leaving a dip in the centre. Smooth mixture round the edge. Tie a double piece of brown paper round the outside of the tin deep enough to stand 1in. above the tin. Cook cake for $6\frac{1}{4}$ hours in all, in centre of oven, pre-heated to 300 deg. F. or Mark 2, but after 3 hours cover cake with three layers of greaseproof paper and after 4 hours reduce heat to 275 deg. F. or Mark 1.
☐ Test your cake by pushing a skewer into the middle. It should be quite clean. If not, cook for a little longer, testing again. Let the cake cool in its tin overnight, then turn out, wrap in clean greaseproof paper and store in a tin.
☐ The top layer is made and baked as instructed for the large layer, using the remainder of the ingredients. Cook the mixture in a round 6in. tin, which must be prepared in the same way as the 10in. tin. Bake for $3\frac{1}{4}$ hours in centre of oven, pre-heated to 300 deg. F. or Mark 2. After 2 hours, cover top of cake with three layers of greaseproof paper.

ALMOND PASTE

$1\frac{1}{2}$lb. icing sugar
$1\frac{1}{2}$lb. ground almonds
3 large eggs
little almond essence—optional
lemon juice
1lb. apricot jam

☐ Sift the icing sugar into a bowl. Add almonds. Beat eggs lightly. Mix in a few drops of almond essence if liked. Make a well in centre of dry ingredients. Add egg mixture. Draw in sugar mixture and mix to a very stiff dough, adding a little lemon juice. Form into a ball. Wrap in waxed or greaseproof paper and leave in a cool place overnight.
☐ Next day, empty apricot jam into a small saucepan. Heat until boiling, then sieve. Keep it hot. Cut tops of cakes flat if necessary. Cut a piece of greaseproof paper $\frac{1}{2}$in. longer than the circumference of the cake and $\frac{1}{2}$in. deeper. Weigh 2lb. almond paste and keep the rest for the small cake.
☐ Divide the 2lb. in half. Brush sides of cake with apricot jam. Roll one half of the almond paste out to fit the greaseproof paper pattern, dusting rolling pin and table with icing sugar. Carefully lift paper and paste and press paste round the cake until edges meet. Peel off paper and smooth the join with

a knife blade. Smooth paste over top edge of cake. Using a clean, straight-sided jam jar, roll jar round sides to smooth any bumps.
☐ Brush top of cake with jam. Cut a piece of greaseproof paper to the size of the cake top. Place remaining paste on greaseproof paper and roll out to the same size. Trim to a perfect circle with a sharp knife. Lifting paper and paste carefully, invert it on the cake. Press firmly. Smooth and square edges using a palette knife. Leave to dry for at least 2 days, covering cake with greaseproof paper. Use the remaining paste for the small cake, covering in the same way.

ROYAL ICING

$3\frac{1}{2}$lb. icing sugar
7 large egg whites
1 tablespoon glycerine
1 roll pink self-adhesive ribbon
30 Carole rosebuds

☐ Sift the icing sugar into a large bowl. Lightly beat egg whites, without beating in too many bubbles. Add half the sugar to the egg whites. Stir with a wooden spoon until thoroughly mixed. Mix in remaining sugar and the glycerine. Beat for 10min. until icing is glossy and white. Cover bowl with a damp tea towel and leave for 1 hour. Keep wetting the tea towel so that the icing does not become hard on top. You can leave it overnight, but transfer the icing to an airtight container and put it in a cool place.

☐ Place a little icing in the centre of a 12in. cake board. Stand large cake on this and leave for 2 hours. Weigh 1¼lb. icing and reserve for the top tier. Spoon about ⅔ of the remaining icing on top of the large tier. Using a clean palette knife work icing backwards and forwards until top is smooth and evenly covered. Remove any icing from sides.

☐ Hold a clean long palette knife or supple plastic ruler at either end, one edge resting on the top edge of the cake away from you. Draw steadily across cake. Repeat this until the top is smooth, replacing icing if layer becomes too thin. Leave for 24 hours to harden, storing remaining icing in an airtight container or polythene bags. Put the cake on a turntable or upturned plate and smooth off any rough edges of icing. Spread remaining icing round sides of cake until smooth. Leave for 24 hours to harden. Using a sharp knife scrape the edges until they are smooth. Repeat process on the small tier. Smooth about 1 teaspoon of icing in centre of large tier. Put small tier in place and leave for 1 hour.

☐ Mix 2 tablespoons cold water with 12 tablespoons of the remaining icing. Add another tablespoon of water, if necessary, to give a smooth flowing coat. Stand cakes on turntable and pour icing over the tiers and the cake board, smoothing it over the board if necessary. Leave for 2 hours. Scrape off any drips from underneath the board. Leave for 2 days to harden.

☐ Sift a little more icing sugar into the remaining icing to make a piping consistency. Spoon into a piping bag fitted with a small star pipe. Cut ribbon into various lengths. Split into strips ½in. wide. Cut off all but ½in. of stalk from the rosebuds. Trim off discoloured petals and the calyx of each. Pipe a large star of icing in centre of small tier and a small star on edge of large tier. Press a piece of ribbon into the top star of icing and twisting it, secure it on star on large tier. Press a rosebud into lower star. Continue in this way, allowing lengths of ribbon to fall naturally, secured on top tier and some secured to bottom tier and some to the board.

☐ Arrange a small bowl of flowers and press this on to the icing on the top tier to keep it firm. Conceal container if necessary with a few more rosebuds or some loops of ribbon.

CUMBERLAND ALMOND PUDDINGS
(Makes four puddings)

4oz. plain flour
pinch of salt
1oz. lard
1oz. margarine
2 level tablespoons raspberry jam
2oz. butter
2oz. caster sugar
2 large eggs
4oz. ground rice
2 level tablespoons ground almonds

☐ Sift the flour and salt into a bowl. Rub in the lard and margarine until the mixture looks like breadcrumbs. Add cold water and mix to a stiff dough. Roll pastry on a floured board and cut rounds to line 4 individual flan rings or ovenproof saucers. Line with the pastry and then prick with a fork. Spread a thin layer of jam over pastry.

☐ Cream butter and sugar together until light and fluffy. Add eggs, one at a time, beating well after each addition, and then work in the ground rice and almonds. Spread the mixture over the jam.

☐ Bake for 40-45min., or until golden brown, in centre of oven, pre-heated to 350 deg. F. or Mark 4. Cover the puddings with greaseproof paper if the tops are browning too quickly.

STRAWBERRY GATEAU

1 packet plain sponge mix
½lb. firm strawberries
½ pint double cream

☐ Make up the plain sponge mix according to the instructions on the packet. Turn into a greased, round 8in. cake tin lined with greased greaseproof paper. Bake according to packet instructions. Turn out on to a wire cake rack and leave until cold.

☐ Wash strawberries. Reserve 10 of the best of them for decoration. Hull remainder and put them in a bowl. Lightly mash, using a fork.

☐ Whip the cream in another bowl until standing in soft peaks. Reserve ⅔ of cream. Lightly stir mashed strawberries into rest of cream.

☐ Cut cake in 3 layers and sandwich together again with strawberry cream mixture. Swirl rest of cream over top and sides of cake—see picture. Cut 6 reserved strawberries in half and arrange round the side of the cake. Cut 3 whole strawberries into slices. Arrange in a circle in the centre of the cake and place a whole strawberry on top. Serve immediately.

LEMON REFRIGERATOR CAKE

4 tablespoons sherry
7½oz. packet semi-sweet biscuits
3½oz. butter
5oz. caster sugar
4 medium-sized eggs
1 large lemon
1oz. flaked almonds
1oz. plain chocolate
5oz. carton double cream

☐ Pour the sherry into a shallow dish. Line the base of a round 7½in. loose-base cake tin with a circle of greaseproof paper. Dip each biscuit into the sherry and arrange a single layer over the base of the tin. Don't bother to fill the gaps.
☐ Cream the butter and sugar until light and fluffy. Separate the eggs. Beat the yolks, one at a time, into the butter mixture. Finely grate the lemon rind. Squeeze out and strain the juice. Beat the rind and the juice into the creamed mixture.
☐ Whisk the egg whites until standing in soft peaks, then carefully fold them into the creamed mixture. Spoon a third of this over the biscuits in the tin. Arrange another layer of biscuits over the lemon mixture, first dipping them in the sherry. Repeat the layers, finishing with a layer of biscuits. Cover the top with a circle of greaseproof paper. Leave in the refrigerator for 2-3 hours. Remove from the refrigerator and place a plate with a weight on it over the greaseproof paper. Replace it in the refrigerator for 24 hours.
☐ Before serving toast the almonds until golden. Break the chocolate on to a plate and stand the plate over a pan of hot water until the chocolate has melted and is smooth. Whip the cream until standing in soft peaks. Spoon into a piping bag fitted with a small star pipe.
☐ Remove the cake from the tin and peel off the circles of greaseproof paper. Place cake on a serving dish. Pipe the cream between the biscuits and in a circle in the centre. Decorate with the toasted almonds. Make a small greaseproof paper icing bag—see page 8 —and fill with the cool liquid chocolate. Snip off the end of the bag and drizzle the chocolate over the almonds and the cream in the centre. Leave for 15min. until the chocolate has set.

SUGAR RINGS
(Makes twenty rings)

1 large egg
4oz. caster sugar
2 tablespoons milk or single cream
1½oz. butter
8oz. plain flour
½ level teaspoon ground cardamom
1 level teaspoon baking powder
oil for deep frying

☐ Whisk egg and sugar together until creamy and thick and whisk will leave a trail when lifted out. Add milk or cream. Melt butter. Sift flour, spice and baking powder. Add flour mixture alternately with butter to egg mixture and mix to a soft dough.
☐ With your hands, roll pieces out to ½in. thick and 5in. long; join each into a ring.
☐ Heat oil to the correct temperature— see page 15. Cook rings until deep golden brown. Drain on kitchen paper.

MERINGUES
(Makes fourteen halves)

3 large egg whites
6oz. caster sugar
½ pint double cream

☐ Whisk the egg whites for at least 7min., or until standing in stiff peaks and fluffy without looking dry. Whisk in 3oz. sugar, a spoonful at a time. Continue whisking for 3min., or until stiff again. Fold in remaining sugar.
☐ Pour a little cold water into a bowl. Dip 2 dessertspoons in water, shake off excess. Take a heaped spoonful of meringue and push it into a blob with the other spoon on to a large baking tray greased and lined with greased greaseproof paper. Rinse the spoons from time to time.
☐ The mixture can also be piped. Spoon the mixture into a large piping bag fitted with a medium-sized star pipe. Pipe a circle 2½in. across and then build up the sides with 2 complete piped circles of meringue—these look like baskets. Dry meringues for 3 hours in lower part of oven, pre-heated to 225 deg. F. or Mark ¼. Turn off the oven and leave to dry overnight.
☐ Whip the cream until standing in peaks and use to sandwich 2 meringue halves together.

PHOENICIAN HONEY CAKES
(Makes about twenty-four cakes)

1lb. plain flour
1 pint and 4 tablespoons olive oil
6oz. caster sugar
4 tablespoons retsina (resinous white wine)
4 tablespoons orange juice
2 tablespoons brandy
¼ level teaspoon ground cloves
¼ level teaspoon ground nutmeg
ground cinnamon
6 level tablespoons honey
juice of ½ large lemon
1 oz. blanched almonds

☐ Sift the flour and work it little by little into the oil with 4oz. sugar, wine, orange juice, brandy, cloves, nutmeg and ½ level teaspoon cinnamon until you have a fairly stiff dough. Add more liquid if too stiff, and more flour if too soft to handle. Knead well for 15min. Pinch off a piece at a time and form into a ball the size and shape of a small egg. Put on an oiled baking tray and flatten slightly.
☐ Bake for 15-20min. or until brown, in centre of oven, pre-heated to 425 deg. F. or Mark 7.
☐ Put the honey, rest of sugar, lemon juice and 6 tablespoons cold water in a small pan and bring gently to the boil, stirring to dissolve the sugar. Boil until frothy. When the cakes are ready, take them from the oven, and immediately drop them one by one into the hot syrup. Leave for 1-2min., then remove and place on a sheet of greaseproof paper to cool. Chop the almonds and sprinkle over the cakes with cinnamon.

YOGURT CAKE

4oz. butter
1lb. caster sugar
6 large eggs
5oz. carton and 4 tablespoons plain yogurt
1 large lemon
1lb. 2oz. plain flour
1 level tablespoon bicarbonate of soda
pinch of salt
icing sugar

☐ Cream the butter and caster sugar.
Separate the eggs and beat the yolks.
Beat yolks into the creamed mixture,
then stir in the yogurt. Finely grate the
lemon rind; squeeze out and strain the
juice.
☐ Sift the flour, bicarbonate of soda and
salt; fold into the creamed mixture
alternately with the lemon rind and juice.
Whisk the egg whites until they form soft
peaks and fold them into the mixture.
☐ Pour into a greased and lightly
floured round 8½in. cake tin. Bake for
15min. in centre of oven, pre-heated to
350 deg. F. or Mark 4, then reduce heat
to 300 deg. F. or Mark 2 and cook for a
further 1¼ hours or until just firm to the
touch and shrunk away from the sides of
the cake tin. Leave in the tin for 15min.,
then turn on to a wire rack. Dust with
icing sugar and leave to cool.

CREAM SLICES
(Makes eight slices)

8oz. puff pastry—see page 18
6oz. icing sugar
½oz. cocoa
5oz. carton double cream
raspberry jam

☐ Roll pastry to a ⅛in. thick rectangle.
Lift on to a wet baking tray and cut into
16 strips, each 1½in. wide and 4in. long.
Cook for 10min. towards top of oven,
pre-heated to 450 deg. F. or Mark 8.
Cool on a wire rack.
☐ Sift 4oz. sugar into a bowl, add just
enough cold water to mix to a coating
consistency. Sift remaining sugar and
cocoa into a small bowl, add a little hot
water and mix to a piping consistency.
Spoon into a piping bag fitted with a
small plain pipe. Whip the cream.
☐ Spread 8 pastry slices with jam and
cream, sandwich together with remaining
pastry slices. Ice tops with white icing
and pipe two chocolate lines along the
top of each cake. Draw a knife across
through the lines at 1in. intervals. Leave
to set then serve.

FRUIT GINGER LOAF

½lb. cooking apples
3oz. soft brown sugar
4oz. golden syrup
3oz. margarine
6oz. self-raising flour
1 level teaspoon ground ginger
½ level teaspoon ground cinnamon
salt
1 standard egg
1 piece preserved ginger
1 piece angelica
2 level teaspoons caster sugar

☐ Peel and core the apples. Slice thinly.
Put into a saucepan with 1 teaspoon cold
water. Cover. Simmer gently for 10min.,
or until apple is soft. Push through a
sieve into a bowl.
☐ Put brown sugar, syrup and margarine
into a saucepan. Heat gently until
margarine melts. Remove from heat and
leave to cool.
☐ Sift flour, ground ginger, cinnamon
and a pinch of salt into a bowl. Beat egg
lightly. Make a well in the centre of the
flour mixture and add the apple purée,
syrup mixture and beaten egg. Beat until
smooth. Pour mixture into a greased 1lb.
loaf tin, lined with greased greaseproof
paper.
☐ Bake for 1½ hours in centre of oven,
pre-heated to 325 deg. F. or Mark 3.
☐ Leave to cool for 30min. in the tin.
Turn on to a wire rack to finish cooling.
When cold, decorate with slices of
preserved ginger and angelica cut into
diamond shapes. Put caster sugar into
a pan and melt over a very low heat.
When melted brush over the cake top.

HUISH CAKE

4oz. plain flour
4oz. butter
8oz. caster sugar
4oz. ground rice
4 large eggs
½ level teaspoon caraway seeds

☐ Sift the flour. Cream butter and sugar
until light and fluffy. Stir in flour and
ground rice. Separate the eggs. Beat the
yolks and stir into the mixture. Whisk
the whites until stiff and standing in
peaks and fold into the mixture with the
caraway seeds.
☐ Turn into a greased 12in. by 8in.
Swiss roll tin. Bake for 1 hour or until
risen and firm, in centre of oven,
pre-heated to 350 deg. F. or Mark 4.

CUMBERLAND CURRANT PASTIES
(Makes twelve pasties)

4oz. currants
2oz. soft brown sugar
½ level teaspoon ground cinnamon
¼ medium-sized cooking apple
2½oz. lard
6oz. plain flour
pinch of salt
1½oz. margarine
caster sugar

☐ Mix currants, brown sugar and
cinnamon. Peel and core the apple. Cut
into small dice. Add to currants. Cut
1oz. lard into small pieces and mix with
the fruit.
☐ Sift flour and salt into a bowl. Rub
in rest of lard and the margarine until
mixture looks like breadcrumbs. Mix to
a stiff dough with cold water. Turn on
to a lightly floured board and roll out.
☐ Cut out 12 circles using a 4in. plain
cutter. Put a small spoonful of fruit
mixture in centre of each circle. Moisten
half the edge of each one and fold over
to form half circles. Press edges with the
prongs of a fork to decorate and seal.
☐ Cook for 20min., or until pale
golden, in centre of oven, pre-heated to
425 deg. F. or Mark 7. Sprinkle with
caster sugar. Cool on wire racks.

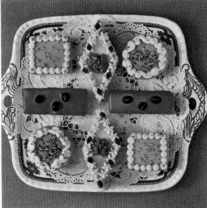

MARZIPAN TARTLETS
(Makes fifteen tartlets)

4oz. plain flour
pinch of salt
4oz. butter
3oz. caster sugar
1 large egg
2oz. self-raising flour
8oz. bought marzipan
red, yellow and green vegetable
colouring
2 level tablespoons apricot jam
1 level tablespoon blackcurrant jam

☐ Sift the plain flour and salt into a large mixing bowl. Rub in 2oz. butter until the mixture looks like fine breadcrumbs. Stir in 1 level teaspoon caster sugar and 4 teaspoons cold water to mix to a stiff dough. Knead lightly on a floured board. Roll out thinly and cut into rounds to fit 15 greased patty tins.
☐ Cream the remaining butter and 2oz. sugar until light and fluffy. Lightly beat the egg in a small bowl and add to the creamed mixture a little at a time, beating well after each addition. Sift the self-raising flour and using a large metal spoon fold it into the creamed mixture. Spoon the mixture into the patty tins.
☐ Cook for about 15min., or until firm to the touch, towards top of oven, pre-heated to 375 deg. F. or Mark 5.
☐ Meanwhile, knead the marzipan to soften it. Divide it into 3 pieces and colour each piece with one of the food colourings. Roll each piece thinly between pieces of greaseproof paper. Cut the marzipan into 15 circles using a 2½in. fluted cutter. Remove centres with small fancy cutters; dredge with sugar.
☐ Colour half the apricot jam pale green and half pale pink.
☐ Place spoonfuls of the pink jam on 5 cakes and top with the pink marzipan circles. Spoon the green apricot jam on another 5 cakes and top with the green marzipan. On the last 5 cakes spoon some blackcurrant jam and top with the yellow marzipan circles.

ICED FANCIES
(Makes twenty-four cakes)

9oz. butter
6oz. caster sugar
3 large eggs
6oz. self-raising flour
pinch of salt
1lb. 2oz. icing sugar
angelica
1 level teaspoon instant coffee
red and green vegetable colouring
silver balls
hundreds and thousands
sweet coffee beans
walnut halves

☐ Make a Victoria Sandwich mixture—see page 142—using 6 oz. butter, the caster sugar, eggs, flour and salt. Spread into a greased and lined 11in. by 7in. cake tin. Cook for 20min., in centre of oven, pre-heated to 375 deg. F. or Mark 5. Turn out; cool.
☐ Cream remaining butter and 6oz. icing sugar together and spoon into a piping bag fitted with a small star pipe. Cut angelica into leaves. Sift remaining icing sugar into a bowl and mix to a coating consistency with a little cold water. Divide into 4 bowls. Dissolve coffee in ½ teaspoon hot water and add to one bowl. Colour one pink, one green and leave the last white.
☐ Cut the cake into squares, circles, oblongs and diamonds. Coat the squares with green icing, circles with pink icing, oblongs with coffee icing and the diamonds with white icing. Decorate with butter icing, the angelica and other decorations, as shown.

CHRISTMAS CAKE

8oz. butter
8oz. soft brown sugar
6 large eggs
1 small lemon
½ level teaspoon ground cinnamon
½ level teaspoon ground nutmeg
1 level teaspoon ground mixed spice
5 level tablespoons black treacle
1lb. plain flour
12oz. stoned raisins
9oz. currants
9oz. sultanas
2oz. chopped mixed peel
2oz. glacé cherries
pineapple juice
1 level teaspoon bicarbonate of soda
1 miniature bottle brandy

☐ Cream butter and sugar. Separate eggs; beat yolks into creamed mixture. Finely grate lemon rind; squeeze and strain juice. Stir in rind, juice, spices and treacle. Alternately fold in flour and dried fruit, peel and cherries, adding some pineapple juice to moisten. Keep the mixture very stiff at this stage as more liquid is added. Mix bicarbonate of soda with a little fruit juice; add to mixture. Whisk egg whites fairly stiffly; alternately fold into mixture with the brandy to form a stiff dropping consistency.
☐ Grease a round 9in. cake tin. Line with greaseproof paper; grease paper. Turn mixture into tin. Tie band of brown paper round tin. Bake for 3-4 hours until well risen and firm to the touch, in lower part of oven, pre-heated to 275 deg. F. or Mark 1. To test if cooked, push a metal skewer down into the cake; if it is clean and very hot when removed the cake is cooked.
Cool and decorate as follows.

1lb. bought marzipan
3 level tablespoons apricot jam
2 large egg whites
6oz. ground almonds
6oz. caster sugar
few drops almond essence
14 glacé cherries
2-3 glacé pineapple rings
1 glacé apricot
13 walnut halves
16 blanched almonds

☐ Knead marzipan until soft. Roll marzipan to fit round side of cake. Heat jam until boiling, then sieve if necessary. Brush jam over cake. Carefully lay marzipan round sides. Press edges together and smooth them.
☐ Whisk egg whites until stiff. Fold in almonds, 3oz. sugar and essence. Spoon into a piping bag fitted with a large fluted pipe. Pipe rosettes round top of cake. Cut cherries in half, pineapple

Christmas Cake

rings into pieces, and apricot into small
cubes. Arrange fruit and nuts on top in
circles. Tie a double piece of greaseproof
paper round cake. Place cake on a thick
pad of newspaper covered with clean
brown paper; cover fruit with foil. Put
in centre of oven, pre-heated to 300 deg.
F. or Mark 2 for about 20min. until
rosettes are pale golden.

☐ Meanwhile, dissolve remaining sugar
in 5 tablespoons water over very low
heat. Bring to boil and boil for 5min.

☐ Remove cake from oven. Peel off
paper. Brush syrup liberally over fruit
and marzipan rosettes. Leave to cool,
then store in an airtight tin.

DURHAM PIKELETS
(Makes twelve pikelets)

8oz. plain flour
pinch of salt
1½oz. caster sugar
½ pint buttermilk
1 level teaspoon bicarbonate of soda
2oz. lard

☐ Sift flour and salt into a bowl. Stir in the sugar. Make a well in the centre and add all but 1 dessertspoon of the buttermilk. Mix to a stiff smooth batter.
☐ Dissolve the bicarbonate of soda in remaining buttermilk and beat into the batter.
☐ Grease a heavy frying pan with a little lard and when hot drop tablespoons of the batter on to the pan, forming each into a round with the tip of the spoon. Cook for 2min., or until golden on the underside, then turn and cook gently for 1min. more. Cook the remainder of the batter in the same way.
☐ Serve hot or cold with plenty of butter and bramble jelly.

CREMPOG
(Makes about ten cakes)

½ level teaspoon bicarbonate of soda
½ pint buttermilk
8oz. plain flour
pinch of salt
1 large egg
1oz. lard

☐ Stir the bicarbonate of soda into the buttermilk. Sift the flour and salt into a bowl. Make a well in the centre and add the egg and the buttermilk. Beat well with a wooden spoon for about 5min.
☐ Grease a heavy frying pan with a little of the lard. Drop 1 tablespoon of the mixture for each cake into the hot pan. Cook for 2min. or until golden. Turn and cook for 1min. on other side. Keep hot while you cook the rest of the mixture.
☐ Serve very hot with a small pat of butter on each cake, and with sugar or golden syrup.

MADEIRA CAKE

6oz. butter
6oz. caster sugar
3 large eggs
grated rind of 1 large lemon
10oz. self-raising flour
salt
3 slices of citron peel

☐ Cream butter and sugar until light and fluffy. Beat eggs lightly. Add gradually to creamed mixture, beating all the time. Stir in the lemon rind. Sift the flour and a pinch of salt together. Fold in the flour using a metal spoon. Mix in 2 tablespoons cold water.
☐ Spoon into a greased, round 7in. cake tin. Cook for 30min. in centre of oven, pre-heated to 350 deg. F. or Mark 4, then reduce heat to 325 deg. F. or Mark 3 and cook for a further 30min., arranging the citron peel on top of the cake after 45min. cooking, leaving the cake in the oven to do this.
☐ Leave cake to cool in the tin for 30min. then finish cooling on a rack.

CHERRY CAKE

☐ Make exactly as for Madeira Cake, see recipe above, but stir 2oz. chopped glacé cherries into the creamed mixture just before adding the flour.
☐ To prepare the cherries. Wash them in hot water to remove their sugar coating. This prevents them from sinking to the bottom of the cake. Dry well and cut in quarters. You will not need the citron peel for decoration.

MAIDS OF HONOUR
(Makes fifteen cakes)

8oz. packet frozen puff pastry
¼ pint milk
1 heaped tablespoon fresh white breadcrumbs
2oz. butter
½oz. caster sugar
1oz. ground almonds
grated rind of 1 small lemon
1 large egg
few drops almond essence

☐ Allow pastry to thaw for at least 1 hour.
☐ Heat milk until almost boiling. Stir in breadcrumbs and leave for 10min. Cut butter into small pieces and stir into milk mixture with the sugar, almonds and lemon rind. Beat egg lightly. Add to mixture with almond essence to taste. Stir well.
☐ Roll out pastry on a lightly floured board to ⅛in. thickness and, using a 3in. fluted cutter, cut out 15 rounds. Press into patty tins. Divide almond mixture between pastry rounds. Bake for 20min., or until golden, in centre of oven, pre-heated to 425 deg. F. or Mark 7. Cool on a wire rack.

JAM AND CREAM SCONES
(Makes ten scones)

8oz. plain flour
2 level teaspoons baking powder
½ level teaspoon salt
2oz. butter
¼ pint milk
4 heaped tablespoons raspberry jam
5oz. carton double cream

☐ Sift the flour, baking powder and salt into a large mixing bowl. Rub in the butter and using a palette knife, mix in the milk to make a soft but not sticky dough. Turn mixture on to a floured board and knead lightly until smooth. Roll out to about ½in. thickness. Using a 2½in. fluted cutter, cut out 10 scones. Place the scones on a greased baking tray and brush them with a little milk.
☐ Cook for 10min., or until golden, towards top of oven, pre-heated to 450 deg. F. or Mark 8. Cool on a rack.
☐ Heat jam gently so that it will spread more easily. Whip the cream to soft peaks.
☐ Cut the scones in half and spread the bottom halves with cream. Spread a little of the jam on top halves; sandwich together and serve.

IRISH WHISKEY CAKE

rind of 1 large orange
5 dessertspoons Irish whiskey
6oz. sultanas
6oz. butter
6oz. caster sugar
3 large eggs
8oz. plain flour
pinch of salt
1 level teaspoon baking powder

☐ Using a sharp knife, peel the rind off the orange leaving all the pith on the fruit. Soak the rind in whiskey for 6 hours or overnight. Discard the rind; add the sultanas to whiskey.
☐ Cream the butter and sugar until light and fluffy. Beat the eggs and beat gradually into the creamed mixture. Sift the flour, salt and baking powder together and fold into the mixture. Lastly, fold in the sultanas and whiskey.
☐ Spoon mixture into a greased round 7in. cake tin lined with greased greaseproof paper. Bake for 1½ hours in centre of oven, pre-heated to 350 deg. F. or Mark 4, reducing the heat towards the end of cooking if the cake seems to be browning too much. Eat while fresh.

CIDER CAKE

8oz. plain flour
¾ level teaspoon bicarbonate of soda
1 level teaspoon ground ginger
¼ level teaspoon ground nutmeg
pinch of salt
4oz. butter
4oz. Demerara sugar
2 large eggs
1½ level tablespoons golden syrup
¼ pint dry cider

☐ Sift the flour, soda, spices and salt. Cream the butter and sugar until light and fluffy. Beat the eggs. Add a tablespoon of egg at a time to the creamed mixture, beating well after each addition. Stir in the syrup. Stir half the flour into the mixture. Whisk the cider until frothy and stir in. Add remaining flour. Beat well until smooth. Pour into a greased, shallow cake tin 7in. by 10in.
☐ Cook for 30min. in centre of oven, pre-heated to 325 deg. F. or Mark 3, then reduce heat to 300 deg. F. or Mark 2 and cook for a further 30min., or until well risen and firm to the touch. Leave to cool in the tin for 30min.
☐ Turn on to a wire rack and finish cooling. Cut into squares to serve. This cake keeps well; in fact, it's better after storing in an airtight tin.

SWISS ROLL

4oz. plain flour
pinch of salt
3 large eggs
5oz. caster sugar
1 tablespoon hot water
3oz. raspberry jam

☐ Sift flour and salt on to a piece of greaseproof paper. Break the eggs into a large bowl. Add 4oz. sugar and stand the bowl over a saucepan of hot water, making sure that the water is not touching the bowl. Whisk for about 10min., until mixture is thick enough to hold the trail from the whisk for 5sec. Remove from heat and whisk for 5min. to cool.
☐ Sift half the flour into the egg mixture and lightly fold in with a tablespoon. Fold in the rest of the flour with the hot water. Pour the mixture into a greased and lined 8in. by 12in. Swiss roll tin. Spread mixture lightly, making sure the corners are filled. Cook for 10min. until well risen, firm to the touch and golden brown, in upper part of oven, pre-heated to 425 deg. F. or Mark 7.
☐ Wring out a tea towel in warm water and spread it on a working surface. Cover it with a piece of greaseproof paper and dust with ½oz. caster sugar. Warm the jam to soften it.
☐ Turn the sponge upside down on to the sugared paper and peel off lining paper carefully. Trim off ¼in. round the sponge. Spread sponge with jam to within ½in. of the edges. Press the back of a knife into one end of the sponge about ½in. from the edge. Lift greaseproof paper at the knife marked end, and gently ease the ½in. to make a fold. Be careful not to split the sponge. Using both hands, firmly roll the sponge away from you, peeling the paper back as you do so. Leave the sponge wrapped in the paper and resting on the cut end for about 2min. Carefully remove the paper and dredge the Swiss roll with remaining caster sugar. Finish cooling on a wire rack.

INVERNESS GINGERBREAD

12oz. plain flour
1 level teaspoon bicarbonate of soda
4oz. fine oatmeal
8oz. butter
4 tablespoons single cream or rich milk
12oz. black treacle
1oz. green root ginger
4oz. candied lemon peel

☐ Sift the flour and bicarbonate of soda into a bowl and mix in the oatmeal. Cream the butter until soft and then beat in the flour mixture and the cream or milk alternately. Heat the treacle until just runny. Peel the ginger until the green just shows. Cut the ginger and lemon peel into fine shreds. Add treacle, ginger and peel to bowl and mix well.
☐ Turn mixture into a greased, shallow, 13½in. by 9½in. cake tin, and bake for 45min. in centre of oven, pre-heated to 325 deg. F. or Mark 3.

GRANTHAM GINGERBREAD

8oz. plain flour
½oz. ground ginger
1 level teaspoon baking powder
4oz. butter
4oz. caster sugar
1 large egg
3 tablespoons milk

☐ Sift the flour, ginger and baking powder together. Cream the butter and sugar until light and fluffy. Separate the egg and beat the yolk into the creamed mixture. Stir in flour mixture. Whisk the egg white until stiff and fold into the mixture, adding the milk to give a stiff dropping consistency.
☐ Spoon into a greased and lined 11in. by 7in. Swiss roll tin. Bake for 30min. until cooked but still pale in colour, in centre of oven, pre-heated to 350 deg. F. or Mark 4.

GINGERBREAD HOUSE

12oz. golden syrup
10oz. caster sugar
5 level teaspoons ground ginger
½ level teaspoon ground cinnamon
10oz. margarine
5 rounded teaspoons bicarbonate of soda
2½lb. plain flour
½ level teaspoon salt
2 large eggs
5-6 large egg whites
3lb. icing sugar
assorted decorations

☐ Heat syrup, caster sugar and spices. Add margarine; stir until melted. Stir in soda. Cool for 5min.
☐ Sift flour and salt. Beat whole eggs and mix into flour with the syrup mixture. Knead until smooth and pliable.
☐ Divide into 3 pieces. Roll each piece on the base of an upturned 13½in. by 9½in. baking tin until a little thinner than ¼in. Cut off ½in. all round one piece.

Cut large piece in half downwards to form roof. Cut off 1½in. border round second piece. Cut off 1½in. strip from one short end. Cut large piece in half to form house sides. Trim off ½in. piece all round third piece. Cut two oblongs each 8in. by 4½in. Measure and mark 4½in. along each 8in. side. To make the triangular tops, measure and mark 2¼in. across tops of rectangles. Cut off slanting pieces from these marks to the 4½in. marks. Roll scraps to a ½in. thickness; cut five 1½in. by 4in. strips for supports and chimney. Carefully place all pieces on lightly greased baking trays.
☐ Cook pieces for 20-25min. or until brown, towards top of oven, pre-heated to 350 deg. F. or Mark 4. Cover if browning too much. Leave on trays for 5min. Loosen with palette knife; cool on wire racks. Should gingerbread spread too much before cooling, trim before assembling. Check pieces fit together well before icing.
☐ Beat 5 egg whites for 1min. Gradually beat in icing sugar using your mixer to form fairly stiff peaks. Spoon into a piping bag fitted with a small writing pipe. Cover remainder with a damp cloth. Pipe windows and snow on side walls. Pipe doors and eaves on end walls. Decorate by pushing round coloured sweets into icing. Leave to set for 15min.

☐ Pipe a thick ridge of icing along base and side of one end wall and along base and side of side piece. Fit together on a 14in. square cake board and hold for 1min. Pipe icing along base and sides of one support; place behind join. Ice and stick together remaining two sides, icing supports each time and fitting them behind the corners to hold walls in place. Leave for 30min. to dry.
☐ Thickly ice top of walls and add the roof pieces. Hold in place for 5min. Pipe icing along top gap to fill and down sides of roof. Leave for 20min. Spread icing over roof using a palette knife. Cut off a slanting piece from remaining post to fit the roof. Stick in place to form the chimney. Leave to dry. Decorate house with various small coloured sweets. Top chimney with icing. Add a very little more egg white to the icing to make it softer and swirl it all over the board. Smooth a path to the door and add figures if liked. Leave to dry overnight. Store in a polythene bag.

LITTLE SPONGE CAKES
(Makes twenty-four cakes)

Victoria Sandwich mixture—see page 142
4oz. butter
1lb. icing sugar
coffee essence
1 level tablespoon cocoa
3 tablespoons hot water
½ level teaspoon finely grated lemon rind
1 teaspoon lemon juice
vanilla essence
2 level teaspoons instant coffee
yellow food colouring

☐ Spoon the Victoria Sandwich mixture in a greased, shallow 7in. by 11in. tin, about 1½in. deep. Smooth well into the corners. Cook for 25-30min., in centre of oven, pre-heated to 350 deg. F. or Mark 4. Leave to cool for 10min., then turn out on to a cooling rack and leave until cold. Then cut into various shapes.

☐ Cream the butter. Sift in 8oz. icing sugar a little at a time, beating well after each addition. The mixture should be smooth and creamy. Divide into 4 bowls and flavour one portion with coffee essence. Dissolve the cocoa in 1 tablespoon hot water and mix well. Leave to cool then beat into a second bowl of butter icing. Add the grated lemon rind and juice to one of the remaining bowls, and a few drops of vanilla essence to the final bowl.

☐ Sift 4oz. icing sugar into a bowl. Dissolve the instant coffee in 1 tablespoon hot water and add to the icing sugar a little at a time, until the mixture is thick and smooth. The icing should coat the back of a spoon fairly thickly.

☐ Sift remaining icing sugar into a bowl. Stir in 1 tablespoon hot water a little at a time until the mixture is thick and smooth. Add a few drops of yellow colouring.

Mandarin Daisies
Cut three 2½in. circles from the sponge. Spread the sides with vanilla butter cream. Roll in almond nibs. Brush the tops with melted apricot jam. Arrange 6 mandarin orange segments on the top. Decorate with stars of vanilla butter cream.

Coffee Triangles
Cut 3 triangles of sponge cake. Spread the sides with coffee butter cream. Coat with toasted almond flakes. Cover the tops with coffee glacé icing. Pipe coffee butter cream round the top. Decorate with sweet coffee beans, available from posh sweetshops.

Chocolate Sponges
Cut 3 squares of the sponge cake and spread the sides with chocolate butter cream. Coat with chocolate vermicelli. Pipe chocolate butter cream on the top and sprinkle with a little vermicelli.

Coconut and Jam Circles
Cut three 2½in. circles from the sponge. Coat the sides with vanilla butter cream or apricot jam. Roll in toasted coconut. Pipe vanilla butter cream round the top and spoon a little raspberry jam in the centre.

Lemon Walnut Slices
Cut three 1in. wide fingers from the sponge. Cut each in half lengthways and fill with lemon butter cream. Sandwich together again. Coat the tops with yellow glacé icing and decorate with walnut halves.

Blackberry Diamonds
Cut 3 diamond shapes from the sponge. Spread the sides with vanilla butter cream and coat with almond nibs. Brush the tops with melted blackberry jam and top with fresh blackberries. Brush the fruit with the melted jam. Pipe vanilla butter cream round the edges.

Honey Rum Balls
These are made with all the trimmings of the sponge cakes. To every 4oz. sponge cake crumbs, add 2 teaspoons coffee essence, 1oz. almond nibs, 1 tablespoon rum, 1 teaspoon water and 1 level tablespoon honey. Stir well until the mixture binds together. Roll into 6 balls. Put chocolate vermicelli on to a plate and roll the balls in it until well covered.

SANDCAKE

3oz. cornflour
2oz. plain flour
1 level teaspoon baking powder
2oz. butter
4oz. caster sugar
2 large eggs
lemon essence

☐ Sift cornflour, plain flour and baking powder together. Cream butter and sugar until light and fluffy. Beat the eggs and add to creamed mixture a little at a time, beating after each addition. Fold in the flour mixture and lemon essence to flavour.
☐ Turn into a greased round 7in. cake tin lined with greased greaseproof paper. Bake for 45min. or until well risen and golden brown, in centre of oven, pre-heated to 350 deg. F. or Mark 4.

ECCLES CAKES
(Makes twelve cakes)

1oz. butter
5oz. currants
2oz. Demerara sugar
¼ level teaspoon ground cinnamon
pinch of ground nutmeg
1 teaspoon lemon juice
8oz. puff pastry—see page 18
½oz. caster sugar

☐ Melt the butter in a pan. Add the currants, Demerara sugar, spices and lemon juice and mix well. Cool.
☐ Turn pastry on to a lightly floured board and roll out to ¼in. thickness. Cut out 12 circles using a 4½in. plain cutter.
☐ Place a heaped teaspoon of the fruit mixture in the centre of each pastry circle. Moisten the edges with water, gather edges and pinch well to seal.
☐ Turn the cakes over and roll until the fruit just shows through. Make three cuts in the top of each with a sharp knife and place cakes on lightly greased baking trays.
☐ Bake for 20-25min. until just coloured, towards top of oven, pre-heated to 425 deg. F. or Mark 7. Remove and cool on wire racks. Sprinkle with caster sugar while they are still hot.

BUNLOAF

8oz. plain flour
pinch of salt
pinch of ground mixed spice
pinch of ground nutmeg
¾ level teaspoon bicarbonate of soda
4oz. butter
4oz. soft brown sugar
¼lb. sultanas
¼lb. currants
¼lb. stoned raisins
1oz. chopped mixed peel
1 level dessertspoon black treacle
buttermilk or milk to mix

☐ Sift the flour, salt, mixed spice, nutmeg and bicarbonate of soda into a bowl. Rub in the butter until the mixture looks like fine breadcrumbs. Stir in the sugar, fruit, and peel. Add the treacle and mix to a fairly stiff dropping consistency with buttermilk or milk.
☐ Turn mixture into a greased 1lb. loaf tin and bake for 2½ hours in centre of oven, pre-heated to 325 deg. F. or Mark 3. Test with a skewer to see if cooked.

SEED CAKE

1lb. plain flour
1lb. butter
1lb. caster sugar
8 large eggs
2oz. caraway seeds
1 level teaspoon ground nutmeg

☐ Sift the flour. Cream the butter until soft, then stir in the sugar. Separate the eggs. Lightly beat the egg whites and beat into the creamed mixture. Beat the yolks into the mixture. Beat in the flour, seeds and nutmeg.
☐ Turn mixture into a greased round 9in. cake tin. Bake for 2 hours in centre of oven, pre-heated to 350 deg. F. or Mark 4. Cool in tin.

CHOCOLATE SPONGE CAKE

3oz. plain chocolate
2 level teaspoons instant coffee
3 dessertspoons boiling water
2oz. butter
3 large eggs
4oz. caster sugar
pinch of salt
2oz. plain flour

☐ Break the chocolate into a small bowl. Dissolve the coffee in the boiling water and add to the chocolate. Put the bowl over a saucepan of very hot water and stir until the chocolate has melted and is smooth. Remove from the heat. Beat in the butter in small pieces until the mixture is creamy.
☐ Separate the eggs. Whisk the yolks in a bowl, then gradually add 3oz. caster sugar and beat until the mixture is light and thick enough to hold a trail of mixture from the whisk.
☐ Whisk the egg whites, remaining sugar and salt together in another bowl until they form stiff peaks. Fold the lukewarm chocolate and coffee mixture into the egg yolk mixture, then fold in a quarter of the egg whites using a large metal spoon. Sift the flour and fold a quarter of the flour into the mixture when the egg whites are partially blended. Continue folding in egg whites and flour alternately until all are used.
☐ Turn mixture immediately into a round 7½in. cake tin which has been lightly buttered and floured. Bake for 30min. in centre of oven, pre-heated to 350 deg. F. or Mark 4. The top will crack and the cake is quite cooked when a large needle pushed into the centre comes out clean.

GATEAU AUX NOISETTES

Victoria Sandwich Cake—see page 142
6oz. unsalted butter
4oz. icing sugar
2 large egg yolks
3oz. ground almonds
1oz. cocoa
4 level teaspoons instant coffee
boiling water
4 tablespoons sherry
5oz. plain chocolate
2oz. shelled walnuts
3 tablespoons double cream

☐ Cut each Victoria Sandwich into 2 layers. Cream 4oz. of the butter with the icing sugar. Beat one yolk at a time into the creamed mixture. Stir in the almonds. Dissolve the cocoa and 2 teaspoons of the coffee in 3 tablespoons boiling water. Dissolve the rest of the coffee in 3 tablespoons of sherry.
☐ Line the base of a round 7in. loose-base cake tin with a circle of greaseproof paper. Mix the cold cocoa into the almond mixture with the rest of sherry. Beat until smooth.
☐ Put a layer of sponge in the base of the tin. Sprinkle with 2 tablespoons of the coffee and sherry liquid. Spread the sponge with a third of the creamed mixture. Repeat the layers, finishing with a layer of sponge. Cover the top with a circle of greaseproof paper. Put a plate with a weight on it on top. Leave in the fridge for 24 hours.
☐ To serve the cake, break the chocolate on to a plate and stand it over a pan of hot water. Stir from time to time until the chocolate has melted and is smooth. Make 5 small greaseproof paper cones, like piping bags—see page 8—and then cut them down so that they are 2in. high. Spoon a little melted chocolate into a paper cone and spread it lightly round the sides so they are well covered. Invert on a plate and leave to set. Make 5 cones.
☐ Add the remaining 2oz. unsalted butter to the chocolate and heat gently until smooth. Chop the walnuts.
☐ Remove the cake from the tin and peel off the greaseproof papers. Smooth half the chocolate round the sides and then roll the sides in the chopped nuts. If the cake is very cold this must be done quickly. Place on a serving plate. Smooth the rest of the chocolate over the top.
☐ Whip the cream until it stands in soft peaks. Spoon into a small piping bag fitted with a small star pipe. Unwrap the cones.
Pipe cream into each one. Pipe the rest of the cream in a large rosette in the centre of the cake. Arrange the cones round the centre Leave for 15min., or until set.

FRUIT AND NUT LOAF

2oz. dried apricots
10oz. self-raising flour
pinch of salt
¼ level teaspoon ground cinnamon
¼ level teaspoon baking powder
5oz. butter
5oz. caster sugar
6oz. stoned dates
1½oz. shelled walnuts
1 level teaspoon bicarbonate of soda
4 tablespoons milk
2 large eggs

☐ Put the apricots into a bowl. Cover with cold water and leave to soak.
☐ Sift the flour, salt, cinnamon and the baking powder into a large bowl. Rub in the butter until the mixture looks like breadcrumbs. Stir in the sugar.
☐ Chop the dates and walnuts. Drain the apricots, chop roughly. Add the fruit and most of the walnuts, leaving some for decoration, to flour and butter. Mix well.
☐ Dissolve the bicarbonate of soda in the milk. Break eggs into a bowl. Beat lightly and add the milk. Make a well in the centre of the dry ingredients and add the egg and milk. Mix to a soft consistency. Spoon into a greased 9in. loaf tin. Sprinkle rest of chopped walnuts on top. Cook for 15min. in centre of oven, pre-heated to 375 deg. F. or Mark 5, then reduce heat to 325 deg. F. or Mark 3 and cook for a further 1 hour or until well risen, golden brown and firm to the touch. If the cake gets too brown before it is cooked, cover the top with a piece of greaseproof paper.
☐ Remove and leave to cool in the tin for 1 hour. Turn out and finish cooling on a wire rack.

WALNUT AND CHERRY LOAF

8oz. self-raising flour
½ level teaspoon salt
2½oz. shelled walnuts
2½oz. glacé cherries
2oz. caster sugar
1oz. butter
2 level tablespoons malt extract
1 large egg
7 tablespoons milk

☐ Sift the flour and salt together. Roughly chop 1½oz. walnuts and 1½oz. glacé cherries. Melt 1oz. sugar, the butter and the malt in a saucepan. Stir dry ingredients into the pan and add the cherries and walnuts. Lightly beat the egg and add to pan with milk. Turn mixture into a greased and lined 1lb. loaf tin.
☐ Bake for 1 hour 5min. until firm and well risen, in centre of oven, pre-heated to 325 deg. F. or Mark 3.
☐ Remove cake from tin and leave to cool on a wire rack.
☐ Chop the remaining cherries and walnuts. Place the remaining sugar and 1 tablespoon water in a small saucepan and heat until the sugar has dissolved. Boil quickly for 1min. Stir in the fruit and then pour this over the loaf.
☐ Serve the loaf, sliced and buttered.

COCONUT CAKE

14oz. plain flour
pinch of salt
4 level teaspoons baking powder
8oz. butter
8oz. caster sugar
2oz. desiccated coconut
4 large eggs
milk to mix

☐ Sift the flour and salt into a mixing bowl. Rub in the butter until the mixture looks like fine breadcrumbs. Stir in the caster sugar and the coconut. Lightly beat the eggs and add gradually to the bowl. Add a little milk if necessary to give a stiff dropping consistency.
☐ Turn the mixture into a greased and lined 7in. cake tin, and bake for 2 hours or until firm to the touch and golden brown, in centre of oven, pre-heated to 350 deg. F. or Mark 4. Turn on to a wire rack and leave to cool.

159

Homemade Biscuits

Enough biscuits to feed the family can be made in one morning because they're quick to mix and as quick to bake. After that it's up to you whether you ice and decorate them, sandwich them together with jam or leave them plain and simple.

SHREWSBURY BISCUITS
(Makes about thirty-six biscuits)

4oz. butter
5oz. caster sugar
1 large egg
8oz. plain flour

☐ Cream the butter until it is soft and light in colour. Add 4oz. sugar. Beat the egg, and add to butter with the flour. Mix well. Turn on to a lightly floured board and roll out to a ¼in. thickness. Cut into rounds using a 2½in. fluted cutter.
☐ Arrange on lightly greased baking trays. Prick with a fork. Bake for 12-15min., or until just coloured, in centre of oven, pre-heated to 350 deg. F. or Mark 4. Sprinkle with rest of caster sugar while still hot, then allow to cool on wire racks.

CURRANT SLICES AND CHERRY CRISPS
(Makes about thirty-six biscuits)

basic Shrewsbury Biscuits mixture—see recipe above
4oz. currants
2oz. glacé cherries

☐ Divide Shrewsbury mixture in half before adding the flour. Add currants to half mixture; chopped cherries to rest.
☐ Roll out to ¼in. thickness and cut into fingers and 3in. rounds. Cut centres out of rounds using a 1in. plain cutter.
☐ Cook as for Shrewsbury Biscuits.

CHRISTMAS COOKIES
(Makes about twelve cookies)

10oz. butter
6oz. icing sugar
6oz. plain flour
2oz. cornflour
pinch of salt
angelica
glacé cherries
nuts
4oz. plain chocolate
1oz. almond nibs
1oz. chocolate vermicelli

☐ Cream 8oz. butter and 2oz. icing sugar until smooth. Sift in the flour, cornflour and salt. Fold in using a large tablespoon until mixture binds together. Spoon into a large piping bag fitted with a ½in. star pipe. Pipe circles, stars, fingers and shells on to greased baking trays. Decorate circles with small leaves cut from angelica; stars with glacé cherry halves, whole hazelnuts, whole almonds and walnut halves.
☐ Cook for 12-15min. or until golden, in centre of oven, pre-heated to 375 deg. F. or Mark 5. Cool on wire racks.
☐ Dust circles and stars with caster sugar if liked. Cream rest of butter and icing sugar. Spoon into a piping bag fitted with a small star pipe. Melt chocolate over hot water. Toast almond nibs. Pipe butter cream on half the fingers and shells. Sandwich with remaining biscuits. Dip ends in melted chocolate. Dip fingers into almond nibs and shells into vermicelli. Leave to set.

ICED BISCUITS
(Makes about forty biscuits)

basic Shrewsbury Biscuits mixture—see recipe left
10oz. icing sugar
1 level teaspoon instant coffee
pink and green vegetable colouring
sweet coffee beans
coloured sugar strands
hundreds and thousands
silver balls

☐ Make and bake as described for Shrewsbury Biscuits but use fancy cutters.
☐ Sift the icing sugar into a mixing bowl and add just enough water to mix to a stiff fairly thick consistency. Divide the icing into 3 bowls. Dissolve the instant coffee in ½ teaspoon hot water and add it to one of the bowls. Colour another lot pink and the last lot green.
Coat biscuits with these icings and add the decorations.

SUGAR CARTWHEELS
(Makes about twenty biscuits)

basic Shrewsbury Biscuits mixture—see recipe left
strawberry and greengage jam
icing sugar

☐ Roll the basic mixture out to ¼in. thickness. Use a 3in. plain cutter and cut out rounds. With a 1in. fluted cutter, cut out the centres of half the biscuits. Cook as for Shrewsbury Biscuits.
☐ When cool, spread jam over the complete rounds. Dredge the ring biscuits with icing sugar and sandwich them together.

Shrewsbury Biscuits, Currant Slices, Cherry Crisps, Viennese Cookies, Sugar Cartwheels, Iced Biscuits—recipes on the opposite page. Recipes overleaf for Nutty Cookies, Chocolate Drops, Almond Crispies and Gingernuts

CHOCOLATE DROPS
(Makes twelve drops)

6oz. plain flour
2oz. cocoa
pinch of salt
5oz. butter
4oz. caster sugar
1 standard egg
4oz. icing sugar
3oz. plain chocolate
12 walnut halves

☐ Sift flour, 1oz. cocoa and salt into a bowl. Rub in 4oz. butter until mixture looks like breadcrumbs. Stir in caster sugar. Beat egg and stir enough into dry ingredients to give a stiff dough.
☐ Roll dough on a floured board to ⅛in. thickness. Cut out 24 rounds using a 2½in. plain cutter. Place 1in. apart on greased baking trays and cook for 15min. above centre of oven, pre-heated to 350 deg. F. or Mark 4.
☐ Cream remaining butter, cocoa and the icing sugar until fluffy. Break chocolate on to a plate over a pan of hot water. Leave to melt. Spread butter cream on half the biscuits and sandwich with remaining halves. Spoon a little chocolate on the top of each biscuit and press a walnut half into the chocolate. Leave to set.

ALMOND CRISPIES
(Make about sixteen crispies)

2½oz. butter
2½oz. caster sugar
1½oz. plain flour
2½oz. flaked almonds

☐ Cream butter and sugar in a bowl until light and fluffy. Sift in flour. Add almonds and stir well. Put teaspoons of the mixture 2in. apart on greased and floured baking trays. Flatten with the back of a fork.
☐ Bake for 5-6min. or until just coloured, in centre of oven, pre-heated to 400 deg. F. or Mark 6. Remove from trays one at a time and place over rolling pin.

GINGERNUTS
(Makes about thirty-six biscuits)

3oz. margarine
6oz. Demerara sugar
9oz. plain flour
pinch of salt
1 level teaspoon bicarbonate of soda
2 level teaspoons ground ginger
1 level teaspoon ground mixed spice
¼ level teaspoon ground nutmeg
4 level tablespoons golden syrup

☐ Cream the margarine and sugar until fluffy. Sift in flour, salt, bicarbonate of soda and spices. Mix thoroughly with a wooden spoon, adding the syrup to give a fairly stiff dough. Form into 1in. balls in the palms of your hands, then flatten each one slightly. Place 2in. apart on greased baking trays and cook for 15min. in upper part of oven, pre-heated to 375 deg. F. or Mark 5. Cool.

NUTTY COOKIES
(Makes about twenty-four cookies)

4oz. whole blanched almonds
3oz. butter
3oz. Demerara sugar
1 large egg
6oz. self-raising flour

☐ Reserve 24 whole almonds, finely chop the rest. Cream butter and sugar until fluffy. Beat egg and add gradually to creamed mixture, beating well after each addition. Fold in the flour and chopped almonds. Shape the firm dough into a long roll about 2in. in diameter. Wrap in greaseproof paper and leave overnight in a cool place or in the refrigerator.
☐ Unwrap and slice the dough into twenty-four ¼in. thick rounds. Press a whole nut on to each round. Place on greased baking trays at least 1in. apart.
☐ Cook for 10min. in upper part of oven, pre-heated to 400 deg. F. or Mark 6. Cool on wire racks.

COCONUT BISCUITS
(Makes about thirty-six biscuits)

½lb. self-raising flour
pinch of salt
5oz. butter
4oz. caster sugar
2oz. desiccated coconut
¼ teaspoon vanilla essence
1 large egg

☐ Sift flour and salt into a bowl. Rub in the butter until the mixture looks like fine breadcrumbs. Stir in the sugar and coconut. Add vanilla essence. Beat the egg and use to bind the mixture to a smooth dough. Knead mixture together with your hands—do not add more moisture, it will bind together.
☐ Turn on to a lightly floured board and knead gently until smooth. Wrap in aluminium foil or place in a polythene bag and chill for 30min. Roll out biscuit dough fairly thinly then cut into 36 rounds using a 3in. plain cutter. Place the biscuits on greased baking trays. Prick well with a fork.
☐ Bake for 12-15min., or until golden, in centre of oven, pre-heated to 350 deg. F. or Mark 4. Leave on trays to cool for about 3min. then transfer to a wire cooling rack. Store in an airtight tin when cold.

CHOCOLATE BISCUITS
(Makes about twenty-eight biscuits)

4oz. butter
4oz. caster sugar
1 large egg
7oz. plain flour
1oz. cocoa

☐ Cream the butter and sugar together until light and fluffy. Beat the egg and add a little at a time to the creamed mixture, beating well after each addition. Sift the flour and cocoa together then sift this, a little at a time, into the creamed mixture. Fold in the flour. Roll to a firm dough. Knead lightly. If the dough is soft and difficult to handle, wrap in greaseproof paper or foil for a while and leave in a cool place.
☐ Roll out biscuit dough to a ¼in. thickness on a floured board. Cut into rounds with a 2½in. fluted cutter. Grease 2 baking trays and place the biscuits on these. Bake for 15-20min., or until very lightly browned, in upper part of oven, pre-heated to 350 deg. F. or Mark 4. Leave to cool on the baking trays for 5min., then remove on to cooling racks.

MACAROONS
(Makes about twenty-four macaroons)

1oz. whole almonds
4oz. ground almonds
8oz. caster sugar
2 large egg whites
½oz. ground rice
½ teaspoon almond essence
2 sheets rice paper

☐ Put the whole almonds in a small saucepan of water and bring to the boil. Drain the almonds and skin. Split them in half. Place the ground almonds, sugar and egg whites in a bowl and beat together for about 5min., using a wooden spoon. Add the ground rice and essence. Mix well.
☐ Put the mixture into a large piping bag fitted with a ½in. plain pipe. Pipe small rounds on to 2 greased baking trays covered with rice paper. Place an almond half in the centre of each. Bake for 20min., or until golden, in centre of oven, pre-heated to 350 deg. F. or Mark 4. Cool on a wire rack.

ROUT DROPS
(Makes about thirty-eight biscuits)

8oz. butter
8oz. caster sugar
1lb. plain flour
8oz. currants
1 large egg
1 teaspoon orange flower water
1 tablespoon rose water
1 tablespoon sweet wine
1 tablespoon brandy

☐ Beat the butter in a large bowl until soft and fluffy. Add the sugar slowly, beating all the time until fluffy again. Sift the flour. Stir in the currants. Gradually add to the butter and sugar mixture, mixing in as much as possible. Then make a hole in the centre. Add the egg, orange flower water, rose water, wine and brandy. Mix well, slowly drawing in the flour from the edge until you have a stiff mixture.
☐ Drop in little heaps from a tablespoon on to greased baking trays, leaving a good space between each one. Bake for 15min. in oven, pre-heated to 375 deg. F. or Mark 5.

SPECIERS
(Makes about thirty-six biscuits)

½lb. butter
¼lb. caster sugar
5oz. plain flour
2oz. blanched almonds

☐ Cream the butter in a large bowl until soft. Beat in the sugar, beating until mixture is light and fluffy. Sift the flour and chop the almonds. Stir both into the creamed mixture. With your hands, work the dough until smooth. Divide the dough into four equal rolls about 2in. in diameter. Wrap in greaseproof paper and leave in the refrigerator overnight.
☐ Next day, slice the rolls thinly. Place biscuits on ungreased baking trays, allowing space for them to spread. Bake for 10min. or until golden brown, in upper and centre parts of oven, pre-heated to 350 deg. F. or Mark 4. Cool on racks.

WALNUT COOKIES
(Makes about fifteen cookies)

4oz. butter
6oz. caster sugar
1 large egg and 1 large egg white
pinch of salt
¾lb. plain flour
3oz. finely ground walnuts
1oz. chopped walnuts
¼ teaspoon lemon essence
4oz. blackberry or blackcurrant jelly

☐ Cream the butter with 2oz. sugar until light and fluffy. Separate the egg and add the egg yolk and salt. Sift flour and stir into the mixture to make a very stiff dough. Pat the dough in a thin layer in a 10in. by 15in. Swiss roll tin.
☐ Whisk egg whites until very stiff and standing in peaks. Gradually add the remaining sugar, beating well all the time. Fold in the ground walnuts and lemon essence. Spread jelly over the dough, then, using a palette knife, swirl meringue over jelly to completely cover the dough. Sprinkle meringue with the chopped walnuts and bake for 30min. in centre of oven, pre-heated to 350 deg. F. or Mark 4. Cut into squares.

SHORTBREAD
(Makes eight pieces)

6oz. plain flour
2oz. caster sugar
4oz. butter

☐ Sift flour and sugar into a bowl. Rub in the butter until the mixture looks like fine breadcrumbs. Knead well to form a smooth ball.
☐ Lightly grease a 7in. sandwich tin and line base with greased greaseproof paper. Press the mixture into the tin and smooth the top. Mark shortbread into 8 sections.
☐ Cook for 30min. in centre of oven, pre-heated to 350 deg. F. or Mark 4, then reduce heat to 325 deg. F. or Mark 3 and cook for another 30min.
☐ Cut right through the sections and cool in the tin.

SOURED CREAM COOKIES
(Makes about thirty cookies)

4oz. butter
6oz. caster sugar
1 large egg
10oz. plain flour
½ level teaspoon bicarbonate of soda
½ level teaspoon baking powder
¼ level teaspoon salt
1 level teaspoon ground cardamom
5oz. carton soured cream
vanilla sugar

☐ Cream the butter until light in colour, then gradually beat in the sugar. Beat in the egg. Sift the flour, bicarbonate of soda, baking powder, salt and cardamom, and stir alternately into the butter mixture with the soured cream, beginning and ending with flour. Put the dough in the fridge or a cold place until firm enough to roll.
☐ Roll dough on a lightly floured board to a ¼in. thickness. Cut out rounds using a 3in. plain cutter. Place on ungreased baking trays. Bake for 12min. or until golden brown, in centre of oven, pre-heated to 375 deg. F. or Mark 5.
☐ Turn on to a wire rack to cool, then sprinkle with vanilla sugar. You can buy vanilla sugar, or simply drop a vanilla pod in a jar of caster sugar and keep for baking days.

FAIRINGS
(Makes about twenty-eight fairings)

8oz. plain flour
2½oz. butter
1oz. lard
½ level teaspoon ground mixed spice
½ level teaspoon ground ginger
4oz. Demerara sugar
4oz. golden syrup
¼oz. bicarbonate of soda
pinch of tartaric acid
2oz. chopped mixed peel

☐ Sift the flour into a bowl. Rub in
butter and lard until the mixture looks
like fine breadcrumbs. Mix the spices and
sugar together. Put the syrup in a bowl.
Bring the bicarbonate of soda to the boil
in 2 teaspoons water. Add to syrup.
Heat the tartaric acid in 2 teaspoons
water until it froths.
☐ Mix all ingredients together. Knead
lightly to a soft paste and roll out on a
lightly floured board to 1in. thick. Cut
into 1in. squares.
☐ Place on baking trays, leaving spaces
between to allow for spreading, and bake
for 30-40min. in centre of oven,
pre-heated to 300 deg. F. or Mark 2.
Cool on wire racks.

SPICE BISCUITS
(Makes about thirty biscuits)

8oz. plain flour
½ level teaspoon baking powder
½ level teaspoon ground cloves
¼ level teaspoon ground allspice
¼ level teaspoon ground cinnamon
4 level tablespoons honey
6 level tablespoons golden syrup
3oz. caster sugar
½oz. butter
½oz. lard
3oz. icing sugar
almond essence
1 tablespoon lemon juice

☐ Sift flour, baking powder and spices.
Heat honey, syrup and sugar until
dissolved. Bring to the boil and remove
from the heat. Add butter and lard and
stir until melted.
☐ Beat in the flour mixture, about 2oz.
at a time. When the batter is smooth,
drop teaspoons of it on to buttered
baking trays, 1in. apart.
☐ Bake for 12-15min., until firm to the
touch and light brown, in centre of oven,
pre-heated to 400 deg. F. or Mark 6.
☐ Mix icing sugar, a few drops of
almond essence, the lemon juice and 1
tablespoon cold water until thin and
smooth. Brush over the biscuits.

STANHOPE FIRELIGHTERS
(Makes about ten pieces)

4oz. rolled oats
4oz. margarine or butter
4oz. caster sugar

☐ Mix all ingredients together in a bowl. Press into a lightly greased square 10in. by 6in. tin.
☐ Cook for 30min. in centre of oven, pre-heated to 350 deg. F. or Mark 4.
☐ Cut into pieces and allow to cool in the tin.

FAT RASCALS
(Makes about fourteen rascals)

1lb. plain flour
8oz. butter
1oz. soft brown sugar
pinch of salt
4oz. currants
milk
caster sugar

☐ Sift the flour into a bowl. Rub in the butter until the mixture looks like fine breadcrumbs. Stir in the brown sugar, salt and currants and mix to a stiff dough with a little milk and water mixed. Turn on to a lightly floured board and roll out to ½in. thickness.
☐ Cut into rounds using a plain 3in. cutter or a glass. Dust with a little caster sugar and place on baking trays. Bake for 20min. in centre of oven, pre-heated to 400 deg. F. or Mark 6.

WIDECOMBE FAIR GINGERBREAD
(Makes thirty-six biscuits)

6oz. self-raising flour
6oz. butter
6oz. caster sugar
1 level teaspoon ground ginger
6 level tablespoons black treacle

☐ Sift the flour into a bowl. Rub in the butter, then stir in the sugar and ginger. Warm the treacle, pour into the flour mixture; mix well.
☐ Drop small pieces the size of a walnut on well-greased baking trays, allowing room for spreading. Bake for 25-30min., or until well browned and flattened, in centre of oven, pre-heated to 300 deg. F. or Mark 2. Leave on the trays for 3min., then cool on wire racks.

SOULING CAKES
(Makes about thirty biscuits)

¾lb. plain flour
½ level teaspoon ground cinnamon
½ level teaspoon ground mixed spice
pinch of ground nutmeg
6oz. margarine or butter
7oz. caster sugar
1 large egg
1½ teaspoons malt vinegar

☐ Sift flour and spices together. Rub in the margarine or butter until the mixture looks like fine breadcrumbs. Stir in 6oz. sugar. Make a well in the centre and drop in the egg and vinegar. Mix well and knead lightly until soft.
☐ Roll out on a lightly floured board to a ¼in. thickness. Cut into rounds using a 3in. plain cutter. Place on lightly greased baking trays. Bake for 20-25min. or until slightly coloured, in centre of oven, pre-heated to 350 deg. F. or Mark 4. Sprinkle with rest of caster sugar while still warm then transfer to wire racks to cool completely.

BOSWORTH JUMBLES
(Makes about thirty jumbles)

3oz. butter
8oz. caster sugar
1 standard egg
4oz. plain flour
1oz. caraway seeds

☐ Cream butter and sugar until light and fluffy. Beat the egg and beat most of it into the mixture. Sift the flour and fold into the mixture with the caraway seeds. Knead well until smooth.
☐ Divide the mixture into even-sized balls and form each into an S shape. Place on baking trays, allowing plenty of room between each one. Brush each with a little beaten egg.
☐ Bake for 10-15min. or until pale brown, in centre of oven, pre-heated to 325 deg. F. or Mark 3. Cool on a rack.

PEPPER CAKES
(Makes forty-eight cakes)

5oz. soft brown sugar
8oz. golden syrup
1 level teaspoon ground ginger
1 level teaspoon ground cinnamon
½ level teaspoon ground white pepper
½ level teaspoon ground cloves
½ level teaspoon ground cardamom
1 heaped teaspoon bicarbonate of soda
5oz. butter
1 large egg
1lb. plain flour

☐ Melt sugar, syrup and spices together. Add bicarbonate of soda; beat well. Put butter in a mixing bowl; pour on hot syrup, stirring, so that the butter melts. Lightly beat egg. Sift flour. When butter has melted, stir in egg. When cool, gradually stir in flour. Allow mixture to stand, covered, until next day.
☐ Work dough until smooth and pliable. Add a little more flour if it seems too soft. Roll out on a lightly floured board to ¼in. thickness, and cut into shapes using fancy cutters. Place on baking trays.
☐ Bake for 15min. in centre of oven, pre-heated to 325 deg. F. or Mark 3. If liked, make up a little Royal Icing, and, using a fine pipe outline shapes.

COCONUT MERINGUES
(Makes twenty meringues)

2 large egg whites
5oz. caster sugar
5oz. desiccated coconut

☐ Whisk the egg whites until very stiff. Stir in the sugar and the coconut.
☐ Pile heaps on a greased baking tray and bake for 1 hour or until dry, in centre of oven, pre-heated to 250 deg. F. or Mark ½.

ORANGE BISCUITS
(Makes forty biscuits)

12oz. plain flour
6oz. caster sugar
3oz. butter
1 level teaspoon baking powder
grated rind of 2 oranges
2 large eggs
milk
icing sugar

☐ Sift the flour and sugar together in a mixing bowl. Rub in the butter until the mixture looks like breadcrumbs. Add the baking powder and orange rind. Lightly beat the eggs and add to the flour and mix to a stiff dough, adding a little milk if the mixture seems too stiff.
☐ Place heaped teaspoonsful on greased baking trays and bake for 25-30min., or until pale golden, in centre of oven, pre-heated to 400 deg. F. or Mark 6.
☐ Remove from the oven and sprinkle with icing sugar.

OATCAKES
(Makes twenty-four oatcakes)

8oz. fine oatmeal
2oz. plain flour
2oz. caster sugar
1 level teaspoon baking powder
pinch of salt
3oz. butter
milk

☐ Mix together the oatmeal, flour, sugar, baking powder and salt. Rub in the butter until the mixture looks like breadcrumbs. Add enough milk to mix to a stiff dough. Leave to rest for 30min.
☐ Roll out on a floured board to ¼in. thickness. Cut into rounds or squares and bake for 20min., or until light brown, in centre of oven, pre-heated to 375 deg. F. or Mark 5.
☐ Serve with butter and jam or marmalade for breakfast.

WALNUT BISCUITS
(Makes forty-eight biscuits)

12oz. plain flour
6oz. butter
5oz. shelled walnuts
4oz. caster sugar
½ large lemon
1 tablespoon rum
1 large egg
granulated sugar

☐ Sift the flour into a bowl. Rub in the butter until the mixture looks like breadcrumbs. Very finely chop the walnuts and add them to the bowl with the sugar. Finely grate the rind from the lemon; squeeze out the juice.
☐ Add rind, juice, rum and the egg to the bowl and mix to a firm dough.
☐ Roll out the dough on a floured board to ¼in. thickness. Cut into rounds using a 2½in. plain cutter. Sprinkle each with a little granulated sugar and place on greased baking trays.
☐ Bake for 15-20min., or until pale golden, in centre of oven, pre-heated to 350 deg. F. or Mark 4. Cool on a rack.

JELLY BISCUITS
(Makes twelve biscuits)

4oz. butter
2oz. caster sugar
1 large egg
4oz. plain flour
pinch of salt
1½oz. desiccated coconut
1 heaped teaspoon redcurrant jelly

☐ Cream the butter and sugar together until light and fluffy. Separate the egg and add the yolk to the creamed mixture, beating well. Sift the flour and salt into the creamed mixture and fold in. Form the mixture into 12 balls.
☐ Beat the egg white. Toss the biscuits in the egg then roll in coconut. Place on greased baking trays and press the centre of each biscuit with your finger to make a slight hollow for the jelly. Fill with jelly.
☐ Bake for 30min. in centre of oven, pre-heated to 325 deg. F. or Mark 3. Cool on a wire rack then store in an airtight tin.

REFRIGERATOR BISCUITS
(Makes forty biscuits)

6oz. butter
7oz. caster sugar
1 large egg
vanilla essence
8oz. plain flour
1 level teaspoon baking powder
pinch of salt
5oz. whole hazelnuts

☐ Cream the butter and sugar together until light and fluffy. Beat the egg lightly and add gradually to the creamed mixture, beating well after each addition. Add a drop of vanilla essence.
☐ Sift the flour, baking powder and salt together and fold into the creamed mixture. Chop the nuts finely and add to bowl; mix thoroughly.
☐ Roll dough into a large sausage shape about 2in. thick. Wrap in greaseproof paper and leave in the refrigerator for 24 hours to chill.
☐ Cut the dough into very thin slices and place them on greased baking trays. Bake for 10min., or until a pale golden colour, in centre of oven, pre-heated to 400 deg. F. or Mark 6. Cool on a rack.

PEANUT BUTTER COOKIES
(Makes sixteen cookies)

2oz. butter
2oz. granulated sugar
2oz. soft brown sugar
1 large egg
vanilla essence
4oz. peanut butter
3oz. plain flour
¼ level teaspoon bicarbonate of soda

☐ Cream butter and sugars together until smooth. Beat the egg and add a little of this at a time to the creamed mixture, together with a few drops of vanilla essence and the peanut butter. Beat the mixture well. Sift the flour and bicarbonate of soda together then fold them into the creamed mixture.
☐ Divide mixture into 16 pieces then shape each into a small ball; flatten each one. Place on greased baking trays.
☐ Bake for 20min., or until golden, in centre of oven, pre-heated to 350 deg. F. or Mark 4. Leave to cool on a wire rack.

LANGUES DE CHAT
(Makes twenty-four biscuits)

3½oz. caster sugar
5oz. carton double cream
4½oz. plain flour
vanilla essence
2 large egg whites

☐ Mix together the sugar and cream. Sift the flour and add to the sugar and cream, with a few drops of vanilla essence.
☐ Whisk the egg whites until very stiff and fold quickly into the sugar mixture using a metal spoon.
☐ Spoon the mixture into a piping bag fitted with a large plain pipe. Pipe small strips on to foil covered baking trays.
☐ Bake for 10min., or until golden, in centre of oven, pre-heated to 400 deg. F. or Mark 6. Cool on a wire rack.

MELTING MOMENTS
(Makes about twenty-four biscuits)

4oz. butter
3oz. caster sugar
1 large egg yolk
vanilla essence
5oz. self-raising flour
2oz. cornflakes

☐ Cream the butter and sugar together until light and fluffy. Beat in the egg yolk and a few drops of vanilla essence. Sift the flour and stir into the butter mixture to make a stiff dough.
☐ Divide into 24 pieces, rolling each piece to a perfect round. Crush the cornflakes and roll each ball in cornflakes to coat. Place on greased baking trays.
☐ Bake for 15-20min. in centre of oven, pre-heated to 375 deg. F. or Mark 5. Cool on wire racks.

Crusty Bread & Buns

Homemade bread, buns and other delicious yeasty things don't take masses of time to prepare. It's the rising times which can be long but they're flexible, so you can do other things at the same time. Here too are recipes for non-yeast breads.

WHITE TIN LOAF AND ROLLS
(Makes one loaf and six rolls)

¼oz. dried yeast
¾ pint lukewarm water
1½lb. strong plain white flour
3 level teaspoons salt
½oz. lard

☐ Sprinkle the yeast on to the lukewarm water. Leave for 15min.
☐ Sift the flour and salt into a bowl; rub in the lard. Make a well in the centre of the flour and pour in all the yeast liquid. Mix with your hands to a soft, smooth, pliable dough.
☐ Turn on to a clean, lightly floured working surface. Knead well for 10min., or until the dough is no longer sticky and is smooth and springy. Shape into a ball and place in a clean, lightly oiled polythene bag. Leave to rise for 1-2 hours at room temperature, or until doubled in size.
☐ Remove the dough on to a lightly floured board. Cut off and reserve 12oz. to make 6 rolls. Lightly knead remaining dough to distribute air bubbles and make dough ready for shaping. Shape dough into an oblong to fit a greased 9in. loaf tin. Place in the tin pushing dough into the corners. Replace in polythene bag—making sure the polythene does not touch the dough. Leave for about 1 hour, or until the dough just reaches the top of the tin.
☐ Meanwhile, divide the 12oz. dough into 6 portions. Knead each piece lightly and form into a ball using palm of left hand and fingers of right. Place rolls on a greased baking tray 1in. apart. Leave under the polythene bag for 30min.
☐ Remove bread from polythene. Bake loaf for 15min. in centre of oven, pre-heated to 450 deg. F. or Mark 8, then reduce heat to 400 deg. F. or Mark 6 and bake loaf for 30min. more. Bake rolls for 20-25min., above the loaf. The bread should sound hollow when tapped underneath with the knuckles. When cooked, cool loaf and rolls on a rack.

CHELSEA BUNS
(Makes eighteen buns)

1lb. plain flour
good pinch of salt
4oz. margarine
½oz. dried yeast
¼ pint lukewarm milk
¼ pint lukewarm water
7oz. caster sugar
1 large egg
2oz. sultanas
2oz. currants
2oz. chopped mixed peel

☐ Sift flour and salt. Rub in 2oz. margarine. Sprinkle the yeast on the mixed lukewarm milk and water. Leave in a warm place for 15min., or until frothy.
☐ Stir 1oz. sugar into flour mixture. Beat the egg and add to bowl with the yeast liquid. Beat well until the mixture is elastic. Oil a polythene bag and put the bowl of dough in it. Leave in a warm place for 30min., or until doubled in bulk. Knead dough well on a floured board. Roll out to 24in. by 9in.
☐ Melt rest of margarine. Stir in 4oz. sugar, fruit and peel. Spread evenly over dough. Roll piece, starting at one long end. Moisten edge; press to seal. Cut into 18 pieces and place in two round 7½in. tins, cut side uppermost. Put in a warm place until buns have joined up.
☐ Bake for 20-25min. or until golden, in centre of oven, pre-heated to 425 deg. F. or Mark 7. Dissolve rest of sugar in 4 tablespoons cold water. Boil for 1min. Turn buns on to a wire rack; brush with the glaze.

POPPY SEED PLAIT AND ROLLS
(Makes one plait and six rolls)

basic dough as given for White Tin Loaf— see recipe left
1 standard egg
poppy seeds

☐ Follow recipe and method for White Tin Loaf until the dough has doubled in bulk. Remove dough from bag; reserve 12oz. for rolls. Knead remaining dough lightly to distribute air bubbles. Cut into 3 equal pieces. Knead lightly and roll into 10in. lengths. Lightly moisten one end of each strip and press firmly together. Lift carefully on to a greased baking tray and plait fairly loosely to form a short fat loaf. (Don't stretch the dough). Moisten loose ends and press together, then tuck under.
☐ Beat egg and 1 tablespoon cold water. Brush loaf with mixture and sprinkle with poppy seeds. Leave to prove under polythene for 30min., or until well risen.
☐ Bake for 15min., in centre of oven, pre-heated to 450 deg. F. or Mark 8, then reduce heat to 400 deg. F. or Mark 6 and cook for 15min. more.
☐ Shape each roll into a smooth ball, then brush with egg and sprinkle with poppy seeds. Bake rolls as basic recipe for White Tin Loaf.

White Tin Loaf and Rolls, Chelsea Buns, Poppy Seed Plait and Rolls—recipes on the opposite page. Recipes for Wholemeal Plait and Rolls, Flower Pot Loaves and Cottage Loaf overleaf

WHOLEMEAL PLAIT AND ROLLS
(Makes one plait and six rolls)

½oz. dried yeast
¾ pint lukewarm water
1lb. wholemeal flour
½lb. strong plain white flour
¾oz. salt
2 level teaspoons caster sugar
1oz. lard
cracked wholewheat grains

☐ Sprinkle the yeast on to the lukewarm water and leave for 15min., until the surface is covered with a thick layer of bubbles.
☐ Mix the flours in a bowl adding ½oz. salt and the sugar. Rub in the lard then make a well in the centre. Pour in the yeast liquid; mix with your hands, adding more water if necessary. Turn on to a lightly floured working surface and knead for 5min. to distribute air bubbles. Cut off 12oz. to make 6 rolls. Cut remaining dough into 3 equal portions. Knead lightly and roll pieces with palms of hands to 10in. lengths. Lightly moisten one end of each strip and press firmly together. Lift on to a greased baking tray and plait fairly loosely. Moisten loose ends and press together, then tuck under.
☐ Dissolve 1 level teaspoon salt in 1 tablespoon warm water and brush this over the bread. Sprinkle with cracked wheat and leave to prove under polythene—making sure it does not touch the dough—for 1 hour or until nearly doubled in size. Cut the reserved dough into 6 portions. Roll with the palm of left hand and fingers of the right, to form small balls. Place 1in. apart on a greased baking tray and leave under polythene for 30min., or until doubled in size. Sprinkle with wheat if liked.
☐ Bake plait for 15min. in centre of oven, pre-heated to 450 deg. F. or Mark 8 then reduce heat to 400 deg. F. or Mark 6 and bake for 45min. more. Bake rolls for 20-25min., at 450 deg. F. or Mark 8, towards top of oven, reducing heat if necessary. Wholewheat bread does take longer to cook than white bread. The bread should sound hollow when tapped on the bottom. Cool on a wire rack.

FLOWER POT LOAVES
(Makes three loaves)

basic bread dough as given for Wholemeal Plait—see this page
three 3½in. flower pots (not plastic)

☐ Follow the recipe for Wholemeal Plait until the dough has doubled in bulk. Remove the dough from the bag on to a lightly floured working surface. Knead for 3min. to distribute the air bubbles. Divide into 3 equal pieces. Knead each piece and form into a cork shape. Put each piece of dough into a well oiled flower pot. Dissolve 1 level teaspoon salt in 1 tablespoon warm water and use to brush loaves. Leave to rise for 30min., or until dough has just risen to the top of the flower pots.
☐ Bake for 40min. in centre of oven, pre-heated to 450 deg. F. or Mark 8, then reduce heat to 400 deg. F. or Mark 6, if the loaves are browning too much. The loaves should sound hollow when tapped on the bottom.

COTTAGE LOAF

basic bread dough as given for White Tin Loaf—see page 168
1 standard egg

☐ Follow recipe and method for White Tin Loaf until the dough has doubled in bulk.
☐ Remove risen dough from bag, cut off ¼ for the top. Knead the larger amount for 3-5min., to distribute bubbles, using as little flour as possible. Shape into a smooth ball and place on a greased baking tray. Knead smaller piece until smooth and form into a ball. Brush top of large ball with water; place smaller ball on top. Flour your finger and push this down the centre of both pieces. Beat the egg and 1 tablespoon water. Brush this over the whole loaf. Leave to prove under polythene— making sure it will not touch the dough —for 30min.-1 hour, depending on room temperature, until it springs back when touched with a finger.
☐ Bake for 15min. in centre of oven, pre-heated to 450 deg. F. or Mark 8, then reduce heat to 400 deg. F. or Mark 6 and continue cooking for a further 30-35min., or until bread sounds hollow when tapped.

QUICK WHITE BREAD

1lb. strong plain white flour
2 level teaspoons salt
¼oz. dried yeast
½ pint lukewarm water

☐ Sift the flour and salt into a warm bowl and put in a warm place. Sprinkle the dried yeast on to ¼ pint lukewarm water and leave in a warm place for 15min., or until frothy on top.
☐ Make a well in the flour, add the yeast liquid and mix to an elastic dough with the remainder of the lukewarm water. Turn the dough on to a floured board and knead for 10min., or until really smooth. Form into a loaf shape and put into a greased 1lb. loaf tin, pressing the dough into the corners.
☐ Cover with a damp tea towel and leave in a warm place to rise until the dough reaches the top of the tin.
☐ Bake for 15min. in centre of oven, pre-heated to 450 deg. F. or Mark 8, then reduce heat to 400 deg. F. or Mark 6 and cook for 30min. more or until the bread sounds hollow when tapped underneath. Cool on a wire rack.

MILK ROLLS
(Makes ten rolls)

½oz. dried yeast
¼ pint lukewarm milk
8oz. strong plain white flour
1 level teaspoon salt
1oz. margarine

☐ Sprinkle the yeast on to the lukewarm milk and leave for 15min., until the surface of the liquid is covered with bubbles.
☐ Sift the flour and salt into a bowl; rub in the margarine. Make a well in the centre of the flour and pour in the yeast liquid. Mix to a fairly soft dough, adding a little more lukewarm milk if necessary. Turn on to a lightly floured working surface and knead for about 10min., or until dough is no longer sticky and is springy to the touch. Form into a smooth ball and place in a clean, lightly oiled polythene bag. Leave until nearly double in size.
☐ Bake for 15min., or until golden, towards top of oven, pre-heated to 425 deg. F. or Mark 7. Remove from tray and cool.

IRISH BROWN BREAD
(Makes two loaves)

10oz. wholemeal flour
5oz. plain white flour
1 level teaspoon baking powder
½ level teaspoon salt
1½oz. caster sugar
4oz. butter
1 large egg
½ pint buttermilk or sour milk

☐ Mix together the flours, baking powder and salt. Stir in the sugar.
☐ Rub in the butter until the mixture looks like fine breadcrumbs.
☐ Beat the egg lightly then stir in the buttermilk, or sour milk, if used. Make a well in centre of dry ingredients and gradually add the egg mixture. Mix to a stiff dough. Divide dough in half and shape into round balls. Flatten tops slightly and cut a cross about ½in. deep with a pointed knife.
☐ Put loaves on greased baking trays and bake for 1 hour in centre of oven, pre-heated to 400 deg. F. or Mark 6. Cool, slice and spread with butter.

ALMOND BUN PLAIT

½oz. dried yeast
¼ pint lukewarm milk and water mixed
8oz. strong plain white flour
pinch of salt
2oz. butter
1 large egg
almond essence
1½oz. caster sugar
1½oz. flaked almonds
3oz. icing sugar

☐ Sprinkle the dried yeast on the lukewarm liquid. Leave it to stand for about 15min., until a froth has formed.
☐ Sift the flour and salt into a mixing bowl and rub in the butter until the mixture looks like fine breadcrumbs. Make a well in the centre of the flour and add the yeast mixture.
☐ Lightly whisk the egg. Reserve a little for glazing. Add remainder with a few drops of almond essence to the flour. Mix the flour and liquid well with the hand until it becomes elastic and leaves the sides of the bowl. Place the dough on a well floured board and knead well to give a smooth texture, and distribute the yeast. Return to the bowl and cover with an oiled polythene bag.
☐ Leave it in a warm place for about 45min., until it has doubled in size, taking care not to let it touch the polythene. Knead in the sugar lightly and form the mixture into sausage shapes—see Wholemeal Plait, for method on page 170. Place on a well greased baking tray and plait the dough, sealing the ends firmly. Leave in a warm place for about 10min. to rise. Don't let it stand too long or it will lose the plait shape.
☐ Brush with reserved egg. Bake for 10-15min. in centre of oven, pre-heated to 425 deg. F. or Mark 7, then reduce heat to 350 deg. F. or Mark 4 and cook for a further 30min., until golden brown. Remove it from the tin and when tapped on the bottom the plait should sound hollow.
☐ Leave to cool on a wire rack. Toast almonds until golden. Make up the icing sugar using a little cold water to make a coating consistency. Carefully pour the icing over the plait and sprinkle on the browned almonds.

OATMEAL CAKES
(Makes about six cakes)

4oz. medium oatmeal
8oz. plain flour
good pinch of salt
2 level teaspoons baking powder
1 level teaspoon caster sugar
½oz. dried yeast
1 large egg
2oz. lard

☐ Put the oatmeal in a basin and just cover with cold water. Leave to soak overnight.
☐ Sift flour, salt and baking powder into a bowl. Stir in sugar. Heat 4 tablespoons water until lukewarm, sprinkle on the yeast and leave for 15min., or until frothy. Beat the egg.
☐ Make a well in the centre of the flour; add yeast liquid, egg and oatmeal and a little of its water. Mix well and beat until you have a thick smooth batter, adding more oatmeal water if required.
☐ Melt a little lard in a heavy frying pan. When hot pour in enough batter to cover base of pan and cook for 2min. on each side or until golden brown. Keep hot while you make remaining pancakes. Serve hot with butter and caster sugar.

OVEN CAKES
(Makes two cakes)

8oz. plain flour
½ level teaspoon salt
1oz. lard
½oz. dried yeast
¼ pint lukewarm milk

☐ Sift flour and salt. Rub in the lard. Sprinkle the yeast on half the lukewarm milk and leave in a warm place for 15min., or until frothy.
☐ Make a well in centre of flour. Add yeast liquid and mix to an elastic dough adding more of the lukewarm milk. Knead well on a lightly floured board until smooth. Divide in two and roll each piece into a flat round. Place on baking trays and prick well down to the tin.
☐ Allow to rise in a warm place, then bake for 15min. or until firm, in centre of oven, pre-heated to 400 deg. F. or Mark 6. Split in half, butter and serve.

PIZZA
(Enough for one or two)

8oz. plain flour
pinch of salt
¼oz. dried yeast
¼ pint lukewarm water
1 dessertspoon olive oil
8oz. tin peeled tomatoes
basil or marjoram
4oz. mozzarella or Bel Paese cheese
1 small green pepper
1 small onion
½oz. butter
1oz. button mushrooms
2oz. lean cooked ham
½in. piece of Italian salami

☐ Sift the flour and salt into a large bowl. Sprinkle yeast on to the lukewarm water and leave it to stand for 15min., or until it becomes frothy. Add to the flour and mix. Knead the dough well on a lightly floured surface. Put it into a clean, lightly oiled bowl, cover with a cloth which has been wrung out in hot water, and leave dough to rise in a warm place for about 1 hour. When it is ready, the dough will retain the impression of your fingers and if you pull it away from the side, it looks stringy.

☐ Turn the dough on to a lightly floured surface and knead it well for about 5min. kneading in most of the oil. Form the dough into a large flat round, about 10in. in diameter. Put it on an oiled baking tray and flatten it again with your fingers so that the edge is slightly raised. Leave in a warm place for not more than 10min. to rise again.

☐ Drain the tomatoes and break them down a little. Spread over the dough. Sprinkle with a little basil or marjoram. Slice the mozzarella cheese, spread it over the tomatoes.

☐ Cut pepper in half. Remove core and seeds. Wash pepper. Cut into strips. Skin and finely chop onion and fry for 5min. in the butter. Rinse mushrooms. Cut into slices downwards, including stalks. Cut ham into cubes, removing fat. Cut salami into fine slices. Scatter ingredients on top of pizza; sprinkle with a little oil.

☐ Bake for 30min. in centre of oven, pre-heated to 425 deg. F. or Mark 7. Halfway through cooking, brush the edge with olive oil. If you're using Bel Paese cheese, slice it and add it to the pizza for the last 5min. cooking time.

☐ If preferred, sprinkle the tomatoes with a little dried rosemary and add slices of mozzarella cheese. Arrange anchovy fillets in a lattice pattern with black olives in between—see the picture.

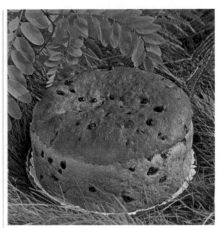

CORNMEAL LOAF

9oz. fine yellow maize flour
1¼ level teaspoons salt
1 level teaspoon caster sugar
¾ pint boiling water
2½ teaspoons olive oil
¼oz. dried yeast
3 tablespoons lukewarm water
8-9oz. plain flour

☐ Put 6oz. maize flour, salt, sugar and boiling water in a large mixing bowl and stir until smooth. Stir in the oil and cool until lukewarm.
☐ Sprinkle the yeast on to the lukewarm water and let it stand in a warm place for about 15min., or until frothy on top.
☐ Stir the yeast into the maize mixture. Gradually add the remaining maize flour and 4oz. plain flour, stirring constantly. Gather the dough into a ball, put it in a bowl and cover bowl with a damp cloth. Allow to stand in a warm place for 30min., or until doubled in bulk. Brush the bottom of a 9in. flan tin with oil.
☐ Knead dough for 5min. on a lightly floured surface, adding 4-5oz. more plain flour to make a firm but not stiff dough. Shape into a smooth round and place in the tin. Cover and allow the dough to rise again in a warm place.
☐ Bake bread for 15min. in centre of oven, pre-heated to 425 deg. F. or Mark 7, then reduce heat to 350 deg. F. or Mark 4 and cook for another 30min., or until golden brown.

SAFFRON CAKE

large pinch of saffron
¼ pint boiling water
milk
½oz. dried yeast
1lb. 4oz. plain flour
¼ level teaspoon salt
3oz. butter
3oz. lard
3oz. sultanas
3oz. currants
1oz. chopped mixed peel
2½oz. caster sugar

☐ Sprinkle the saffron on to the boiling water in a jug. Leave for 5min., strain and make the saffron liquid up to ½ pint with milk. Sprinkle yeast on the warm liquid; leave for 15min. or until frothy.
☐ Sift the flour and salt into a large bowl. Rub in the butter and lard until the mixture looks like fine breadcrumbs. Stir in fruit, peel and sugar. Make a well in the centre of the flour and pour in the yeast liquid. Draw in the dry ingredients and mix to a smooth soft dough. A little more warm water may be added if the dough is too dry. Knead in the bowl or on a floured working surface for 5-10min., until the dough is smooth and springy to the touch. Put into a lightly oiled polythene bag and leave for about 1½ hours in a warm place until doubled in bulk.
☐ Remove from the bag and knead for about 5min. Form into a ball, flatten it and press into a greased and lined 8in. cake tin pushing it into the corners. Leave to prove for 45min. under a polythene bag (make sure the bag is not touching the cake), or until the dough has reached the top of the tin. Brush with milk.
☐ Cook for 30min. in centre of oven, pre-heated to 400 deg. F. or Mark 6, then reduce heat to 350 deg. F. or Mark 4 and continue cooking for 1 hour more. Leave in the tin for 2 hours to cool. Turn out and finish cooling on a wire rack.

DOUGHNUTS
(Makes twelve doughnuts)

8oz. strong plain white flour
good pinch of salt
2oz. butter
2oz. caster sugar
¼oz. dried yeast
¼ pint lukewarm milk
1 medium-sized egg
4 level tablespoons raspberry jam
oil for deep frying

☐ Sift the flour and salt into a large mixing bowl. Rub in the butter and add 1oz. caster sugar. Dissolve the dried yeast in the lukewarm milk. Leave to stand for about 15min. until frothy.
☐ Lightly beat the egg and add it to the flour with the yeast liquid. Knead the dough for about 10min., and place it in an oiled polythene bag and leave to stand in a warm place for about 1 hour until it has doubled in size.
☐ Lightly knead the mixture and divide it into 12 pieces. Form each piece into a ball and place on a well greased baking tray. Leave the dough for about 10min. Push a well floured index finger into the centre of each doughnut and spoon in a small quantity of jam. Close up the hole and leave the dough to stand for a further 10min.
☐ Heat the oil to the correct temperature —see page 15. Carefully lower in 3 doughnuts at a time and cook for about 3min., until golden brown. Don't try to fill the basket as the doughnuts puff up. Drain well and dredge with remaining caster sugar.
☐ If preferred, roll out the dough on a lightly floured board to ½in. thickness. Cut out rounds using a 2½in. plain cutter and cut out centres using a 1in. plain cutter. Fry as described.

DANISH PASTRY
(Makes eighteen pastries, six types)

½oz. dried yeast
¼ pint and 2 tablespoons lukewarm milk
1lb. plain flour
11oz. unsalted butter
1oz. caster sugar
½ level teaspoon ground cardamom
½ level teaspoon salt
2 large eggs

☐ Sprinkle the yeast on to the lukewarm milk and leave it in a warm place for 15min., or until frothy.
☐ Sift the flour into a bowl, then rub in 2oz. butter. Stir in sugar, spice and salt. Make a well in the centre. Beat the eggs and add to the flour with the yeast liquid. Mix to an elastic dough. Turn on to a lightly floured board and knead for 3-4min. or until smooth, soft and pliable. Cover pastry and allow to rise in a warm place until doubled in bulk.
☐ Work remaining butter with a palette knife until soft. Shape butter into a square block. Roll out pastry to a 12in. long piece and allow to cool for 10min. Put butter on the pastry, then pat the butter over the entire surface, working quickly with your fingertips. Fold nearest third over middle, then fold remaining third over to make 3 layers. Chill for 15min. in the fridge.
☐ Roll out pastry quickly to an oblong about ½in. thick and fold in 3 as before. Chill again. Repeat the rolling, folding and chilling process twice more. Roll again to ½in. thickness and fold pastry in half. Chill for 30min.
☐ Line baking trays with foil to prevent the butter oozing over the oven floor. Cut off a third of the pastry and set aside. Roll rest of pastry with a chilled rolling pin to a 12in. by 16in. oblong. Cut out twelve 4in. squares. Roll reserved third to a 12in. by 6in. strip. Cut in half lengthways.
☐ Use pieces to make Triangles, Buckles, Carnival Buns, Cushions and Brushes and Combs.

WATER ICING

6oz. icing sugar

☐ Sift icing sugar into a bowl. Add 2 tablespoons water gradually and mix to a smooth icing.

VANILLA CUSTARD

1oz. plain flour
1oz. caster sugar
1 large egg
¼ pint milk
½ teaspoon vanilla essence

☐ Mix flour and sugar. Beat egg and mix with the flour and sugar. Heat milk to just below boiling point and pour on to flour mixture, stirring well. Return to pan and cook for 3-4min. over a low heat until very thick and smooth. Stir in vanilla essence and leave to cool. Use half for Triangles and half for Buckles.

TRIANGLES
(Makes three triangles)

½ quantity of vanilla custard
three 4in. squares of Danish pastry
little egg yolk
1oz. shelled walnuts or almonds
water icing

☐ Place 1 heaped teaspoon of vanilla custard in the middle of each pastry square and fold in half to form a triangle. Press edges well to seal in filling. Cut edges 5 times with a sharp knife. Place on prepared baking trays.
☐ Beat the egg yolk and chop the nuts. Brush pastries with egg yolk and sprinkle with the nuts. Allow to rise in a warm place for 15min.
☐ Cook for 15-20min., or until golden brown, just above centre of oven, pre-heated to 400 deg. F. or Mark 6. Spoon a little water icing on each while still warm. Cool on a wire rack.

CUSHIONS
(Makes three pastries)

3 heaped teaspoons raspberry jam
three 4in. squares of Danish pastry
little egg yolk
water icing

☐ Place 1 heaped teaspoon of raspberry jam in the centre of each pastry square. Fold the corners into the centre and pinch together. Beat the egg yolk and brush over the pastries. Allow to rise, then bake and complete as for Triangles.

BRUSHES AND COMBS
(Makes six pastries)

½oz. butter
1oz. caster sugar
3oz. ground almonds
1 standard egg
almond essence
two 12in. by 3in. strips of Danish pastry
1oz. shelled walnuts or almonds
1oz. granulated sugar

☐ Cream the butter and caster sugar. Stir in ground almonds. Beat the egg and add enough to give a stiff spreading consistency. Add a few drops of almond essence. Spread a pencil thick strip of almond filling down the centre of the strips of Danish pastry. Fold one third of one pastry strip lengthways over filling. Brush folded over pastry with egg. Fold the other third over the middle to give 3 layers. Press strip lightly to flatten. Turn over and brush smooth side with egg.
☐ Finely chop the nuts and combine with the granulated sugar. Cut the dough into 3 pieces making diagonal cuts. Dip smooth sides into sugar and nut mixture and place on prepared baking trays.
☐ To shape the combs, fold one third of remaining strip lengthways over filling. Cut the strip into 3 pieces making straight cuts. Brush with remaining egg and sprinkle with the sugar and nut mixture. Using a sharp knife, cut unfolded side 5 or 6 times to within ⅛in. of the filling but without touching the filling.
☐ Allow to rise, then bake as for Triangles. These pastries don't need icing after baking.

CARNIVAL BUNS
(Makes three buns)

½oz. stoned raisins
3oz. chopped mixed peel
three 4in. squares of Danish pastry
little egg yolk
water icing

☐ Place a few raisins and a little mixed peel in the centre of each pastry square. Fold the two opposite corners over the fruit and pinch together. Beat the yolk and brush over pastries. Allow to rise, and bake and complete as for Triangles.

BUCKLES
(Makes three buckles)

½ quantity of vanilla custard
three 4in. squares of Danish pastry
little egg yolk
water icing

☐ Place a heaped teaspoon of vanilla
custard in the centre of each pastry
square. Cut each corner towards the
middle to within ¼in. of the filling. Fold
alternate points into the centre and
pinch together. Place on the prepared
baking trays. Beat the egg yolk and
brush over the pastries. Allow to rise,
and bake and complete as for Triangles.

BARA BRITH

1½lb. plain flour
pinch of salt
¼ pint and 4 tablespoons milk
½oz. dried yeast
4oz. lard
4oz. sultanas
4oz. currants
4oz. stoned raisins
1oz. chopped mixed peel
1 large egg

☐ Sift flour and salt into a warm bowl.
Mix milk with an equal amount of
water. Heat until lukewarm. Sprinkle
yeast on top and leave for 15min. or
until frothy. Make a well in the flour
and add yeast liquid. Mix well, then
knead in the bowl until elastic. Put bowl
in an oiled polythene bag and put in a
warm place for 1½ hours or until the
mixture has doubled in bulk.
☐ Melt lard and mix into the risen
dough using your hands. Knead in fruit
and peel. Beat the egg and add to bowl.
Mix in. Turn dough on to a floured
surface and knead very well, pushing
back any fruit that falls out as you
knead. Form into an oblong and put
into a greased 2lb. loaf tin. Leave to
rise in a warm place until the dough
reaches top of tin.
☐ Cook for 1 hour or until firm, in
centre of oven, pre-heated to 375 deg. F.
or Mark 5. Tap the bottom of the loaf
with your knuckles. It will sound hollow
when done. Cool on a wire rack and
serve cut into slices and thickly buttered.

BARMBRACK

1lb. plain flour
½ level teaspoon ground nutmeg
pinch of salt
2oz. butter
½ pint milk
½oz. dried yeast
2 level tablespoons caster sugar
2 large eggs
½lb. sultanas
½lb. currants
4oz. chopped mixed peel

☐ Sift flour, nutmeg and salt into a
bowl. Rub in the butter. Warm the milk
until lukewarm, sprinkle on the dried
yeast and leave in a warm place for
15min., or until frothy.
☐ Stir the sugar into the flour mixture.
Beat the eggs well. Add the yeast liquid
and most of the eggs to the mixture,
beating well with a wooden spoon to a
stiff but elastic mixture. Beat for 5min.
more. Mix in the sultanas, currants and
peel.
☐ Turn mixture into a buttered 2lb. loaf
tin. It should only half fill the tin. Cover
with a cloth and leave to rise in a warm
place until the dough has reached the
top of the tin.
☐ Brush top with remaining beaten egg.
Bake cake for 15min. in centre of oven,
pre-heated to 400 deg. F. or Mark 6,
then reduce heat to 350 deg. F. or Mark
4 and cook for a further 45-50min. Test
by pushing a skewer through the middle.
If it comes out clean, the cake is cooked.
Leave in the tin for 3min. to cool, then
turn on to a wire rack to finish cooling.
Cut into thin slices to serve and spread
with butter.

LARDY CAKE

1lb. 2oz. plain flour
1 level teaspoon salt
½oz. dried yeast
½ pint lukewarm water
3oz. lard
2½oz. caster sugar
1 level teaspoon ground mixed spice

☐ Sift 1lb. flour and the salt. Sprinkle
dried yeast on the lukewarm water; leave
in a warm place for 15min. or until
frothy. Add to flour and mix well. Knead
well with your hands in the bowl until
the dough is elastic and leaves the sides
of the bowl clean. Put dough into an
oiled polythene bag and leave in a warm
place until doubled in bulk.
☐ Turn dough on to a floured board and
knead well. Roll out risen dough on a
lightly floured board to an oblong 12in.
by 4in. with one short end near you. Dot
half the lard over the nearest two thirds.
Mix the sugar and the spice. Sprinkle
half over the lard. Sprinkle with a third
of the remaining flour.
☐ Fold farthest third over middle and
nearest third over again to make 3
layers. Turn dough so folded edges are
at the sides. Roll out and dot with lard
and sprinkle with spice mixture and
flour as before. Fold, turn and roll out
again.
☐ Sprinkle with remaining flour; fold
and roll into a 7in. round. Put in a
greased round 7in. tin and leave in a
warm place for 15min. until dough has
reached the top of the tin. Cook for
50min. in centre of oven, pre-heated to
425 deg. F. or Mark 7. Serve hot slices
spread with butter.

SODA BREAD

1lb. plain flour
1 level teaspoon salt
1 heaped teaspoon baking powder
1oz. butter
¼ pint and 3 tablespoons buttermilk

☐ Sift flour, salt and baking powder
into a bowl. Rub in the butter.
Mix in the milk to give a soft dough.
☐ Flour your hands and mould the
dough into a round about 1½in. thick.
Make a cross cut on the top of the loaf.
Bake for 30-35min. in centre of oven,
pre-heated to 425 deg. F. or Mark 7.

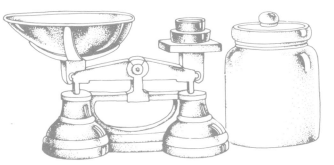

CHRISTSTOLLEN
(Makes two cakes)

8oz. stoned raisins
4oz. currants
1lb. 12oz. plain flour
4oz. butter
2oz. lard
6oz. granulated sugar
½oz. dried yeast
½ pint lukewarm milk
2 large eggs
2oz. chopped mixed peel
icing sugar

☐ Clean raisins and currants. Sift flour. Rub in butter and lard until mixture looks like breadcrumbs. Stir in granulated sugar. Sprinkle yeast on to the milk and leave for 15min. until frothy. Beat eggs; stir into yeast liquid. Make a well in dry mixture, pour in yeast liquid and mix to a stiff dough with your hand. Knead it in the bowl until elastic. Cover with a clean tea towel wrung out in hot water; leave in a warm place for 1 hour to rise.
☐ Turn dough on to a floured board and knead well. Knead in fruit and peel. Grease a 2lb. and a 1lb. loaf tin. Pull off a third of dough. Shape both pieces into oblongs and put into tins. Leave, covered, in a warm place for 1 hour, or until well risen. Bake for 1 hour in centre of oven, pre-heated to 375 deg. F. or Mark 5, then reduce heat to 325 deg. F. or Mark 3 and bake for 1 hour more.
☐ Leave to cool then dredge heavily with sifted icing sugar.

HOT CROSS BUNS
(Makes eighteen buns)

½oz. dried yeast
½ pint and 3 tablespoons lukewarm water
1lb. 5oz. strong plain white flour
½ level teaspoon salt
4 level teaspoons ground mixed spice
½ level teaspoon ground cinnamon
2oz. lard
5oz. granulated sugar
1 large egg
3oz. currants
1oz. sultanas
½oz. chopped mixed peel
4 tablespoons milk

☐ Sprinkle the dried yeast on to the lukewarm water. Leave to stand for about 15min. or until frothy on top.
☐ Meanwhile, sift 1lb. 4oz. flour, salt and spices into a large bowl. Rub in the lard. Stir in 3oz. sugar. Make a well in the centre. Beat the egg and add to the flour mixture with the yeast liquid. Mix to a soft but not sticky dough. Turn the dough on to a floured board and knead for 10min., or until the dough is smooth and springy. Flour your hands from time to time but don't put too much flour on the board or the dough will become too dry.
☐ Sprinkle a little flour into a clean bowl. Form the dough into a smooth ball and place in the bowl. Lightly oil a large clean polythene bag and place the bowl and dough inside. Leave in a warm place for about 1 hour or until doubled in size.
☐ Turn the risen dough on to a lightly floured board and make a well in the centre. Add the fruit and peel. Knead dough until fruit is evenly distributed. Divide the dough into 18 equal pieces. Knead each piece into a ball and place 2in. apart on lightly greased baking trays. Mix remaining flour with 2 tablespoons cold water to form a smooth thick paste. Spoon the paste into a piping bag fitted with a small plain pipe and pipe a cross on each bun.
☐ Place the buns inside greased polythene bags. Keep the polythene well above the buns. Leave for about 30min. or until doubled in size.
☐ Remove buns from bags. Cook for 12-15min., until risen and golden, towards top of oven, pre-heated to 425 deg. F. or Mark 7. If the oven is too hot the buns will crack on the top.
☐ While buns are cooking, heat rest of sugar and milk until the sugar has dissolved. Bring to the boil and remove from heat. Remove the cooked buns on to cooling racks and immediately brush with the sugar glaze. Leave to cool.
☐ Heat the buns for 10min. in oven before serving.

YULETIDE CAKE

4oz. caster sugar
½ level teaspoon ground cinnamon
½ pint lukewarm milk
¼oz. dried yeast
1 standard egg
1oz. butter
14oz. plain flour
2oz. chopped mixed peel
4oz. stoned raisins
8oz. icing sugar

☐ Mix caster sugar, cinnamon and milk in a bowl. Stir in yeast and leave for 15min. until it is frothy. Beat egg. Melt butter. Stir into bowl. Sift flour; make a well in it. Add liquid and mix to a dough. Beat until smooth. Leave in a warm place, covered with a damp tea towel until doubled in bulk.
☐ Grease and flour a 2lb. ring tin. Knead dough well. Knead in peel and raisins. Turn into tin, cover and leave in a warm place until well risen.
☐ Bake for 10min. in centre of oven, pre-heated to 425 deg. F. or Mark 7, then reduce heat to 375 deg. F. or Mark 5 and bake for 20-25min. more. Leave to cool in tin inverted on a wire rack.
☐ Mix icing sugar with enough cold water to make a fairly stiff icing. Coat top of cake, letting icing dribble down.

BATH BUNS
(Makes eight buns)

8oz. plain flour
pinch of salt
1oz. butter
2oz. caster sugar
milk
¼oz. dried yeast
1 large egg
1oz. currants
1oz. chopped mixed peel
1 small lemon
6 sugar lumps

☐ Sift flour and salt into a warm bowl. Rub in butter. Stir in caster sugar. Heat 3 tablespoons milk with 3 tablespoons water until lukewarm. Sprinkle on dried yeast and leave in a warm place for 15min., or until frothy.
☐ Beat the egg. Make a well in the flour mixture and add the egg and the yeast liquid. Mix to a smooth dough, beating it with your hands until it becomes elastic, adding a little more lukewarm water if required. Put dough into an oiled polythene bag and leave in a warm place for 1 hour or until dough has doubled in bulk.
☐ Turn dough on to a floured board and knead well, kneading in currants and peel. Finely grate the lemon rind and knead into the dough. Form dough into 8 buns, flouring your hands each time. Place on greased baking trays. Leave buns in a warm place for 20min.
☐ Brush buns with a little milk. Crush sugar cubes into pieces and sprinkle over buns.
☐ Cook for 20-25min. or until golden brown, in centre of oven, pre-heated to 400 deg. F. or Mark 6. Cool on a rack.

HUNGARIAN CAKE

10oz. plain flour
5oz. butter
7oz. caster sugar
¼oz. dried yeast
13 tablespoons lukewarm milk
1 large egg
6oz. shelled walnuts
4oz. sultanas

☐ Sift flour into a bowl. Rub in 3oz. butter. Stir in 1oz. sugar. Sprinkle yeast on 8 tablespoons milk and leave for 15min. until frothy. Separate egg and stir in yolk. Add to flour mixture and work to a fairly stiff dough. Knead well. Cover bowl with a damp tea towel; leave dough to rise in a warm place for 30min. or until doubled in bulk.
☐ Dissolve rest of sugar in rest of milk. Chop walnuts very finely, add to pan. Stir over a gentle heat for 1min. Beat in rest of butter and sultanas. Cool mixture.
☐ Knead dough well on a floured board for 5min., then roll out to a large oblong. Spread on filling, roll up like a Swiss roll. Leave on a greased baking tray in a warm place for 10min. to rise, then brush with unbeaten egg white. Bake for 15min. in centre of oven, pre-heated to 450 deg. F. or Mark 8, then reduce heat to 400 deg. F. or Mark 6 and bake for 15-20min. more. Serve sliced.

SCARBOROUGH MUFFINS
(Makes about eight muffins)

1lb. plain flour
pinch of salt
½ pint milk
¼oz. dried yeast
1 large egg

☐ Sift flour and salt into a bowl; make a well in flour. Warm the milk until lukewarm and stir in the yeast. Leave for 15min. until thick and frothy on top. Beat the egg and add to the milk; pour into flour. Work the flour into the milk mixture to make a stiff dough. Roll out on a lightly floured board to ½in. thickness. Cut into rounds using a 3in. plain cutter. Allow to rise for 30min. in a warm place.
☐ Bake for 10min. in centre of oven, pre-heated to 450 deg. F. or Mark 8, then reduce heat to 350 deg. F. or Mark 4 and cook for 20min. longer.

QUICK BUNS
(Makes eight buns)

8oz. plain flour
¼ level teaspoon salt
2 level teaspoons baking powder
3oz. butter
1oz. sultanas
4oz. caster sugar
1oz. shelled walnuts
1 large egg
milk

☐ Sift the flour, salt and baking powder into a bowl. Rub in the butter until the mixture looks like fine breadcrumbs.
☐ Add the sultanas and 2oz. sugar. Chop the walnuts and add to the bowl. Beat the egg and add enough egg and milk to mix to a fairly stiff dough.
☐ Turn the dough on to a floured board and divide into 8 equal portions. Form these into rounds and place on greased baking trays. Bake for 15–20 min., or until golden, towards top of oven, pre-heated to 425 deg. F. or Mark 7.
☐ While the buns are cooking put the remaining sugar and 2 tablespoons cold water into a small pan. Heat gently until the sugar has dissolved. Boil for 2min., until thick and syrupy. Brush hot buns with the glaze and cool.

RIPON SPICE CAKE

1lb. plain flour
pinch of salt
1 level teaspoon ground mixed spice
1½oz. butter
1½oz. lard
½oz. dried yeast
½ pint lukewarm milk
1 large egg
2oz. caster sugar
3oz. currants
1oz. chopped mixed peel
2oz. stoned raisins

☐ Sift the flour, salt and spice into a warm bowl. Rub in butter and lard until the mixture looks like fine breadcrumbs. Sprinkle the dried yeast on the lukewarm milk and leave for 15min. in a warm place until frothy.
☐ Make a well in the centre of the flour and pour in the yeast mixture. Sprinkle with a little flour from the sides of the bowl and wait for the yeast to break through. Beat egg and add to bowl with sugar, currants, peel and raisins. Beat dough well. Put into an oiled polythene bag and leave in a warm place for 20min., or until doubled in bulk.
☐ Knead dough on a lightly floured board, shape into a loaf and put in a greased 2lb. loaf tin. Leave to stand for 20min. in a warm place until dough has just reached top of tin.
☐ Bake for 15min. in centre of oven, pre-heated to 425 deg. F. or Mark 7, then reduce heat to 375 deg. F. or Mark 5 and cook for 30min. more or until cooked. Tap bottom of loaf with your knuckles. It will sound hollow when done. Turn on to a wire rack to cool.

DEVON CHUDLEIGHS
(Makes eighteen buns)

½oz. dried yeast
¼ pint lukewarm water
6 tablespoons milk
1oz. lard
2oz. butter
1lb. plain flour
¼ level teaspoon salt
raspberry jam
clotted cream or whipped cream

☐ Sprinkle dried yeast on to the lukewarm water. Leave for 15min. or until thick and frothy. Put the milk, lard and butter into a small saucepan and heat gently—do not boil—until fat has melted. Cool.
☐ Sift the flour and salt into a large bowl; pour in the yeast liquid and the milk mixture. Mix with your hands to a soft, but not sticky dough. Turn on to a lightly floured surface and knead well for 5min. or until smooth. Put into a lightly oiled polythene bag and leave in a warm place for 1 hour, or until doubled in bulk. Knead for about 3min.
☐ Divide dough into 18 equal pieces; form into smooth balls.
☐ Place the Chudleighs ½in. apart on lightly greased baking trays in a warm place. Leave until the buns are just touching.
☐ Cook for 20min. or until well risen, towards top of oven, pre-heated to 400 deg. F. or Mark 6. The buns should sound hollow when cooked. Wrap in a tea towel until cold—this keeps the bread soft.
☐ Split each bun and fill with jam and thick cream.

MALT BREAD
(Makes two loaves)

¾lb. wholemeal flour
8oz. strong plain white flour
1 level teaspoon salt
½oz. dried yeast
½ pint lukewarm milk
2 level tablespoons caster sugar
1 level tablespoon golden syrup
1oz. malt extract
1oz. sultanas
2 tablespoons cold milk

☐ Sift the wholemeal and plain flours together. Add the salt. Sprinkle the dried yeast on ¼ pint lukewarm milk. Leave for 15min., or until the top is thick and frothy.
☐ Make a well in the flour and add the yeast liquid. Add 1 tablespoon caster sugar, the golden syrup, malt extract and sultanas. Add the other ¼ pint lukewarm milk. Mix to an elastic dough and knead. Place in an oiled polythene bag. Leave to rise for about 45min., until it has doubled in bulk.
☐ Turn on to a floured board and knead lightly to distribute the air. Divide the dough in half and place each half in a greased 7in. loaf tin. Leave until the dough rises almost to the top of the tins.
☐ Heat the remaining sugar with 2 tablespoons milk and brush the loaves. Bake for 40-45min. in centre of oven, pre-heated to 450 deg. F. or Mark 8.
☐ When cooked, turn out of the tins and tap the bottom of the loaves. They should sound hollow.

MILK LOAF
(Makes two loaves)

2lb. plain flour
1 level teaspoon salt
½oz. dried yeast
1 pint lukewarm milk
1 large egg

☐ Sift the flour and salt together. Sprinkle yeast on to the lukewarm milk and leave to stand for 10min., or until thick and frothy. Make a well in centre of the flour and add the yeast liquid. Mix to a soft dough. Knead well then cover with a damp tea towel. Leave to rise for 1–2 hours until doubled in bulk.
☐ Knead the dough on a floured board and form into 2 rounds. Put on greased baking trays. Leave to rise for a further 30min.
☐ Beat the egg and brush the loaves. Bake for 10min. in centre of oven, pre-heated to 425 deg. F. or Mark 7, then reduce heat to 375 deg. F. or Mark 5 and bake for a further 35min. Cool.

QUICK WHOLEMEAL BREAD

1lb. wholemeal flour
¼oz. salt
1 level dessertspoon black treacle
½ pint and 4 tablespoons lukewarm water
½oz. dried yeast

☐ Mix the flour and salt in a warm bowl and put the flour to warm. Mix the treacle with the lukewarm water and sprinkle on the yeast. Leave in a warm place for 15min., or until frothy on top.
☐ Add the yeast liquid to the wholemeal flour and mix well—the dough should be quite soft and wet. Put the mixture into a greased 6in. sandwich tin, cover with a damp tea towel and leave the dough in a warm place for about 30min. to rise.
☐ Bake for 30-40min. in centre of oven, pre-heated to 400 deg. F. or Mark 6. The loaf should sound hollow when tapped on the bottom. Cool on a wire rack.

BLINI
(Makes about twenty pancakes)

2 level teaspoons dried yeast
½ pint and 4 tablespoons lukewarm water
12oz. plain flour
1oz. butter
2 large eggs
½oz. caster sugar
pinch of salt
½ pint milk
oil for frying
1 large onion
5oz. carton soured cream
3½oz. jar of lumpfish roe (Danish caviar)

☐ Sprinkle the yeast on to the lukewarm water and leave for 15min., or until frothy on top. Sift the flour and put half in a large bowl. Add the yeast liquid gradually to the flour in the bowl, beating to a smooth batter. Cover and leave to rise for about 30min., or until doubled in size and covered with bubbles.
☐ Melt the butter. Gradually add the remaining flour with the melted butter to the batter. Separate the eggs and beat yolks, sugar and salt into the batter. Beat until smooth.
☐ Heat the milk to lukewarm and add gradually to the mixture beating well. Cover and leave to rise as before.
☐ Whisk the egg whites until standing in stiff peaks and fold them into the batter using a large metal spoon. Leave the batter to rise until doubled in size and covered in bubbles.
☐ Heat 1 tablespoon oil in a heavy frying pan. Pour about 3 tablespoons batter into the pan and with the tip of a spoon form it into a 4in. round. Cook for about 1min., or until the underside is golden brown, turn and cook the other side. Place each one as it is cooked on a wire rack and put into a warm oven to keep hot, while you cook the remainder of the batter.
☐ Skin and roughly chop the onion. Spoon the soured cream into a bowl and spoon the onion into another bowl. Turn out the lumpfish roe and spoon it into another bowl.
☐ Serve the blini hot, one to each person and flat on the plate. Spoon on chopped onion, lumpfish roe and soured cream and mix. Eat with a knife and fork.

Sweets & Candies

Making your own sweets and toffees can be a great deal of fun and it's not as hard as it seems at first glance. I do recommend that you buy a sugar thermometer because other methods of testing are not accurate and one degree often matters

BRAZIL WHIRLS
(Makes fourteen chocolates)

8oz. plain chocolate
3 drops of glycerine
14 shelled Brazil nuts

☐ Break chocolate into a small bowl and stand it over a pan of fairly hot water. Don't allow the water to become too hot or the chocolate will lose its gloss and will get a mouldy look when it cools.
☐ Remove from the heat and add the glycerine. Stir until the mixture starts to thicken. Spoon into a piping bag fitted with a small star pipe. Pipe a little on to the base of the Brazils and stand them on greaseproof paper. Pipe chocolate round each nut, completely encasing it. Leave in a cool place to set.

PEPPERMINT CREAMS
(Makes about thirty creams)

1lb. icing sugar
1 teaspoon glycerine
2 standard egg whites
oil of peppermint
green vegetable colouring

☐ Sift icing sugar into a basin. Add the glycerine and a little beaten egg white. Knead to a firm consistency. Add a few drops of peppermint; colour pale green. Roll mixture out to ¼in. thickness. Cut out rounds using a 1½in. plain cutter. Leave on baking trays to harden.

COCONUT ICE
(Makes about thirty-five pieces)

1lb. granulated sugar
4 tablespoons milk
5oz. desiccated coconut
red vegetable colouring

☐ Put the sugar, milk and 4 tablespoons water into a large saucepan and heat very gently to dissolve the sugar. Bring to the boil and boil for 10-12min., until the temperature reaches 240 deg. F., or forms a soft ball when a little mixture is dropped into a bowl of cold water. Remove from the heat and stir in the coconut. Quickly pour half the mixture into a greased 6in. square tin.
☐ Colour the remainder pink and spread it over the white layer. This must be done quickly or the two layers will separate and will not turn out well. Mark into 1in. cubes when half set. Break when cold.

HAZELNUT CLUSTERS
(Makes about twenty clusters)

1lb. Demerara sugar
½oz. butter
2 teaspoons white vinegar
8oz. shelled hazelnuts

☐ Put the sugar, butter, vinegar and ¼ pint cold water into a large saucepan. Heat gently until all the sugar has dissolved. Bring to the boil and boil quickly until the temperature reaches 375 deg. F., or the syrup forms a brittle ball when a little of the mixture is dropped into a bowl of cold water.
☐ Remove from the heat and drop 5-6 nuts at a time into the toffee. Remove with a metal spoon and leave to harden on a greased baking tray. Repeat the process until all the nuts have been used.

CRISPY CHOCOLATE
(Makes sixteen pieces)

4oz. whole blanched almonds
8oz. plain chocolate
½oz. butter
2 large egg yolks

☐ Chop almonds fairly finely. Melt chocolate. Remove from the heat and cool. Stir in the butter and egg yolks. Replace over the hot water and stir for 2min. Stir in half the almonds and leave to cool. Toast remaining almonds.
☐ Roll mixture into 16 small balls and toss in the toasted almonds.

Brazil Whirls,
Coconut Ice,
Peppermint Creams,
Hazelnut Clusters
and Crispy Chocolate
recipes opposite.
Recipe overleaf for
Fondant Creams

FONDANT CREAMS
(Makes about eighty fondants)

1lb. granulated sugar
¼ level teaspoon cream of tartar
green, red and yellow vegetable
colourings
almond, vanilla and lemon essences
chocolate powder

☐ Put the sugar, cream of tartar and
¼ pint cold water into a large saucepan
and heat gently until the sugar has
completely dissolved. Keep a bowl of
cold water and a pastry brush at hand to
brush down the sides of the pan when
the mixture boils, to prevent crystals
forming. Bring to the boil and boil for
about 10min., until the temperature
reaches 240 deg. F., or test by dropping
the syrup into a bowl of cold water and
if ready, in a few moments you can form
a soft ball with your fingers.
☐ Sprinkle a little water on to a baking
tray and pour on the syrup. Leave it for
a few moments until a skin forms over
the surface. Using a palette knife, work
the mixture quickly in a figure of eight
until it whitens and becomes grainy in
texture. Knead the mixture in your
hands until it is smooth. Don't colour
the fondant all at once as each bowl will
need melting before it can be used.
☐ Divide the fondant between 4 bowls;
add a few drops of green colouring to 1
portion and flavour with almond essence.
Stand the bowl over a pan of hot water
and heat gently until the fondant
softens. It may be necessary to add a
little water. Put a teaspoon of fondant
into each section of a lightly-oiled
fondant mat.
☐ Colour the second bowl with pink
colouring and vanilla essence. Colour
the third bowl chocolate with chocolate
powder, and colour the fourth bowl
yellow with yellow colouring and add
lemon essence.
☐ If a rubber fondant mat is not
available, the fondant should be softened
slightly by heating in a bowl. Then roll
it out on a dry surface and cut with
fancy cutters. If liked, you can colour
one lot of fondant with pink, green and
yellow to get pale mauve. Flavour with
almond or vanilla essence.

PEANUT BRITTLE
(Makes about 2lb. brittle)

4oz. granulated sugar
6oz. soft brown sugar
6oz. golden syrup
2oz. butter
¼ level teaspoon bicarbonate of soda
12oz. unsalted chopped peanuts

☐ Put the sugars, syrup and ¼ pint cold
water in a saucepan and heat gently to
dissolve the sugar. Add the butter and
bring to the boil; simmer gently until the
temperature reaches 300 deg. F., or
when a little of the syrup forms brittle
threads when dropped into cold water.
Add the bicarbonate of soda and nuts.
☐ Pour the mixture into a greased 7in.
square tin and leave to set. Just before it
has set, mark into squares.

CANDIED ORANGE SLICES
(Makes about twenty slices)

3 large oranges
6oz. lump sugar
1oz. liquid glucose

☐ Wash the oranges and cut them into
¼in. slices, leaving their peel on. Remove
as many of the pips as you can. Put the
slices in a large pan. Cover with cold
water. Bring to the boil and drain.
☐ Put the sugar, glucose and 4
tablespoons cold water in a very large
saucepan. Heat very gently until the
sugar has dissolved. Stand a sugar
thermometer in the pan. Bring syrup to
the boil. Do not stir, but brush the sides
of the pan with a small brush dipped in
cold water to prevent the sugar crystals
from clinging to the sides. Boil for
2-3min. or until a temperature of 220
deg. F. has been reached.
☐ Dip the orange slices in the syrup,
using a skewer or fork, and lay them on
a wire rack.
☐ When they are all coated, stand the
rack on a baking tray to catch any
drips, and dry the fruit slowly in a warm
place, turning occasionally. If you have
any syrup left, use it for stewed fruits.

HONEYCOMB TOFFEE
(Makes about 1lb. toffee)

1lb. granulated sugar
pinch of cream of tartar
2 level tablespoons golden syrup
1 level teaspoon bicarbonate of soda

☐ Put the sugar, cream of tartar and
golden syrup into a saucepan with ¼
pint cold water. Heat gently to dissolve
the sugar; bring to the boil and boil until
the temperature reaches 300 deg. F. or
when a little of the syrup forms brittle
threads when dropped into cold water.
Remove from the heat.
☐ Blend the bicarbonate of soda with 2
teaspoons cold water and add to the
toffee, stirring well. Pour into a 9in.
greased tin and stand tin on a baking
tray. Leave to set for 20min.
☐ Just before it sets completely, mark
into squares with a sharp knife and
leave until cold. Break into pieces.

TREACLE TOFFEE
(Makes about 1lb. toffee)

1lb. Demerara sugar
¼ level teaspoon cream of tartar
4oz. black treacle
4oz. golden syrup
3oz. butter

☐ Put the sugar into a large saucepan
with ¼ pint cold water. Dissolve the
sugar slowly and add the cream of
tartar, treacle, syrup and butter. Bring to
the boil and boil rapidly until the
temperature reaches 300 deg. F., or if the
mixture is dropped into a bowl of cold
water it should form brittle threads.
☐ Pour the toffee into a well greased 6in.
by 8in. shallow tin and allow to cool for
about 5min. Mark into squares using a
sharp knife. Leave to set for 30min., and
break when cool.

MARZIPAN FRUITS
(Makes about twenty sweets)

4oz. icing sugar
1 large egg yolk
6oz. ground almonds
red, yellow, brown and green vegetable
colourings
little angelica

☐ Sift the icing sugar into a large mixing bowl. Add the egg yolk. Boil a large pan of water. Whisk the sugar and egg over the hot water until the mixture is thick and will hold a trail when the whisk is lifted out of the bowl. Work in the ground almonds and knead to a smooth paste using your hands. Add a little more sugar and almonds if the mixture is too wet.
☐ Divide mixture into 4 parts. Colour first part orange, using a mixture of red and yellow colouring. Form into neat round orange shapes. Mixing the yellow and brown, colour second part fairly deep yellow and form into banana shapes. Colour the third part yellow and form into lemon shapes. Colour the last part green and form into small round apple shapes. Finish the green apples by giving them a rosy blush with red colouring, using a clean paint brush or your finger. Add a stalk of angelica to each.
☐ With a cocktail stick, mark the top of each orange into the star shape of the calyx—the dried flower. Dip the stick in brown colouring and colour the indentations. Press each orange gently against the fine side of your grater to pit the surface. Pit the surface of the lemons in the same way. Using a clean paint brush and brown colouring, mark the bananas in the natural way with a few brush strokes down their length. Store the fruit in an airtight tin.

TRUFFLES
(Makes about twenty-five sweets)

4½oz. plain chocolate
4 tablespoons double cream
1 dessertspoon aromatic bitters
3oz. cocoa
4oz. icing sugar

☐ Melt the chocolate in a small bowl over a pan of hot water. Cool.
☐ Whip the cream until stiff. Fold in the chocolate and aromatic bitters. Leave until cold.
☐ Sift together 2oz. cocoa and the icing sugar. Beat into the chocolate mixture and shape into small balls. Coat in the remaining cocoa.

TURKISH DELIGHT
(Makes about 1lb. sweets)

1lb. caster sugar
¼ level teaspoon citric acid
½ pint hot water
1oz. powdered gelatine
vanilla and almond essences
cochineal
2oz. icing sugar
1oz. cornflour

☐ Add the sugar and citric acid to the hot water. Heat slowly until the sugar has dissolved. Bring to the boil and boil for 20min. Remove from the heat, sprinkle in the gelatine and leave to stand for 10min. without stirring.
☐ Add a few drops of vanilla and almond essences and stir well. Divide the mixture and pour half into a well greased 6in. square tin. Colour the remaining half with a few drops of cochineal and pour over the first layer. Leave to set for 24 hours.
☐ Sift the icing sugar and cornflour together and sprinkle it over greaseproof paper. Turn the Turkish delight on to the icing sugar and cut it into squares. Toss well in the sugar. To store pack in greaseproof paper in an airtight tin.

VANILLA FUDGE
(Makes about 1½lb. fudge)

1lb. granulated sugar
2oz. butter
¼ pint evaporated milk
¼ pint milk
vanilla essence

☐ Place the sugar, butter and 2 milks into a large saucepan and heat gently until the sugar dissolves. Bring to the boil and boil gently, stirring all the time until it reaches 240 deg. F., or if you drop some of the syrup into a bowl of cold water it should form a soft ball when squeezed between the thumb and finger. Remove the pan from the heat and add 3 drops vanilla essence. Beat well until the mixture becomes thick and texture becomes grainy.
☐ Pour into a well greased 8in. by 11in. shallow tin and leave for about 30min. to set. Just before it has completely set mark into cubes with a sharp knife. When it is firm break the fudge along the marked lines.

LAST-MINUTE SWEETS
(Makes about fifty sweets)

1lb. icing sugar
1 teaspoon glycerine
2 standard egg whites
lemon, almond and vanilla essences
yellow and red vegetable colourings

☐ Sift the icing sugar into a basin. Add the glycerine and a little beaten egg white. Knead to a firm dough, adding more egg white as necessary.
☐ Divide into thirds. Flavour 1 third with lemon essence and colour lemon yellow. Flavour another with almond essence and colour pale pink. Leave the third piece white but flavour with vanilla. Roll out all pieces to ¼in. thickness and cut into small shapes using fancy cutters. Place on baking trays dusted with a little extra icing sugar and leave to harden.

All kinds of Drinks

Refreshing drinks for summer, mulled wines for winter, smashing fizzy drinks for children and delicious punches and cocktails for people who don't like alcohol as well as recipes for Turkish Coffee and a thick spicy chocolate drink from Spain

FRUIT CRUSH
(Enough for eight)

two 25 fluid oz. bottles pure apple juice
½ pint soda water
4oz. granulated sugar
1in. stick of cinnamon
1 large lemon
1 large red eating apple
1 large orange
1in. piece of cucumber
2oz. strawberries
1oz. black grapes

☐ Chill the apple juice and soda water in the refrigerator for 3 hours or overnight. Put the sugar and ¼ pint cold water in a pan. Heat gently until the sugar has dissolved. Boil for 1min. Remove from the heat and add the cinnamon.
☐ Wash and thinly peel the lemon. Add the rind to the hot syrup. Leave until cold. Squeeze out and strain the lemon juice. Pour juice into a large jug or bowl with the chilled apple juice and soda water. Wash the apple and slice thinly, removing the core. Wash and thinly slice the orange. Wash and halve the strawberries and grapes, removing grape pips.
☐ Add all the fruit to the apple juice and strain in the cold sugar syrup, discarding the cinnamon and lemon rind.

LIME FIZZ
(Enough for six)

24 fluid oz. bottle lemonade
6 tablespoons lime juice cordial
green vegetable colouring
sprigs of mint

☐ Pour the lemonade and lime juice cordial into a jug and mix well, adding a little green colouring.
☐ Chill well and serve with mint.

RASPBERRY DELIGHT
(Enough for four)

4 tablespoons raspberry cordial
24 fluid oz. bottle of lemonade
2oz. white grapes
2oz. small strawberries
few cocktail cherries

☐ Chill the cordial and lemonade and mix well. Wash the grapes and strawberries. Thread the fruit on to cocktail sticks, alternating the fruits.
☐ Pour the lemonade into glasses and add one fruit stick to each glass.

ORANGEADE
(Enough for six)

3 large oranges
1 large lemon
3oz. caster sugar
1¼ pints boiling water

☐ Wash the fruits and peel thinly, leaving behind all the white pith as this will make the orangeade bitter. Put the rinds and sugar into a bowl or jug and pour on the boiling water. Cover and leave until cold.
☐ Pour into a liquidiser and blend for 3min. Strain into a jug. Squeeze out and strain the fruit juices; stir into the cold liquid. Chill and serve.
☐ This orangeade is not suitable for bottling as it keeps for about 5 days.

CITRUS SQUASH
(Enough for twelve)

1lb. granulated sugar
2 large grapefruit
1 large orange
3 level teaspoons tartaric acid

☐ Put sugar and 1½ pints cold water into a saucepan. Stand it over a low heat and stir until the sugar has dissolved. Bring to boil and boil for 10min.
☐ Meanwhile, wash fruit and finely grate rinds of both fruits. Put rinds and tartaric acid into a bowl. Pour on the syrup and leave overnight.
☐ Next day squeeze out and strain the fruit juices. Stir into the cold liquid. Bottle and label. To serve, dilute with water or soda water.

GRAPE CUP
(Enough for eight)

24 fluid oz. bottle red grape juice
24 fluid oz. bottle white grape juice
2oz. black grapes
2oz. white grapes

☐ Chill the grape juice overnight in the refrigerator. Wash the grapes and cut them in half. Remove the pips. Pour the grape juices into a jug, add the grapes and serve chilled.

Top, left to right
Orangeade, Lime Fizz, Fruit Crush.
Bottom, Citrus Squash, Grape Cup,
Raspberry Delight

MOCHA SHAKE
(Enough for four)

4 level tablespoons drinking chocolate
1 level tablespoon instant coffee
3 tablespoons boiling water
1½ pints milk
small block vanilla ice cream

☐ Dissolve the drinking chocolate and instant coffee in the boiling water. Leave to cool.
☐ Pour the milk into a large bowl or into a liquidiser. Add the chocolate mixture and the ice cream. Whisk until frothy. Serve in tall glasses.

BREAKFAST CHOCOLATE
(Enough for four)

8oz. bar plain chocolate
pinch of ground cinnamon

☐ Break the chocolate into pieces and put it in a small pan. Add 1½ pints cold water and bring slowly to the boil, stirring all the time until the chocolate has melted. Then simmer for 30min., or until the chocolate is very thick like cream. Stir in the cinnamon and serve.

TURKISH COFFEE
(Enough for four)

3oz. very finely ground coffee
3oz. caster sugar
few drops rose water

☐ Put the coffee, sugar and 1 pint of cold water in a very small saucepan. Stir over a medium heat until the mixture comes to the boil and becomes frothy. Remove from the heat and when the froth has subsided, replace the pan over a high heat and stir until boiling and frothy again. Repeat this twice more.
☐ Just before serving, add a tablespoon of cold water to settle the coffee grounds and add a few drops of rose water. Pour into small cups and serve with Turkish Delight—see page 183.
☐ Never mix milk with Turkish coffee, but you can add more or less sugar than I've suggested.

KENTUCKY MINT JULEP
(Enough for six)

6 sugar lumps
finely crushed ice
bourbon
sprigs of mint

☐ Chill six tumblers on ice for 1 hour. Dissolve the sugar lumps in 1 tablespoon water over a very low heat. Cool.
☐ Crush the ice by wrapping ice cubes in a tea towel and hitting them hard with a rolling pin on a hard surface. Fill each tumbler with ice and add enough bourbon to cover the ice. Stir until the outside of the tumbler is heavily frosted.
☐ Stir the sugar syrup into the glasses and tuck 3 sprigs of mint into the ice so that they stand above the glass.

SPICED FRUIT PUNCH
(Enough for eight)

1lb. 12oz. tin apricot halves
two 1in. pieces of cinnamon stick
½ teaspoon whole allspice
6 cloves
1 level teaspoon ground ginger
2 blades of mace
1 large lemon
1lb. 3oz. tin pineapple juice
½ pint orange juice
½ pint grapefruit juice

☐ Drain ½ pint juice from the apricot halves and pour it into a pan. Add ½ pint cold water, the cinnamon sticks, allspice, cloves, ginger and mace. Bring to the boil, then simmer for 10min.
☐ Squeeze out and strain the lemon juice and pour it into another pan. Add the pineapple, orange and grapefruit juices.
☐ Push the remaining apricot juice and apricot halves through a sieve to make a purée or liquidise. Add to the pan with the juices. Bring to boiling point. Remove from the heat and strain in the spiced syrup, discarding spices. Stir well.
☐ Pour into heatproof glasses and float slices of orange on top.

STRAWBERRY MILK SHAKE
(Enough for four)

1 pint milk
4 tablespoons strawberry milk shake syrup
4 large tablespoons strawberry ice cream

☐ Chill the milk in the refrigerator. Pour it into a deep bowl and whisk with the syrup until it is frothy. Pour the milk shake into 4 tall glasses and top each with a tablespoon of ice cream. Serve at once with a couple of straws.

HUCKLE-MY-BUFF
(Enough for four)

8 large egg yolks
4 tablespoons brandy
4 tablespoons beer
1oz. caster sugar

☐ Beat the egg yolks until thick and pale. Beat in the brandy, beer and sugar and serve at once in 4 glasses.

IRISH COFFEE
(Enough for four)

freshly made strong black coffee
4 level teaspoons caster sugar
Irish whiskey
5oz. carton double cream

☐ Heat 4 stemmed glasses rinsing them with hot water. Pour in the strong black coffee to within ¾in. of the top of the glass.
☐ Stir 1 level teaspoon sugar and 2 tablespoons Irish whiskey into each glass and stir well to dissolve the sugar. Gently pour the cream on to the coffee over the back of a spoon with its tip just held against the coffee.

THE BISHOP
(Enough for eight)

2 large lemons
14 cloves
5oz. cube sugar
1 level teaspoon ground ginger
½ level teaspoon ground nutmeg
½ level teaspoon ground cinnamon
½ level teaspoon ground mixed spice
½ pint port
1 bottle red wine
8 Maraschino cherries
8 cinnamon sticks

☐ Wash the lemons and stick one of them with the whole cloves. Roast this on a baking tray for 30min., in centre of oven, pre-heated to 350 deg. F. or Mark 4.
☐ Meanwhile, rub the cube sugar over the remaining lemon skin. Put the sugar, ginger, nutmeg, cinnamon and mixed spice into a large pan. Add ½ pint water, the port and red wine.
☐ Bring to the boil slowly, removing from the heat once it has boiled. Leave to stand for 30min., covered.
☐ Add the lemon and boil to simmering point. Pour into heatproof glasses. Add a Maraschino cherry and 1 cinnamon stick to each glass.

WIDECOMBE FAIR SPICED ALE
(Enough for six-eight)

1 quart of ale
1 large red eating apple
4 cloves
pinch of ground mixed spice
¼ level teaspoon ground nutmeg
3 level teaspoons caster sugar

☐ Heat the ale very slowly, but do not let it boil. Wash the apple, core and slice, but do not peel it. Add the spices and sugar to the ale. Stir well to dissolve the sugar and strain.
☐ Serve hot in glasses with apple slices.

GOLDEN APPLE PUNCH
(Enough for six)

two 1in. pieces of cinnamon stick
3 whole cloves
good pinch of ground nutmeg
2oz. granulated sugar
1 large lemon
1½ pints apple juice
½ pint tinned orange juice
sprigs of mint

☐ Pour ¼ pint water into a saucepan. Add the cinnamon sticks, cloves, nutmeg and sugar. Bring to the boil. Reduce heat and simmer for 10min.·
☐ Wash the lemon. Thinly peel off the rind and cut into long strips ¼in. wide. Wind these round a clean pencil and leave.
☐ Squeeze out and strain the lemon juice, and pour this, together with the orange and apple juices into a large bowl. Strain in the spicy syrup, discarding the spices. Cool, then chill for 2-3 hours in the refrigerator.
☐ Take the lemon off the pencil and cut into smaller pieces. Decorate the glasses with a twist of peel and float a sprig of mint on top. One or two ice cubes may be added to each glass before serving.

SANGRIA
(Enough for four-six)

½ large orange
½ large lemon
½ large eating apple
3oz. caster sugar
1 bottle dry red Spanish wine
4 tablespoons brandy
1 large bottle soda water

☐ Wipe the orange and lemon and cut them into ⅛in. slices. Core the half apple and cut into thin slices.
☐ Put the fruit, sugar, wine and brandy into a very large jug. Stir until well mixed. Chill in the fridge for 1 hour. Chill the soda water separately.
☐ Just before serving, add the soda water. Stir and pour into chilled glasses. Garnish the jug with mint.

MULLED WINE
(Enough for ten)

1 bottle medium-dry white wine
1 bottle rosé
3oz. granulated sugar
3 whole cardamom seeds
1 blade of mace
1in. piece of cinnamon stick
1 bay leaf
1 small orange
2oz. stoned raisins
1 miniature jar of peach with brandy conserve or
3 tablespoons peach and brandy conserve

☐ Pour the white and rosé wines into a large pan. Add the sugar. Tie the cardamom seeds, mace, cinnamon and bay leaf in a muslin bag, and add to pan. Thinly peel the rind from the orange and add, together with the raisins. Bring to the boil slowly then remove from the heat. Cover for 30min.
☐ Add the peach conserve to the pan and bring to simmering point. Remove the spice bag and pour into glasses.

LAMBS WOOL
(Enough for four)

1 pint brown ale
½ bottle dry white wine
pinch of ground nutmeg
pinch of ground ginger
2oz. soft brown sugar
½ pint milk

☐ Put the ale and wine in an enamel pan and heat, but don't boil. Stir in the spices and sugar.
☐ Heat the milk in another pan and stir into ale mixture until it froths. Serve hot.

Delicious Preserves

Traditional methods of preserving fruits and vegetables are bottling, jam-making and making pickles and chutneys; all of them easy to do. Here are many recipes plus lots of information on preserving including the newest method of all—freezing

Jams & Marmalades

Jam and marmalade making isn't difficult at all and it is so rewarding. Once you've made your first pots and tasted the real fruit you'll want to make more until you can have home made preserves every day. You don't need masses of equipment and you'll probably find everything in your kitchen. You must have a large saucepan. If you haven't got one large enough, invest in a preserving pan. Aluminium pans, 12in. in diameter, are not too expensive, and of course you can use it for things other than jam. You also need a wooden spoon, a small jug, plenty of jars and a few packets of jam-pot covers which include labels. Inspect all your jars first, making sure they are not chipped or cracked. Wash them in warm soapy water and rinse them well in clean water, drain and leave upside down. It's not necessary to dry them. If you've got some jars that are very dirty, put them in a big saucepan and cover them with cold water. Bring the water to the boil and boil gently for 5min. Lift out the jars using tongs and leave them to drain upside down. Once drained, the jars must be warmed. Easiest way is to put them in the oven. Don't pre-heat it, but set it to 225 deg. F. or Mark ¼.

Choosing your fruit
Fruit for jam-making should be under-ripe, but a mixture of ripe and under-ripe fruit is satisfactory. During many tests it has been found that pectin —the natural substance found in all fruit in different quantities, and the substance which produces the set—is released more easily from under-ripe fruit. The presence of acid in the fruit is also essential and like pectin it is present in all fruits but in different quantities. Acid is essential as it helps extract the pectin to get a good set, it brightens the colour of the jam and can improve the flavour and prevent crystallisation of sugar.
Fruits rich in pectin and acid are:
Apples, black and redcurrants, damsons, gooseberries and plums.
Fruits less rich in pectin and acid include: apricots, blackberries, greengages, loganberries and raspberries.
Fruits which have little pectin or acid are: cherries, pears and strawberries.
Pick your fruit over carefully discarding, over-ripe, bruised fruit and those that are not perfect. Remove stalks or hulls and take out large stones.
Put the fruit in the pan with the amount of water stated in the recipe.
Don't fill your pan more than halfway so that the jam has plenty of room.
Cook your fruit at simmering point until it is reduced to a pulp. The amount of water required does vary. You need more in a large pan where evaporation is quick. Juicy fruit requires less than dry fruit. If you increase the quantities of a recipe you will need less than the increased amount of water.
If you wish you can add acid to fruits which are deficient—such as strawberries, late season blackberries, pears, sweet apples and cherries. The following quantities are sufficient for 4lb. fruit: 2 tablespoons lemon juice or ½ level teaspoon citric or tartaric acid.
Marmalades are usually made with Seville oranges which are in the shops at the beginning of the year. But you can make marmalade with any of the citrus fruits such as lemons, grapefruits and tangerines.

Adding the sugar
When the fruit has been cooked until it is soft, add the sugar. You can use preserving sugar bought specially for the job, but granulated or lump sugars are as good. Warm the sugar in the oven with the jars so that it will dissolve more quickly—this is important with jams which are boiled for a very short time. Sugar has a hardening effect on skins of fruit so don't add it until you're sure. Once the sugar is in, you can't make the tough skins soft by longer boiling. Stir the sugar all the time while it's dissolving and make sure it has dissolved before you boil the preserve.

Boiling for the second time
Boiling should be done as rapidly as possible and the time varies between 3 and 20 minutes depending on the size of the pan, quantity and kind of fruit.

Testing for a set
There are several ways. One very satisfactory method, if you've got some good scales, is to weigh the pan. Weigh the empty pan before you start. You should have 10lb. preserve for every 6lb. sugar used.
If you've got a sugar thermometer, put this in the pan right from the first boiling. It must register in degrees right up to 230 deg. F. Stir the mixture thoroughly before you read the temperature, and if it reads 220 deg. F. or no more than 222 deg. F. you will get a good set.
The cold plate test is of course less accurate, but useful to know. Take the pan off the heat when you think it's ready. Spoon a little preserve on to a cold saucer and put it in the fridge for a minute. If the jam will give a good set, you'll find a skin will wrinkle when you push the preserve on the saucer. If it doesn't boil again.

Tangerine

Grapef[...]

Dark Thick

Lemon

Tangerine, Grapefruit
and Lemon Jelly, Dark
Thick and Three Fruit
Marmalade, recipes
overleaf

Jams & Marmalades

Filling your pots

Remove the pan from the heat and remove any scum with a perforated spoon dipped in boiling water and dried. Pour at once into the pots using a clean small jug. Fill right to the top with the preserve, to allow for some shrinkage during storage.

For jam with whole berries in it such as strawberries, let the jam stand in the pan until a thin skin forms on the top. Stir the jam gently and pour into the jars. This thickens the jam slightly and prevents the fruit from rising. Press a well fitting waxed disc on the surface of the jam. Wipe the rims with a cloth wrung out in hot water. Cover with cellophane circles and secure with rubber bands. Label with the name and the date.

Store your jams and marmalades in a dry, dark, cool, airy place. Too much heat and damp encourages mould to grow on the top.

Making a jelly

Prepare and cook the fruit as described for jam, but before you add the sugar the fruit must be strained to remove stones and skins. You can buy a jelly bag of felt but this is quite expensive and a bit messy and not necessary for household jams and marmalades. I use four layers of muslin, each corner tied to the leg of an upturned stool. Rinse the muslin and a large bowl with boiling water. Place bowl underneath the bag. Pour the cooked fruit into the bag gently and allow the juice to drip through undisturbed. Don't try to push it through as this will cloud the jelly. Of course, it doesn't alter the marvellous flavour but it looks so much better when crystal clear.

Return the juice to the pan, bring to boiling point add the sugar and finish exactly as described for jam.

BLACKBERRY AND APPLE JAM
(Makes about 5lb.)

1lb. cooking apples
2lb. blackberries
3lb. preserving sugar

☐ Wash, peel and core the apples. Tie the peel and cores in a piece of muslin. Slice the apples and put them in a large saucepan with ¼ pint cold water. Cover and simmer until the apples are soft.

☐ Meanwhile, pick over the blackberries and put in a preserving pan with ¼ pint cold water and the muslin bag of peel and cores. Simmer for 20min. or until soft.

☐ Remove the muslin bag from the pan and add the apples to the blackberries. Add the sugar and heat gently until it has dissolved, stirring from time to time. Bring to the boil and boil rapidly for 8-10min., or until the setting point is reached.

☐ Pour the jam into clean, warm jam jars and cover and seal as described.

WHOLE BERRY JAM
(Makes about 5lb.)

3lb. small firm strawberries
3lb. preserving sugar
1½ large lemons

☐ Hull the strawberries; rinse them and gently wipe dry. Put strawberries and sugar into a preserving pan. Heat very, very gently until all the sugar has dissolved.

☐ Wipe lemons. Squeeze out and strain the juice. Add to the pan. Bring quickly to the boil and boil rapidly for 20-25min., or until setting point is reached.

☐ Leave jam to cool for 15min., or until a thin skin has formed. Stir gently. Using a large cup, pour jam into clean, warm jars. Cover and seal as described.

DARK THICK MARMALADE
(Makes about 9lb.)

2lb. Seville oranges
2 large lemons
6lb. preserving sugar
1 level tablespoon black treacle

☐ Wash the fruit well. Cut in half and squeeze out the juice and the pips. Cut peel into thick shreds, cutting away some of the white pith if it is too thick. Tie pips and excess white pith in a small piece of muslin. Put the juice, peel and muslin bag in a large preserving pan with 6 pints cold water. Or if you only have a large saucepan add 4 pints cold water. Bring to boil and simmer for 2 hours or until the peel is soft.

☐ Remove the muslin bag, squeezing it to remove the juice. Add sugar and black treacle, and dissolve over a gentle heat, stirring all the time. Bring to boil and boil rapidly for 3min. or until a set is reached. Remove any scum that has formed and leave to stand for about 15min. Stir gently and pour into jars. Cover and seal as described.

TANGERINE JELLY
(Makes about 4lb.)

2lb. tangerines
1 large grapefruit
2 large lemons
preserving sugar

☐ Wash the fruit well. Peel the fruit. Cut the peel into small pieces. Chop the fruit into rough pieces. Put peel, fruit, pith and pips in a preserving pan or large saucepan with 5 pints cold water. Bring to the boil and simmer for about 2 hours, or until the peel is soft.

☐ Strain through muslin as described. Measure the liquid into a clean pan and add 1lb. sugar for every pint. Heat slowly, stirring to dissolve the sugar, then boil rapidly for about 3min. or until setting point is reached. Remove any scum that has formed and pour jelly into clean, warm jars. Cover and seal as described.

GRAPEFRUIT JELLY
(Makes about 7lb.)

4lb. grapefruit
3 large lemons
preserving sugar

☐ Wash the fruit well. Peel all the fruit. Cut both the peel and the fruit into small pieces and put peel, pith, fruit and pips in a preserving pan or large saucepan. Add 6 pints cold water. Or if you only have a large saucepan, add 4 pints cold water. Bring to the boil, then simmer gently for 2 hours.
☐ Strain as described. Measure juice into a clean pan; add 1lb. sugar for every pint. Stir over gentle heat until dissolved, then bring to boil, and boil rapidly for about 3min. or until setting point is reached. Remove any scum that has formed and pour into clean, warm jars. Cover and seal as described. Label jelly.

PLUM JAM
(Makes about 6lb.)

4lb. plums
4lb. granulated sugar

☐ Wash the plums and remove the stalks. Put the fruit into a large saucepan or preserving pan. Add 1 pint cold water, or, if the plums are large and juicy, add only ¾ pint water, as the fruit will not require as long to cook. Cover. Heat gently until the fruit simmers. Reduce heat and continue to simmer for 30min. if the fruit is hard or 15min. if it is ripe. Add the sugar. Stand the pan over a low heat and stir until the sugar has completely dissolved.
Bring quickly to the boil. Boil rapidly for 10min. Using a perforated spoon, lift out the stones as they rise to the surface. Test for a set. Remove any scum. Leave for about 10min. before pouring into jars.
☐ Using a cup, pour the cooled jam into clean warmed jam jars. Cover and seal as described.

CRANBERRY JELLY
(Makes about 2lb.)

1lb. cooking apples
2lb. cranberries
¼ pint strained fresh lemon juice
preserving sugar

☐ Wash and chop the apples. Don't peel or core them. Wash the cranberries. Put apples, cranberries and lemon juice in a large pan. Just cover with cold water. Bring to boil. Reduce the heat and simmer for 40min.
☐ Skim and strain as described. When the jelly has finished dripping, measure the juice into a large clean pan. Add 1lb. sugar for every 1 pint juice. Heat gently, stirring all the time until the sugar has dissolved. Bring to boil and boil for about 5min. or until a set is reached. Pour into jars and cover and seal as described. Label jelly.

RASPBERRY JAM
(Makes about 8lb.)

5lb. raspberries
5lb. preserving sugar

☐ Hull fruit. Wash only if really necessary. Heat gently until the juice flows and fruit softens. Add sugar and stir until dissolved. Bring to the boil and boil for 5min. Test for a set.
☐ Pour immediately into clean, warm jam jars. Cover and label. When cold, store in a cool, dry cupboard.

GOOSEBERRY JAM
(Makes about 10lb.)

6lb. gooseberries
7½lb. preserving sugar

☐ Top, tail and wash the fruit. Put it into a large preserving pan with ¾ pint water. Bring to the boil and simmer gently for 30min., until the fruit is pulpy. Stir frequently. Remove from the heat and add sugar. Gently dissolve the sugar and boil for 5min., or until setting point is reached. Skim the surface. Remove from heat and pour the jam into warm jars. Cover as described.

LEMON JELLY
(Makes about 6½lb.)

4lb. large lemons
3 Seville oranges
preserving sugar

☐ Wash the fruit well. Carefully cut the peel from the lemons so that no white pith is removed. Cut the lemon peel into fine shreds and tie them in a small piece of muslin. Remove the peel from the oranges and cut into small pieces. Chop the fruit roughly. Put the fruit, peel, pith and pips in a preserving pan or large saucepan. Add the muslin bag of shreds and 6 pints cold water. Or if you only have a large saucepan, add 4 pints cold water. Bring to the boil and simmer for 2½ hours, removing the bag of shreds after 1 hour. Rinse them in cold water and drain.
☐ Strain as described. Measure the juice into a clean saucepan and add 1lb. sugar for each pint of juice.
Heat gently, stirring until the sugar has dissolved. Add the shreds and boil rapidly for about 3min., or until setting point is reached. Remove any scum that has formed. Leave to stand for about 15min. Stir gently and pour into clean, warm jars and cover and seal as described. Label and store.

REDCURRANT JELLY
(Makes about 4lb.)

6lb. redcurrants
preserving sugar

☐ Wash the fruit, but don't cut off the stalks. Put it into a large pan with 2 pints of cold water. Simmer gently for 40min., or until the currants are really soft and pulpy. Strain through a large piece of muslin as described.
☐ Measure the amount of strained juice and return it to the pan. Add 1lb. preserving sugar to each pint of juice extracted. Stir the liquid well and dissolve the sugar slowly. When it has dissolved bring to the boil and boil rapidly, until a set is obtained. Skim, pot, cover, and label as described.

Pickles &
Chutnies

Pots of homemade pickles and chutneys
always give me immense satisfaction.
Apart from the achievement of actually
making them, I know that meals of cold
roast on Monday will be thoroughly
enjoyable instead of an anti-climax to
the Sunday dinner. They're easy enough
to make if you follow some general rules.

Rules for pickles
1. The vegetables or fruit must be
salted and left overnight to prevent the
growth of bacteria, then well rinsed. If
the vegetables or fruit still taste too
salty, rinse again until palatable—too
much salt can ruin the pickles.
2. Jars must always be sealed airtight,
otherwise the vinegar will evaporate and
the pickles at the top of the jar will
discolour. Best covering is a circle of
greaseproof paper topped by a layer of
cotton tied securely. Then brush with
wax (melt a white household candle).
3. Prick all whole fruit before you heat
it to avoid shrivelling. This applies to
Spiced Plums.

Rules for chutney
1. Cut up all the ingredients fairly
finely and cook them slowly for at least
1 hour.
2. Don't use metal sieves or spoons;
they can impart a metallic taste. And
don't use your old brass, copper or iron
preserving pans for the same reason.
Enamel-lined pans are good; so are
aluminium pans.
3. Make sure the cover is as airtight
as you can make it, then the chutney
won't shrink during storage. Use the
same covering as you would for pickles.
4. Use brown sugar because it gives a
better colour.
5. Make enough for the whole year;
you'll find your chutney will improve
with age. A good chutney will be
mellow tasting no matter what the
ingredients.
Store your pickles and chutneys in a
cool, dry, airy place, away from light.

Tomato and Apple Chutney, Mixed Vegetable Pickle, Pickled Orange Rings, Spiced Plums recipes on this page. Recipe for Apple and Apricot Chutney overleaf

TOMATO AND APPLE CHUTNEY
(Makes about 5lb.)

3lb. red tomatoes
boiling water
2½lb. cooking apples
8oz. sultanas
1½oz. fresh cloves of garlic
1½ pints distilled malt vinegar
1¼lb. Demerara sugar
1 heaped teaspoon ground ginger
1 level teaspoon ground mixed spice
1 level teaspoon pepper

☐ Remove tomato stalks. Cover tomatoes with boiling water for 1min. Drain and skin. Wash apples, peel and core them. Cut in slices. Wash sultanas. Skin garlic cloves and cut in quarters. Put tomatoes, apples, sultanas and garlic through a coarse mincer and then into a 12in. preserving pan with rest of ingredients.
☐ Simmer gently, uncovered, for 1 hour. or until liquid has evaporated and mixture has thickened. Pour into warm jars.
☐ Seal as described.

MIXED VEGETABLE PICKLE
(Makes about 7lb.)

1 medium-sized cauliflower
1lb. pickling onions
¼lb. green beans
1 large cucumber
4oz. salt
1¾ pints distilled malt vinegar
2 level teaspoons ground allspice
6 blades of mace
6 peppercorns
three 2in. pieces of cinnamon stick

☐ Trim off cauliflower leaves and stalk. Break head into small florets and leave in cold water. Skin onions. Wash beans, trim ends and string it. Cut into 1in. pieces. Wash cucumber and cut into ½in. dice. Layer all vegetables in a large bowl, sprinkling each layer with salt. Cover bowl with a clean tea towel and leave to stand overnight.
☐ Pour vinegar into a saucepan, add spices and bring to the boil. Pour into a large jug. Leave until cold, then strain through muslin. Rinse vegetables well to remove all salt, drain and pat dry in a clean tea towel. Pack into clean jars using the handle of a wooden spoon to fit them in neatly. Fill jars with spiced vinegar, cover as described. Label and store when cold.

PICKLED ORANGE RINGS
(Makes about 1½lb.)

5 large oranges
1 pint white vinegar
1lb. granulated sugar
3 level teaspoons ground cloves
two 1in. pieces of cinnamon stick
6 whole cloves

☐ Wipe oranges, cut into ¼in. slices, discarding first and last slices, and put into a large pan. Add cold water to just cover. Simmer for 45min., or until rind is tender.
☐ Remove orange slices on to a large plate. Add the vinegar, sugar, ground cloves and cinnamon to water. Bring to the boil and simmer for 15min. Replace orange slices a few at a time and simmer for 15min., or until rind clears slightly. Pack into clean jars arranging smaller slices down the sides and leaving ½in. space at the top. Boil syrup for 15min., or until it starts to thicken Add whole cloves. Fill jars with syrup and seal as described.

SPICED PLUMS
(Makes about 5lb.)

3lb. Victoria plums
whole cloves
1½lb. granulated sugar
1 pint distilled malt vinegar
1 level teaspoon ground cinnamon

☐ Wash plums and remove stalks. Prick each plum and stick a whole clove into it. Dissolve sugar in the vinegar over a gentle heat, stirring frequently. Stir in cinnamon. Arrange plums in a single layer in a baking tin and pour enough sugar vinegar over them to just cover. Add a little more vinegar if necessary. Cook for 1 hour in centre of oven, pre-heated to 300 deg. F. or Mark 2, until starting to split. Leave plums cooling in the tin overnight.
☐ Next day, pack into clean jars. Pour syrup into a large saucepan; bring to boil. Simmer, uncovered, for 1 hour or until thick and syrupy. Cool for 15min., then fill jars with syrup.
☐ Seal as described, label and store.

APPLE AND APRICOT CHUTNEY
(Makes about 7lb.)

12oz. dried apricots
4lb. cooking apples
1lb. onions
1lb. stoned raisins
1lb. soft brown sugar
1 pint distilled malt vinegar
1 level tablespoon salt
1 level tablespoon ground cinnamon

☐ Put apricots into a bowl, cover with cold water and leave to soak overnight.
☐ Peel, core and slice the apples. Skin and slice onions. Wash raisins. Drain apricots and chop roughly. Put all ingredients into a 12in. preserving pan and simmer gently, uncovered, for 1 hour, or until mixture thickens and there is no liquid on the surface.
☐ Pour into warm jars. Seal as described, label and store.

ELDERBERRY CHUTNEY
(Makes about ¾lb.)

1 small onion
1lb. elderberries
2 level tablespoons caster sugar
½ level teaspoon ground ginger
½ level teaspoon ground mixed spice
½ pint vinegar
pinch of salt

☐ Skin and finely chop the onion. Wash elderberries; remove the stalks. Put the berries in a basin and mash them well. Put into a large pan. Add the onion, sugar, ginger, mixed spice, vinegar and salt. Cook slowly for 40-45min., stirring frequently to prevent the chutney from burning.
☐ Pour hot chutney into warm jars. Cover and seal as described.

BLACKBERRY CHUTNEY
(Makes about 6lb.)

6lb. blackberries
2lb. cooking apples
2lb. onions
2lb. Demerara sugar
1oz. salt
2oz. mustard powder
2oz. ground ginger
2 level teaspoons ground mace
1 level teaspoon Cayenne pepper
2 pints malt vinegar

☐ Remove stalks from the blackberries. Peel, core and chop the apples. Skin and chop the onions. Put all the ingredients in a preserving pan and bring to the boil. Simmer uncovered until the liquid has evaporated and the mixture is thick.
☐ Pour into hot jars. Cover and seal as described.

APPLE AND BANANA CHUTNEY
(Makes about 5lb.)

3lb. cooking apples
5 large bananas
½lb. stoned raisins
2 medium-sized oranges
6 whole cloves
1½ pints malt vinegar
2lb. Demerara sugar

☐ Peel and core the apples. Chop roughly and put them into a large preserving pan. Peel the bananas and chop roughly. Add to the apples with the raisins. Mix well. Grate the orange rind and squeeze out juice. Tie the cloves in a small piece of muslin. Add to the pan with the vinegar, orange rind and juice.
☐ Bring to the boil, then simmer until the fruit is soft and pulpy, stirring occasionally. Add the sugar to the pan and heat gently until sugar dissolves. Boil rapidly until the mixture has thickened, stirring occasionally.
☐ Discard the muslin bag and bottle the chutney immediately in warm jars. Cover and seal as described.

SPICED PEARS
(Makes about 2lb.)

1 level dessertspoon whole cloves
1 level dessertspoon whole allspice
1in. piece cinnamon stick
small piece of root ginger
small piece of lemon rind
8oz. granulated sugar
½ pint white malt vinegar
2lb. hard cooking pears

☐ Tie cloves, allspice, cinnamon, ginger and lemon rind in a small piece of muslin. Put in a pan with sugar and vinegar. Heat gently, stirring, until sugar has dissolved.
☐ Peel and core pears. Cut into halves; put in a pan with the syrup. Cover. Simmer for 10-15min. or until tender but still whole. Lift out of syrup. Discard muslin bag. Boil syrup for 5min., or until slightly thickened.
☐ Meanwhile, pack the pears into clean, warm jars. Pour over the syrup and leave to cool. Cover as described.

PEAR SAUCE
(Makes about 2½lb.)

8 large ripe eating pears
2oz. caster sugar
¼ level teaspoon ground mixed spice
¼ level teaspoon ground cinnamon
pinch of ground cloves

☐ Peel, core and chop the pears. Put in a large pan with ¾ pint water, sugar and spices. Bring to boil. Cook for 10min., or until tender and broken up. Push through a nylon sieve. Return to the rinsed saucepan and boil for 5min. Put into warm jars and seal.

PLUM CHUTNEY
(Makes about 5lb.)

3½lb. plums
½lb. shallots
½lb. stoned raisins
¼lb. stoned dates
1lb. soft brown sugar
½oz. salt
½oz. ground ginger
2½ pints malt vinegar

☐ Stone and chop the plums, skin and chop the shallots. Chop the raisins and dates. Mix ingredients in a pan; bring to the boil. Simmer for 2½-3 hours.
☐ Pour into hot jars, cover and seal.

PICKLED RED CABBAGE
(Makes about 4lb.)

2 pints malt vinegar
2oz. mixed pickling spice
3lb. red cabbage
3oz. salt

☐ Put vinegar and pickling spice into a large saucepan. Cover with a lid and bring to the boil. Boil for 2min., then leave overnight in a cool place, with the lid on.
☐ Remove any discoloured leaves from the cabbage. Quarter the cabbage and then shred finely. Layer the cabbage and salt in a large bowl and leave overnight to stand.
☐ Next day strain the spiced vinegar, discarding the spices. Drain the cabbage but do not rinse. Press the cabbage well to remove any extra liquid. Pack the cabbage into jars and fill with the cold vinegar—fill right to the top. Cover as described.
☐ Leave for 1 week before eating, but it doesn't keep for very long.

PICCALILLI
(Makes about 6lb.)

1 large cucumber
1 small marrow
1lb. runner beans
1lb. green tomatoes
½lb. small pickling onions
1 small cauliflower
1lb. salt
2 pints distilled vinegar
10oz. granulated sugar
¾oz. mustard powder
½oz. ground turmeric
1½ level teaspoons ground ginger

☐ Peel the cucumber and cut into small dice. Peel the marrow. Cut into small dice removing the seeds. String the beans; cut into 1in. lengths. Wash the tomatoes; cut into eighths. Skin the onions. Wash the cauliflower and break the head into small florets. Mix the vegetables and put them in layers into a large bowl, sprinkling each layer with salt. Cover and leave to stand overnight.
☐ Next day, drain off liquid and wash off excess salt. Put the vinegar into a large saucepan. Add the sugar, mustard, turmeric and ginger. Bring slowly to the boil, then add the vegetables. Simmer for 20-30min., stirring occasionally. Pour the mixture into warm jars. Cover and seal as described.

PICKLED ONIONS
(Makes about 12lb.)

9lb. small pickling onions
½lb. salt
4 pints malt vinegar
2oz. mixed pickling spice

☐ Skin the onions and place them in a large bowl. Add the salt, cover bowl and leave to stand overnight. Meanwhile, put the vinegar and pickling spice into a large saucepan. Bring to the boil, reduce the heat and simmer for 30min. Cool.
☐ Next day, drain the onions, wash off excess salt and pack them into clean jars. Strain the vinegar and pour it over the onions. Cover and seal as described.

PICKLED BEETROOT
(Makes about 5lb.)

4lb. small raw beetroot
boiling water
2 pints malt vinegar
½oz. allspice
4oz. granulated sugar

☐ Wash the beetroot, but do not break the skins. Put into a large pan and cover with boiling water. Simmer for 1½ hours, or until tender.
☐ Meanwhile, put the vinegar, allspice and sugar into a large saucepan. Bring to the boil, cover the pan with a tight fitting lid and simmer for 10min. Allow to become cold.
☐ Drain the water from the beetroot. Rub off the skins and cut the beetroot into thin slices or small dice. Put into clean jars then pour in the cold spiced vinegar. Cover and seal as described.

TOMATO CHUTNEY
(Makes about 4lb.)

6lb. tomatoes
boiling water
1lb. cooking apples
1lb. onions
2 medium-sized carrots
1lb. Demerara sugar
½oz. ground ginger
1 level teaspoon Cayenne pepper
8 dried chillis
1 level tablespoon salt
1 pint distilled malt vinegar

☐ Drop the tomatoes in boiling water, leave for 1min. then drain. Skin and chop the tomatoes. Peel, core and chop the apples. Skin the onions, peel the carrots and chop both roughly. Put all the ingredients into a saucepan and bring to the boil. Simmer for 1-1½ hours, or until the mixture is thick.
☐ Pour into clean, dry jars. Cover and seal as described.

MARROW CHUTNEY
(Makes about 7lb.)

4lb. marrow
3oz. salt
2lb. cooking apples
1lb. small onions
1 small piece of green root ginger
6 red chillis
6 peppercorns
1lb. granulated sugar
3 pints distilled malt vinegar

☐ Peel the marrow; cut into small pieces, removing the seeds. Put into a large bowl, sprinkling each layer with salt. Cover the bowl and leave to stand overnight.
☐ Next day, drain and wash off excess salt. Wash the apples, peel and core. Chop up roughly. Skin the onions. Put marrow, apples and onions in a preserving pan. Bruise the ginger and tie with the chillis and the peppercorns in a piece of muslin and add to the pan. Cook for 15min. or until the marrow is soft.
☐ Add the sugar and vinegar. Heat gently until the sugar dissolves, then bring to the boil. Cook for 15-20min., stirring occasionally, until the chutney is the consistency of jam. Remove muslin bag; put chutney into warm jars and seal immediately as described.

Bottling

Like most other forms of cooking, there is a right and a wrong way to bottle. The object when bottling is to heat the fruit to a temperature high enough to kill natural yeasts and moulds which are always present, and to prevent them re-entering the jar. At the same time, the heat inactivates the enzymes in fruit. These enzymes are always present to ripen the fruit but if not inactivated in some way they will finally cause rotting. The first job is buying your jars. I use Kilner jars which come in three sizes— 1lb., 2lb. and 3lb. The rubber ring is attached to the lid and a screwband keeps the lid in place. Examine each of your jars to see that they are perfect. If you find any chips in the rim, discard the bottle. It is wisest to buy new lids each year. A bent lid or perished ring can result in a faulty seal. Wash the jars, lids and screwbands in warm soapy water, using a bottle brush if necessary to remove any dirt. Rinse them well in warm clear water and leave upside down to drain. Don't dry the bottles because the fruit slips easily into place if the insides are wet. Soak the lids and rubber rings in a bowl of warm water for about 15min. before using them.

Recipes for bottled Golden Plums,
Gooseberries, Tomatoes, Apricots
and Gooseberries, Cherries and
Peaches overleaf

Sugar syrup for bottling

Fruit can be preserved in sugar syrup or water; both are suitable. But fruit bottled in sugar syrup has a better flavour and colour even after a long storage than the same fruit bottled in water. Unfortunately sugar syrup tends to make the fruit rise in the bottle, but I think the improved flavour and colour is well worth a bit of space at the bottom. The strength of the sugar syrup can be varied according to taste, but an average proportion is 8oz. sugar to 1 pint water. This is suitable for plums, gooseberries, apple and pear quarters, but for fruit which packs closely, when less syrup will be needed, make a stronger syrup using 1lb. sugar to 1 pint of water.

Making your sugar syrup

Use granulated or loaf sugar and add it to the quantity of water you need. Dissolve the sugar very slowly, and once dissolved, bring this syrup to boiling point and boil for 1min. Strain through muslin or a fine sieve.

Preparing your fruit

See the table overleaf. Tight packs containing more than 11oz. fruit need the stronger syrup.

Packing the bottles

Pack the fruit tightly without bruising it, filling the bottle. Pour on boiling syrup, water or brine, depending on what you're bottling, to within 1in. of the top. Trapped bubbles can be removed by rotating the bottle gently in opposite directions, or by using a very fine knitting needle, being careful not to pierce the fruit. Clean the top of the jars and add lids.

Preserving your fruit

Oven method

To my mind this is the simplest way of bottling, but unsuitable for apples, pears, peaches, apricots or any fruit where the appearance is very important. Stand the filled jars on a baking tray lined with several thicknesses of newspaper. The jars should not touch each other. Put into centre of oven, pre-heated for at least 15min. to 300 deg. F. or Mark 2. Leave for the time indicated in the table. Remove from oven when ready, screw on the bands tightly and leave overnight. Test in the morning by removing the screwbands and trying to lift the jar by the lid. If it doesn't move, the seal is perfect. If it does, re-sterilise.

Preserving your fruit

Hot water bath method

This method is useful for all types of fruit and must be used for apples, pears, peaches, apricots or any fruit where the appearance is important. After filling the jars with syrup, add the lids and screwbands, turning them back a $\frac{1}{4}$ turn to allow steam and air to escape. You need a deep saucepan with a lid and something to make a false bottom so that the bottles do not touch the metal. Newspaper thickly wadded or an oven cloth will do well. Put the jars in the pan, making sure they are not touching each other or the sides of the pan. Pour in cold water. Ideally it should cover the bottles completely, but at least it must come to the shoulders of the bottles. Cover the pan with the lid, using a tea towel doubled underneath if the seal isn't perfect. The water should be brought very slowly to simmering point taking about $1\frac{1}{2}$ hours, and maintained at simmering for 20min. Remove on to a wooden surface and tighten the screwbands. Test seal in the morning.

Storage

Store bottles in a cool place protected from strong light which destroys the colour of the fruit. Wipe the inside of each screwband with oil and replace loosely. Label each jar.

To open

Insert point of knife under ring and lever gently until air enters.

Times for bottling in the oven

Fruit	Time (min.) 1-4lb.	Time (min.) 5-10lb.
Blackberries	30-40	45-60
Currants	30-40	45-60
Loganberries	30-40	45-60
Mulberries	30-40	45-60
Raspberries	30-40	45-60
Strawberries	30-40	45-60
Gooseberries* (for pies)	30-40	45-60
Rhubarb* (for pies)	30-40	45-60
Damsons	40-50	55-70
Tomatoes (whole)	60-70	75-90

*Gooseberries and rhubarb for desserts (not pies) should be processed for 10min. more

BOTTLED PLUMS

1½lb. granulated sugar
4lb. plums
boiling water

☐ Put the sugar and 3 pints cold water into a saucepan. Heat gently until the sugar dissolves. Stir well. Bring to the boil and boil for 1min. Leave to become quite cold.

☐ Wash the plums. Remove stalks and use only perfect, slightly under-ripe fruit. Wipe with a soft cloth to remove the bloom. Pack tightly into clean jars. You may find it easier to pack the fruit using wooden spoon handles.

☐ When the syrup is cold, pour it into the jars, filling them to overflowing. Try to get out as many air bubbles as possible, using a fine knitting needle dipped first in boiling water. Be careful not to pierce the fruit.

☐ Dip the rubber seals into boiling water and place them on top of the jars. Screw down the metal band, then turn it back a quarter to allow air and steam to escape. Put a thick piece of towelling in the base of a very deep pan. Stand the jars on this; do not allow them to touch the sides of the pan or each other. The water should cover the bottles or at least reach the shoulders. Cover. Heat very gently, bringing the temperature up to 180 deg. F., or just to simmering point, in 1½ hours. Lower the heat for a while if the water gets too hot. Leave the jars for 15min. once the temperature is at simmering point. Scoop out some of the water. Carefully lift the bottles on to a board. Tighten each screwband as you take the bottle out. Leave to cool for 24 hours.

☐ Unscrew the band, and gently lift each bottle holding only the lid. If the seal is perfect, add the screwbands; label and store in a cool dry place. If the rubber seal comes away from the jar, either bottle the fruit again as described or make a pie.

BOTTLED APRICOTS WITH GOOSEBERRIES

3lb. ripe apricots
¼lb. ripe gooseberries
1½lb. granulated sugar

☐ Insert a knife at the stalk end of each apricot and cut round the stone. Twist halves round stone in opposite directions.

☐ Cut small slices off the tops of the gooseberries when topping and tailing them.

☐ Dissolve the sugar in 3 pints water and boil for 1min. Strain.

☐ Place a gooseberry in each apricot—where the stone was—and pack tightly into prepared jars.

☐ Process by the hot water bath method.

BOTTLED CHERRIES

3½lb. ripe cherries
1½lb. granulated sugar
⅛oz. citric acid

☐ Remove stones from cherries using either a cherry stoner or knife. Collect the juice.

☐ Dissolve the sugar in 3 pints water and boil 3min. Strain. Add the citric acid.

☐ Pack the cherries and juice tightly into prepared jars without bruising them. Cover with syrup.

☐ Using one of the sterilisation methods, process the cherries.

☐ Seal as described.

BOTTLED PEACHES

3½lb. ripe peaches
1½lb. granulated sugar

☐ Dip the peaches in boiling water for 1min. then cool in cold water. Remove skins. Halve and remove stones—or they may be left whole.

☐ Have ready the syrup—dissolve the sugar in 3 pints water and boil for 3min. Strain.

☐ Working quickly, before the fruit discolours, pack the fruit tightly in prepared jars. Cover with syrup and process by the hot water bath method.

☐ Seal as described.

BOTTLED PEARS

6lb. pears
1½lb. granulated sugar
3 pints boiling water
salt

☐ Choose firm, even sized, slightly under-ripe pears.

☐ Dissolve the sugar in the boiling water over a gentle heat. Boil for 1min., then strain through a fine strainer or fine muslin. Leave to get cold.

☐ Peel pears, using a stainless steel knife, then cut the pears in half. Remove the cores, using a teaspoon. Leave in slightly salted water. Pack the jars with the fruit. Pour sugar syrup into the jars to overflowing and remove all bubbles. Place on lids and screwbands, giving screwbands a quarter turn back.

☐ Place a thick wad of newspaper in the base of a large pan. Stand the jars in the pan, so they don't touch the sides or each other, then fill the pan with water to cover jars or at least cover the shoulders of the jars. Bring slowly to simmering point, taking 1½ hours, then simmer for 40min.

☐ Take out and place on a wooden board and tighten screwbands. After 24 hours test seal as described.

BOTTLED TOMATOES

3½lb. tomatoes
boiling water
salt
caster sugar

☐ Choose medium-sized tomatoes which are well ripened but firm, and of an even shape.

☐ Remove the stems. Drop tomatoes into boiling water and leave for 1min. Drain water; remove skins.

☐ Pack small fruit whole, and quarter or halve larger tomatoes. Add 1 level teaspoon salt and ½ level teaspoon of sugar to each 1lb. tomatoes and pack tightly into the jars so no liquid is needed.

☐ Process for 70-80min. in oven, pre-heated to 300 deg. F. or Mark 2. Remove on to wooden boards, cover with lids and screwbands. Test for a seal 24 hours later.

BOTTLED GOOSEBERRIES

3lb. granulated sugar
6 pints water
6lb. gooseberries

☐ Put the sugar and water in a pan and heat slowly to dissolve the sugar. Boil mixture for 1min. Strain through a fine sieve or muslin.

☐ Pick over fruit, discarding gooseberries which are bruised. Wash the fruit then pack into the jars, prepared as described. Preserve the fruit for 1 hour 15min. in oven, pre-heated to 250 deg. F. or Mark ½. When gooseberries are ready, reboil syrup. Lift jars out on to a wooden board to prevent cracking. Fill to overflowing with boiling syrup. Remove any air bubbles with a sterilised fine knitting needle. Wipe outside of jars then cover with lids.

☐ Place screwbands in position and seal tightly. Test seals after 24 hours.

FRUIT	PREPARATION	Prepared fruit oz. per 1lb. jar
Apples	Peel, core, cut into slices. Prevent discolouration by putting into salty water (¼oz. per pint). Rinse quickly in cold water before packing.	10
Apricots (whole)	Remove stalks; rinse in cold water.	9-11
Apricots (halved)	Insert knife at stalk end and cut round the stone. Twist halves round stone in opposite directions. Pack quickly before cut surfaces brown.	10-12
Blackberries	Remove unsound fruit, stalks and leaves.	10-12
Blackcurrants	Remove stems, also calyx if liked.	12-15
Cherries (whole)	Remove stalks and rinse fruit in cold water.	11-12
Cherries (stoned)	Remove stones, collecting juice and putting with fruit.	12
Damsons	Remove stalks, wipe off bloom and rinse fruit in cold water.	11-12
Gooseberries	When preserving in syrup, cut small slices off the top when topping and tailing to prevent shrivelling.	10-12
Greengages	Remove stalks and rinse in cold water.	9-11
Mulberries	Remove over-ripe fruit, handling as little as possible.	10-12
Peaches	Dip in boiling water for ½min., put in cold water to remove skins. Halve and remove stones—see apricots. Preserve before fruit discolours.	9-12
Pears (dessert)	Peel, halve and remove cores with a pointed teaspoon. Prevent discolouration by dropping into salty acid water (½oz. salt, ¼oz. citric acid per quart of water). Rinse in cold water and pack quickly. Cooking pears are not recommended for bottling as they darken.	8-10
Plums (whole)	Remove stalks, rinse in cold water and wipe bloom off dark varieties.	9-11
Rhubarb	Remove base and leaves and cut into 1in. lengths.	9-10
Strawberries	Remove calyx and plug. Rinse fruit in cold water. Choose medium-sized even fruits.	9
Tomatoes (whole in brine)	Choose small even fruit, rinse in cold water. Pack into containers. Use brine made from ¼oz. salt to 1 quart water instead of syrup.	10

Freezing

If you're thinking of buying a freezer, I can thoroughly recommend it as a time saver. It's the most useful addition to my kitchen. There are plenty of makes on the market now and prices are lower, and for people with a tiny kitchen (and this seems to be most of us) there are some very small freezers available. Many of the modern fridges have a freeze compartment in the top, but generally this compartment is for storing food once frozen and *not* for freezing food.

A freezer will run at a temperature of 0 deg. F. or below and some makes now have a boost switch to set an hour before you want to freeze food, which lowers the temperature still further. Once the food is frozen, click off this switch and the freezer will run at the normal temperature of about 0 deg. F.

How it works
When you freeze food the whole object is to process at a low enough temperature to discourage large crystals forming in the food and the pack and to discourage the growth of moulds and bacteria. The lower the temperature the faster the freezing time and the less chance there is of large crystals forming or any organisms remaining active.

Containers for freezing
You can use boxes, bags, tubs or suitable wrapping material, whichever best suits the food you're preparing. But all forms of wrapping must have these essentials.
1. It must be moisture-proof and the seams leak-proof.
2. It must be vapour-proof so that food does not lose moisture and dry out or pick up smells from other foods.
3. It must withstand the low temperatures and not become brittle. Use waxed cartons, aluminium foil, polythene bags and the clear film which you buy in a roll and which seals on being moistened. (Grocers use it round their cheese). You'll need covered wire

fasteners for polythene bags. Square cartons are more economical than round ones or other odd shapes. And for this reason, it's a good idea to freeze food inside polythene bags in a box. When removed you'll have a neat package. When you wrap raw food press the wrapping closely to the surface to exclude all the air. Cover wing tips of poultry or bones of meat with a double thickness of aluminium foil before you wrap for freezing to prevent puncturing the final wrapping.

Preparation of food
Prepare fruit and vegetables just as though you were eating them fresh that day. Steaks and chops should be in single portion size; don't fold steak. Cakes, bread and pastry pies should be frozen whole. Prepare small savouries or cocktail snacks as you would to serve, including their garnish. You can also freeze butter, cheese, cream, ice cream, stock, fruit juices (leaving room in the carton for them to expand) cooked meats, pâtés, left-over poultry and meats for sandwiches, biscuits and pastry. Don't freeze salad vegetables; they're not successful because of their high water content, neither are onions, marrows and melons, for the same reason. Bananas go black if frozen and fresh milk and mayonnaise separate. Hard-boiled eggs become leathery, celery loses its crispness. You can freeze separated eggs, marking the cartons clearly with the number of whites or yolks. Yolks require salt or sugar, using ½ teaspoon salt or 1 level teaspoon caster sugar to prevent coagulation. Mark the carton clearly, so you don't use salty eggs for sweet dishes.

Sugar or sugar syrup?
Most fruits are nicer if frozen in dry sugar or sugar syrup. Soft fruits such as raspberries and currants are best frozen in dry sugar using 4oz. caster sugar to a pound of fruit.
Harder fruits such as gooseberries and those with stones, e.g. plums, should be packed in syrup. Make a sugar syrup using ½-1lb. sugar to 1 pint water. Freeze gooseberries whole but take the stones out of other fruit as they take up space and can flavour fruit during storage. Make sure fruit is covered with syrup and leave ½in. space at the top to allow for expansion during freezing. Apples are best puréed. Cook them and mash them or sieve them until they are smooth. Sweeten to taste, and pack leaving room for expansion.

Blanching vegetables
This applies to vegetables—all of them should be blanched in boiling water to retard the action of enzymes which will cause spoilage of colour and flavour during storage if blanching is not done. See the table giving times for various vegetables.
Use a large container which will hold 3 or 4 pints of water. Put in only 1lb. of vegetables at a time using a wire mesh basket for easy removal. The water should be fast boiling. Bring the water quickly back to the boil and time from the moment it reaches boiling point. Time them carefully. When blanched for the correct time, lift the food in the strainer and plunge it into plenty of iced water. Leave in the iced water for the same time as for blanching. Drain the vegetables, dry well on a clean tea towel, then pack in the container you've chosen and chill in the fridge before transferring to the freezer.

Labelling your container
This is most important and should be accurate. If you're storing for 6 months you'll forget exactly what is in the pack. And all cartons look alike once frozen. You'll need a wax crayon for cartons, tie-on labels for bulky packages, self-stick labels for all other parcels. Your label should tell you what the contents are, what their number or weight is, whether you have added anything (amount of sugar if necessary), and the date before which you will want to eat the contents.

Storage Times

Food	Storage Time
Vegetables	up to 12 months
Fruit	up to 12 months
Beef and lamb	12 months
Mince and offal	2 months
Bacon	1 month
Chicken	12 months
Duck	6 months
Giblets	3 months
White fish	6-12 months
Oily fish	4 months
Eggs	9 months
Butter	6 months
Cream—double	9 months
Soft cheese	6 months
Baked cakes and pastry	6-9 months
Uncooked pastry	6 months
Soups, sauces, stock	6 months
Cooked dishes, stews, curries, etc.	6 months

Freezing

Put the packets in the coldest part of the freezer, which is usually the top. Don't stack them tightly, but allow plenty of room for air to circulate. Don't freeze more than about 5lb. of food at any time if you've got a small freezer, but you'll find the exact amount in the instructions book which is obtainable with all freezers.

Thawing

Thawing gently in the fridge overnight gives the best results. Leave food in the carton or bag. Dessert fruits should be served still slightly frozen. Fruit which originally had stones should be thawed quickly to prevent discolouration. Fruits for stewing can be put in the pan in the frozen state and heated gently while you break the block carefully with a fork. Fruit for pies must be thawed before covering or the pastry becomes soggy. Cook vegetables while still frozen. You only need about ½ pint or less boiling salted water. Bring the water back to the boil as fast as possible with the lid on the pan. Frozen vegetables do not take as long to cook as fresh vegetables. In most cases the time is just about halved.

What to do in a power cut

You can insure your contents against a very long power cut, but this is only worthwhile if you have an enormous chest-type freezer. During the normal power cut, your frozen food will remain frozen, provided you don't open the door at all. If you open the door, warm air rushes in and the power isn't there to freeze it.

Defrosting your freezer

Do this at least once a year and when the freezer is at its emptiest. Remove all the food and wrap it securely in some newspapers and an old blanket. Put it in the coldest place you can find. Ideally, pick a freezing cold day, and put all your frozen food outside. Leave the freezer wide open with bowls of boiling water on the shelves to thaw the ice quickly. You can scrape frost off the sides if you use a flat wooden spatula, but it must be blunt and you must be careful not to damage the interior. Finally wash the walls well with plenty of hot water with a little bicarbonate of soda dissolved in it. Dry thoroughly and switch on. Return the food at once. Take this opportunity to make a check on length of storage times of articles and whether their condition is still good. Renew labels and put food to be used first in the front.

VEGETABLE	PREPARATION	Blanching and cooling times (same for both)
Asparagus	Grade according to thickness of stem and cut to fit container. Don't tie.	thin, 2min. thick, 4min.
Aubergines	Wash and cut into ½in. slices. Put into salted water (3 level teaspoons to 1 pint) to prevent discolouration.	4min.
Beetroot	Freeze only young small beets. Leave whole and cook until tender. Rub off skins.	Don't blanch
Broccoli	Choose compact heads. Trim stalks down to even lengths, cutting off woody ends.	3-4min., according to thickness of stalks
Carrots	Use only small whole carrots, the first of the season. Cut off tops and roots and skin after blanching.	5min.
Cauliflower	Break into florets of even size.	3min.
Corn on the cob	Remove husk and silk. Must be new and tender cobs.	4-6min. according to size.
Corn kernels	Remove husk and silk. Scald cobs in boiling water for 4min. Cool quickly and strip off kernels.	
Courgettes	Wash and cut into slices.	3min.
French beans	String and cut off ends. Cut into 1in. lengths—straight across. Retains better flavour than slicing diagonally.	cut, 2min. sliced, 1min.
Leeks	Remove outer coarse leaves and trim ends. Wash well under running cold water. Leave whole or slice.	2-4min. depending on size
Mixed vegetables	Prepare and blanch according to their kind. Mix after cooling.	
Mushrooms	Wash and dry thoroughly. Should not be peeled unless they're ragged. Do not blanch. If desired mushrooms may be sautéed in butter. Cool quickly.	Don't blanch
Peas	Choose very young tender peas. Pod and sort carefully.	1min.
Runner beans	As for French beans.	
Spinach	Pick over leaves carefully and remove any thick ribs. Wash well. Blanch only small quantities at a time so that the leaves do not stick together.	2min.
Sprouts	Choose tight small sprouts of uniform size. Trim off outer leaves.	3min.
Root vegetables	Freeze only very young vegetables. Peel and dice or slice.	3min.
Tomatoes	These soften after freezing but are good for cooking. Skin by immersing in boiling water and cut into quarters.	Don't blanch
New potatoes	They lose some of their texture after freezing. Select potatoes of a similar size. Scrape and wash.	4min.
Peppers	Wash, remove seeds and ribs inside. Halve or shred.	2min.

Index

continued overleaf

continued overleaf

continued overleaf

Acknowledgements

Design
Stanley Glazer
Illustrations
Ken Brasier
Cover photograph
Bob Cramp
Other photographs by
Bob Cramp
Don McAllister
Len Fulford
Tony Copeland
Michael Boys
Penny Tweedie
George Nicholls
John Cross
Philip Pace
Tom Belshaw
David Price
Mike Leale
David Davies
Peter Bolton
Ron McFarlane
Derry Brabbs
Rod Ebdon